THE
BACKPACKER'S
FIELD MANUAL
revised and updated

a comprehensive guide to mastering backcountry skills

Rick Curtis

DIRECTOR, PRINCETON UNIVERSITY
OUTDOOR ACTION

THREE RIVERS PRESS • NEW YORK

The publisher gratefully acknowledges permission to reprint excerpts from Mountain Safety, Research Inc.'s instructions for the Whisperlite stove and for artwork illustrating the Whisperlite stove; Arc'teryx for providing a backpack for the cover art; the Leave No Trace Center for Outdoor Ethics for permission to use the Leave No Trace logo; MapTech, Inc. for U.S.G.S. quadrangle maps generated from MapTech Terrain Navigator Pro; Sierra Club Books for excerpts from *Weathering the Wilderness,* by William E. Reifsnyder; artwork showing the SAM splint from the Seaburg Company; the MapTools UTM grid artwork from John Carnes at MapTools.com; *The Physician and Sports Medicine Journal* for excerpts from the article "Self-reduction of Anterior Shoulder Dislocation" by Dr. Elizabeth Joy (November 2000); Prentice Hall for an illustration of the Situational Leadership Model from *Management of Organizational Behavior* by Paul Hersey, Kenneth Blanchard, and Dewey Johnson.

Published in the United States by Three Rivers Press, an imprint of the Crown Publishing Group, a division of Random House, Inc., New York.

www.crownpublishing.com

THREE RIVERS PRESS and the Tugboat design are registered trademarks of Random House, Inc.

Originally published in different form by Three Rivers Press, an imprint of the Crown Publishing Group, a division of Random House, Inc., New York, in 1998.

Library of Congress Cataloging-in-Publication Data

Curtis, Rick.
    The backpacker's field manual : a comprehensive guide to mastering backcountry
    skills / Rick Curtis.—Rev. and updated.
    Includes bibliographical references and index.
    1. Backpacking—Handbooks, manuals, etc.   2. Camping—Handbooks, manuals,
    etc.   3. Low-impact camping—Handbooks, manuals, etc.   I. Title.
GV199.6.C87   2005
796.51—dc22   2004023668

ISBN 1-4000-5309-9

Printed in the United States of America

Design by Jennifer K. Beal

10   9   8   7

First Edition

ACKNOWLEDGMENTS

I want to thank the many close friends with whom I have traveled the trails, peaks, and rivers over the years: Liz Cutler and Tom Kreutz; John Gager; Ed Seliga; Philo Elmer; all the other folks and places who have enriched my outdoor experiences; and especially my mom, Ann Curtis, for all her love and encouragement throughout my career in outdoor education.

In writing this second edition I've relied on my own thirty years of experience in the outdoors as well as seeking out some of the best experts in different fields to bring you the most complete information possible (and still fit within my publisher's page limits). One thing I've learned over the years is to recognize what I know and what I don't know; a lot of people have been essential at helping fill in my knowledge gaps. For all their help and guidance with the first edition I want to thank Tod Schimelpfenig at the National Outdoor Leadership School for his review of Chapter 9. For this second edition I want to thank Charlie Schimanski of the Mountain Rescue Council for his help with the Search and Rescue sections; Ben Lawhon from the Leave No Trace Center for Outdoor Ethics for his help with Chapter 5; Professor Stephen Herrero of the University of Calgary for his review of the information on bears and bear attacks; Dr. Martin Uman, John Gookin, and Richard Kithil for helping me to understand the physics of lightning; my friend Brent Bell, director of Harvard University's Freshmen Outdoor Program for information about dealing with diabetes on the trail; Dr. Robert "Brownie" Schoene, former President of the Wilderness Medical Society, for his help on altitude illnesses; and my good friend Bill "Tigerpaw" Plonk, who gave me firsthand information about ultralight hiking after his successful 2002 ultralight through-hike of the Appalachian Trail.

Finally, I want to thank all of the Princeton University students who have been leaders in the Outdoor Action Program since 1973 and have helped to develop and implement our principles of outdoor education. These wonderful people have volunteered their time to teach others the joy of being in the wilderness. To all of you, especially to the many Leader Trainers who I have spent so much wonderful time with, thank you so much. You all have made me so proud of what you have accomplished at Princeton with your peers, and how you have taken your leadership skills out into the world to make a difference. Over the years more than 13,000 Princeton students have participated in the program, and Outdoor Action has become one of the leading college outdoor programs in the country. Outdoor programs from across the country and around the world look to Outdoor Action for help in developing their programs and training leaders. Through our educational efforts on campus, this book, and our Web publishing at www.princeton.edu/~oa, www.outdoored.com, www.outdoorsafety.org, and www.backpackersfieldmanual.com, we hope that you will have a productive and safe learning experience wherever you go.

CONTENTS

INTRODUCTION

Back in 1996, when I was writing the first edition of *The Backpacker's Field Manual,* the World Wide Web was still in its infancy. Since then the Internet has revolutionized the way we search for information and interact with one another. Backpacking and outdoor sports are no exception to this, from finding hiking trails to searching for gear reviews. Backpacking and outdoor recreation, like everything else, have become "information-driven." Your knowledge base is a key part of maximizing your enjoyment, your safety, and your stewardship of the natural world.

Since the first edition, backpacking itself has changed. Advances in gear design now mean that a seven-day trip no longer means a seventy-pound pack. We've expanded our comfort range in all sorts of seasons and learned how to hike thousands of miles with less than twenty pounds of gear in our packs. We can use GPS receivers to pinpoint our exact location and tell us how to hike to our next campsite. At the same time, backpackers face new challenges today. The growth of outdoor recreational sports has put millions of more people on the land. Leave No Trace practices and wilderness conservation have become increasingly important to safeguard the wild lands we all love. We've also seen new hazards emerge like West Nile Virus and Crypotosporidium.

With all our advances in technology, there still exists a set of core skills that people need to travel in the outdoors. We seem to forget that the earliest "backpackers," in the United States and Canada, from native peoples to backcountry explorers like Lewis and Clark, didn't have Gore-Tex, polypropylene ultralight tents, and a gas stove. They survived the harshest conditions with wool, leather, canvas, and yes, even cotton, through their deep knowledge of how to take care of their own needs in the outdoors.

With all these changes it was time to write a new edition of *The Backpacker's Field Manual.* I've used the first edition as our main textbook for teaching new outdoor leaders at Princeton University. Other schools and outdoor programs across the country use it as a textbook for backpacking and outdoor recreation courses and as a staff field manual. The first version of this book was a twenty-page manual written for our trip leader back in 1985. The manual continued to grow each year until 1996, when I began working with Random House to produce a book-length version. This new edition brings the book up to date with changes in backpacking and expands the book to cover more aspects of outdoor leadership and education. It's a great book for beginners who need comprehensive instruction for planning and running their own outdoor trips. For experienced hikers it's a solid reference manual and re-fresher for your next trip. There are lots of good backpacking books out there, and I reference a lot of them in the Bibliography. Unlike any other book on the market, *The Backpacker's Field Manual* is designed not only to be something to read on the couch at home when you are planning your trip but also to be a manual you take with you in the field. Every part of the book is designed to allow you to get the information you need as quickly as possible.

DISCLAIMER

As a risk-management expert I know that traveling in the backcountry can be hazardous. I've dealt with group emergencies on the trail and had my own share of close calls. By balancing your skills, experience, and gear with the right trip you can have enjoyable and safe experiences. This book is designed to be a resource to help you on your way. It can't be a replacement for per-sonal experience and professional training in specialized skills such as first aid and CPR. The author, Random House, and Princeton University assume no li-ability for any personal injury, illness, or property damage or loss that may arise out of use of this material.

Specific equipment, such as stoves and water filters, is discussed in this book. There are many other products that could have been included but were not due to space considerations. The inclusion of these items does not imply any endorsement of these products.

Trip Planning

BASIC TRIP PLANNING

Planning a trip requires more than simply deciding where to go and when. Whether it's a weekend trip with friends, a formal outdoor program, or a major expedition, you need to evaluate your trip across a number of categories and develop a solid plan. One or two people may take on the role of planner, or the process of planning can be spread out among the entire group. After planning and running trips for thousands of people both around the United States and around the world, I can tell you that these are the elements you should keep in mind when planning any trip.

GROUP SIZE AND ABILITY

Whenever you're planning a trip, you need to determine if the route should fit the group or the group fit the route. The group may have a range of experience levels, physical conditions, and goals, in which case, your goal should be to plan a trip that is appropriate for everyone. Other times, you may have a specific trip you want to do that may be challenging or require special skills. For this kind of trip, you need to select a group that has the right qualifications to participate. Here's a checklist of questions to ask when planning a group trip:

- What kind of group is it? Is it an informal group of friends or a formal group like an outdoor education program? Are the participants friends, students, volunteers, or paying customers? Formal groups may have specific policies and protocols that must be followed.
- What are the goals of each group member? Are people required to attend? (This factor can have a significant impact on how committed or not the group is to the wilderness experience.) Does the group have collective goals?
- What is the experience level of each member? What is the average experience level?
- Are there people in the group with the necessary skills to lead and manage the group, or do you need to find other people to provide leadership? (See Chapter 10, "Outdoor Leadership.")
- How big is the group?
- What is the age range of group members?
- What is the physical condition of each member? What is the average physical condition of the group?
- Do people have particular health issues that could impact their participation?

Determine the level of experience, physical ability, etc., as much as possible *before* you set out. This will enable you to plan a smoother and more successful trip. More important, it will diminish the potential for dangerous situations. (See Chapter 8, "Safety and Emergency Procedures.") Keep the group's parameters in mind as you evaluate the other categories, thinking in terms of both optimal challenge and safety. Be aware that you will often have a great range of experience levels and physical abilities, so plan the trip at a level that will be fun, educational, challenging, and safe for everyone. Think about the high end and the low end of the experience level and physical condition, and err in the direction of the low end. Gathering physical fitness and basic health information will help you determine different abilities and experience levels (for a sample form, see page 408).

Group Dynamics

- How are costs going to be handled—equipment, food, transportation, permits, etc.? If you have to buy gear, who keeps it after the trip? It's really important to work these things out before the trip, otherwise serious tensions can arise later.
- How will leadership be handled during the trip? (See Chapter 8, "Safety and Emergency Procedures," and Chapter 10, "Outdoor Leadership.")

ACTIVITIES

When planning the activities for a particular trip, you need to consider the following:

- What activity(ies) do you want to do on your trip (backpacking, peak climbing, and/or glacier travel, for example)?
- What are the goals for the trip?
- What skills will people need? Do they already have the skills, or do they need to learn them?
- How do you integrate time for teaching skills with time for traveling?

Once you've evaluated the group members' abilities, you can adapt your goals to an appropriate level. Plan activities that will be both appropriately challenging and safe. Be aware of how mileage, elevation change, and time for teaching and learning skills will affect your route (see "Estimating Travel Times," page 12). Start easily and increase the level of difficulty gradually so that everyone can be progressively challenged at appropriate levels, rather than placing someone in a situation that is beyond their abilities.

LOCATION AND WEATHER

Research Your Destination

- Investigate the availability of guidebooks and maps.
- Contact area rangers or land managers to get more information. Inquire about permits required, safety issues like hunting season, and seasonal hazards like wildfires.
- Talk with other people who have been to the area before. If possible, check their trip logs, which may have important information not found in guidebooks.

Trip Planning Questions

- How long is the trip? Can the trip be self-supporting in terms of equipment and food, or will you need to resupply? How will you handle the resupply—cache items ahead of time, hike out, or have someone hike in? (See "Resupply Issues," page 15.)
- How remote is the trip from "civilization" and help in case of an emergency?
- What are the trail conditions?
- Are there special places you want to see?
- Are there places you want to avoid like high-use areas?
- Are shelters available on a daily basis, or do you need to bring your own?
- Where is parking and trailhead access?
- What is the water availability and water quality on a daily basis?
- Are there safety issues—hunting season, off-road vehicles, etc.?
- Are there any special natural hazards—flash floods in desert canyons, wildfires, etc.? (See "How Accidents Happen," page 225.)
- What Leave No Trace practices will you need to implement to safeguard the environment? (See Chapter 5, "Leave No Trace Hiking and Camping.")

Regulations and Permits

Each location can have its own unique set of regulations and requirements. It is important to check these out in detail before you go. Here are some of the possible issues to research:

- Are permits needed, and how do you obtain them?
- How far in advance do you need to apply for a permit?
- Is there a cost for the permit?

- Are their any special regulations about rescue? (Some parks, like Denali in Alaska, may require that you pay for your own rescue.)
- Are there limitations to group size?
- Where is camping allowed and not allowed?
- Are there any restricted areas, hazardous zones, protected areas for endangered species, and such?
- Are fires allowed? If fires are allowed, will wood be available? Or will you need to bring a stove?
- Are there special regulations about Leave No Trace practices such as disposing of human waste?

Weather

- How many hours of daylight will there be? Check the Web at sites like the Weather Channel *(www.weather.com)* for sunrise and sunset times and average high and low temperatures.
- How will the season determine the weather? Are storms or particular weather patterns likely? (See Chapter 7, "Weather and Nature.")
- How will weather affect trip activities? How might it affect the safety of the group?
- Will altitude changes during the trip have an impact on weather or temperature?

EXPECT THE UNEXPECTED

When planning a trip, remember that the ultimate goal is for people to have fun. Here are some tips to planning a trip that everyone can enjoy:

- Make a plan that can be modified during the trip. All sorts of factors—bad weather, changing trail conditions, broken equipment, ill-prepared participants, an injury—may require you to change your itinerary.
- Don't plan long or difficult hikes on every day of the trip. Vary the mileage so that you have some days when you can get a later start or get to camp early.
- On longer trips, schedule a rest day every five to seven days.
- Make sure that people have some time during each day to kick back—to read, watch the sunset, write, etc.
- When hiking at high altitudes, people acclimatize at different rates. You may have to adjust your trip to give people time to properly acclimatize before going higher, especially if people are coming straight from sea level to a high altitude. (See "Altitude Illnesses," page 380.)

EQUIPMENT

Once you have determined your trip activities and location, you need to put together an equipment list. Sample equipment lists are provided in the Appendix, but remember that they should be used only as guidelines. Each trip and each person may have special requirements.

FOOD

It is important to have food that is both nourishing *and* edible. On longer trips, with specialized activities, or in different climates (e.g., cold-weather trips), it may be necessary to plan a menu that supplies a specific number of calories per day and stresses certain food groups over others. On any trip, it is essential to be aware of special dietary requirements for each trip member—food allergies, vegetarians, and kosher eaters—and plan a menu accordingly. Check this information on the Fitness and Health Information Form for each person on the trip (see page 408). For food, nutrition, and menu planning guidelines, see Chapter 3, "Cooking and Nutrition."

COSTS

Before going on a group trip, talk about how costs will be distributed. This includes food, fuel, travel expenses, and first aid supplies. You'd be surprised how friendships can get strained because people did not work out the finances beforehand.

SKILL DEVELOPMENT

Depending on the type of group you're traveling with, people may have varying levels of experience. There are specific skills that people need before the trip, such as how to pack a pack, and some that need to be taught on the trip, such as how to set up camp or how to use a backpacking stove. There are so many different skills I use on a backcountry trip that I find it hard to remember them all—many I just do automatically. Take the time to make a list of these skills so you don't overlook anything (a sample Teaching Plan is included in the Appendix). If you are a trip leader, or if you're just traveling with friends who are less experienced, plan time to cover the important subjects both ahead of time and on the trail.

For advanced-level trips, you may need to do a more formal skill assessment. For example, if you are going to be traveling across glaciers, does everyone have experience traveling on snow, handling an ice axe, and being roped up? Will people need to know special techniques like self-arrest or crevasse rescue? Sometimes this assessment is done by reviewing people's previous trip experiences, or you may have the group go out on a supervised practice trip to review and test special skills.

TRIP PREPARATION CHECKLIST

Use this checklist to help organize all the tasks that need to be accomplished before, during, and after your trip. If you are going on an extended expedition, expand the list and establish specific timelines for each task. For example, trips to remote areas might require you to apply months or even years in advance for a permit.

PRE-TRIP

This is a general list of things to accomplish before the trip, in a loose chronological order.

- Contact participants and arrange meetings to talk about the trip (activities, experience level, individual and group goals, etc.).
- Make lists of necessary personal equipment and group equipment, based on trip activities, location, and weather.
- Identify potential hazards: environmental, equipment, and human. (See "How Accidents Happen," page 225.)
- Have all participants fill out a Fitness and Health Information Form (page 408).
- If appropriate, have people turn in a trip résumé to gauge their experience.
- Evaluate the physical ability of each participant and develop a route appropriate for all members of the group.
- In planning the route, consider transportation time, hours of daylight, time needed to set up camp, teaching time, rest days needed, changes in elevation, and other factors.
- Make arrangements for any permits needed.
- Develop a menu based on personal preferences and special dietary needs.
- Assemble the group equipment and first aid kit.
- Purchase and repackage the food.
- Meet to distribute the group equipment and food for final packing.
- Put together a trip packet with cash, credit cards, vehicle keys, maps, emergency numbers, travel directions, and the like.
- Designate an emergency contact (someone who is not going on the trip) and give that person your Trip Logistics Plan and Trip Safety Plan (pages

411 and 412), showing your planned starting and ending points, daily route, campsites, and return time, along with the appropriate emergency numbers and instructions about who to call if you are overdue.

- Contact area rangers for last-minute trail information.
- Check the weather.

DURING THE TRIP

- Keep track of all expenses on a Trip Expenses Form (page 417).
- Fill out your Trip Log (page 418) as you hike so you have detailed information on hiking times, campsite locations, and water availability for future trips.
- Document any close calls, accidents, or first aid treatments. These should be reviewed after the trip. (See Chapter 8, "Safety and Emergency Procedures.")

ON YOUR RETURN

- Notify your emergency contact person as soon as you return, and let him or her know you have returned safely.
- Return any borrowed personal or group equipment.
- Clean all gear. Water bottles and water containers should be treated with iodine or chlorine bleach solution if they have contained potentially contaminated water. (See "Water Purification," page 94.)
- Dispose of garbage and properly dispose of human waste if you packed it out. (See Chapter 5, "Leave No Trace Hiking and Camping.")
- Dispose of any medical waste properly (see page 121).
- Settle up finances.
- It's good to talk about the trip afterwards and see how well it met the goals you set out as a group and each individual's goals. Are there things that you'd do differently next time? Identify and discuss any problems on the trip, including close calls or accidents. (See Chapter 8, "Safety and Emergency Procedures," and Chapter 10, "Outdoor Leadership.")

ROUTE DIFFICULTY

Whoever decides to plan the route should first determine the physical condition of the people going, which can be difficult. It's best to rely on some form of objective measurement rather than counting on the "Yeah, I'm in great shape" reply. After reviewing thousands of health and fitness forms from college students I'm still amazed how often people either overestimate or underestimate their physical fitness level. Assessing physical fitness ranges from asking some basic questions about health and exercise activities to administering a required physical exam. Base your degree of assessment on the level of difficulty for the trip: If the trip is of low to moderate difficulty, staying relatively close to civilization, then you'll have greater resources to fall back on in case of a problem. If the trip is more difficult or ventures into a remote location with limited access for evacuation or medical care, you need to do a much more thorough screening. In some cases, you may even require a specific conditioning regimen. Part of making sure that a person is going on the right trip is giving the individual as detailed information as possible about what the trip will entail. Having someone attempt a trip that is too physically demanding can lead to friction within the group as well as real safety issues.

TRIP DIFFICULTY RATING

Wouldn't it be great if you could look in a guidebook and find out how easy or difficult a particular hike would be? Unfortunately there is no commonly used system for rating trail difficulty. Lots of other outdoor sports, like rock climbing and whitewater paddling, have systems for rating the difficulty of a climbing pitch or a whitewater river. These systems are very useful for matching your skill level with the difficulty of the trip.

There are so many factors that can slow down or speed up a hiker that rating the difficulty of a trail is extremely subjective. Take the Appalachian Trail in Pennsylvania: In the southern part of the state, it is on a fairly flat ridge with good trails, then it moves northward and you enter the dreaded "rock zone," where the trail requires constant rock-hopping for miles that slows down hikers significantly. I look at the following factors and rely on my own hiking experience as a gauge.

- Daily mileage
- Daily elevation changes—how many feet/meters you go up or down over the course of the day
- Steepness of ascent or descent
- Trail conditions (smooth, rocky, switchbacks, off trail, etc.)
- Amount of weight the person is carrying, as a percentage of their body weight. (See "The Backpack," page 38.)
- If you are over 8,000 feet (2,438 meters), consider the effect of reduced oxygen and acclimatization on hiking pace. (See "Altitude Illnesses," page 380.)

PLANNING A ROUTE
GUIDEBOOKS

I like to start with guidebooks when planning a trip. Since the maps that you would typically take on a trip are pretty specific (and buying lots of maps can get expensive), it's best to focus on the general area that you are interested in first, and a good guidebook is indispensable. Most guidebooks will give you an overview of the area and some basic maps, so you can get an idea of where to go. A good guidebook will also have specific trails and trips described in detail with mileages, elevation changes, campsites, places to visit, etc. Since guidebooks are so regionally specific, there are lots of different publishers, and finding guidebooks outside your local area can be difficult. Whenever I travel I make it a habit to stop at local bookstores or outdoor shops to see what local-area guidebooks and maps they have. Here are a few of the larger publishers you might check out:

- Appalachian Mountain Club *(www.outdoors.org)*
- The Globe Pequot Press *(www.globepequot.com)*
- Menasha Ridge Press *(www.menasharidge.com)*
- The Mountaineers Books *(www.mountaineersbooks.org)*
- Stackpole Books *(www.stackpolebooks.com)*
- Wilderness Press *(www.wildernesspress.com)*

Once you've located a specific area, get some maps and start working out the details of your trip. (See "Maps and Map Reading," page 134.)

- See "Estimating Travel Times" (page 12) to determine how long each day's hike will take. For each day, establish a Time Control Plan that includes your hiking time along with other factors to calculate your total travel time for the day. During the day, monitor your Time Control Plan; you may have to modify the trip if you are not able to keep to your planned schedule.
- Use the Trip Logistics Plan (page 411) to help document your route and to give to your emergency contact person.
- As you plan your route, develop a daily evacuation plan and document it on your Trip Logistics Plan. For each day of the trip, know, in general, where you would go to get help in case of an emergency. Obviously, this information will change all the time, but you should know the area well enough to find nearby roads or towns or other resources in case of a problem.

TRAVEL LOGISTICS

- Where is your starting point? Where is your ending point? What type of road or other access is there to the trail?
- Is everyone traveling together to get to the trailhead or going separately?
- Is this a loop route, or an in-and-out route back to your original starting point (A to A), or a one-way route (A to B)? If A to B, do you need to get back to A to get to your car? Can you do your own shuttle? Or do you need to be picked up at B? Are there taxis or public transportation available?

Once you are out on your trip, keep an accurate daily trip log about where you went, what you saw, how long it took, and so on. This will be a great help in planning your next trip.

🍁 TRICKS OF THE TRAIL

Timing is Everything There are a lot of environmental factors that can impact your trip route. For example, in mountainous regions like the Rockies, afternoon thunderstorms are very common in the summer. If you are going to travel on exposed ridges or summits, you want to plan your day to leave very early and be back down off exposed areas by the early afternoon. Another mountain issue is snowmelt. The stream crossings in Denali National Park in Alaska are legendary. During the summer, as the temperature rises during the day, there is greater snow and ice melt. What can be an easy low-water crossing in the early morning can become a dangerous or impassable current by the afternoon.

CHOOSING CAMPSITES

Trip planning is often done from campsite to campsite. You need to make sure that at the end of the day, you will have a place to set up your tent or tarp that isn't in the middle of a bog or perched on a steep rockslide. A lot of campsite selection can be done using guidebooks and maps. Select a site that allows your group to set up a good Leave No Trace campsite. (See Chapter 5, "Leave No Trace Hiking and Camping.") Unfortunately, sometimes you don't have the information you need to determine a good campsite in advance, and you'll have to locate a spot as you hike. More than once, I've looked at the map contours and thought, "That looks flat; there must be a good campsite there," only to discover thick underbrush with no open spaces. Here are some general guidelines for campsite selection:

- **Water Availability**   Preferably you want a site near a water source; otherwise, you may need to carry in enough water for dinner, breakfast the next day, and possibly the next day's hike. Is the water source reliable at all times of year? Is it drinkable or must it be treated?
- **Campsite Space**   You want a site that provides enough open space for sleeping, cooking, and washing. (These areas do not have to be right next to each other.) In locations like bear country, it is best if you have a campsite with enough space to keep these areas separate (see page 180).
- **Campsite Location**   If you don't know of a specific campsite, start looking for campsites early in the day. It's better to stop at a good campsite earlier on and make up the mileage the next day, rather than continue hiking, only to find nothing there—which means either backtracking or continuing to hike on, which could be difficult or even dangerous if it's getting dark.
- **Private Land**   Be sensitive about hiking on private land. In some cases hiking through is permitted but overnight camping is not. If conditions (bad weather, an injured group member) require it, you may decide you need to. If so, recognize that you may be breaking the law and must live with the consequences. Most people are understanding about emergency situations.
- **Restricted Areas**   Don't camp in a restricted area (unless a group member's safety is at stake). The area is restricted for a reason. If you choose to camp in a restricted area, recognize that you may be subject to tickets, fines, or even arrest. Explain your situation to rangers or other officials and ask for their assistance. Get them involved as allies in helping you in a difficult situation rather than as law-enforcement officials prosecuting you for an offense. In most cases involving safety (like an injury), rangers and wilderness managers are very understanding. They may still require you to move but may be helpful in finding another location.

ESTIMATING TRAVEL TIMES

As part of planning your route you want to figure out how long it's going to take you each day. Getting a truly accurate estimate of travel times for your trip is difficult since there are so many factors: your physical condition, condition of the trail, elevation gain/loss, amount of weight you are carrying, rest stops, how much you want to stop and enjoy nature, etc. Guidebooks can be a real help here, since some give estimates of how many hours are required for the hike.

Here is a *general* formula for estimating travel time for backpacking trips. Use this *only* as an estimate: On a day hike with less gear or if you are going ultralight, you will move faster than with a heavy pack; a packed dirt trail will be faster than sand dunes or powder snow. In a group, people with different physical abilities or of different ages may move faster or slower, changing the pace of the entire group. This gets back to our earlier discussion about physical condition levels. If you have a broad range of physical condition levels, it may be hard to find a pace that everyone is comfortable/satisfied with. Talk about this before the trip and arrive at a decision that the whole group can live with. As a rule of thumb, the larger the group, the more slowly it moves (there are more stops for pack adjustments, bathroom breaks, etc.).

General Travel Time Guidelines

- An average person's hiking speed on generally flat terrain is 30 minutes per mile (1.6 kilometers), so 1 hour equals 2 miles (3.2 kilometers). If you know that your hiking speed is faster or slower than this, adjust the formula.
- Add 1 hour for each 1,000 feet (305 meters) of ascent.
- Plan about 5 minutes of rest for each hour of hiking. The more people you have, the more rest stops, bathroom breaks, and equipment adjustments there will be, so adjust accordingly.

Calculating Miles per Hour

Divide the number of miles to be hiked by 2. Calculate the total feet of ascent, divide it by 1,000, and multiply that number by 1 hour. Add up all the hours to find the total hiking hours for the day.

> (miles traveled ÷ 2 mph) + (elevation gained ÷ 1,000) + (miles traveled × 5 minutes) = travel time

Example: A group hikes 8 miles (12.8 kilometers) in Rocky Mountain National Park. The day includes a total ascent of 2,000 feet (610 meters). The estimated time to hike this route would be:

> 8 miles ÷ 2 miles per hour = 4 hours + (2,000 ÷ 1,000) × 1 hour [ascent]
>
> 4 hours + 2 hours = 6 hours + (6 × 5 minutes for rest breaks) = 6 hours 30 minutes

Calculating Kilometers per Hour

Using the same example, divide the number of kilometers to be hiked by 1.6. Calculate the total meters of ascent, divide it by 305, and multiply that number by 1 hour. Add up all the hours to find the total hiking hours for the day.

Using the same example from above, the estimated time to hike this route would be:

12.8 kilometers ÷ 1.6 kilometers per hour = 4 hours + (610 ÷ 305) × 1 hour [ascent]

4 hours + 2 hours = 6 hours + (6 × 5 minutes for rest breaks) = 6 hours 30 minutes

These calculations will give you basic transit time. This *doesn't* include longer stops for meals, stops for scenic views and photos, etc. You will need to add time in for these things each day based on information from maps and guidebooks or personal experience with the area. Once you are hiking, check your actual time against the time you calculated for your route. By keeping a daily Trip Log (page 418) with information on hiking times, trail conditions, rest breaks, etc., you can refine your estimates. Use your actual travel time to revise your estimates for the next day of your trip. If there is a significant discrepancy, you may need to revise your route plan.

TIME CONTROL PLAN

A Time Control Plan is just that: a plan for controlling your time on the trail each day. Creating a daily Time Control Plan will help you get to your planned destination on time and reduce the potential for accidents. (See Chapter 8, "Safety and Emergency Procedures.")

Here's an example. You are planning a summer day hike to the top of Mt. Princeton at 14,197 feet (4,327 meters), in Colorado, in late July. There won't be any snow on the trails at that time. The hike starts at 8,900 feet (2,712 meters). It's 6.25 miles to the summit (10 kilometers). You know that afternoon thunderstorms are common, and you need to be off the exposed ridgelines of the peak by early afternoon. You calculate that it will take you 5 hours to reach the summit including rest breaks. It will then take you 2 hours to get back to treeline at 11,000 feet (3,352 meters). You decide to start hiking at 5:00 A.M. Your plan has you arriving at the summit at 10:30 A.M. You plan for 30 minutes for lunch on the summit, with a departure time of 11:30 A.M. to start heading back (an extra 30 minutes of buffer time). This gets you back to treeline at 1:30 P.M.—within your window of safety for afternoon storms. As you can see, this is just a one-day hike and there were lots of time-control parameters.

The following table will help you plan each day. Start with what time you will get up, and then fill in times for each day's activities. Remember all of the factors discussed earlier to help determine your route, such as participant age, experience, and physical condition, as well as trail conditions, pack weight, and weather. Add up all the times and then subtract that from the hours of daylight.

If your result is a negative number, you're likely to end up arriving after dark. Look at the route and see if hiking in the dark would put you on a difficult section of the trail. If that presents a problem, go back to the drawing board and make some changes—cut down the mileage, decide if you can hike faster, or get up earlier.

TIME REQUIRED

+ ___ minutes	How long will it take you to break camp?
+ ___ minutes	Are there any special places you want to explore?
+ ___ minutes	Based on your estimated travel time, how long will your group take to hike the distance?
+ ___ minutes	Are there any hindrances to travel, such as river crossings or bushwhacks, that will add additional time?
+ ___ minutes	How much time is needed for rest breaks and meals?
+ ___ minutes	How long it will take to set up a proper Leave No Trace camp?
= ___ hours ___ minutes	Add all of the above for your total time.
− ___ hours ___ minutes	Subtract the number of hours of daylight.
___ hours ___ minutes	Total Planned Travel Time—if this is a negative number, you don't have enough hours of daylight, so think about replanning.

LONG-DISTANCE TRIPS

Planning a long-distance trip is a whole different ballgame from a few days or a week. Once you get into multiweek or multimonth trips, you can't carry all of your food on your back, so you have to start thinking about resupply. There are far too many things to cover about long-distance backpacking in the space provided here, but these general guidelines will get you started, and the Bibliography includes references for long-distance hiking.

RESUPPLY ISSUES

- Are there resupply locations within a reasonable hike from the trail at the intervals you need? Hike out, buy food, and hike back in.
- Can someone meet you along the trail for resupply?
- Can you mail items to yourself care of General Delivery? This works for nonperishable food items. Pack food for the period between post offices and mail it to yourself. You'll need to know where the post offices are and plan how you'll get to them from the trail. For trails like the Appalachian Trail, all of this information is well documented for through-hikers.

- Do you develop some sort of meal rotation so you don't have to eat the same mac & cheese dinner every night and also don't have to plan a ridiculous number of meals? Don't plan too much—many through-hikers find that their tastes change as they go through the trip.
- What other items besides food will you need to replenish (fuel, batteries, etc.)? Many hikers handle some of these needs through a "bump box" or "drift box." They mail things ahead of themselves to the next General Delivery site and can pick up items they need temporarily, like toenail clippers and a razor, then send them on again and not have to carry them.

How you answer these questions is going to have a big impact on both your route and food planning. It might be 5 days between your resupply one week and 8 days the next.

✺ GOING ULTRALIGHT

Many of us go to the wilderness for a sense of freedom. We leave civilization behind and feel this great connection with the outdoors. It's funny how we also tend to bring everything but the kitchen sink with us in order to feel "comfortable" in the outdoors. All that weight has an impact on hiking speed, your joints, how much mileage you can cover, what you can see, and just the pure pleasure of hiking. Think about those great day hikes you've been on with lightweight boots and a small daypack on your back; you just eat up the miles. Then you come back to the same place for a multiday trip and you've got 50+ pounds (22+ kilograms) on your back. Where you were flying before, you're now just trudging along. But there is an alternative. Ultralight backpacking is as close to flying on the trail as you can get, and throughout the book I'll give you tips on how to incorporate ultralight practices in your backpacking trips. Watch for the feather logo and the GOING ULTRALIGHT heading to help you plan your lightweight getaway.

Ultralight backpacking evolved from long-distance through-hikers on trails like the Appalachian Trail (AT) and the Pacific Crest Trail (PCT). When you're hiking every day for six months you really come to understand what it means to carry extra weight, and these hikers quickly learn just what they need and what they don't need on the trail. Talk to people who have completed one of these trails, and they will tell you about all the stuff they shipped home along the way because they just weren't using it.

I've always been an "overpacker," bringing stuff I think that *maybe* I might need or just want to have. I end up huffing and puffing with a huge pack, and a good 20 percent of it never gets used. During my first trip to New Zealand I had to cut way back on what I took with me, and that changed my perspective dramatically. If you know the area and the conditions you are going to encounter, and if you know your own body (what you need to keep warm, dry, and comfortable), you don't have to carry tons of gear. There's been a revolution in the availability of ultralight clothing, sleeping bags, packs, stoves, and shelters, so you can now go out and be comfortable without breaking your back. The person who is perhaps best known for leading this revolution is Ray Jardine, whose book *Beyond Backpacking* is a classic text for anyone who is serious about the ultralight approach. Ray is a visionary who accomplished his goals of dramatically reducing equipment weight through his own ingenuity. He went from a 75-pound (34 kilogram) pack on his first PCT through-hike to under 12 pounds (5.4 kilograms).

Trained as an engineer, Ray has always been an inventor, so sewing his own clothing, packs, and shelters wasn't anything new. Most of us aren't visionaries and don't have time to sew our own gear. Thankfully, major equipment manufacturers like GOLITE, Gregory, Mountain Hardwear, Sierra Designs, and others have recognized the demand for ultralight gear and now produce a wide range of products, including clothing, packs, shelters, and sleeping bags. The very lightest gear can be too fragile for commercial production, so the cutting edge of this type of design is often done by hard-core ultralight techies. Check out some of the resources in the Bibliography.

When you are planning a route, you make a set of assumptions on miles per day based on the 2 miles per hour formula (3.2 kilometers). That's an *average* hiking speed for an *average* person carrying an *average* weight pack. As you drop equipment weight, your daily hiking mileage is going to increase. Experienced ultralight hikers routinely cover 25 to 30 miles per day (40–48 kilometers). So keep this in mind if you are planning a trip with ultralight gear. One caveat: just taking lighter gear doesn't mean you can hike long distances. Through-hikers have either trained or build up to those mileages. Of course, just because you can hike farther doesn't mean you have to. You may head to the same place as you would with a heavier pack and have more time for exploring side hikes along the way, a long stop for nature photography and journaling at lunch, etc. If you are planning a trip with friends and some have ultralight gear and others heavier gear, you'll need to talk about the goals for the trip and how you will manage different hiking paces and timelines.

One important thing to understand about the ultralight approach is that it is both a philosophy and a continuum. The philosophy is to *take only what you need and need only what you take*. The continuum is your personal choices and strategies. You might reduce weight with clothing, sleeping bag, and backpack choices and still decide to take a tent because it's black fly season, and for your enjoyment of the outdoors (or so you don't go insane) you'd like to be in a tent. Someone else might be comfortable with a lighter weight tarp and a mosquito headnet. Here are the principles my friend Bill "Tigerpaw" Plonk suggests based on his ultralight through-hike of the Appalachian Trail.

- Take only what you need.
- Take the lightest gear that will do the job.
- Use gear with multiple functions.
- Reassess regularly and discard whatever you haven't used.

There isn't one "right" lightweight approach (and don't let purists try to convince you otherwise), but I can guarantee you, once you start to shed pounds, you'll never go back.

CHAPTER 2
Equipment

EQUIPMENT ASSESSMENT

The idea of being able to live with *just* what you carry on your back is one of the things that makes backpacking such an enticing activity. At the same time, that means that *what* you carry on your back becomes incredibly important—clothing, boots, sleeping bags, tents, stoves, first-aid gear, water filters, etc. This chapter is designed to help you think about the major pieces of equipment you'll need for your trip. When it's time to get your gear together, there are sample equipment lists in the Appendix, including personal equipment, group equipment, and first-aid equipment to help you gather what you need.

Whether you're going for a one-day hike on a local trail or a month-long expedition to a remote area, you need to thoroughly plan what equipment to bring. The equipment assessment for your trip should cover the following areas:

PERSONAL EQUIPMENT

- **Clothing**   Shirts, pants, boots, hats, and so on
- **Travel**   What is needed for travel—just your feet or a canoe, a bike, cross-country skis, etc.
- **Storage**   What you use to carry personal and group equipment—a backpack, bike panniers, waterproof bags for canoeing, etc.
- **Sleeping**   Sleeping bag, foam/inflatable pad
- **Miscellaneous**   Water bottles, toiletries, personal items

GROUP EQUIPMENT

- **Shelter**   Evaluate the type of shelter required for the size of the group and anticipated weather conditions—tarp, tent, or shelters on the trail.
- **Cooking**   Stoves, pots and pans, utensils
- **Hygiene**   Items for water purification, handwashing, going to the bathroom
- **First aid**   See page 406 for a list of first-aid essentials
- **Repair**   Anticipate what might break and have the necessary replacement parts and tools.

When deciding what equipment to bring, review your planned route and answer the following questions:

- How long is the trip?
- How many people are going? How does that affect the amount of group equipment needed?
- Are people providing their own personal equipment?

- Who is providing group equipment?
- What season is it? What are the typical maximum and minimum temperatures during the day? What is typical weather (foggy morning, afternoon thunderstorms, etc.)? What is atypical weather (can it snow in July)? (See Chapter 7, "Weather and Nature.")
- What is the altitude? What effect will the altitude have on temperature? (See "Temperature Ranges," page 194.)
- What are the trip activities? What equipment will be needed for different activities?
- Where is the trip? Is it remote or accessible?
- Is equipment resupply a possibility or will you have to carry everything?
- Do you need any special equipment for Leave No Trace camping? (See Chapter 5.)
- How will you deal with equipment repair if things break? What equipment items are more likely to break? What equipment items, if broken, would create serious problems for the trip (e.g., stoves)?

THE ESSENTIALS

No matter where you are going, and whether you are out for a day or a month, there are some pieces of equipment that are considered *essential* for safe backcountry travel. There are countless tales of hikers who have gotten into trouble, even on short day hikes, because they neglected these essentials.

- Map
- Compass (and knowledge of how to use it)
- Extra food
- Extra clothing (polypropylene, fleece, or other insulating clothing)
- Water bottle (full, 1–2 quarts)
- Flashlight/headlamp with extra batteries
- Rain gear
- Pocketknife
- Matches/lighter (best to have at least two sources for lighting a fire)
- Candle or firestarter to help light a fire
- First-aid kit
- Sunglasses and sunscreen

Other recommended items include:

- Watch
- Water purification system

- Large garbage bag, space blanket, tube tent, or small tarp for emergency shelter
- Foam or inflatable sleeping pad for ground insulation

CLOTHING

Knowing what to buy and wear is hard. There are so many different materials out there that do similar things, and everything has a fancy name that ends in something like *-ex* or *-tec*. As you are reading this, some industrial chemist in a lab somewhere is developing the next generation of smart fabrics while garment designers dream up innovative features. Clothing manufacturers crank out new lines so frequently that it isn't possible to give you specific information on what's available now, so here are some general guidelines to help you choose the best clothing for your trip.

REGULATING YOUR BODY TEMPERATURE

In order to plan the right clothing for a trip, you need to understand how your body reacts to the temperature and weather conditions you are likely to experience. Balancing the heat you are losing to the environment with the heat you generate from exercise and absorb from the environment is called thermoregulation. According to *The Outward Bound Wilderness First Aid Handbook,* if you gain more heat than you lose, you experience a heat challenge. (See "Regulating Body Temperature," page 329.) If you lose more heat than you gain, you experience a cold challenge. The ability to regulate body temperature is critical for preventing hyperthermia and hypothermia. (See "Heat-Related Illnesses," page 342, and "Hypothermia," page 332.)

One way to regulate body temperature is to wear the right clothing and layer your clothing properly. Clothing items should be versatile enough to meet the various seasonal and weather conditions you may encounter. Since each person's body is different, experiment to determine your individual requirements.

How Your Body Loses Heat

Heat leaves your body in the following ways:

- **Conductive Heat Loss** occurs when contact is made between your body and a cooler surface. It can be minimized by not sitting on the cold ground, especially on snow. Conduction occurs 25 times faster with wet clothing than with dry. *Prevention:* Thickness of insulation.
- **Convective Heat Loss** occurs when your body heat warms the air adja-

cent to your body; that air then rises and moves away from your body and fresh colder air replaces it. Wind increases the speed of heat loss through convection. The impact of heat loss from convection is measured by the windchill factor. (See "Windchill Index," page 331.) This same process happens when you are submerged in cold water, but it happens much faster than in air because of the greater density of water. An important element in dressing for the backcountry is trapping the air around the body. *Prevention:* Windproof garments.

- **Radiant Heat Loss** is caused by the escape of infrared radiation from the body. It is minimized by wearing insulative fabrics or those with reflective fabric that reflects the heat back to the body. *Prevention:* Thick layers of insulation or reflective material.

- **Evaporative Heat Loss** occurs when perspiration (water) on the skin evaporates, drawing heat from the body. Changing water from a liquid to a gas takes a lot of energy. This is why sweating helps cool you off when you are hot. In hot weather, evaporation is essential in cooling your body down to prevent heat illnesses. (See "Heat Challenge," page 342.) However, when it's cold you want to minimize the amount of sweating to reduce evaporative heat loss. *Prevention:* Fabrics that move water away from the skin and vapor barriers (page 24).

Trapping Your Body Heat

Clothing insulates you from the environment by trapping your body heat. The best insulation is a layer of static, unmoving air close to your body, known as "dead air." This air is warmed by heat given off by your body (through radiation, conduction, and convection) and maintains a warm microclimate around your body. Clothing insulates by creating pockets of dead air. How much a particular clothing fabric insulates is based on its loft or thickness—the greater the loft, the more dead air space. Also, different fibers are better at creating dead air space than others. The goal is to find a fiber that creates lots of dead air space and at the same time doesn't weigh very much. This is known as the warmth-to-weight ratio. A really light fiber like down has an excellent warmth-to-weight ratio.

Not all clothing is designed to insulate. In hot desert environments, thin layers of clothing with negligible loft are worn not to insulate but to provide shade from the sun to minimize overheating. You want something loose-fitting that ventilates and allows your sweat to evaporate, cooling you off.

THE LAYERING PRINCIPLE

By wearing multiple layers of different types of fabrics you can maintain a comfortable body temperature without excessive sweating (which can lead to heat loss). Throughout the day, you "layer up" or "layer down" as temperature conditions and/or activity levels change. By experimentation, you can determine which of the base layer, insulating layer, and shell layers you require in various situations. The layers should not restrict your movement and the outer layer, especially, should not be too tight, since tight outer layers squeeze the layers beneath and actually compress the dead air space in layers below, reducing their insulation value. You can modify one or all of the following factors to properly thermoregulate.

- **Clothing Layers** The number and type of layers you wear allow you to create sufficient dead air space for insulation and protection from external conditions (wind, rain, etc.). Extra layers may be added in the cooler hours of the morning or evening, or when your activity level drops, like at a lunch break.
- **Activity Level** Increasing or decreasing your activity level increases or decreases the heat you generate.
- **Staying Dry** An important factor in retaining heat is to minimize wetness, since you can lose heat 25 times faster in wet clothing than in dry. Moisture comes internally from perspiration generated by exercise or externally from rain or snow. You want clothing layers that minimize the buildup of moisture close to your skin and also protect you from external moisture.
- **Ventilation** Opening up or closing the layers of your clothing allows you to decrease or increase heat loss as needed, without having to actually remove or add a layer. As you move, a bellows action occurs in clothing that pumps your accumulated warm air out through openings and pulls the cooler air in. In some conditions, this bellows action can reduce your body's insulation by 50 percent or more, so unzip if you are too hot and zip up if you are cold. Ventilating also prevents moisture buildup from perspiration. Look for clothing that allows for easy ventilation, such as full-zip outer shell jackets, armpit zippers in shell jackets, zip-front turtlenecks, button-down shirts, and side-zip pants. Rolling up sleeves and pants legs is another way to ventilate.

THE CLOTHING LAYERS
The Base/Wicking Layer

The base/wicking layer keeps the skin dry and comfortable. This layer transports moisture from body perspiration away from the skin to the outside of the fabric. This layer should dry quickly. In cool weather, wear close-fitting layers to provide insulation. In warm weather, wear loose-fitting layers to maximize ventilation and absorption of moisture for the skin to keep cool and dry. There are a number of different ways to wick moisture away from your body:

- **Hydrophobic/Hydrophilic Fibers**   These are synthetic fibers often made of polyester or polypropylene that do not absorb water (as cotton does). They are extremely effective worn directly against the skin to keep it dry and reduce evaporative heat loss. In addition to not absorbing water, many of these fabrics are hydrophobic ("water-hating") on the inside, so they push the water vapor from the area of highest concentration (next to your skin) to the outside of the fabric. Some fabrics are hydrophilic ("water-loving") on the outside and pull the water outward. Others are bicomponent and use both a hydrophobic inner layer and a hydrophilic outer layer. The hydrophobic or hydrophilic nature is accomplished either by the physical characteristic of the fabric itself or by applying a chemical coating to the fabric. *Examples:* Capilene, Lifa, and Dryline.
- **Micro-channel Fibers**   These are synthetic fibers with tiny channels or capillaries within the individual fabric threads. These fabrics rely on what is known as "capillary action" to transport moisture through the channels from next to your skin to the outside of the fabric. Some fabrics are bicomponent with an inner layer of macrofiber yarn and an outer layer of microfiber yarn. The outer layer has a much greater surface area, which helps "pull" the water to the outside of the fabric. *Examples:* CoolMax and Polartec PowerDry.

🍁 TRICKS OF THE TRAIL

Vapor Barriers A vapor barrier is a clothing item that is waterproof, serving as a barrier to the transportation of water vapor. When worn near the skin, it keeps water vapor near the skin. Eventually the humidity level rises to the point where the body senses a high humidity level and shuts off perspiration. This stops evaporative heat loss and slows dehydration. Vapor barriers are typically worn on top of a light wicking layer, not directly against the skin. There is no doubt that a vapor barrier system is effective for some people in some conditions. Before using a vapor barrier, consider your activity level, the amount you naturally sweat, and your "moisture comfort." One common use of vapor barriers is socks. Feet are susceptible to cold since they have a high surface-to-volume ratio and we rarely put as much insulation on our feet as we do on our upper bodies. A vapor barrier sock can help make your feet warmer. If the temperature drops and your feet aren't able to stay warm, put plastic bags on your feet over your liner socks.

Some of these fabrics have a definite "inside" and "outside." If you wear a bicomponent garment inside out, you defeat the purpose of the garment. Garments that rely on the physical characteristics of the fabric itself rather than a chemical coating continue to function regardless of the number of times they are washed, while those that rely on a chemical treatment may eventually "wear out." There are different thicknesses of these fabrics, generically called lightweight, medium weight, and heavy or expedition weight. The thicker fabrics offer great insulative value along with their wicking properties. *Pro:* Excellent inner layer. Minimizes moisture next to the body, where high conductive heat loss can occur. *Con:* Not windproof, so best used as an inner layer. Some fabrics retain odor more than others.

The Insulating Layers

The main purpose of the insulating layer is to create dead air space for insulation. It also absorbs some of the wicking layer's moisture, keeping the moisture away from your skin, so you want it to easily pass moisture. Depending on the temperature this can be one layer or many layers.

- **First Layer** Your first insulating layer is typically shirts and pants. This could be an extension of the wicking layer—for example, wearing middle-weight to expedition-weight polypropylene that both wicks and provides insulation. Layers that allow you to "open" and "close," like zip-front turtlenecks or button-down shirts, allow for ventilation during periods of high heat-producing activity. Synthetics like polypropylene or Thermax work well in this layer.
- **Second Layer** If you need more loft for insulation, add another insulating layer like synthetic fleece or wool pullovers, sweaters, jackets, and pants.
- **Outer Layer** If it is really cold, you may need to add an even thicker layer like an insulated parka or pants. These typically have an outer and

---

🍁 TRICKS OF THE TRAIL

Loose fill versus continuous fill Insulating fibers can either be loose fill, like down, or continuous fill, like Polarguard. Loose fills are made up of small individual fibers. In order to keep the fibers equally distributed throughout the sleeping bag or garment, the manufacturer has to sew in interior "walls" of fabric known as baffles to create individual compartments to hold the fill. This adds a lot to the manufacturing cost.

Continuous-fill fibers are made in large sheets that can be cut into the right shape and sewn directly into the sleeping bag or garment without baffles.

inner layer of fabric and either down or some synthetic insulating fill sandwiched in between. These layers are often worn at the beginning and end of the day in camp, when activity levels are low or in temperatures below freezing.

The Insulating Materials

Fleece is a synthetic fabric often made of a plastic (polyester, polyolefin, polypropylene). It has a "fuzzy" 3-D quality that imitates a sheep's fleece and gives it insulating properties. It remains warm when wet, does not absorb moisture, and dries very quickly. This material has an insulative capacity similar to that of wool. Fleece is manufactured in a variety of thicknesses, offering different amounts of loft and insulation and numerous layering possibilities. Some fleece garments are made from recycled plastics or with a middle windproof layer. *Pro:* Fleece is able to provide the equivalent warmth of wool at half the weight. *Con:* Fleece by itself has poor wind resistance and almost always requires an additional wind-resistant layer. *Examples:* Polartec 100, Polartec 200.

Wool derives its insulating quality from the elastic, three-dimensional wavy crimp in the fiber that traps air. Depending on the texture and thickness of the fabric, as much as 80 percent of wool cloth can be air. Wool can absorb a fair amount of moisture without imparting a damp feeling because the water "disappears" into the fiber spaces. Even with water in the fabric, wool retains some dead air space and will still insulate you. The disadvantage to wool is that it can absorb a lot of water, making it very heavy when wet. Maximum absorption can be as much as one-third the garment weight. Wool releases moisture slowly, with minimum chilling effect. *Pro:* Tightly woven wool is quite wind resistant. Wool clothing can often be purchased cheaply. *Con:* Wool garments can be heavy, take a long time to dry, and can be itchy against the skin. Some people are allergic.

Down The very soft underbody plumage of geese or ducks provides excellent insulation and dead air space for very little weight. (Goose down is finer quality than duck.) Down is rated by its fill power, or how many cubic inches of volume an ounce of down will fill. Fill power goes from 550 cubic inches up to 800—a 700-fill sleeping bag lofts better and is more thermally efficient than a 550-fill bag. Most high-end sleeping bags are made of 700 fill; 800 fill is mostly for expedition-quality garments and sleeping bags.

Since down is a loose fill, sleeping bags and clothing must have a series of small compartments sewn in with baffles to hold the fill evenly throughout, which adds to the manufacturing cost. Down is useful in sleeping bags since it tends to conform to the shape of the occupant and minimizes convection areas. It is also very compressible, which is an advantage when packing. But the same compressibility means that your body weight compresses the down beneath you, significantly reducing your insulation from the cold ground, so you need an insulating pad underneath you more so than with a synthetic bag. *Pro:* Excellent insulator. Incredible warmth-to-weight ratio. Compresses to extremely compact size. Long life span if cared for properly (up to 20 years). *Con:* When down gets wet it simply clumps together and loses almost all of its insulative value *and* is almost impossible to dry in the field. Use depends on your ability to keep it dry. When using a down sleeping bag, take special care to prevent it from getting wet. For example, a vapor barrier sleeping bag liner in a down bag will help the bag stay dry from the inside and a waterproof-breathable bivy sack will help the outside keep dry. Keeping the bag in a waterproof stuff sack will protect it during the day. In wet conditions a down-fill outer parka may get soaked, and a synthetic-fill would be better. Down is a loose fiber fill that requires baffles (see "Tricks of the Trail," page 26.) Expensive. Some people are allergic.

Synthetic Fibers There is a multitude of different synthetic fibers used for garment and sleeping bag fills. Most are based on some form of polyester. These are primarily used in sleeping bags and heavy outer garments, like parkas. The fibers are fairly efficient at providing dead air space (though not nearly as efficient as down). Some products like Polarguard are made in large sheets. Others create additional dead air space by having hollow channels within the fiber (e.g., Quallofil). *Pro:* They do not absorb water and dry fairly quickly. Some fibers are produced in sheets that do not require baffling. *Con:* Heavy. Not as efficient an insulator as down. Hard to compress to a small size. Some are loose fibers that require baffling. Fibers produced in sheets tend to break down over time, losing their loft more quickly. *Examples:* Polarguard 3D, Polarguard Delta, Quallofil.

"Superthin" Fibers These synthetic fibers are based on the principle that by making the fiber thinner you can increase the amount of dead air space around the fiber. Some superthin fibers are close to the weight of down for an equivalent fiber volume. They stuff down to a small size and have similar warmth-to-weight ratios as down without the wetness issue. *Pro:* Lightweight and thermally efficient. Good compressibility for stuffing. They do not absorb water and dry fairly quickly. Some fibers are produced in sheets that do not require baffling. Can be stuffed down to a small size. *Con:* Some are loose fibers that require baffling. Some superthin fibers like Thinsulate are heavy and therefore aren't good insulators for larger items like parkas and sleeping bags but are very effective in smaller items such as gloves and boots. *Examples:* Primaloft, Lite Loft, Thinsulate.

Phase Change Materials These materials use tiny spheres or microcapsules either laminated to or embedded within the fabric surface. What is unique about this approach is that the microcapsules can be manufactured to absorb or release heat at a specific temperature. In products designed for cold weather, the microcapsules absorb and retain body heat during periods of activity, and then release the heat back during periods of inactivity—sort of like taking off a layer and putting one back on. For clothing designed for warmer temperatures, the microcapsules absorb body heat, providing a cooling effect. Currently used mostly in gloves and boots. *Pro:* Absorbs heat to keep you cool in high activity. Releases heat back in low activity. *Con:* Expensive. Fabric is "tuned" to either cold temperatures or warm temperatures. *Example:* Outlast.

The Shell Layers

The shell layer consists of an outer jacket and pants layer that protects from wind, rain, snow, and sun. It is essential to have an outer layer that is windproof and at least water resistant, if not waterproof. Acting as a windbreaker, the shell layer minimizes convective heat loss, containing the warmth trapped by layers beneath. If your shell layer is waterproof but not breathable, moisture buildup from perspiration is possible, so look for garments that provide ample ventilation options, such as full-front zips and armpit zippers. Waterproof/breathable fabrics provide both wind and rain protection and still allow some perspiration moisture to escape. However, in a driving rain, there is almost nothing you can do to stay *totally* dry when you are being active. You will either zip up and get moist from sweat or ventilate and get wet from rain, so the goal is to *minimize* moisture. One thing to think about with shells is sizing—something that fits snugly over a shirt or blouse in the store is not going to work over your wicking layer and two insulating layers. In those cases you need a garment cut large enough to handle most of your inner layers. At the same time, it is not likely that you would buy something so big that you can fit your shell over a down or synthetic parka, so you need to ask yourself if the outer parka also needs to be waterproof.

Wind Shell A wind shell is just that—a shell that projects you from the wind. It is breathable, lets moisture out, and keeps wind out. Typically these are made from fairly lightweight materials such as nylon or nylon blends. They are tightly woven so there are no open spaces for the wind to penetrate. They dry quickly and make excellent outer shells for being active in dry conditions. *Pro:* Windproof. Allows body moisture to escape. Lightweight. Inexpensive. *Con:* Not waterproof. *Examples:* Ripstop Nylon, Pertex.

Soft Shell Soft shells are a step up from a wind shell. These are wind-resistant and water-resistant shells. They are made of synthetic materials with an open weave that allows body heat and built-up moisture from inner layers to escape but is still tightly woven enough to repel light wind and rain. They perform best in active sports where heat production from activity helps draw the moisture out. The heat transfer also works to keep precipitation from entering the fabric. These will keep you dry in "gentle rain" but are not designed to be completely waterproof. They dry quickly and make excellent outer shells. *Pro:* Wind resistant. Water resistant. Allows body heat and moisture to escape. Lightweight. Dries quickly from body heat. *Con:* Not completely windproof. Not waterproof. Expensive. If the garment gets totally wet and is in contact with wet inner layers, you can quickly chill from fast water-driven conduction. *Examples:* Conduit Soft Shell, Polartec Power Shield, Schoeller Dryskin.

Hard Shell Hard shells are waterproof and are designed to keep you dry in pouring rain conditions. There are two approaches to hard shells:

- **Waterproof Shell** These are fabrics that use some type of impermeable waterproof coating (i.e., coated nylon). These will keep you dry from rain but allow water vapor from perspiration to build up in layers underneath. *Pro:* Very waterproof. Windproof. Inexpensive. *Con:* Allows for significant body moisture buildup.
- **Waterproof and Breathable Shell** There are a number of ways to make a waterproof and breathable outer shell. All rely on the principle that water droplets from rain are more than 20,000 times larger than water vapor. With a fabric that has a layer with very tiny pores, water *vapor* can pass through from the inside to the outside while the outside remains impenetrable to water *droplets*. With all of these fabrics there is always a trade-off between the degree of waterproofness of the fabric and its breathability. Some fabrics use a microporous membrane that is laminated to the fabric (Gore-Tex, Sympatex); others have a microporous coating on the fabric (Ultrex, Triple Point Ceramic, Entrant). *Pro:* Degrees of waterproofness. Degrees of breathability. Windproof. *Con:* Degrees of waterproofness. Degrees of breathability. Some body moisture buildup. Expensive.

All hard shells require some form of seam sealing. While the fabric itself may be waterproof, any place where there is stitching means a hole going through the fabric that can let water in. There are a number of approaches to seam sealing including glue, heat sealing, and seam tape.

> 🍁 **TRICKS OF THE TRAIL**
>
> **Bringing Your Rain Gear Back to Life** After frequent use, all water-proof and breathable fabrics start to lose their edge. You can revitalize them by washing with a mild nondetergent soap, machine drying, and then lightly ironing the outer fabric on a medium temperature setting. The washing helps restore the membrane or coating's effectiveness, and the heat of the iron helps bring back the ability to resist water.
>
> Many fabrics (waterproof and waterproof/breathable) have a DWR (durable water repellant) chemical coating on the outside of the fabric. This is what makes water bead up on the surface of your jacket. It's like your car after a new coat of wax. Over time these coatings wear off, allowing water to seep into the fabric. The garment may still be waterproof, just soaked on the outside and heavier. You can revitalize your DWR finish with spray-on products like Revive-X or by machine-washing it back in with a liquid treatment, like NikWax TX-Direct or McNett ReviveX.

The Head Layer

This is for sun and rain protection, and to reduce heat loss. Up to 70 percent of the body's heat can be lost through radiation and convection at the head in cold weather. Wearing a hat (preferably wool or synthetic) will conserve heat, allowing the body to send more blood to cold peripheral areas (hands, toes, feet). Other items like wide-brimmed hats can help in a downpour, keep sun off your face, and provide shade to help prevent overheating.

The Hand Layer(s)

These insulate your hands in cold conditions. Gloves and mittens come in all shapes and sizes with lots of different fabrics for insulation. They should fit snugly, not tightly. Gloves provide greater flexibility for your hands, but they are colder than mittens since they have greater surface area at the fingers for radiating heat. A combination of thin synthetic glove liners and fleece or wool mittens is excellent for cold weather. Also good are mitten shells, which add a windproof/waterproof layer. Fingerless gloves or flip-top mittens are great for cooking or other activities that require dexterity.

The Feet Layers

These serve as insulation and cushioning on your feet and help prevent blisters. You should wear a lightweight, synthetic liner sock, which helps pass moisture away from your foot. It's helpful to use a liner sock that has wicking properties. On top of the liner, wear a medium to heavy wool, wool-nylon blend, or synthetic hiking sock. Having two sock layers means that your socks will slide against each other, so the friction from your boots is absorbed by the sock layers rather than rubbing your skin (friction against the skin leads to blisters; see page 317). The outer sock provides cushioning and passes the moisture from your foot outward, keeping your foot dryer. If your feet stay damp, they get wrinkled and are more prone to blisters. *Don't* wear cotton socks. The cotton absorbs and retains the sweat from your feet, keeping your feet wet throughout the day and increasing the potential for blisters or trenchfoot (see page 341). Before putting your boots on, smooth the socks of all wrinkles to prevent blisters. You should always carry extra socks, with a recommended rotation of one set to wear, one to dry, and one always dry. I typically take three pairs of liners and two pair of wool/synthetics on multiday trips.

CLOTHING TECHNIQUES

- When you first get up in the morning, your activity level will be low, as will the air temperature. You will need to have many, if not all, of your layers on until you become active.
- As your activity level increases, you will need to shed some layers, since you will start generating heat. A good rule of thumb is, just before you get ready to hike, strip down until you feel just cool, not chilled. Then start hiking. If you begin with too many layers on, you will only start overheating and sweating and you'll have to stop 10 minutes down the trail to take layers off. Opening or closing a zipper, rolling sleeves up or down, taking a hat off or putting one on all help with temperature regulation.
- If you stop for more than a few minutes, you may need to add a layer to keep from getting chilled, so keep an extra layer close at hand.
- Different parts of your body may require different layering combinations. In winter conditions I need a lot of layers on my trunk to stay properly regulated, but my arms and legs don't need as many layers. Vests provide insulation where you need it most, around the torso, and weigh less than a full jacket.
- If your clothing gets wet—not just damp—take it off and change into something dry. You won't be able to warm up if you are in soaking wet clothing. Remember, wetness can lead to hypothermia. (See "Hypothermia," page 332.)
- At the end of the day, as activity decreases and temperature drops, you'll need to add layers. Once you start to cool down, it takes a lot of the body's resources (calories) to heat up again, so layer up immediately, before you get chilled. If your base layer is totally soaked, change into some-

thing dry before layering up. It may be good to put on more than you think you need; it will only get colder. If you are too warm, you can open up the layers and ventilate to reach the proper temperature.

🍁 TRICKS OF THE TRAIL

Cotton What's the worst thing to bring on a backpacking trip? Blue jeans. In temperate climates and environments, you should minimize your use of cotton clothing. Although cotton is comfortable to wear, cotton fibers absorb and retain water (hydrophilic). Once wet, cotton loses heat 25 times faster than dry clothing. Wet cotton clothing can be a significant factor in hypothermia (see "Hypothermia," page 332). Never wear cotton in cold conditions as a form of insulation. In warm weather, some cotton-synthetic blends can be used, since they dry more quickly than 100 percent cotton and do not absorb as much water. *Pro:* Comfortable when dry. *Con:* Absorbs water, causing increased heat loss. Loses all insulating value when wet. Difficult to dry.

🪶 GOING ULTRALIGHT—CLOTHING

Ultralight clothing is ultimately about understanding the environment and knowing yourself. In order to get the most out of an ultralight approach to clothing, you have to understand how your body works in particular temperatures and customize what you bring. I used to think about how cold it might get at night and then toss in a heavy fleece jacket as an extra layer when, in fact, a lightweight fleece vest underneath my rain jacket keeps me just as warm. Ultralight hikers develop a whole interconnected system where the layers complement one another in different combinations. Doing this can save you lots of weight without needing to buy specialized "ultralight versions" of everything. Experienced ultralight hikers know their bodies in different weather conditions and know just how to layer and delayer throughout the changing conditions of the day to keep warm, cool off, stay dry, etc. Some hikers have literally spent years refining their clothing system by fabric type, thickness, and number of layers to get it down to the least possible weight. Most people don't have the time to spend years working all this out, so look for what the experts have to say. There is a rich set of Web sites devoted to ultralight gear and lots of people who test and review things (see the Bibliography).

If you want to cut off even more weight, then buy specific ultralight gear. Weight is reduced by choosing particular fabrics that are thin and light, and by cutting out frills in the design that add weight. There are companies like GOLITE *(www.golite.com)* that specialize in ultralight gear. These companies have developed a set of interconnected products based on certain assumptions. If you go this route, you'll need to determine if their assumptions about layering fit your body needs.

This step can get expensive, especially if you already have "regular" backpacking gear, so I suggest taking it a bit at a time. However, there aren't "ultralight" versions of *every type* of garment. Instead, look for the lightest weight garment that provides the amount of insulation you need. For example, buy the lightweight fleece jacket and pair it with your rain gear for the same amount of insulation as a heavyweight fleece.

Don't be fooled into thinking that the only factor you need to look at is weight. Flexibility in a garment, like its venting capability, can make something useful over a much broader temperature range. Also, some "garments" can serve dual purposes, such as a rain poncho that doubles as a tarp for an emergency shelter. Ultralighters hate duplication, so they will take a multifunction item over a single function item every time. Ask typical AT through-hikers and see what they started carrying at first and what they ended up carrying as they learned just what they needed and how to get different clothing items to work together.

One caveat about going ultralight: it's going to change the way you treat your gear. One of the reasons that things like packs are so heavy is not that manufacturers can't make them lightweight. It's that people abuse them so much. So the manufacturer adds a "super-double-extra-kevlar-cordura bottom panel" to the pack so the fabric doesn't rip when you drop it on a rock. Ultralight gear is specifically not built this way, so you need to handle it carefully.

BOOTS

Your boots are among the most important pieces of equipment that you bring into the backcountry. With every step, they are the direct interface between you and the land. Boots come in an almost infinite array of heights, weights, materials, soles, etc. They should be selected according to your needs—day trip versus multiday, packweight, terrain, season and temperature, your hiking style (traditional versus ultralight), and personal characteristics (e.g., weak ankles), to name a few. And there isn't one boot that is best for every condition. The boots that are best for a day hike are not the best boots for a multiday winter camping expedition. Boots are an investment. Selecting, fitting, breaking in, and caring for your boots will help them last a long time and will maximize your own comfort.

WHAT KIND OF BOOTS

There's no one boot that does it all, although there are boots that will handle a pretty wide range of uses and conditions. It's generally estimated that every pound (2.2 kilograms) of weight in your boots is the equivalent in energy expenditure of adding 5 pounds (11 kilograms) to your back. Lifting your feet up for thousands of steps each day takes a lot of energy.

When you are looking for boots, go with the lightest weight boot that meets your needs. I think about what I need in a boot in relation to what I am doing on the trail. If I am doing an extended mountaineering trip and I've got a 60-pound (27 kilogram) pack, I want a stiff boot that extends well over the ankle to provide me with the kind of support I need. This boot is going to somewhat heavy. If I'm going on a multiday trip and carrying 40 pounds (18 kilograms), I'll be fine with a lightweight boot that extends just over the ankle. If I'm on a day hike or an ultralight multiday with less than 20 pounds, I can use trail shoes or running shoes. You'll notice that I defined all of this in terms of *my* personal needs. I've got notoriously weak ankles, so I always opt for a lot of ankle support. Someone else might not need this much support (boot weight) while others might need more. As with clothing systems, you need to decide what your body needs and look for the lightest thing that meets those needs.

Some people bring a second pair of "camp shoes" for use in camp. After a long day it feels good to get out of your boots and air out your feet, especially if they are wet from sweat or rain. Changing to camp shoes can also help reduce your impact at camp. (See Chapter 5, "Leave No Trace Hiking and Camping.") There is an interesting weight issue here: The heavier your boots, the more important it may be to change into camp shoes. That means even more weight from carrying a second pair of shoes. Ultralight hikers who wear low-cut trail or running shoes don't need camp shoes. Sandals like Tevas are popular for in-camp use and are also helpful in stream crossings when you want to keep your boots dry. Many ultralight backpackers hike in sandals, which have the advantage of drying quickly, especially in rainy weather or after stream crossings. Gaiters, a boot "add-on," are boot covers, usually waterproof, that go over your boots and socks. They help keep your boots dry as well as protect your lower legs.

FITTING BOOTS

Proper fitting of boots is essential, and whole treatises have been written on the subject. One thing to know about boots is that all boots are constructed on what's called a *last,* a representative "average" foot mold (length, width at toes, width at heel, etc.) that the boot is built around for each shoe size. Some boot makers use a unisex last for each size while others have a separate last for women's boots and men's boots (and there are lasts for children's boots). I've found that some manufacturers' lasts just don't work with my feet while others seem to be just right. Finding that winning combination of a boot that has the features you want and the correct last is your goal.

You should try new boots on in the afternoon, since your feet swell during the day. Select a sock combination of a liner sock and outer sock that you plan to wear on the trip, and try the boots on. Bring your own socks. A lot of times I've forgotten to bring my own socks to the store and end up using socks from some random pile the store has. Then when I get home it turns out that with my own socks the boots don't fit right. With the boot unlaced, slide your foot all the way to the toe end of the boot. You should be able to get your index finger to fit between the back of your heel and the back of the boot. Lace up the boots with moderate tension. The laces should hold the boot in an "intermediate position"—that is, that you still have room to crank tighter, pulling the boot together more, or loosening them up, so you can tighten or loosen the boots as needed. You should be able to wiggle your toes inside the boot. With your foot flat on the ground, hold the boot heel down and try to lift your heel inside the boot. There should be only ¼ to ½ inch (6 to 12 millimeters) of heel lift. Too much heel lift will lead to friction and possible heel blisters. You also want to check the boot length. With the boot firmly laced, do some good hard kicks against a post or the floor. Do your toes smash into the front of the boot? If so you've discovered "boot bang." This is a serious problem. On long downhill stretches your toes smashing into the front of the boot can result in lost toenails and other foot problems. Whatever boot bang you experience in the store will be magnified when you are going downhill with a heavy pack. If you are getting boot bang, try lacing differently, another size, different sock combination, or another boot.

As we get older our feet tend to get longer—no, we aren't still growing, but most people's arches begin to flatten out and without that curve the feet get longer. So if you haven't been hiking for a while you might be in trouble if you pull that five-year-old pair of boots out of the closet and expect them to fit like they used to. If it's been a while, wear them around *before* your trip and make sure it's not time to buy a new pair.

BREAKING IN BOOTS

Before you leave the store with your new boots, make sure that you can bring them back if they don't fit. Most stores are good about this if you only wear them indoors and bring them back in good condition and in a reasonable period of time. Start wearing your boots around the house to be sure you have the right fit. Once you are happy with the fit, you need to break the boots in to your feet. Always break in a pair of new boots well before your trip. Most medium to heavyweight boots will require some use to soften up and conform to your particular feet. Even old boots should get a little break-in if you haven't worn them for a while. Begin with short walks and gradually increase the time you wear them. Easy day hikes are a good way to break in boots. Each time you lace your boots, take the time to align the tongue and lace them properly; otherwise, the tongue will set into a bad position, which can lead to hot spots and blisters.

BOOT CARE

Boot care varies with the type of material—leather, synthetic leather, nylon, and combinations of these. If you have all-leather hiking boots, find out what type of leather it is. Oil-tanned leather is usually treated with wax or oil, chrome-tanned leather with silicone wax (a beeswax-silicone mixture is recommended). The primary reason for treating boots is not to completely waterproof them, but to make them water repellent and to nourish the leather to prevent it from drying and cracking. Boots should be treated when they are new and on a regular basis to keep the leather supple.

Wet boots should be air-dried slowly or with low heat (put them in the sun). Don't try to dry boots quickly (for example, near a fire or a radiator)—different thicknesses of leather dry at different rates, which leads to cracking and curling. I've seen boots peel apart from drying too fast near a fire. While walking on the trail, the heat from your foot will help dry the boot. At the end of the day, when you take off your boots, open them up as much as possible to help them dry out. (This will also make them easier to put on in the morning.) You may want to leave your boots upside down at night to prevent dew from forming inside.

When you return from a trip, always clean your boots before you store them, or the dirt will corrode the stitching at the seams. Use a stiff, nonwire brush to remove caked-on dirt. For leather boots, rub them with moistened saddle soap. Wipe off the residue, air-dry them thoroughly, then apply a

🍁 TRICKS OF THE TRAIL

Warm Up Those Cold Boots On a cold night, turn your sleeping bag stuff sack inside out and put your boots inside. Sleep with the stuff sack in your sleeping bag, between your legs. The coated nylon of the stuff sack will keep the wet boots from soaking your sleeping bag, and your body heat will keep the boots warm and help dry them out a bit so you don't have to face cold or even frozen boots in the morning.

generous coating of wax or sealer. Store your boots in a cool, dry place to prevent mildew. Boot trees can help maintain the shape of your boot and cedar boot trees can absorb moisture from the inside of the boot, helping it dry slowly.

THE BACKPACK

There are two basic types of packs: external and internal frame. The purpose of the frame is to transfer most of the weight of your gear onto your hips, so the strong muscles in your legs carry the load, rather than your shoulders. If you remember trying to carry loads of books home from school in a day pack, you know what I mean. The ideal distribution is about 70 to 80 percent of the weight on your hips and 20 to 30 percent on your shoulders. This split in weight also lowers your center of gravity, making you more stable. Recent advances in pack design offer an incredible range of sizes and options.

- **External Frame** The external-frame pack helped revolutionize backpacking. Suddenly, much larger amounts of weight could be easily and safely carried, allowing for longer trips. External-frame packs typically use a ladderlike frame of aluminum or plastic. The hip belt and shoulder straps are attached to the frame (see diagram below). A separate pack bag attaches to the frame, usually with clevis pins and split rings. Pack bag volumes range from 3,000 to 4,500 cubic inches (49 to 73 liters). There is also space for attaching large items like a sleeping bag to the outside of the frame so the actual carrying capacity of the pack is more than the

External-Frame Pack   Internal-Frame Pace

pack bag volume. Some external-frame packs come in specific sizes based on the length of your spine; others are adjustable to fit a range of sizes. Look for good lumbar padding, a conical hip belt, recurved shoulder straps with good padding, and a chest compression strap. *Pro:* Good for carrying weight. The external frame allows for some air space between your back and the pack bag so your back doesn't sweat as much. The weight is carried higher in the pack, allowing for a more upright posture. Frame extension bars and space for a sleeping bag outside of the pack allow you to strap on lots of gear when you need to, making the carrying capacity of the pack more versatile. Less expensive than many internal-frame packs. *Con:* Since external-frame packs carry the load higher, they raise your center of gravity, making you more "top heavy" and less stable. Most external-frame packs don't hug your body as well, so the pack tends to wobble from side to side as you walk. This is usually not a problem on a regular backpacking trip, but can throw you off balance if skiing or snowshoeing. Airline baggage-handling machines are notorious for bending frames. Don't take it on an airplane unless you have boxed it up.

- **Internal Frame** Internal-frame packs use a wide variety of materials—aluminum stays, carbon fiber, plastic sheets, and foam—to create a rigid spine to which the hip belt and shoulder straps are attached (see diagram, page 38). The pack bag runs the full height of the pack, although it may be divided into several compartments. Pack volumes range from 3,000 to 7,500 cubic inches (49 to 122 liters). Some internal-frame packs come in specific sizes based on the length of your spine; others are adjustable to fit a range of sizes. As with an external-frame pack, you should look for good lumbar padding, a conical hip belt, recurved shoulder straps with good padding, and a chest compression strap. A removable top pocket and a bivy extension (a fabric layer sewn around the top opening of the pack bag that, when pulled up, adds to the overall pack volume) on the pack bag will let you lift the top pocket and store more gear. Also, make sure that the pack has side compression straps to squeeze the pack down if you are carrying a smaller load. *Pro:* Good for carrying lots of weight. Conforms to the body for better balance. Generally more comfortable to wear for long periods. *Con:* Since the pack bag and frame are directly against your entire back, back perspiration can be a problem. Since the weight is carried lower in the pack, you may have to bend over more. You can't put as much on the outside, so the overall carrying capacity of the pack is somewhat fixed by its internal volume. Tends to be more expensive than external frame packs.
- **Day packs** Day packs typically forgo a frame and use a foam or plastic sheet for the back panel. This provides some rigidity and helps distribute

weight to the hips (up to a point). How much of a frame you need depends on how much weight you plan to carry. For heavier weights, look for well-padded shoulder straps, a foam hip belt rather than just a webbing strap, and a chest compression strap. Day pack volumes range up to 3,000 cubic inches (49 liters).

GOING ULTRALIGHT—PACKS

If you are going ultralight, then the size and weight of your pack can decrease substantially. The ultralight approach means three things—bringing less stuff, bringing lighter stuff, which means less *volume* of stuff. That means that ultralight packs don't need to be so large; most are under 3,000 cubic inches (49 liters). Since you are carrying less weight, the pack doesn't need to have a huge and heavy frame system to transfer the weight, so it can be made of lighter weight material. Since you aren't carrying 50+ pounds (110 kilograms), you don't need all that padding on the hip belt and the shoulder straps—you might not even need a hip belt. You can just feel the pounds melting off.

- **Ultralight Internal-Frame Packs** have a lightweight internal frame with simple shoulder straps and a foam or webbing hip belt. Most of these packs weigh between 1 and 3 pounds (0.4 to 1.3 kilograms).
- **Ultralight Rucksacks** forgo a frame altogether. They are typically just a bag with shoulder straps and weigh a pound (2.2 kilograms) or less. By stuffing the inside full of your gear or by adding a rolled foam pad, you "build" enough of a "frame" to transfer the weight. Some have a very light hip belt or no hip belt at all. If you keep the weight low enough you can comfortably carry all the weight on your shoulders. Some are made of lightweight mesh to reduce weight.

PACK SIZE

Size is an important factor when selecting a pack. You need to make sure that you can adequately carry all the equipment and food you will need for the length of your trip. Keep in mind that the pack bags of external-frame packs are smaller than those of internal-frame packs. This is because there are spaces on the external-frame pack to strap large items directly to the frame. For example, a sleeping bag in a stuff sack may be anywhere from 700 to 1,500 cubic inches (11 to 25 liters). Here are some rough guidelines on pack size related to trip length:

Length of Trip	External-Frame Pack Volume	Internal-Frame Pack Volume
2–4 days	1,500+ cubic inches (25+ liters)	3,500+ cubic inches (57+ liters)
5–7 Days	2,000+ cubic inches (33+ liters)	4,500+ cubic inches (73+ liters)
8–10 days	3,000+ cubic inches (39+ liters)	5,500+ cubic inches (90+ liters)

❋ TRICKS OF THE TRAIL

Buying a Pack When you go to the store and try on a pack, the salesperson will help you adjust it, and it will feel great. Then she will give you a few sandbags (25–30 pounds or 11–13 kilograms) to add some weight. Chances are it will still feel good. The real test is when you get home and try to carry 50 to 70 pounds (22–31 kilograms). Make sure that the store will take the pack back if it doesn't feel right. I bought a pack once without doing this test until I hit the trail. With 60 pounds in the pack, the hip belt slipped off my butt and I ended up carrying most of the weight on my shoulders. I hiked in discomfort for days.

SIZING A PACK

It is essential to have a pack that fits properly. The major measurements are your spine length, waist size, and shoulder width to get a pack the correct length and one with the correct size hip belt and shoulder straps. Packs vary from company to company, so check the manufacturer's instructions for both fitting and loading. Many packs come with different size hip belts and/or shoulder straps and some are specifically designed for women's bodies. The idea behind a frame pack is to have the frame transfer most of the weight to your legs through the hip belt. Therefore, when fitting a pack, the place to start is with the hip belt. Here are some general fitting guidelines:

- Put on the pack and adjust the hip belt to fit your hips. Wear the hip belt on the hip bones just underneath the rib cage. The center of the hip belt is about at the crest of your pelvis. The buckle will be about at your navel. Wearing the hip belt higher transfers weight onto major muscle groups. Wearing the belt too low on the hips can compress arteries and nerves and lead to poor circulation and numbness in the legs.
- With the hip belt on and properly positioned, tighten the shoulder straps and note their position. Some packs will allow you to adjust the height at which the shoulder straps attach to fine-tune your fit. For an *external-frame pack* the straps should come off the frame about even with the top of your shoulders. If the straps drop too far down, the pack is too small, and too much weight will be pulled onto your shoulders. If the straps go too far up, the pack is too large, and too little weight will go onto your

shoulders. For an *internal-frame pack* the frame stays or frame structure should extend 2 to 4 inches above your shoulders. The shoulder straps should follow the contour of your shoulders and join the pack approximately 2 inches (5 centimeters) below the top of your shoulders. The position of the shoulder harness can usually be adjusted. The lower ends of the straps should run about 5 inches (12.7 centimeters) below your armpits. On both types of packs be sure the width of the shoulder straps is positioned so that they neither pinch your neck nor slip off your shoulders. On the shoulder straps you may find load lifters that connect to the pack at about ear level and connect to the shoulder straps in front of your collarbone. These help pull the top of the pack onto your shoulders.

- Some *internal-frame packs* allow you to bend the frame stays to adjust them to match the curvature of your back.
- In both types of packs the sternum strap should cross your chest below your collarbone. If the pack is properly fitted, you can adjust the load lifters and other fine-tuning straps to make the pack hug your back. Adjustments can also be made while hiking, periodically shifting the weight distribution to other muscle groups, which makes hiking less tiring.

PACKING YOUR PACK

Loading an External-Frame Pack

The major consideration in loading a pack is how best to distribute the weight. There are two basic principles: for trail hiking over generally flat ground, the weight of the pack should be high and relatively close to the body. The heavier items should sit between your shoulder blades. For consistently

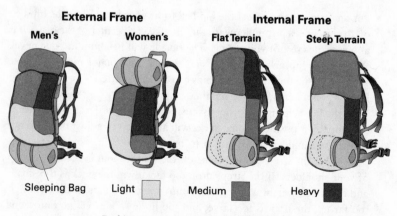

Packing External- and Internal-Frame Packs

steep or rough terrain, carry the weight lower to give you better balance and avoid falls from having a higher center of gravity. In this case, heavier things should be placed more toward the middle of your back. To achieve either arrangement, load the heavier, bulky items into the large top compartment in the position where you want most of the weight. Then fill this and the remaining compartments with lighter items. Tents and tarps can be lashed to the extender bars at the top of the pack and sleeping bags can usually be lashed to the frame at the bottom of the pack. In either case, the horizontal weight distribution should be balanced so that the left side of the pack is in balance with the right. A woman's center of gravity is generally lower than a man's. So, for women, the heavier items should be placed close to the body but lower in the pack, as in the case for rough terrain, described above. Packs designed especially for women take this into account by lowering the pack bag on the frame. Load these packs as described above and then lash sleeping bags and tents or tarps to the extender bars at the top of the packs.

Loading an Internal-Frame Pack

Your gear will help form the structure of support for an internal-frame pack. For easy, level hiking, a high center of gravity is best. To achieve this, load bulky, light gear (e.g., your sleeping bag) low in the pack and stack heavier gear on top of it. For steeper terrain, a lower center of gravity is best because it lessens the chance of falls from a top-heavy pack. In this case, place heavier items a little lower in the pack and closer to your back than normal. Women may prefer this arrangement under all circumstances.

GENERAL PACKING SUGGESTIONS

- Stuff your clothes into the pack or pack items in stuff sacks rather than fold them. This serves to fill all the available space of the pack better so that things don't shift around and allows you to get more into the pack.
- The more common weight distribution (general trail hiking) has the lighter, bulkier items on the bottom: the sleeping bag and clothes. The heavier items such as food, stoves, and fuel go into the upper section or on top of the pack, with the heaviest items closest to the pack frame. A general rule is that 50 percent of the weight should be in the upper third of the pack.
- For consistently steep or rough terrain, carry the weight lower to give you better balance.
- The horizontal weight distribution should be balanced so that the left side of the pack is in balance with the right.

- Your hip belt should have enough room to allow you to loosen or tighten it for different layers of clothing beneath. If the belt is too loose, socks or shirts can be inserted between the belt and your body. This adds an extra layer of padding to the belt as well, which may increase the comfort of the fit.
- Avoid hanging things all over the outside of your pack—no one wants to listen to you clank and clang your way down the trail; also, all that junk can snag branches. If you find yourself having to tie things on all the time, either your pack is too small or you are carrying too much (or both).
- Think about the things you will need during the day and have them relatively accessible so that it doesn't take a complete emptying of your pack to find lunch, the first-aid kit, or your rain gear. Also, group and store items according to function. For example, keep toiletries together. Small stuff sacks help organize your gear.
- For protection from rain, line your sleeping bag stuff sack and main pack compartments with plastic garbage bags. These can be reused on subsequent trips and recycled when you are through with them. They also work as emergency shelters. Pack rain covers are also useful.
- Fuel bottles should be placed below any food items or in pockets on the outside of your pack.

How Much Weight?

How much weight to carry depends on your size, weight, and physical condition. The general rule for a multiday backpacking trip is to carry no more than 15 to 25 percent of your body weight. On longer expeditions or trips with more gear (such as winter camping), this figure may go up. The bottom line is, don't carry more than you need or more than you can handle. Many a hiker has blown out knees, ankles, or back by hauling more weight than she could handle. Here are some things to do to make your trip as comfortable as possible:

- Try on your loaded pack at home before you leave.
- Fiddle with the pack and adjust it at home (you probably won't take the time to do this at the trailhead while your friends are waiting).
- Weigh your pack and compare that to your body weight. Figure out the percent of your body weight that you are carrying. Is it too much?
- Take a good look at what you are bringing. Prune out the nonessentials.
- Look and see what other people are carrying and how the whole group

can share the load in a way that makes sense for each member, given size, weight, physical condition, and experience.

Checking Your Pack Before a Trip

- Take a look at the shoulder straps, hip belt, and other compression and load-carrying straps.
- Check all pack buckles.
- Check all zippers.
- Check the pack bag itself for rips or tears.
- If the pack is an external-frame pack with a pack bag mounted onto the frame, check the attachment pins (typically clevis pins and split rings).

Putting on a Heavy Pack

There are a number of methods for putting on a heavy pack to avoid straining.

1. With the pack on the ground and the shoulder straps facing you, lift the pack up and rest it on one extended knee. Slide one arm through a shoulder strap. At this point, your shoulders will be slightly tilted, so that the shoulder strap is sliding onto your shoulder toward your neck. Lean forward slightly and rotate your body to swing the pack onto your back. Slide your other arm through the other shoulder strap. Adjust the hip belt first. The easiest way to do this is to bend over at the waist so the weight is being carried on your back rather than your hips and the hip belt is free to be snugged up tightly. Then you can straighten up and adjust the shoulder straps. Aim for 70 to 80 percent of the weight on your hips.

Putting on a Pack

2. Follow the same technique with a friend to help stabilize your pack. This is especially helpful if you are carrying a large or very heavy pack.
3. Lift the pack up onto an object that is about waist high (rock, log). Stabilize the pack and slip your arms through both shoulder straps. Pull on the pack and tighten the hip belt.

I *don't* recommend putting your pack on while sitting on the ground and then trying to stand up. This can place too much strain on your lower back. Instead, ask a friend (or two) to pull you up.

SLEEPING EQUIPMENT

SLEEPING BAGS

When selecting a sleeping bag, you need to consider a number of factors. Unlike clothing layers, a sleeping bag doesn't offer much in the way of ventilation to control your body temperature. As a result, you might have more than one bag: a summer-rated bag for hot conditions, a three-season bag for spring and fall, and a winter bag for serious cold-weather conditions.

Sleeping Bag Temperature Ratings

Sleeping bags come with temperature ratings to give you a general idea of how cold it can get and if the bag will still provide adequate insulation to keep you warm. These ratings are averages and should be used only as guidelines. Some people sleep "colder" than others, so you may need a bag with more or less insulation to be comfortable at a particular temperature. Also, ratings differ from manufacturer to manufacturer. To calculate the temperature rating you will need, look at the lowest normal temperature for the trip location and season you are going, and then subtract 10° or 15°F (9° or 12°C) from that temperature. This gives you a margin of safety in case the temperature is colder than expected. For example, if the usual nighttime temperature is 50°F (10°C), bring a bag that goes to about 35°F (2°C). Here are some general guidelines for sleeping bag ratings:

Season	Temperature Rating
Summer	40° to 60°F (4° to 16°C)
Three-season	20° to 40°F (−6° to 4°C)
Cold-weather	0° to 20°F (−17° to −6°C)
Winter	−30° to 0°F (−34° to −17°C)

Sleeping Bag Styles

The following are three general styles for sleeping bags:

- **Mummy**   A form-fitting bag with a hood. The bag tapers in width from the shoulders to the legs, with little room. This snug fit means that there is less convective heat loss in the bag, making for a warmer bag. Mummy bags use less fill than comparable rectangular bags and will weigh less.
- **Rectangular**   Simple rectangular bag typically without a hood. These are the roomiest bags but also are heavier since they are just as wide at the feet as they are at the shoulders.
- **Semi-rectangular**   This bag is rectangular at the top without a hood and it tapers somewhat to the feet. It is not as warm as a mummy bag but provides more room, and weighs less than a comparable rectangular bag.

Specific Features to Look for

- A hood allows you to insulate your head to prevent heat loss in cold weather. If this is a summer weather bag, a hood may not be necessary.
- The draft tube is an insulated tube that runs along the zipper line and prevents cold spots at the zipper.
- A draft collar provides a closure at the neck area to reduce the bellows action of heat leaving the bag. Good for cold-weather bags.
- Well-designed zippers allow you to open and close your bag easily from the inside and allow some level of ventilation.

Sleeping Bag Fit

Fit is as important in a sleeping bag as it is in clothing. In sleeping bags, you want the bag to snugly conform to your body. If the bag is too big, you will have large spaces for convection currents and you'll be cold. You might even need to wear extra clothing layers to help fill up the space. If the bag is too tight, the insulation may actually be compressed, decreasing its effectiveness. How comfortable you feel in the bag can also affect your night's sleep—some people feel confined in a snug sleeping bag and need more "wiggle room" than others.

Insulation Types

When we talk about how warm a sleeping bag is, we mean the loft of the bag. Loft is the amount of dead air space created by the fill used in the sleeping bag. There are a variety of fills for sleeping bags, but they break down into two categories: synthetic fibers and down (see pages 27–29 for details).

Sleeping Bag Care

Keep in mind that sleeping bags age. Over years of use, the fibers that create the loft in the bag break down and dead air space diminishes even though the bag stills weighs the same. This means that the bag is no longer capable of keeping you warm at its original temperature rating. Here are a few things you can do to prolong the life of your bag:

- Stuff your sleeping bag into its stuff sack rather than rolling it. Rolling compresses and ultimately breaks the fibers in the same direction, decreasing loft faster. Stuffing is a random pattern of compression that helps your loft last longer.
- Don't keep your sleeping bag in its stuff sack between trips. Keep the bag unstuffed in a large breathable bag like a laundry bag.
- Follow the manufacturer's instructions for washing your bag and wash the bag only when necessary (repeated washings tend to reduce the loft of the bag).

Sleeping Bag Extras

Here are a number of sleeping bag extras that can be useful on your trip:

- **Sleeping Bag Liner** Sleeping bag liners can serve as a lightweight cover for sleeping on top of your bag in hot weather. Tightly woven fabrics like silk can even work as mosquito netting. In cooler weather, a lightweight liner of Thermolite weighs only a few ounces and can add 10° to 15°F (8° to 9°C) of warmth to the rating of your bag. For long-distance hikers, you can mail the liner home when you no longer need it. Liners also can help keep the inside of your bag clean, reducing the number of times the bag needs to be washed.
- **Vapor Barrier Liner** A vapor barrier liner (page 25) can add about 10°F (9°C) to the rating of your bag by reducing evaporative heat loss. You may feel a little moist inside, so wear polypropylene or other hydrophobic wicking layers against your skin.
- **Bivouac (Bivy) Sack** This waterproof outer shell can add 10° to 15°F (8° to 9°C) to the rating of your bag.
- **Overbag** This is actually another lightweight rectangular sleeping bag cut to fit over a regular bag. Depending on the amount of insulation, an overbag can add 10° to 25°F (8° to 11°C) to the rating of your bag. A properly matched sleeping bag/overbag system can be a great combination. The overbag alone can be used for a summerweight bag. The sleeping bag alone can be used for fall and spring, and the combined bags can

be used for cold weather (but may not be warm enough for a full winter trip).

🍁 TRICKS OF THE TRAIL

Sleeping Warm Your sleeping bag will be whatever the ambient air temperature is. Here are some tricks for warming things up before you crawl into your bag to sleep:

- After dinner, fill a water bottle with hot water. Put the hot bottle inside your bag before you get in to preheat the bag. The water should stay warm all night. (Make sure you have a bottle that seals tightly.)
- Get in your bag and do a bunch of sit-ups. The surge of body heat will warm you and the bag.
- Change into dry clothing (like polypropylene) before getting into your bag.
- Wear extra clothing, if necessary. How much clothing to wear in your bag depends on how much extra space there is around your body in the bag, whether you are adequately hydrated, and whether you sleep "warm" or "cold." If there is space, wear extra layers to increase the dead air space around your body. Remember, you will need to warm up all your layers as well as the bag.
- Head out or head in? Some people like to pull the hood drawcords so tight that only their nose is sticking out. This makes me feel a little claustrophobic, so I'm a head-outer. But that makes me colder, so I bring a good fleece hat. In buggy weather I have a mosquito head net.

SLEEPING PADS

Sleeping pads serve two functions: comfort, cushioning your body from rocky ground; and more important, insulation. In cold conditions, a sleeping pad is essential to maintain your body heat by preventing conductive heat loss to the colder ground. Sleeping pads come in two basic types: closed-cell foam such as Ensolite or inflatable pads such as Therm-A-Rest pads. Closed-cell foam pads are lightweight and roll up to a small diameter. They tend to get a little stiff in cold weather. Inflatable pads are typically open-cell foam covered with coated nylon and have an inflation valve at one end. Some people feel that inflatables are more comfortable, although they tend to be a little slippery—tough if your tent is pitched on a slope. With inflatable pads you should carry repair items (good old duct tape) to patch any holes that develop in the nylon outer layer. A leaky inflatable is almost useless.

For three-season camping, a pad that is ⅜ inch thick (10 millimeters) is adequate. In colder conditions, you should have ½ inch (12 millimeters) of insulation between you and the ground. Pads are available in either full length or partial length (three-fourths or two-thirds). You can save weight by not using a full-length pad. Full-length pads are essential only in very cold environments, so that no part of your sleeping bag is in contact with the cold ground.

GOING ULTRALIGHT— SLEEPING BAGS AND PADS

You can cut down on sleeping bag weight in a couple ways: fill and features. Going with a "superlight" synthetic fill or a down bag will decrease the weight for a particular temperature range of bag. For warm weather camping you don't need features like draft tubes that add weight. You can get 40° F (4° C) sleeping bags that weigh 2 pounds (4.4 kilograms) or less.

While I like the comfort of an inflatable pad, and there are ones that are very light, I think a foam pad is actually a better choice in an ultralight setting. Foam pads have many more uses than just insulating your body from the ground. If you are carrying a frameless rucksack, your rolled foam pad can create the "frame" for additional support. In first-aid situations, they can be cut up for splints; you can pad your blistered heels with them; insulate pots from the cold ground; and on and on.

SHELTER

When planning your trip, you need to know whether you should bring your own shelter or there will be shelter options available on a daily basis along the trail. If you need to bring your own shelter, there are a number of options:

- **Tarps** *Pro:* Lightweight. Inexpensive. Less condensation. *Con:* Not as weatherproof as a tent. Does not provide bug protection. May require trees to set up.
- **Tents** *Pro:* Good weather protection. Good bug protection. *Con:* More condensation. Heavier. More expensive.

GENERAL SHELTER TIPS

- Whenever you use a tent or tarp, think carefully about site placement so that you leave no trace. A tent or ground sheet on grass for more than a day will crush and yellow the grass beneath, leaving a direct sign of your presence. Stakes can damage fragile soils, and guylines and tarp lines can damage trees.

- Find a resilient or already highly impacted location. Try to find a relatively flat location; hollowed-out areas pool water in a storm.
- If possible, identify the prevailing wind direction and set up your tarp or tent accordingly. If rain is a possibility, set up so that the openings don't face the oncoming wind.

TARPS

Tarp setup can be an art. You typically use a ground sheet underneath to provide a floor and protect your sleeping bag and gear from wet ground. You need trees located an appropriate distance apart in order to set up a tarp, although you can also rig a tarp from overhead branches or trekking poles. There are many variations, but the most weatherproof is the basic A-frame.

A-Frame Tarp Setup

Select an appropriate location in your campsite to set up your tarp (see page 50). Have a tarp line of sufficient diameter (¼ inch or 6 millimeter braided nylon) to prevent knots from slipping.

Tree Method Secure one end of the tarp line to a tree using a bowline knot (see "Bowline," page 190) at an appropriate height for the size of your tarp, and stretch the running end to the other tree. You can set your tarp line height so that the bottom edges of the tarp will lie several inches/centimeters above the ground sheet, allowing for ventilation, or wrap the edges of the tarp under the ground sheet for better weather protection (but less ventilation).

Wrap the running end of the tarp line around the second tree and tie it off using an adjustable knot such as a tautline hitch or a trucker's hitch (see "Tautline Hitch," page 190; "Trucker's Hitch," page 192). This will allow you to set and later reset the tension of your tarp line. To tighten the tarp line, simply slide the tautline hitch or pull on the trucker's hitch and tie it off. The tautline hitch is preferred since it can be easily retensioned.

Place the tarp over the tarp line and stake out the corners of the tarp at 45 degree angles. This can be done using stakes or by tying the guylines to rocks or other trees. Make sure the tarp is adequately guyed out so that strong winds won't tear it down. Or you can fold the edge of the tarp underneath the ground sheet and weigh it down with rocks on the inside to create a very rainproof shelter.

Pole Method If you don't have trees available, you can use sticks or

A-Frame Tarp

trekking poles at either end of the tarp. Stake out the four corners of the tarp at 45 degree angles. Raise the pole at one end of the tarp and either use two half-hitches (see page 189) or a simple tension wrap around the top of the pole, then run the guyline down to the ground and stake it out. Do the same on the other side. You will need to make sure both ends are staked down well and the entire line is under tension in order to properly support the tarp. Some tarps have side lifters that, when guyed out, prevent sagging and increase headroom under the tarp.

Tree Method A simple tarp setup is to locate the entrance next to a tree and guy the center point onto the tree while guying the front corners out. The rear end can be staked out with a pole or stick for more ventilation or flattened out to reduce the number of stakes and lines needed.

Tarp Tips

- To prevent rainwater from running down the tarpline into the tarp, tie a bandanna on the line just outside the tarp. It will redirect the water drips to the ground.
- You can create your own grommets for guylines by placing a small stone on the inside of the tarp and tying parachute cord around it from the outside. The free end of the parachute cord can then be staked out. This is useful if grommets are broken or if more support is needed for the tarp.
- Rain ponchos can be used as makeshift doors to prevent wind and rain from blowing in through the ends of the tarp.
- If there aren't trees around, try boulders, rock outcroppings, or other objects to string up your tarp.

TENTS

A multitude of tents are available—everything from simple A-frames to complex geodesic domes. When selecting a tent, consider the following:

- The size of your group and how many people each tent sleeps.
- Freestanding tents are generally preferred over nonfreestanding tents. A freestanding tent has a pole arrangement that maintains the tent's functional shape without the need for guylines. However, in windy conditions nothing is really freestanding, so all tents come with guylines and you should be prepared to stake the tent down and stake the sides out.
- Single-wall Tent versus Double-wall Tent. Most tents use a rain fly—an outer waterproof layer that is separated from a breathable layer beneath. This double-wall system allows moisture inside the tent to pass through the breathable layer and then escape, reducing condensation in the tent while the waterproof layer overhead keeps rain out. It also helps provide better insulation by increasing the layers of still air. There are also single-walled tents. Some are completely waterproof and rely on ventilation systems to reduce condensation inside the tent. Others are made of waterproof–breathable material. A single-wall tent will be lighter than a comparable double-wall tent. Single-wall nonbreathable tents are prone to interior condensation.
- Examine the floor space of the tent and the usable internal volume. Dome-style or arch-style tents typically have greater usable overhead space than A-frame tents.
- What season(s) the tents are designed for. *Summer tents* are double-walled tents with much of the inner breathable layer being mosquito netting. They are lightweight and allow for lots of ventilation in hot weather. *Three-season tents* do well in three-season conditions but are not sturdy enough to take heavy snow loads. *Convertible tents* are four-season tents where you can leave off some poles to make the tent lighter. *Four-Season tents* have stronger poles and are designed to be able to withstand snow loading. They can also be used as three-season tents but weigh more.
- *Fastpack* tents have a tent fly that can be rigged with the poles and attached to a tent footprint as a floor, leaving the rest of the tent at home. Basically you are building a tarp and ground sheet with poles. This is a nice feature to look for when buying a tent as it allows you to cut down on weight when you don't need a full tent.

Tent Tips

- Each tent comes with its own set of instructions. Practice how to set up your tent *before* your trip so you can do it in the dark, in bad weather, or in bad weather in the dark. I set up mine at home the first time to get to know the tent, then try to do it outside at night with a headlamp.

- Make sure you bring pole splints or extra poles with you in case a pole breaks.
- Make sure that you have the right tent stakes for your environment. Ever try to hammer one of those narrow wire tent stakes into rocky soil and watch it bend at a right angle? Lightweight/strong steel or titanium stakes are much better than the cheap aluminum ones. In soft surfaces like sand or snow, you will need a stake with a much greater surface area (especially for sand). In snow, you can create a "dead man" by tying your guyline to a branch and then burying the branch in the snow and packing the snow down on top. When the snow sets, the dead man will be solidly fixed. (You may have to chop it out when it's time to go.) In sand, fill a stuff sack with light bulky items, tie your guyline to it, and bury it.
- Use a tent ground sheet, a space blanket, or a tarp to help protect your tent floor from rips and tears (better to put a hole in the cheap tarp than your expensive tent).
- Always stake your tent down if you are going to be in windy areas or will be leaving your tent during day excursions.
- Avoid cooking in a tent. The material most tents are made of is flammable, and the water vapor from cooking leads to extensive condensation inside the tent. Carbon monoxide gas released from a burning stove in a confined space like a tent can lead to suffocation and death. (See "Carbon Monoxide," page 351.)

GOING ULTRALIGHT–SHELTER

If you are going ultralight, the first question is, Do you need a shelter at all? If you are on a trail like the Appalachian Trail designed for through-hikers, there will be shelters at hikeable mileages for the entire trip. Of course, you can't be sure that you can always make the mileage, so you should carry a basic tarp or bivy sack as an emergency shelter, but you don't need to carry a full tent.

If you are bringing a shelter, there are a number tarps that weigh under a pound (454 grams) and some superlightweight tarps weighing less than 8 ounces (226 grams). Ultralight tarps are often made of silicon-impregnated nylon (sil-nylon). This is one of those lightweight fabrics that takes care to keep from puncturing or tearing it. There are also ultralight tents from companies like Big Agnes, GOLITE, Mountain Hardware, MSR, and Sierra Designs that weigh under 2 pounds (900 grams).

COOKING EQUIPMENT

Basic cooking gear is listed in the general equipment list on pages 404–406, but here are a few necessary items:

- **Pots** It's best to bring at least two pots. A pot set that nests is easiest to carry. The pot size depends on the size of your group: for one to three people, use a 1.5-liter and a 2.5-liter pot. For groups of six, try a 2-liter and a 3-liter pot, and for eight or more, go with at least a 2-liter and a 4-liter. Pots should have lids that seal well. Flat lids allow you to build a small fire on top of the lid for baking. Having a rim on the outside of the pot is essential for picking it up with a pot-gripper. Stainless steel pots weigh a little more than aluminum but will last longer. There is a great debate about pots with nonstick coatings. The nonstick coating makes it easier to clean the pots, but you can't use harsh abrasives to clean them, which eliminates some of the best natural cleaning materials, such as sand.
- **Frying pan** One per trip is usually plenty. Choose your size based on the size of your group (or how big you like your pancakes). Frying pans are generally available in 8-, 10-, and 12-inch models. Using a frying pan with a cover will reduce your cooking times. A pot cover that fits your frying pan saves weight.
- **Utensils** Lexan plastic utensils are basically indestructible. Be careful cleaning them. Harsh abrasives can create scratches that will hold dirt and bacteria.

GOING ULTRALIGHT–COOKING GEAR

Titanium is lighter than either steel or aluminum and just as durable. You can cut down on weight by using titanium cooking pots, cups, fry pans, and utensils. The only drawback is that titanium items are significantly more expensive. For solo hikers, bring only one small pot and lid. A spoon is the only utensil you'll probably need.

BACKPACKING STOVES

There are three basic types of backpacking stoves based on what they burn: liquid fuel, compressed gas in a canister, and stoves that use solid fuels like a fuel pellet or wood. Most backpackers rely on liquid fuel stoves.

- **Liquid Fuel Stoves** burn Coleman fuel (a.k.a. white gas), kerosene, or alcohol. *Pro:* Fuel readily available (alcohol and kerosene available worldwide). *Con:* Require more maintenance. Some stoves don't simmer well. Alcohol doesn't burn well at high altitude (over 7,000 feet or 2,133 meters). *Examples:* MSR Whisperlite, MSR Simmerlite, Coleman Featherweight 442, Coleman Apex II, Primus Omni Fuel, Trangia, and the Brunton Optimus Nova.
- **Compressed Gas Stoves** burn butane, isobutane, or propane. *Pro:* Easy on and off. Low maintenance. Easy to control temperature. Both the stove and the fuel canister are lighter than liquid fuel stoves. *Con:* Don't work as well at colder temperatures. Difficult to tell amount of fuel left. Disposal of pressurized canister. Butane doesn't burn well at high altitude (over 7,000 feet or 2,133 meters). *Examples:* MSR Pocket Rocket, Jet-Boil, Coleman Exponent, SnowPeak GigaPower.
- **Solid Fuel Stoves** burn flammable pellets or wood. *Pro:* Easy on and off. Practically zero maintenance. *Con:* Pretty much either off or on, hard to control temperature. Small, hard to use for large group cooking. *Examples:* Ezbit Stove, Sierra Stove.

How Gasoline/Kerosene Liquid-Fuel Stoves Work

The fuel is stored in a separate tank. In most cases, this tank uses a pump to help pressurize the stove. The tank should be filled only to the ¾ point, leaving some air in the tank. The pump forces air through a one-way valve into the tank, increasing the pressure inside. Opening the fuel flow valve allows the pressurized liquid fuel to flow from the tank through the fuel line to the generator tube that passes over the stove burner and back to the base of the stove, where it comes out a small opening called the jet and into the priming cup. Initially, vent only a small amount of fuel into the priming cup, then shut off the fuel flow valve. When you light this small amount of fuel, it will heat up the generator tube. This process is known as "priming the stove." It can also be accomplished by using a separate priming source such as alcohol or priming paste. Once the generator tube is hot, the fuel flow valve can be opened and the stove burner lit. The pressurized fuel from the tank flows through the heated generator tube, where it is vaporized. The fuel that now flows through the jet is vapor. It strikes the flame spreader on the burner and ignites. The flame spreader redirects the flame from a single, vertical "candle" flame to a wider flame for more efficient heating. When the stove is properly primed, you should see a blue flame similar to that on a gas range. If the flame is yellow or orange, it means that the fuel is not being completely vaporized in the generator. As the generator heats up further, it may begin to run properly, or you may have to turn off the stove and reprime it. (See page 60 for detailed sample instructions.)

Lighting Other Stoves

- **Alcohol Stoves**   Alcohol stoves don't require any priming. Because alcohol doesn't have the explosive combustible properties of gasoline, it doesn't need to be vaporized in order to burn. You just pour the alcohol into the burner container and light it. You can burn either denatured alcohol or grain alcohol (ethanol). In cold temperatures you may have to warm up the alcohol (by putting it next to your body) before lighting.
- **Compressed Gas Stoves**   The fuel canister has a screw attachment on the top. The stove burner either screws directly onto the top of the canister or the burner sits on the ground off to the side and there is a flexible fuel tube that runs from the burner to the fitting on the canister. Once the canister is connected you simply turn the fuel knob to ON and light the stove.
- **Solid Fuel Stoves**   This varies from stove to stove depending on the type of solid fuel. With a pellet stove like the Esbit, the fuel pellets are flammable. You insert the pellet into the stove and light it. The pellets will light even when cold or wet.

Stove Safety Guidelines

- Know how to operate a stove properly *before* you light it.
- Make sure your stove has enough fuel *before* you light it.
- When cooking on a stove, always work from the side where the on/off control is located. Never reach over the stove to work on it or put your face or body directly over the burner.
- Do not overfill a liquid fuel stove.
- A windscreen will help the stove work more efficiently and save fuel as well as keep the flame from being blown out.
- If using a stove with a separate fuel bottle, make sure that the fuel bottle is designed to hold pressure (such as MSR bottles). Also make sure that the bottle is in good shape. I've seen plenty of banged and dented fuel bottles that I just don't trust to hold pressure. These should not be connected to a stove.
- Be careful if a hot stove goes out. Do not relight it until it has cooled down for at least 15 minutes. Priming a hot stove with fuel can result in *instantaneous and violent ignition.*
- *Never* use a stove inside a tent, snow cave, or other enclosed or poorly ventilated space. Stoves give off carbon monoxide, which could lead to asphyxiation in a poorly ventilated area (see "Carbon Monoxide," page 351).

- Fuels should always be stored a safe distance from the stove when it is being used. Care should be taken to note the wind direction in relation to the fuel storage area so that fuel fumes cannot reach the flame source or sparks reach the fuel source. Always refill stoves far from any source of flame or heat.

What to Do if Your Stove Catches Fire

I've seen a number of models of stoves leak and catch fire. The first thing to do is to back away quickly. The best methods for putting out a stove fire are dousing with liberal amounts of water and dumping sand or dirt on the stove. If none of these is available you can also try tossing an empty pot over the stove. The hope is that lack of oxygen will put out the fire; however, the pot also concentrates the heat, which could cause a more violent ignition before the fire is extinguished. Toss baking soda at the base of the flame. It gives off CO_2 gas, which should extinguish the fire.

Be careful with stove fuel and plastic pumps. Make sure that you don't spill fuel on stoves with plastic pumps. If there is fuel on the outside of the pump while the stove is lit, it can catch fire. A fire on a plastic pump can melt the pump, allowing more fuel to flow out and ignite, a potentially explosive situation.

How Much Fuel to Bring

The amount of fuel you need depends on the size of your group and the type of items on your menu. Cooking at high altitude (see page 77), boiling water for purification, or melting snow for water will increase your fuel requirements. The following are guidelines for typical three-season trips cooking for breakfast and dinner:

WHITE GAS FUEL GUIDELINES

Season	Fuel/Person/Day
Summer	⅙ quart (157 milliliters)
Spring and fall	¼ quart (236 milliliters)
Winter or at high altitude	½ quart (473 milliliters) if you need to melt snow for water

USING A WHITE GAS STOVE

Operation

White gas stoves fall into two categories: those where the fuel bottle/pump is integrated with the burner, like the Coleman Peak 1 Feather 442 and no assembly is required; and component stoves with a separate burner, pump, and fuel bottle, like the MSR Whisperlite, the Coleman Apex II, Primus Omni Fuel, and the Brunton Optimus Nova. Component stoves need to be assembled before use, and proper assembly is essential for safe stove operation.

Read the product literature that comes with your stove carefully for the latest instructions and information on how to assemble and use your stove properly. The following instructions are representative of component stoves and are based on MSR stove instructions with permission of MSR. Always follow the instructions that came with your stove, as this information may not be the most current.

Assembling the Stove

1. Fill an MSR Fuel Bottle to the marked Fill Line. Use only MSR fuel bottles. Non-MSR fuel bottles may result in fuel leakage and/or separation from the Pump. Fuel may ignite, possibly resulting in injury or death. (Make sure the bottle is not dented. Small holes can cause pressure loss or fuel leaks.)
2. When you open a fuel bottle the contents may be under pressure, so hold it away from you and others as you unscrew the cap so that fuel doesn't spurt into your face.
3. Screw the Pump snugly into the Fuel Bottle. Make sure the Control Valve is all the way in the OFF (−) position.

MSR Whisperlite White Gas Stove with Fuel Bottle, Pump, and Burner
(Image courtesy of Mountain Safety Research)

4. Pump the Plunger until firm resistance is felt, 15 to 20 strokes if the Fuel Bottle is full, 40 to 55 pump strokes if the bottle is half full.

5. Check for any leaking fuel at any of the O-ring seals on the pump. Don't light the stove if you see fuel leaks.

6. Lubricate the end of the fuel line with saliva or oil and insert the Fuel Line into the hole in the pump.

7. Snap the Catch Arm securely into the slot on the Pump. Failure to lock the catch arm can result in the fuel line and fuel tank detaching from the stove during operation, an extremely hazardous condition. I always teach "click and lock, ready to rock." Don't light the stove until the catch arm locks into place with a click.

8. Snap the pot support legs into place and put the stove on a suitable flat, insulated surface before lighting.

Operating the Stove

Before lighting the stove make sure that:

- The stove assembly has no fuel leaks.
- The catch arm is locked and stove is properly assembled.
- The area is clear of flammable material and spilled fuel.

Priming

The stove must be preheated or "primed" in order to operate properly. Insufficient preheating may result in flare-ups or poor performance.

1. Open the Control Valve and allow approximately 1 teaspoon of fuel to flow through the jet opening in the burner into the priming cup at the base of the burner. (Alcohol may be used as an alternate priming fuel to reduce soot buildup from the preheat process.)
     Note: Do not overprime. Do not fill the priming cup with fuel. Only a small amount of fuel is needed. Excess fuel can result in a dangerous flare-up.

2. Turn the Control Valve off.

3. Check for any leaks at the Control Valve, Pump, Jet, and Fuel Line. If leaks are found, do not use the stove.

4. Light the Priming Fuel.

5. Place the Windscreen around the stove. Make sure the pump and fuel bottle are kept outside the windscreen.

Turning the Stove On

1. When the preheating fuel has burned to a small flame or gone out completely, open the Control Valve gradually and light the stove at the burner. You should get a steady blue flame.
2. If the stove:
   - Goes out, turn the Control Valve off. Wait for the stove to cool and return to the "priming" step.
   - Burns with erratic yellow flame when you first start it, close the Control Valve and allow the stove to preheat longer. (Priming with a separate fuel source like a small squeeze bottle of alcohol is helpful here.)
   - Burns intermittently with yellow and blue flames, turn the Control Valve down but not off until the stove burns with a steady blue flame, then slowly turn the Control Valve up.
3. While the stove is in operation periodically pump the Plunger 3 to 5 strokes as needed to keep enough pressure in the Fuel Bottle.

Turning the Stove Off

1. Close Control Valve firmly. The flame will burn for 1 to 2 minutes as excess fuel in the fuel line is exhausted. Wait for the stove to cool before disassembling.
2. To remove the burner, unlock the Catch Arm, making sure that you are away from heat, sparks, or flame, and remove the Fuel Line from the Pump.
3. Keep the Pump assembled in the Fuel Bottle or, to be sure the Control Valve does not open by mistake, remove the Pump and replace it with the Fuel Bottle Cap. The fuel bottle will be under pressure, so hold it away from you and others as you open it.

LIGHTWEIGHT/ULTRALIGHT CARTRIDGE STOVES

Cartridge stoves and fuel weigh less than typical white gas stoves. There are a number of models that are light enough to creep into the ultralight category:

- **MSR Pocket Rocket**   For those times when you want a lightweight stove for cooking for larger groups, the MSR Pocket Rocket is one of the lightest cartridge stoves available. It sets up quickly and boils a quart/liter (1000 milliliters) of water in under 3.5 minutes.
- **JetBoil**   The JetBoil is an innovative approach to a lightweight cooking system. It merges a canister stove and burner with an integrated insulated cooking mug so you leave your pots behind. Unlike other canister stoves it has its own integrated windscreen and a built-in heat exchanger that

captures heat typically lost with other stoves. This makes the unit more fuel efficient per canister of fuel. It boils 2 cups (473 milliliters) of water in 2 minutes.

GOING ULTRALIGHT—STOVES

Trust Appalachian Trail and other through-hikers to come up with the lightest weight stoves. A number of these stoves simplify the stove to its most basic element — the burner — losing the fuel bottle, pump, and fuel line. With this simplicity comes some loss of functionality. Don't expect these stoves to let you control the flame to a low simmer; they are pretty much on-and-off stoves, whose main purpose is to do one thing: boil water. Some stoves provide a metal shield to move over the flame to block some of the heat as the "simmer control." Here are some of the ultralight options:

Alcohol Stoves There are a number of commercial alcohol stoves on the market. The Trangia Stove from Sweden is one example and is generally sold as a stove/pot system *(www.trangia.com)*. One of the benefits of the stove is its simplicity. It consists of a burner cup that fits inside a windscreen. Fill the burner with alcohol, assemble the stove, and light. *Pro:* Lightweight. No complicated parts to break or fuel lines that clog. Alcohol is available around the world as a fuel. *Con:* Not easy to adjust temperature. Limited burn time.

Aluminum Can Stoves—Alcohol Fuel These lightweight stoves are designed for small cooking loads — 1 to 4 cups of water. It's a boil-water-only stove. The stove is made from two aluminum cans, a smaller 12-ounce can soldered inside a larger 14-ounce can. These stoves are designed to burn alcohol only. You don't get any lighter than this. You can find instructions for how to build this stove at the PCTHiker Web Site *(www.pcthiker.com)*.

Esbit Tablet Stoves The Esbit stove is a folding steel stove. When opened there is space for a small flammable stove tablet about the size of a boxes of matches. Light the pellet and place it in the stove. Like other ultralight stoves it has only two cooking levels, on and off. One tablet will bring 1 pint of water (473 milliliters) to a rolling boil in under 8 minutes. You typically get 12 to 15 minutes of usable burn time per tablet. The Esbit Wing Stove is an even simpler, more compact, and lighter weight version.

Sierra Stove This stove burns twigs, bark, pine cones, and other wood as well as charcoal and other solid fuels. It has an adjustable speed fan that creates a forced ventilation system providing more efficient burning. It boils a quart/liter of water in about 4 minutes *(www.zzstove.com)*.

MISCELLANEOUS GEAR

We all have our favorite little things that we bring on the trail. Here are a few gadgets you might want to consider on your next trip:

- **LED headlamp** One of my most indispensable items on any trip. An LED headlamp is lightweight, is easier to use in camp than a flashlight, and will go for hundreds of hours on a few batteries.
- **Good trowel** When digging catholes, a strong lightweight metal trowel is a real help. It's also good for building a mound fire. Forget the cheap plastic ones—they snap the first time you hit a rock.
- **Multitool** For years it was a Swiss Army knife, but that's now been re-placed with a lightweight multitool. These have the advantage of having other tools like a pair of pliers useful for fixing stoves and packs. If you are being weight-conscious, the little multitools weigh much less and offer almost as much as the big ones do.
- **Camp chair** I admit it, it's a bit of a luxury, but I really like pulling out my Crazy Creek chair at the end of the day and relaxing with a cup of tea and a good book. As a feeble attempt to justify the added weight, you can use the chair for a sleeping pad, and the chair itself makes a good leg splint *(www.crazycreek.com)*.
- **Mosquito Netting Hat** Combined with a good wide-brimmed sun/rain hat, this will keep the bugs and the DEET out of your face.
- **Portable Power** If your trip requires you to bring electronic gear with you (satellite phone, digital camera, PDA, laptop), you need to have power. The Brunton SolarRoll is a collapsible solar power cell. It weighs 17 ounces and can produce 14 watts of power—enough to juice up your PDA, cellphone, or digital camera. It can also charge larger items like lap-top computers *(www.brunton.com)*.

TECHNOLOGY IN THE WILDERNESS

Technology is all around us, and more and more technology is coming into the backcountry. In a broad sense we all use technology outdoors—everything from high-tech clothing to LED headlamps, pocket stoves, waterproof-breathable rain gear, internal-frame backpacks, and ultralight tents.

For many people, the word *technology* really refers to taking electronic gadgets into the outdoors. Some view this as an intrusion on the experience of the wilderness; others feel it is perfectly appropriate. If you choose to bring a music or DVD player, that's your personal choice. You should just be aware that the people in the next campsite may not be at all interested in hearing your device, so bring headphones.

Outside of entertainment devices there are devices designed to help you on your wilderness experience. Here are some of the things out there:

- **Cellphones or satellite phones** Cellphones are now ubiquitous, so it's no surprise that people take them along on backcountry trips. A cellphone or a satellite phone can be a big help in an emergency situation, allowing you to contact help almost immediately (if you have reception).

  There is a great deal of discussion in outdoor programs about the use of cellular phones, satellite phones, and radios. Some people feel that these are essential backcountry safety devices, some feel that they intrude on the experience of being in the wilderness, and others feel they are mistakenly used as a crutch. They can be useful tools in an emergency situation. However, it is important to recognize that none of these communication technologies works in every location and therefore shouldn't be relied upon completely. A lot of people assume that satellite phones work everywhere. Not true—sat phones require a clear view of the sky in order to establish a connection with a satellite. You often can't make a connection in deep forests, canyons, deep gorges, or other locations. And any electronic device can run out of power or break, so never rely on it in place of first-aid training, knowledge of the area, and a good trip plan.

  If you carry a phone or a radio, don't delude yourself that help is only a phone call away. Even with a phone, it still may take rescue personnel hours or even days to get to you, so you must be prepared to deal with the situation. At a conference on wilderness safety someone told the story of a fellow who went hiking with his cellphone. He got lost and called the rangers to tell him where to go. They asked him what landmarks were nearby, and there weren't any obvious ones. It turned out he had no map or compass and had absolutely no idea where he was. He assumed that because he had a cellular phone, all he had to do was call and ask for directions. But the rangers couldn't figure out where he was or how to help him find his way back. At the same time hikers and mountaineers have been seriously injured and called for help on a cellphone. Without the phone to speed the rescue people would have died.

- **Global Positioning System (GPS) Receivers** GPS receivers use satellites to identify your exact position. They can be a great help in planning your route, keeping track of your location, and navigating from place to place. Even so, a GPS is not a replacement for knowing how to use a map and compass. For more on GPS, see page 162.

- **Personal Radios** Personal radios using the FRS or GMRS have become increasingly popular in the backcountry. They can be helpful for larger groups who split up. FRS radios have a range of about ½ mile (0.8 kilometer), while GMRS have ranges up to 5 miles (8 kilometers).

- **Personal Locater Beacons (PLBs)**   Personal Locator Beacons are another satellite technology. This is a land-based version of rescue beacons that have been in use by mariners for some time. When activated the beacon sends an emergency signal to a satellite along with your exact position. This is not a phone, so all the signal means is "I have an emergency." All PLBs must be registered so the responding agency knows who initiated the call (in part to discourage false activations). If a signal is received, the Rescue Coordination Center telephones the beacon's owner and/or emergency contact to check to see if the beacon going off is a false alarm. If it cannot be determined that the signal is a false alert, SAR teams are dispatched to locate the person in distress. Pushing the button means mobilizing a potentially huge rescue effort, so it had better be a real emergency. There are certainly real uses for these devices, particularly for people who travel in remote parts of the world.

The ongoing debate about the use of these types of technology in the backcountry is that carrying these devices creates a false sense of security, the "Hey, if something goes wrong we just use the Satellite Phone, PLB, GPS, etc." approach. Some people are justifiably concerned that people may go into the backcountry without sufficient experience because they assume they can always get rescued, or don't take a map because they have a GPS receiver. What's important to remember is that these are just tools and have limitations. They get left in camp, batteries die, somebody steps on the thing or drops it off a cliff. If you don't have it or it doesn't work, you'd better have the skills to handle the situation. These devices should be used as an adjunct for emergency assistance or navigation, not as a replacement for sound training and good judgment.

CHAPTER 3
Cooking and Nutrition

Food can be one of the most important and complicated elements to plan for a trip. You have to be aware of nutritional requirements, individual dietary needs, and amounts required to feed the entire group. Plus, the food should be appetizing—there is nothing better than a delicious hot meal to bolster morale after a long, hard day of hiking, and nothing worse than trying to keep up your strength while staring into a cup of disgusting mush. Seasoned through-hikers may be more concerned with weight than taste or variety, but it can be difficult to get people, particularly inexperienced backpackers, to eat a meal that doesn't taste good.

ENERGY AND NUTRITIONAL REQUIREMENTS

Good nutrition is just as important, if not more so, in the backcountry as it is at home. Food supplies energy to your body to fuel your physical activity and keep you warm. Food also provides essential nutrients that your body cannot produce: vitamins, minerals, certain amino acids, and certain fatty acids. The amount of energy the body takes in from food is measured in units of heat energy called calories. When planning a menu for a trip, it is important that the foods be high in calories in order to meet these requirements.

CALORIC REQUIREMENTS

Below are the general ranges for calories required to maintain good health, and what you will typically need to carry. Keep in mind that the food weights are averages, since carrying only dehydrated foods, for example, would mean carrying less weight. Also, at higher altitudes the caloric requirements per day increase.

Activity	Caloric Requirement/day	Food Weight/day
Your body's basal metabolism	1,500–2,000	
Three-season backpacking or normal exercise output	2,500–3,000	1.75–2 pounds (0.8–0.9 kilograms)
Cold-weather backpacking or strenuous exercise output	3,500–4,000	2–2.25 pounds (0.9–1 kilograms)
Winter backpacking or very strenuous exercise output	4,500–6,000	+2.5 pounds (+1.1 kilograms)

FOOD SOURCES

Carbohydrates (4 calories/gram, energy released quickly) regularly make up about 50 percent of a person's daily caloric intake. For hiking trips you may need to increase this to 70 percent of the daily caloric intake. Starches and sugars provide both quick energy and longer-term fuel. Processing and refining can reduce the nutritional value of carbohydrates, so it is best to use whole grains, raw sugar, and other unprocessed foods in your menu. Simple carbohydrates (sugars such as trail snacks or candy) are broken down very quickly by the body for quick energy release, and complex carbohydrates (such as pasta) release energy more slowly.

Fats (9 calories/gram, energy released slowly) are another important source of energy in the backcountry. It is recommended that about 25 percent of your daily intake be fats (during the winter this should increase to about 40 percent). Fats take longer to break down than carbohydrates and thus are a better source of long-term energy. For example, adding a spoonful of butter or margarine to a cup of hot chocolate will increase the caloric rating and the length of time the energy is released.

Proteins (4 calories/gram, energy released slowly) are an essential part of any diet. Proteins are the essential building blocks of all tissue. Each protein in the body is made up of twenty-two amino acids. Fourteen of these amino acids are produced in the body, and the other eight, known as the "essential amino acids," are not. Both types are essential to a complete diet. Foods such as meat, poultry, fish, eggs, and milk products are called "complete proteins" since they contain all eight essential amino acids. However, there are limitations to carrying fresh meats, poultry, and eggs due to weight or spoilage. Canned or vacuum-sealed pouches of fish or precooked chicken can be carried. Soybeans and soy products are also complete proteins.

Foods such as beans, lentils, peanuts, cereals, vegetables, and fruit are incomplete proteins since each of them doesn't contain all eight amino acids. However, by using proper combinations, a backcountry menu can be planned that allows you to get all eight amino acids daily. An easy way to remember this is using the "Nutritional *N*" to create food combinations. The *N* contains four elements: dairy, grains, legumes, and seeds. Any two adjacent food groups in the *N*, when combined, provide complete protein.

- **Dairy**   Cheese, milk, yogurt
- **Grains**   Breads, crackers, pasta, granola and other cereals, rice, couscous, bulgur, bran, potatoes, corn, oats
- **Legumes**   Beans, peas, lentils, peanuts, tofu
- **Seeds**   Sunflower, sesame

The phrase "Don't Get Love Sick" (Dairy, Grains, Legumes, Seeds) may help you remember the four groups and the *order* in which they form the nu-

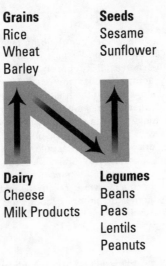

Grains
Rice
Wheat
Barley

Seeds
Sesame
Sunflower

Dairy
Cheese
Milk Products

Legumes
Beans
Peas
Lentils
Peanuts

Complete Protein Combinations

tritional N. Just string the four elements together in alphabetical order. A combination of any two consecutive initial letters of the phrase will provide complete proteins. Dairy and Grains (D & G), for instance, will form a complete protein together, whereas dairy and legumes will not. The other two complete protein combinations are Grains and Legumes (G & L) or Legumes and Seeds (L & S).

Sample Complete Protein Combinations

- **Dairy (or eggs) and grains**   Macaroni and cheese; cheese and crackers; pasta with Parmesan cheese; milk and cereal.
- **Grains and legumes**   Rice and beans; refried beans and flour tortillas; peanut butter and bread; rice or bread and tofu.
- **Legumes and seeds**   Peanuts and sunflower seeds in gorp (see page 70).

BASIC FLUID RECOMMENDATIONS

Water is an essential part of personal nutrition on the trail. It aids digestion, regulates body temperature, keeps cells healthy, and carries waste from the body. Dehydration leads to headaches, fatigue, and irritability. Mild dehydration is often easily relieved by drinking half a quart (½ liter) or more of water. Remember that these general recommendations are for backpacking in temperate forest conditions. You may need to increase your fluid intake based on

Gorp Everyone has his or her own favorite recipes for "gorp," which stands for Good Old Raisins and Peanuts. I start with equal parts raisins and peanuts and then add a quick sugar source. You can increase the variety of the mix by adding smaller amounts of different sugar sources. When using chocolate, consider the melting factor. Also, if you use items like sunflower seeds that are smaller than most of the other things in your mix they will eventually filter down to the bottom of the bag, so be prepared on the last day to find a bag full of sunflower seeds. Here are some items to consider: dried papaya, pineapple, apples, apricots, dates, banana chips, mango, or cranberries (Craisins); coconut; almonds; cashews; brazil nuts; peanuts; chocolate, butterscotch, or carob chips; chocolate malt balls; M&M's; chocolate-covered raisins, peanuts, or almonds; yogurt-covered raisins, peanuts, or almonds; sunflower seeds; rice crackers; dried green peas; pretzels; sesame stix. Be inventive!

your own metabolic needs, physical condition, medical condition, age, sex, or different weather conditions (such as high temperature and humidity), high altitude, or in specific ecosystems (such as desert climates).

Water is always being lost by the body through the "—tions": respiration, perspiration, urination, and defecation. Strenuous activities like backpacking result in increased water loss. Dehydration is one of the most preventable backcountry problems but also one of the most ignored. I've seen people avoid drinking for all sorts of reasons: it was too much trouble to get the water bottle out of their pack or they didn't want to have to urinate. The bottom line is, *stay hydrated*. Failure to stay adequately hydrated can lead to serious and even life-threatening conditions. (See "Fluid Balance," page 326; "Heat-Related Illnesses," page 342; "Hypothermia," page 332; "Hyponatremia," page 327.)

Keep your water bottles handy and keep drinking all day long. Drink 16+ ounces (500 milliliters) before starting to hike and then 10 to 12 ounces (200 to 300 milliliters) every 20 to 30 minutes while hiking. It is easier on your body to handle small amounts of water spread out rather than sucking down a whole quart at once. The sensation of thirst comes *after* the body is already low on fluid, so don't wait until you are thirsty to drink. If your mucus membranes are dry (lips and mouth), then you are low on fluids. The best way to tell if you are adequately hydrated is to check your urine output. It should be "copious and clear."

Keep your daily route and the availability of water in mind when you are planning your menu. If water will be scarce, you need to plan meals that do not require lots of water for cooking or rehydrating.

Season/Weather	Amount/day	Explanation
Fall and spring backpacking*	2–3 quarts (1.8–2.8 liters)	This is what an average person will need on a daily basis in a general temperate climate.
Hot-weather backpacking*	3–4 quarts (2.8–3.7 liters)	In hot and humid weather, you lose additional fluid through sweating, which must be replaced.
Winter backpacking*	4+ quarts (3.7+ liters)	In the winter, you lose moisture through evaporation to the dry air and especially through respiration. Dry air entering the lungs heats up and is exhaled saturated with moisture.
*High-altitude, all seasons	Add 1 quart (0.9 liters)	At high altitudes the body loses more fluid. Increase your fluid intake if you are traveling at high altitudes (over 8,000 feet/2,438 meters).

Remember that these are general recommendations only. You may have different fluid requirements based on your own metabolic needs, physical condition, medical condition, age, sex (e.g., during her menstrual period, a woman will need more fluid), or different weather conditions.

TRICKS OF THE TRAIL

Hydration gear If your water bottle is buried in your pack there's a good chance you won't stop to get to it as often as you need to stay properly hydrated. There are a number of water bladders, like the Camelback and the Platypus, that use a collapsible plastic bag in a fabric liner along with a drinking tube. You can place the carrier in your pack, hang the tube on your shoulder strap, and drink as you hike. I find I stay much better hydrated with a water bladder.

MENU PLANNING

When planning food for a backpacking trip, you need to decide if cooking is a group task or a personal task. A group menu is where everyone in the group plans centralized meals and cooks and eats together versus each person cooking on his or her own. Either way there are two approaches to planning meals that can be taken. The first is a menu planned meal-by-meal (breakfast on day 1 is this, dinner is that); the second is a ration system in which you bring lots of different ingredients (pasta, rice, dried veggies, etc.) and the group creates its own menu on-the-fly. On short trips (two to six days), a meal-by-meal menu often works best. The ration approach is useful on longer trips (seven to ten+ days), as it provides room for greater flexibility and creativity. Proper menu planning means less weight to carry, less wasted food, and less garbage to pack out. Below are some important things to think about when planning your menu.

HOW LONG ARE YOU GOING TO BE OUT?

The length of your trip is essential when planning a menu. You need to bring enough food to feed everyone, but you don't want to carry too much heavy food. For any trip, you can start with a variety of fresh fruits and vegetables, which will typically last several days.

- **Less than a week**   Carry any type of fresh food that won't spoil. At the beginning of a trip if weight is not an issue you can freeze pre-cooked foods and take them with you.
- **Seven to ten days**   Add some dehydrated or freeze-dried foods to cut down on weight.
- **Greater than ten days**   Increase the proportion of dehydrated or freeze-dried foods, or arrange for food resupply.

On longer expeditions, the types of foods you can carry become more limited. You may need to supplement your diet with vitamins and minerals to make up for nutrients that you may not be getting.

EASE OF PREPARATION

One of the things to think about in your menu planning is how you are going to cook. Are you bringing a stove, cooking on fires, or not cooking at all? If you have a stove, is it designed for extended cooking, like the MSR Whisperlite, or just to boil a small amount of water, like the Ezbit stove or the JetBoil? If you are going ultralight and have a simple "boil a cup of water" stove, then you are limited in the types of food you can cook (more prepackaged things like instant oatmeal, ramen noodles, and good old mac 'n' cheese). Knowing *how* you are going to cook is a key factor in deciding *what* foods you are going to bring.

The one-pot meal approach is used by lots of backcountry travelers. By planning your meal around the ability to cook it in one pot you can decrease cooking time and reduce the amount of fuel needed, another important weight factor for you ultralighters.

You can be much more creative with a multipot meal, but it also may require multiple stoves. Also, think about the activities of the trip. For example, on a winter camping trip where you may be having to melt snow for water, you may need a lot of your fuel and time for that task, so a quicker one-pot meal may be best.

WEIGHT

You understand what a good diet is and how many calories each person is going to need. But how are you going to carry all that? For three-season backpacking, assume that each person needs about 2 pounds (0.9 kilograms) of food per day (this increases in winter). You need to plan your menu with the weight of the food in mind. On some trips, like a rafting trip, weight may not be an issue. Here are a few things to keep in mind:

- Some foods are lighter than others, and packaging, especially cans, adds weight.
- Fresh foods, such as fruit or vegetables, are heavy because they contain water, but they provide a welcome treat on the trail.
- You can save weight by eliminating the water carried in foods. For example, carry dried beans instead of canned beans, which contain water. Beans, chickpeas, and black-eyed peas require soaking. You can rehydrate them on the trail by placing them in a full water bottle overnight. Once soaked they will be rehydrated and ready to cook. (This also decreases the cooking time and saves stove fuel.) If you plan to rehydrate, think about water availability on your route. The other way to rehydrate beans is to place them in water, boil them for two to three minutes, and then let them soak for at least an hour. The longer the beans soak, the softer they get (but don't soak more than 24 hours).

🍁 TRICKS OF THE TRAIL

Freeze-dried foods Cooked or fresh food is frozen and then the water is allowed to sublimate off. This removes about 99 percent of the water and leaves most of the nutritional value.

Dehydrated foods Dehydration is a process using heat to evaporate water slowly. About 90 percent of the water is removed during the dehydration process. Some nutrients are also lost. Dehydrated foods can take longer to cook, which adds weight back into your pack in terms of extra stove fuel.

Both freeze-dried and dehydrated foods save on weight but require significant amounts of water to rehydrate. In situations where water is limited, these foods may be a problem. Whenever you are thinking of packing prepared freeze-dried or dehydrated foods, try them out at home first. You want to know that you will like the taste and know how much it actually makes. It may say it feeds four, but after a long day of hiking, it might only feed three.

- Plan your meals to use the heaviest items first and then move to lighter-weight items at the end. This way you will quickly reduce the amount of weight you will be carrying.
- You can feed yourself pretty cheaply on the trail. Dried and freeze-dried foods are lightweight, but you pay more for someone to do the processing. If you have the time, you can dehydrate foods yourself with a food drier.

PACKAGING/REPACKAGING

This is important in terms of weight and minimal impact. (See Chapter 5, "Leave No Trace Hiking and Camping.") Glass, cans, and foils should be avoided as much as possible since they add weight and must be packed out. Glass containers are obviously unwise to carry in a backpack, unless, for example, you want to scrape the honey off the inside of your pack. A simple way to repackage any food is to use sealable plastic bags such as Ziploc or plastic bags tied with loose knots at the top. Double-bagging is important with powders and grains to prevent leakage if one bag tears. Spices often can be purchased in small plastic containers. Whenever possible, bag all the contents of a meal together and label it "Lunch Day 2," "Dinner Day 3," etc. Another approach is to put food items in separate stuff sacks—breakfast, lunch, and dinner.

Leave No Trace camping begins at the store. The idea is to be environmentally conscious when buying items by evaluating the packaging of different foods and brands.

- **Reduce** the amount of packaging you buy by buying in bulk. Choose items that are bulk packaged rather than individually wrapped. Many local supermarkets and health food stores sell items in bulk, which you can repack on your own. This can also reduce your costs.
- **Recycle** all cardboard, glass, and other original packaging when you repack your food. Look for food brands with recyclable packaging.
- **Reuse** After a trip, plastic bags that have no holes can be washed out and reused. Other containers are reusable, too (e.g., a plastic peanut butter jar). Tupperware or other plastic containers can be reused.

SPOILAGE

On longer trips, and even short trips in hot weather, it is usually not possible to carry fresh foods or meats for very long because of spoilage. Here are some guidelines for how long different foods will keep:

Fruits and Vegetables

- Fruits stay fresh for different lengths of time. Harder fruits like apples, oranges, and tangerines are best. If you buy softer fruits like pears, peaches, or nectarines, buy them before they ripen and let them ripen on the trail. Avoid putting easily smushed fruits like bananas in your pack unless you are very brave. Think about using items that are in season or grown locally over items that are brought in from far away. Reducing the impact of what we buy and where it comes from is another part of the Leave No Trace ethic.
- Carrots, potatoes, garlic, onions, and other root vegetables can keep for two to three weeks.
- Dried fruits last for months.

Cheeses and Dairy

Note: The ability of cheese to keep unrefrigerated for extended periods of time is primarily based on the moisture content of the cheese. Any cheese can be out for a few hours, but only some cheeses are appropriate for multiday trips.

- **Grated and grating cheeses** (moisture content 34 percent or less) Parmesan and Romano do not need refrigeration.
- **Hard cheeses** (moisture content 36 to 43 percent) Cheddar, Colby, and Swiss can go without refrigeration for up to a week. Over time, high temperatures result in oiling off of liquefied milk fat. Though unsightly, this is not a spoilage problem. Waxed bricks or wheels hold up best.
- **Semisoft cheeses** (moisture content 44 to 52 percent) Brie, Camembert, blue cheese, Monterey Jack, and Muenster should be refrigerated.
- **Soft cheeses** (moisture content greater than 50 percent) Cream cheese, ricotta, and cottage cheese require refrigeration for long-term storage.
- **Milk** Most people take powdered milk to conserve weight. UHT (ultra-high-temperature pasteurized) milk such as Parmalat can be carried for months unopened without refrigeration. Once opened, the UHT milk must be refrigerated, but if you use it up at one meal, it's fine.
- **Clarified butter** Butter with the milk solids removed. It will last up to three weeks unrefrigerated in the backcountry.
- **Margarine/oils** Famous (or infamous) Squeeze Parkay lasts for several weeks unrefrigerated. Or you can bring olive, sesame, or other oils to cook with instead of butter or margarine.

Meats

- Hard salami, pepperoni, smoked meats, and jerky all last for weeks without refrigeration.
- Canned meats and fish last "almost" forever.

Eggs

- It used to be suggested that eggs could be carried unrefrigerated on trips if kept in water. Because of increases in Salmonella bacteria in chickens and the need for eggs to be cooked completely to kill the bacteria, this is no longer recommended.

🍁 TRICKS OF THE TRAIL

Cook before you go A number of delicious meals or add-ons can be made ahead of time and packed with you. Fresh breads, biscuits, muffins, and deserts can add a lot to a trip. Cold salads such as bean salad, hummus, and tabouli can also be made ahead of time.

Pre-cook and freeze For special meals early in the trip you can pre-cook meals and freeze them in a plastic container. Seal the container well with tape. The food will slowly melt, but should be fine for the first 24 hours. Reheat on the stove for a quick dinner.

EATING ON THE TRAIL

Everyone has different preferences for mealtimes. When hiking, you are expending energy all the time, so you constantly need to replenish that energy. This typically means eating three meals a day. Some people prefer to get up, have a light breakfast, get an early start, and then stop for a bigger meal at midday. Whatever your preference, you should have an ample supply of water and snacks during the day to keep up your energy level. Remember that more falls and injuries take place on hiking trips around 11:00 A.M. and again at 3:00 P.M. than at any other time because blood sugar is low and people are dehydrated. Plan snacks and rest breaks around these times. (See Chapter 8, "Safety and Emergency Procedures.")

It is also important to take into consideration the different eating habits of the group members. There may be people with food allergies, vegetarians, and those who keep kosher. It is also important to plan a variety of foods, especially for longer trips. Asking trip members about specific dietary needs before shopping will help make everyone on the trip feel included. Finally, a tip for cooking for people with particular dietary restrictions: cook whatever food cannot be eaten by everyone *separately*. Put it aside in a separate dish for people to add to their own plates.

GENERAL COOKING GUIDELINES, INGREDIENTS, AND RECIPES

- **Hygiene** Before anyone handles food, make sure the person washes his or her hands thoroughly (see "Keeping Clean on the Trail," page 88).
- **Avoid Burning Your Meals** Cooking on a backpacking stove is a challenging affair, since some stoves don't simmer well and none offers the same control as a kitchen stove. Start with a clean pot to avoid burning last night's dinner. Turn the stove on full only when you are boiling water. Otherwise, turn it down to let the food cook slowly and evenly. It may take longer to cook, but once you burn food in the pot, you'll taste it the rest of the meal. Check periodically to see if food is sticking to the bottom. If so, turn down the heat or add water. If you are using large pots or frying pans over a small stove burner, you may need to move the pot around frequently to make sure the heat is distributed evenly.
- **Avoid Overcooking or Undercooking** The major cause of overcooking or undercooking is adding ingredients in the wrong order. Start with freeze-dried foods first in cold water and boil for 10 to 15 minutes to rehydrate. Next add rice or pasta. The last thing to add is thickeners like flour, potato pearls, milk, or cheese.
- **Spices** Spices bring your meal to life. Remember that many sauces, dehydrated soups, and other stocks are already salty. It is best to let people add their own salt when the food is done, rather than oversalt while you're cooking. Use only a little bit of spice at a time. It takes 5 to 10 minutes for spices to flavor food, so wait and taste before adding more.
- **Pots** If you have extra pots, put water on the stove to boil for hot drinks as soon as you take the dinner pot off. This will also give you hot water for washing.
- **Leftovers** Any solid food left over should be placed in a plastic bag and packed out. Do *not* bury solid food waste; animals will only dig it up.
- **Don't Pack Fuel Near Food** Fuel vapors are heavier than air and sink in your pack. They can penetrate plastic bags and contaminate food like trail mix. Food contaminated with fuel is considered a toxic substance and enough of it can make you sick. Carry fuel in an outside pocket of your pack away from food or in the bottom of your pack with the food packed higher up.
- **Cooking at Altitude** At higher altitudes, the air pressure is lower. This

allows water to boil at lower temperatures, so you'll need to plan longer cooking times. For foods that cook in 20 minutes or less at sea level, add 1 minute of cooking time for each 1,000 feet (310 meters) of elevation. For items that take more than 20 minutes at sea level, add 2 minutes of cooking time for each 1,000 feet (310 meters) of elevation. Something that takes 20 minutes to cook at sea level can take twice as long (40 minutes) to cook at 10,000 feet (3,048 meters). This also means that you may need significantly more stove fuel if your trip is at high altitude.

Elevation	Boiling Point of Water	Cooking Time
Sea level	212°F (100°C)	10 minutes
5,000 feet (1,524 meters)	203°F (95°C)	15 minutes
7,500 feet (2,286 meters)	198°F (95°C)	18 minutes
10,000 feet (3,048 meters)	194°F (90°C)	20 minutes
15,000 feet (4,572 meters)	185°F (85°C)	25 minutes

SAMPLE RECIPES

To me, cooking is a lot like carpentry—the old adage, "measure twice, cut once" becomes "measure twice, cook once." Once, when I was on a backcountry skiing trip, I read a biscuit recipe too quickly and added too much water. In order to salvage the batter, I had to make enough biscuits to feed a small army for a week. By the end of the trip we were all very tired of eating biscuits. In the sample recipes below, you should adjust the quantities to fit the size (and appetites) of your group. Don't be afraid to invent your own recipes, or check out some of the excellent backcountry cookbooks available (see the Bibliography).

Most meals will be one-pot meals. These are often based on pasta, rice, or other grains. Here are the basic cooking directions for pasta and rice:

Pasta   Use two parts water to one part pasta. Bring the water to a boil. Add salt (1 teaspoon per quart of water). Add the pasta and boil it gently for 10 to 15 minutes or until done. You can use the drained water for soups or carbo-loaded hot chocolate.

Instant Rice   Use equal amounts of rice and water. Bring the water to a boil, add margarine (as desired) and salt (1 teaspoon per quart of water). Stir in the rice. Cover, and remove from heat. Let stand for 5 minutes, fluff with a fork and serve.

HUMMUS

This chickpea spread is a great energy food full of protein and calories. You can make it before the trip or on the trail and pack it in a Ziploc or Tupperware, where it will easily last a week. It makes a great lunch food on pita or crackers or a nice appetizer before dinner.

2 (12-ounce) cans chickpeas
2 tablespoons olive oil
6 tablespoons sesame tahini
  Juice of 3 lemons
4 garlic cloves, minced

Mash the chickpeas with a fork. Add the olive oil, tahini, and lemon juice. If the mix is too thick, add a tablespoon or two of water. Add the garlic. Mix until smooth. Serve with slices of pita bread. If you want to carry less weight, bring dry hummus, which can be mixed with water on the trail.

Serves 6

TUNA MELTS

This is a great hot lunch or appetizer for the days when you're feeling lazy and don't want to spend a lot of time cooking.

1 tablespoon margarine or oil
6 (10-inch) tortillas or pita bread
2 (8-ounce) cans/packets tuna fish, drained
1 cup diced Cheddar cheese

Melt the margarine or heat the oil in a frying pan over medium heat. Place a tortilla in the pan and top with a thin layer of the tuna and cheese. Fold in half and cook over medium heat until the cheese is completely melted. Repeat with remaining tortillas and filling.

Serves 6

Note: If you prefer, you can use pita pockets instead of tortillas. Slice the pocket open before placing in the frying pan, and follow the recipe, closing the pita when the recipe tells you to fold the tortilla.

What to do with the remains:

Tuna juice Buy tuna packed in water rather than oil. Depending on how you eat the tuna, you may be able to just pour the water into your pot. However, if you are eating tuna straight out of the can for lunch, you should properly dispose of the tuna juice. Pouring it over the tuna on sandwiches is best. Tuna and chicken are available in foil packets with no juice. It is also easier to pack out the foil pouches than the cans.

Noodle water Anytime you cook pasta, you are left with noodle water. If possible, use this for something else later in the meal, such as hot chocolate. The chocolate will hide the pasta flavor, and you'll get the benefit of the extra carbs in the water. This is much better than putting the water in a sump hole (see "Wastewater," page 122).

BURRITOS

Packed with protein and carbohydrates, burritos are another great energy meal. Repack the beans and salsa into water bottles before your trip, or use instant beans, so you aren't lugging cans around. The cumin makes a huge difference in flavor; don't forget to include it in your spice kit.

    1   tablespoon margarine
    ½   onion, chopped
    1   green bell pepper, chopped
    3   (4-ounce) cans/packets chicken
    2   (12-ounce) cans refried black beans
    2   (12-ounce) cans salsa
    1   teaspoon ground cumin
    6   tortillas
        Cheddar cheese, sliced, for topping

In a large frying pan over medium heat, melt the margarine and sauté the onion for 1 to 2 minutes. Add the green pepper and chicken, and continue to sauté, stirring frequently, until the onion is translucent, 3 to 5 minutes. Add the beans, salsa, and cumin, and cook over medium heat, stirring frequently, until hot. Divide the mixture among the 6 tortillas, sprinkle each with cheese, fold, and serve immediately.

Serves 6

PITA PIZZAS

This meal takes a while if you have to cook one pizza at a time, but it's lots of fun to make. This recipe makes 18 small pizzas.

    3   tablespoons margarine
    2   green bell peppers, chopped
    1   onion, chopped
        Pepperoni stick, sliced
   18   small whole-wheat pitas
    1   (16-ounce) can tomato or pizza sauce
    1   pound Cheddar cheese, sliced

In a large frying pan over medium heat, melt 1 tablespoon of margarine and sauté the green peppers, onion, and pepperoni slices until the onion is translucent, 3 to 5 minutes. Set aside in a bowl. Slice a 4-inch-long opening along the edge of each pita. Fill each one with sauce, cheese, onion, and green pepper. Fry each pita individually in margarine (added to the pan as needed) over medium heat until the pita is browned and the insides are warmed.

Serves 6

QUESADILLAS

Quesadillas are a wonderful excuse to use up any leftover cheese and tortillas you're carrying around. The longer your trip, the more you start fantasizing about fresh vegetables. Spinach is a good solution because it's light and full of vitamins and fiber. Make sure it comes prewashed so you don't use up water washing off sand and dirt.

    3   tablespoons margarine
    1   pound pre-washed spinach
    2   green bell peppers
    2   onions, chopped
    1   cup chopped Cheddar cheese
    6   tortillas

In a large frying pan over medium heat, melt 1 tablespoon of the margarine and sauté the spinach, green peppers, and onions until the spinach is wilted and the onions are browned, 5 to 10 minutes. Set aside in a bowl. Fill a tortilla with one-sixth of the spinach mixture, sprinkle with cheese, and fold in half. Reheat the frying pan and cook each quesadilla over medium heat until the cheese melts, adding margarine as needed. This can be a very sloppy procedure, but the meal is so delicious it's worth the mess.

Serves 6

MACARONI AND CHEESE

Mac and cheese is a meal that I don't think to fix at home, but after a long day on the trail, even something this simple tastes good. Must be all those carbs.

2   pounds elbow macaroni or rigatoni noodles
1   pound cheddar cheese, chopped (using various cheeses adds to the flavor)
4   tablespoons margarine
1   garlic clove, minced

Bring a large pot of water to a boil. Add the noodles, and cook over medium heat until tender, 5 to 10 minutes, depending on the type of noodle. When the noodles are tender, pour the water out (see "Noodle Water," page 80), leaving enough water in the pot to just barely cover the noodles. Add the cheese, margarine, garlic, salt and pepper to taste, and stir until the cheese melts. Serve immediately.

Serves 6

Variation: You can spice this meal up by stir-frying some veggies (broccoli, green peppers, etc.) in a separate pan with a little margarine until tender, and adding them in at the cheese-melting stage.

PESTO SAUCE

Make a batch of pesto before your trip and you'll have a quick and easy meal for those long days when you're too tired to cook.

2   cups fresh basil leaves
⅓   cup olive oil
1   teaspoon lemon juice
2   garlic cloves, minced
¼   cup pine nuts
2   teaspoons red wine or balsamic vinegar

Add all the ingredients to a blender or food processor and grind until smooth. Store the pesto in a Tupperware container (tape it closed all the way around or you'll find oil and basil all over your pack). Serve over your favorite pasta, fish, or chicken.

Makes 2½ cups, to serve 6

CHICKEN FAJITAS

    16 ounces refried beans
    30 ounces canned/packet chicken, drained
     3 tablespoons margarine
     2 green bell peppers, sliced
     2 onions, sliced
    12 (10-inch) flour tortillas
    16 ounces salsa
        Grated cheese (optional)

In a large frying pan, heat the refried beans over medium heat until warm, then set aside in a separate bowl. Drain the chicken (save the juice to add to your frying pan as needed). Add 1 tablespoon margarine to the frying pan over high heat. When the pan is hot, lightly scorch the peppers, onions, and chicken until brown but still tender. (For easier frying, cook only ¼ to ½ of the filling at a time, storing the finished filling in a separate covered pot.) If desired, warm the tortillas in a large frying pan; fry 2 tortillas at a time over medium-high heat, adding a small amount of margarine to the pan as needed. Fill the tortillas with the beans and chicken mixture. Cover with salsa and grated cheese, if desired.

Serves 6

DHAAL-BHAT (SHERPA RICE)

Dhaal-bhat, or curried rice and lentils, is a staple for the people of the Himalayas. I grew to love this simple dish while trekking in Nepal.

    ½ cup lentils
    ½ cup barley
       Salt
     3 cups instant rice

1 onion, chopped
2 green bell peppers, chopped
2 apples, chopped
Curry powder
Ground cinnamon

Soak the lentils and barley for about 2 hours by putting them in a water bottle (you can do this earlier in the afternoon and they will be rehydrated by the time you get to camp). Add salt to a large pot of boiling water. Stir in rice, barley, and lentils. Reduce to a simmer, then add onion, green peppers, apples, and spices. Cover tightly and simmer for 30 minutes.

Serves 6

CURRIED CHICKEN WITH RICE

3 cups instant rice
Salt
1 onion, diced
1 teaspoon minced garlic
1 tablespoon margarine
30 ounces canned/foil pack chicken
2 apples, chopped
½ cup raisins
1 to 2 tablespoons curry powder

Boil 2½ cups water, add rice, and boil for 1 minute with 1 tablespoon salt. Simmer, covered, until done. Drain excess water, if necessary. In a fry pan, sauté onion and garlic in 1 tablespoon margarine until tender. Add the chicken, apples, raisins, and curry and heat for a few minutes. Add chicken mixture to rice and serve.

Serves 6

OUTDOOR BAKING

Baking in the backcountry is an art that requires patience. In order to bake, you need to be able to provide heat on both the top and the bottom of your pan. There are a number of cooking pans and devices, such as the BakePacker and the Outback Oven, that enable you to do this. Another technique is to create a Dutch oven using a pot with a lid. You can do this on a fire (if building a fire is appropriate) or on a backpack stove: place coals from the fire, or build a twig fire, on top of the pot lid. (Lids designed with a rim to contain the fire make this much easier.) Hold your hand about 6 inches above the pot-lid coals. Your hand should feel hot but not burn. Once baking begins, gently remove the lid periodically using pot grips and check your progress, and then quickly replace the lid. You will have to continue to feed the coals to maintain heat.

Outback Oven

The Outback Oven works on the convection oven principle. The unit comes with its own pot and lid. A grate lifts the pot off the stove so that it is not directly on the flame. A heat reflector around the stove burner reflects heat up and underneath an insulated pot cover. This heated air surrounds the pot and does the baking. The pot lid has a small thermometer knob marked "Warm Up—Bake—Burn." By changing your stove setting you keep the pot at the correct temperature. The heat capture is so efficient that you can cook on a low flame on your stove. This means that you have to have a stove that can simmer or you'll just burn everything. The insulated pot cover can also be used by itself to help your pot retain heat, making your stove more efficient.

According to the Backpacker's Pantry folks, you can bake anything in the Outback Oven that you bake in your home oven: potatoes, casseroles, pies, breads, rolls, muffins, etc. Scones and cakes bake in 15 to 20 minutes; pizzas bake in about 30 minutes *(www.backpackerspantry.com)*.

BakePacker

The BakePacker is a 2-inch-high (5 centimeter) metal grid that is placed in the bottom of a pot. The grid is partially covered with water. When the water boils, each subcompartment of the grid acts as a small heat exchanger. The BakePacker is able to transfer significant amounts of heat energy at a relatively low temperature (212°F/100°C at sea level), which allows you to cook and bake foods that would require much higher temperatures in a regular oven. Mix your recipe ingredients in a plastic bag, roll the bag closed but don't seal it, and place the bag on top of the grid. Keep the water at a medium boil throughout the cooking process. Heat transfers evenly into the bag, cooking things completely *(www.bakepacker.com)*.

FOOD EQUIVALENTS

Here are some common menu items with information on how weight or volume converts to the number of servings:

Food Item	Raw Weight/Amount	Finished Volume	Number of Servings
Instant rice	½ cup	⅔ cup	1
Macaroni noodles	1 pound (6 cups)	1 cup	4
Oatmeal	½ cup	1 cup	1
Spaghetti noodles	1 lb	10 cups	6–8
Drink mix	21 ounces	6 quarts	24
Potato buds	⅔ cup	⅓ cup	1
Pancake mix	2 pounds	40 pancakes	10
Tuna fish	7 ounces	¼ cup	2–3
Hot chocolate	1 ounce (4 tablespoons)	1 cup	1
Lipton Cup-o-Soup	1 envelope (14 grams)	2 cups	1
Ramen noodles	3 ounces	2 cups	1
Peanut butter	18 ounces	2 tbsp	15

MEASUREMENT EQUIVALENTS

1 tablespoon	= 3 teaspoons				
1 fluid ounce	= 2 level tablespoons				
¼ cup	8 level tablespoons				
1 cup	8 ounces	16 tablespoons	236 milliliters		
1 pint	2 cups	16 fluid ounces	473 milliliters		
1 quart	4 cups	2 pints	32 fluid ounces	946 milliliters	
1 gallon	16 cups	8 pints	4 quarts	128 fluid ounces	3.78 liters
1 pound	16 ounces	454 grams			

Hygiene and Water Purification

Maintaining proper hygiene is a challenge in the wilderness. After hiking down a muddy trail all day you are just covered with gunk. Add sweat, sunscreen, and bug repellant and you can be a mess. While part of the joy of backpacking is returning to a more basic existence, giving up the luxuries of hot and cold running water, toilets, showers, and the like, sometimes we surrender *too* much to the dirt that surrounds us and that can lead to actual health problems. Dirty and open blisters or cuts and scrapes are a ripe environment for infection. Bacterial infections can spread through poor cleaning of cookware and poor personal hygiene before handling food. Get into the habit of using good cleaning practices for a safer and more enjoyable trip. It's not just your cleanliness; someone else's lack of good hygiene could cause you to become sick. (See below.)

KEEPING CLEAN ON THE TRAIL

One of the most common health problems in the backcountry is gastrointestinal illnesses like diarrhea, which are spread by fecal-to-oral transmission. Fecal-borne pathogens get into your system through one of several routes:

- Direct contact with feces (even using toilet paper leaves germs on your hands)
- Indirect contact with hands that have contacted feces (shaking hands, for example)
- Contact with insects that have contacted feces
- Contact with contaminated drinking water

Imagine that you stop for a rest along the trail. While the group snacks on trail mix, Jim grabs the toilet kit and heads off the trail. He comes back to the group and unthinkingly reaches into the trail mix bag to grab a handful. The next day, he and several others are showing signs of a gastrointestinal infection. The best way to reduce the risk of fecal-oral contamination is to utilize a strict handwashing protocol. Wash your hands before handling or cooking food and after each bowel movement. Think about all those "Employees wash your hands" signs you see in restaurant bathrooms. You don't want people with unwashed hands preparing your food in a restaurant and you don't want it on the trail, either.

HANDWASHING

As soon as you get into camp (before you start cooking), set up a handwashing station. (See Chapter 6, "Wilderness Travel.") There are two common approaches:

Waterless Hand Sanitizers

Probably the best cleanliness invention for backpackers has been waterless hand sanitizers like Purell. These are alcohol-based liquids with moisturizers. Pour a small amount on your hands and rub your hands together until it evaporates. The alcohol kills up to 99 percent of bacteria so your hands will actually be cleaner than washing with soap. The ease of use means that you can easily clean your hands in just a few seconds after that quick jog off the trail instead of trying to set up a soap-and-water handwashing station. They also save water, which in some situations may be in short supply. Keep your hand sanitizer in with your toilet kit so that when someone heads off to go she can wash up immediately afterward.

The one disadvantage to waterless hand sanitizers is that, since there is no "rinsing action" as with soap and water, not much dirt actually leaves your hands (it just moves it around). If your hands are really covered with dirt that you want to remove, do a quick rinse with water before using a hand sanitizer. Note that alcohol-based products like Purell do not contain antibacterial agents as do some other cleaning products and therefore do not contribute to making more resistant bacteria. In fact, these products are so effective that the Centers for Disease Control and Prevention recommends using them instead of antibacterial soap. Foil-pack alcohol towelettes or unscented baby wipes are other alternatives. The disadvantage is that you have to pack out the used towelettes as trash.

Soap and Water

You will need a collapsible water jug with a nozzle that can be easily opened or closed, a small bristle brush, and biodegradable soap. Orient the water jug with the nozzle facing down, perhaps hanging over the edge of a rock. Make sure that the area beneath the jug will be minimally impacted by the soap and water's landing there (e.g., rock). Keep the soap and the hand brush next to the container. This station should be at least 200 feet (61 meters) from any water source. The cleaning procedure is as follows:

1. Wet your hands thoroughly.
2. Add a small amount of soap.
3. Lather up, especially your fingertips. Use a small hand brush to get out deep dirt and clean under fingernails (keeping your nails trimmed helps).
4. Rinse with water, then soap up a second time, brush, and rinse again.
5. Dry with a clean towel or bandanna.
6. Make sure you eliminate any signs of your handwashing station before you leave.

Another method is to hang a water jug from a tree. Just beneath the closeable spout of the jug, attach a small drinking cup with small holes in the bottom. Fill the cup with water, and it will slowly trickle out the holes like a showerhead. One cupful of water will be enough to wet your hands. Then lather up. Filling of the cup again should give you enough water to rinse.

Using Soap

Soap poses a potential conflict between Leave No Trace camping and personal health. Most commercial soaps contain phosphates, which, when released into water supplies, stimulate the growth of algae. These algae blooms quickly use up significant amounts of oxygen in the water. When the algae die off, the lowered oxygen content often kills other microorganisms, plants, and even fish. For this reason, *never* use soap directly in any water source (stream, river, or lake). If you are going to use soap, you should only use soaps that are phosphate-free and biodegradable, like Campsuds or Dr. Bronner's Soap. Keep in mind that "biodegradable" means that the soap will *eventually* break down in the soil, not that it has zero impact. This is why all washing with soap should be done at least 200 feet (61 meters) from any water source. The soapy water filters through the ground slowly and breaks down before it reaches the groundwater. Because biodegradable soap has some, albeit small, impact, whenever possible, it's good to avoid using soap if you don't need it (for example, if just a good water rinse will do). However, there are situations when soap or other cleaners are essential to maintaining good health.

PERSONAL BATHING

Getting the whole body clean is a bit more of a challenge in the backcountry. Collapsible water bags with shower attachments (shower bags), such as the MSR Dromedary Bag or a SunShower, make this process much easier. You can also use a large cooking pot. Make sure you have an adequate water supply available and ready at your washing site before you start (so you don't run screaming around camp with soap in your eyes, looking for water). Again, your washing site should be at least 200 feet (61 meters) from any water source and on a resilient spot that won't turn into a soapy mudpit as you wash. Here's the procedure:

1. Rinse yourself off. Use a shower bag, large water container, or cooking pot. If the only thing you have on you is dirt, you can rinse off in a

stream. If you have "contaminants" on your skin (excessive body salt, sunscreen, insect repellent), avoid rinsing directly in a water source since *these chemicals can contaminate a small water source* (see "Tricks of the Trail," below). The rinse might be the end of your washing if you don't plan to use soap.

2. Lather up, using the *least* amount of biodegradable soap possible; you don't need a lot to get clean.

3. Rinse yourself off with the shower bag or pots of water. The help of a friend always makes this easier. The soapy water will soak into the ground and be filtered by the soil.

🍁 TRICKS OF THE TRAIL

Body Salts and Toxic Chemicals After a day of hiking in hot weather, you may be covered with a variety of nasty things—loads of salt, sunscreen, and insect repellant. You know better than to wash with soap directly in a stream or lake, but people often forget about swimming. They see a cold pool and dive in. Think about what you are "wearing" on your skin before you dive in and look at the size of the water source. In small pools and sinkholes you can leave behind a load of body salts and possibly a toxic chemical slick (e.g., DEET from insect repellant). This can have a major impact on aquatic and other life, especially in small pools or potholes. Small pools in desert areas, like those that form after rains, shrink as they dry up, which further concentrates any salts and chemicals in the water. If your body is carrying contaminants, think about rinsing off on land before going in for a swim.

WASHING CLOTHES

Unless you are out for weeks at a time or take a nasty fall in a swamp, clothes usually can be adequately cleaned by thoroughly rinsing and wringing them out in the water. This is how much of the world has been cleaning clothes for thousands of years. Don't rinse your clothes directly in a water source if they have been contaminated by chemicals (insect repellents, sunscreen). It is best not to use soap on clothes, as it is difficult to rinse out all the soap, and residual soap on clothes can cause skin irritations and rashes.

WASHING DISHES, POTS, AND UTENSILS

Dishwashing is probably one of my least favorite chores on any camping trip. However, with the right equipment and a proper system, it can be done quickly and effectively. Depending on the environment, you may be able to avoid using soap by cleaning with natural materials (grasses, pinecones, sand, snow—see Chapter 5, "Leave No Trace Hiking and Camping"). Remember, natural materials can contain germs. If you are using soap, make sure that you rinse dishes thoroughly, since soap residue can cause diarrhea. (See "Gastrointestinal Infections," page 370.) Never wash dishes directly in a stream, lake, or river. If you are using soap and water is *not* in short supply, here is a recommended washing procedure:

Cleaning Equipment

- Pot
- Biodegradable soap
- Hard-bristle scouring brush (easily rinsed out and does not collect food particles). Avoid scouring pads that get gunked up with food particles and become a source for bacterial growth.

Pot-Cleaning System

1. Make sure people have gobbled up all the food from the pot before cleaning.
2. Boil a large pot of water; this can be the same water you use for hot drinks.
3. Pour some hot water into the pot as soon as people have finished eating.
4. Scour food residue from the pot using the brush or natural materials. Collect any large particles of food and pack them out with garbage. Depending on your ecosystem, pour any remaining liquid residue into a sump hole or scatter it. (See "Wastewater," page 122.)
5. Add more hot water and a small amount of biodegradable soap to the pot. Wash using the brush.
6. Rinse thoroughly with hot water, and pour your water into a sump hole or scatter it. Then rinse again with hot water to make sure that all soap residue is gone. Once rinsed, the items can be air-dried.
7. Properly dispose of waste water after everything has been cleaned.

If the trip is for more than seven days, you should do a sterilization about once a week. Clean the items as described above, then prepare a rinse pot. Add a sterilization compound like chlorine bleach to a large pot of cool water (don't use hot water; it deactivates the sterilization chemical). Use the same proportion as you would for purifying water. Rinse all cups, spoons, pots, and utensils with this water and then air-dry. Then rinse again with boiling water. Use a pot gripper to avoid scalding your hands.

WOMEN'S HYGIENE ISSUES

Both women and men need to be comfortable talking about menstruation in the wilderness. For women who have not been in the backcountry before, the physical exertion of the trip can cause their period to start early or not to occur at all. Neither of these is uncommon or dangerous, but for a woman who is used to being very regular, it may be cause for concern.

Proper hygiene is important in minimizing the possibility of infections. Women should clean themselves daily, washing from front to back to keep fecal bacteria from entering the vagina or urethra. Wash your hands thoroughly before and after cleaning yourself. Premoistened, unscented cleaning towelettes can be a good way of preventing contamination from dirty hands.

TAMPONS VS. PADS

Some women have a definite preference for one form of protection. There are also some considerations for the backcountry. Tampons take up less space and may be more comfortable for strenuous hiking. To avoid infections, use tampons with applicators; tampons without applicators require scrupulously clean hands for insertion and are not recommended in the backcountry unless you can ensure that your hands are clean. Make sure you have sufficient supplies for the trip, even if you are not expecting your period. For some women, the increase in physical activity can bring on an early menstruation.

DISPOSING OF TAMPONS, PADS, AND TOWELETTES

These should be packed out. Bring a colored plastic bag with you. Invert the bag over your hand and pick up the used tampon or pad. Fold the bag back over the tampon or pad. A crushed aspirin or a wet tea bag will minimize the odor from soiled tampons and pads. If you use hand towelettes you can put this in with the pad to control odor. Another method is to use a small piece of aluminum foil that can be wrapped around the tampon or pad and sealed. Don't try to burn tampons or pads in a fire. It takes an extremely hot fire to burn them completely.

WATER PURIFICATION

Dipping your head into a cold mountain stream and taking a long refreshing drink is an experience that has vanished from most of the wilderness areas around the world. With the increased use of the wilderness there has also been an increase in the amount of bacteriological contamination of backcountry water supplies. The U.S. Environmental Protection Agency reports that 90 percent of the world's water is contaminated in some way. There are a variety of microscopic organisms that can contaminate water supplies and cause potentially serious, even fatal, illnesses among wilderness travelers. The major danger in the backcountry from these infections is fluid loss due to diarrhea and vomiting, which can lead to hypovolemic shock and possibly death. (See "Diarrhea or Vomiting," page 368; "Rehydration Solutions," page 329; "Shock," page 274.) Does this mean that every single stream is contaminated? Of course not. The problem is that it's very hard to know what is and what isn't, and something that was safe last year might be contaminated now.

To be safe, unless you are really sure about a particular water source, you should be prepared to treat it. Gastrointestinal (GI) infections like *Giardia* can be serious and if left untreated can cause long-term GI problems (see "Gastrointestinal Infections," page 370). Remember that infections can also be spread through poor personal hygiene—something that purifying your water won't prevent. For information on daily fluid requirements, see Chapter 3, "Cooking and Nutrition." For information on emergency water sources and survival, see Chapter 8, "Safety and Emergency Procedures."

There are a number of approaches to treating water. I'll go into detail on each method so you can decide what's best in your particular circumstance.

Biologically Contaminated vs. Toxic Water

Biologically contaminated water is water that contains microorganisms such as *Giardia,* bacteria, or viruses that can lead to infections. (See "Gastrointestinal Infections," page 370.) *Toxic* water sources contain chemical contamination from pesticide run-offs, mine tailings, and so on. Boiling, filtering, or chemically treating water can remove or kill microorganisms, but it will *not* remove chemical toxins. This is also the case when using a solar still (see page 254).

BOILING

Boiling is the most certain way of killing all microorganisms. It won't remove chemical contaminants, but it kills all the little beasties. It was once thought that you had to boil for 5 minutes. According to the Wilderness Medical Society, water temperatures above 160°F (70°C) kills all pathogens within 30 minutes and water above 185°F (85°C) within a few minutes. So in the time it takes for the water to reach the boiling point (212°F or 100°C) from 160°F (70°C), all pathogens will be killed, even at high altitude. To be extra safe, let the water boil rapidly, covered for 1 minute, especially at higher altitudes since water boils at a lower temperature. (See "Cooking at Altitude," page 77.) If boiling is your primary method of water purification, make sure you take that into account for the amount of fuel you plan to bring.

CHEMICAL PURIFICATION

There are two main types of chemical treatment: those using iodine and those using chlorine. There are a variety of products on the market, so follow the manufacturer's instructions. Be advised that some of these products will have an expiration date and become ineffective after that point. Also, with some tablet products, once the bottle has been opened, the tablets must be used within a certain period. If you have an open bottle and you can't remember when you last used it, buy a new bottle. *Note:* Some chemical treatments are not effective against all microorganisms. According to the Centers for Disease Control, many chemical treatments using either iodine or chlorine-based products have *not* been shown to be effective against *Cryptosporidium* (see pages 96–97).

General Procedures for Chemical Treatment

- The effectiveness of *all* chemical treatment of water is related to the temperature, pH level, and clarity of the water. Cloudy water often requires higher concentrations of chemical to disinfect.
- If the water is cloudy or filled with large particles, strain it, using a cloth, *before* treatment.
- Add the chemical to the water and swish it around to aid in dissolving. Splash some of the water with the chemical onto the lid and the threads of the water bottle so that all water areas are treated.
- The water should sit for at least 30 minutes after adding the chemical to allow purification to occur. If using tablets, let the water sit for 30 minutes after the tablet has dissolved.
- The colder the water, the less effective the chemical is as a purifying agent. Research has shown that at 50°F (10°C), only 90 percent of *Giardia* cysts

were inactivated after 30 minutes of exposure. If the water temperature is below 40°F (4°C), double the treatment time before drinking. It is best if water is at least 60°F (16°C) before treating. You can place the water in the sun to warm it before treating.

Iodine Treatment   *Be aware that some people are allergic to iodine and cannot use it as a form of water purification.* Persons with thyroid problems, people who are taking lithium, women over fifty, or pregnant women should consult their physician prior to using iodine for purification. Also, some people who are allergic to shellfish are also allergic to iodine. If someone cannot use iodine, use another method of purification. Iodine is light-sensitive and must always be stored in a dark bottle. It works best if the water is over 68°F (21°C). The water can be warmed in the sun before treating or hot water can be added. Iodine has been shown to be more effect than chlorine-based treatments in inactivating *Giardia* cysts. *Note: iodine-based products are not effective against* Cryptospirodium.

Generally, the procedure is for using iodine is as follows:

- **Liquid 2% Tincture of Iodine**   Add 5 drops per quart/liter when the water is clear. Add 10 drops per quart/liter when the water is cloudy. Wait time is 30 minutes for water over 68°F (21°C).
- **Polar Pure Iodine Crystals**   Fill the Polar Pure bottle with water and shake. The solution will be ready for use in one hour. Add the number of capfuls (per quart of water treated) listed on the bottle, based on the temperature of the iodine solution. If the water is cloudy, double the number of capfuls. The particle trap prevents crystals from getting into the water being treated. It is important to note that you are using the iodine *solution* to treat the water, *not* the iodine crystals. The concentration of iodine in a crystal is poisonous and can burn tissue or eyes, so be sure to avoid pouring crystals into the water. Let the treated water stand for 30 minutes before drinking. In order to destroy *Giardia* cysts, the drinking water must be at least 68°F (20°C). Refill the treatment bottle after use so that the solution will be ready one hour later. Crystals in the bottle make enough solution to treat about 2,000 quarts/liters.
- **Potable Aqua**   This is an iodine tablet product. Follow the manufacturer's instructions for use. Use 2 tablets per quart and wait 30 minutes. Potable Aqua Plus includes a second agent that removes the iodine taste. After waiting 30 minutes of treatment, add 2 tablets of PA Plus per quart, stir well, and wait 3 minutes before drinking. Each bottle contains 50 tablets, enough for 25 quarts.

Chlorine Treatment   Chlorine can be used for persons with iodine allergies or restrictions. Remember that water temperature, sediment level, and contact time are all elements in killing microorganisms in the water. *Note: many chlorine-based products are not effective against* Cryptosporidium.

- **McNett Aqua Mira (AquaMira)**   This is a chlorine dioxide–based chemical water-treatment kit. It is an easy-to-use, two-part system. Place 7 drops Aquamira (Part A) and 7 drops Activator (Part B) in the mixing cap. Wait for 5 minutes until the solution turns yellow and pour the solution into the water to be treated. Wait for about 15 minutes. If *Cryptosporidium* is suspected, double the dose of Part A and Part B and wait for at least 30 minutes. Turbid water with high organic load should be pre-filtered with a charcoal filter before using Aqua Mira. After treatment there is no aftertaste. The kit treats up to 30 gallons of water. Aqua Mira has a shelf life of four years. If stored properly after opening, the product will remain effective until the expiration date.
- **Katadyn MP1 Purification Tablets**   These are chlorine dioxide. They are effective against *Cryptosporidium, Giardia,* bacteria, and viruses. One tablet treats 1 quart (1 liter) of water. Bacteria and viruses are killed in approximately 15 minutes with water at 68°F (20°C). Cryptosporidium *purification takes about four hours.* The tablets do not leave an unpleasant aftertaste.
- **Household Bleach**   You can purify water using a household beach such as Clorox. Make sure that it contains only bleach (sodium hypochlorite) and no other perfumes or additives (check the label before using). Bleach comes in different concentrations. For bleach that is 4 to 6% sodium hypochlorite, add 2 drops of bleach per quart/liter of water if the water is clear, 4 drops if the water is cloudy. Mix thoroughly and wait 30 minutes. The water should have a slight chlorine odor to it. If it doesn't, repeat the dosage, mix, and allow the water to stand for another 15 minutes. The water should be at least 68° F (20° C) before adding the bleach.

MIXED-OXIDANT SOLUTIONS

Another approach to water purification is using mixed oxidants. This technique, originally developed for municipal water systems, has been miniaturized for backpackers. The MSR Miox pen uses basic salt (sodium chloride) in fresh water to create a salt solution. By applying electricity to the solution, it is broken up into an oxidant solution of chlorine and hypochlorite. The oxidant solution is then poured into your water to destroy any microorganisms. It takes about 15 minutes for the solution to kill bacteria and viruses. The solution will kill *Cryptosporidium* (see pages 96–97), but it takes *four hours,* which shows you how difficult this little bug is to kill.

An important feature of using simple salt as the disinfectant source is that salt has an infinite shelf life, so the purifier will still function even if has been stored for a long period of time. The purifier will treat approximately 200 liters of water on one set of batteries. At standard doses the disinfectant solution does not leave an aftertaste, unlike chlorine or iodine tablets. The Miox is about 6 inches (15 centimeters) long and only weighs 3.5 ounces (99 grams). It uses two CR123 lithium batteries. Like any battery-powered system, if the batteries fail, it won't work.

The Miox can be set to create an oxidant solution for from ½ quart (500 milliliters) to 1 gallon (4 liters). Once the oxidant solution has been generated by the Miox unit, it is poured into the water to be purified. Shake or stir the water so that the oxidant is thoroughly mixed, then test it with one of the included test strips. If the strip gives a positive reading, wait 10 minutes and check again with a test strip. If the second test is positive, splash treated water in the threads of the water container and wait 20 minutes before drinking. If the first test is negative, create another batch of oxidant, retreat, and retest. *Note: to treat water with* Cryptosporidium *you need to wait for four hours after the test strip shows positive before drinking.*

✤ TRICKS OF THE TRAIL

Water treatment backups   What happens if you are planning to boil all your water and your stove breaks? Any of the methods for water purification can fail, so always have at least one backup method. This can be any combination of methods (boiling, filter, chemical, etc.). I'm the cautious type, so I usually have two backup methods: water filter and 2 percent tincture of iodine or Polar Pure iodine crystals, and I can always boil the water. If boiling is your backup method, make sure you have enough fuel.

Fix the taste   Chemically treated water can be made to taste better after treatment by aerating it (pouring it back and forth between containers). Adding vitamin C (about 50 milligrams) to iodized water completely eliminates any taste or color of iodine. The vitamin C in drink mixes like Tang has the same effect. Other methods include adding a pinch of salt per quart. You must wait until after the chemical has completely purified the water before adding flavorings.

ULTRAVIOLET LIGHT

Ultraviolet (UV) light has been used for years as a form of sterilization in hospitals and other settings. UV radiation at certain frequencies kills microorganisms, so carefully applied frequencies of UV light can be used to purify water. Such techniques do not remove chemical contaminants in the water.

Hydro-Photon Steri-Pen

This is a battery-operated UV water purifier. Using a calculated dose of UV light, it takes less than a minute to purify 16 ounces (0.4 liters) of water. There are a few caveats to using the Steri-Pen. It should not be used in discolored water or water containing particulate matter since the UV light can't kill what it can't penetrate, and it is designed to generate only enough UV to purify 16 ounces (0.4 liters) at one time. The Steri-Pen kills all microorganisms including protozoa, bacteria, and viruses. When immersed in water, the UV lamp is basically safe, but UV light can be harmful to eyes and skin, so it should never be turned on except when it is immersed in water. The other issue with any electric device is battery or other failure *(www.hydro-photon.com)*.

FILTRATION

There are a number of devices on the market that filter out microorganisms. A water filter pumps water through a microscopic filter that is rated for a certain-size organism. The standard size rating is the micron (the period at the end of this sentence is about 600 microns). Depending on the micron rating of the filter, larger organisms like *Giardia* are filtered out.

Not all filters are created equal. Filters are rated in three size categories—filter, microfilter, and purifier—based on the size of microorganisms they will catch. Be cautious when selecting a filter. If the device is listed as a "water purifier," then it removes *all* microorganisms either through filtration or through a combination of filtration and chemical treatment. You should know what potential organisms you need to treat for. You don't want to go to an area where a virus like hepatitis A is present in the water (a problem in some developing countries); that would require a *purifier* with a *filter* that will handle only large organisms like *Giardia*. Below are common microorganisms and the filter size needed:

Organism	Examples	General Size	Filter Type	Particle Size Rating
Protozoa	*Giardia, Cryptosporidium*	5 microns or larger	Water filter	1.0–4.0 microns
Bacteria	*Cholera, E. coli, Salmonella*	0.2–0.5 microns	Microfilter	0.2–1.0 microns
Viruses	Hepatitis A, rotavirus, Norwalk virus	0.004 microns	Water purifier	to 0.004 microns

Common Practices for Using a Water Filter

- Filter the cleanest water you can find. Dirty water or water with large suspended particles will clog your filter more quickly.
- Prefilter the water either through a prefilter on the pump or strain it through a bandanna or cloth.
- If you must filter very cloudy water, let it stand for several hours for particles to settle out.

Types of Water Filters

- **Membrane filters** use thin sheets with precisely sized pores that prevent objects larger than the pore size from passing through. *Pro:* Relatively easy to clean. *Con:* Clog more quickly than depth filters. *Example:* Katadyn Hiker.
- **Depth filters** use thick porous materials such as carbon or ceramic to trap particles as water flows through the material. *Pro:* Can be partially cleaned by backwashing. Activated carbon filters also remove a range of organic chemicals and heavy metals. *Con:* Rough treatment can crack the filter, rendering it useless. *Examples:* MSR WaterWorks II, Katadyn Pocket, Aqua Mira Water Bottle Filter.
- **Combination methods** use both a membrane filter and a chemical treatment. *Pro:* The filter typically has larger pore sizes and therefore only removes larger organisms (like the hard-to-kill *Cryptosporidium*), then the chemical treatment, either iodine or chlorine-based, kills smaller organisms including viruses. This is a good alternative to waiting for hours for a chemical-only treatment to get rid of *Cryptosporidium. Examples:* The Katadyn Exstream is a combination filter and iodine cartridge. The Aqua Mira Water Bottle Filter and Aqua Mira chlorine treatment use an activated charcoal filter, and then you would treat the water using the Part A and Part B Aqua Mira chemicals described above.

How Do You Know if Your Filter Will Work?

There are no current required certifications for water filters and purifiers. The Centers for Disease Control provides basic scientific information about the different microorganisms and what it takes to remove/kill them *(www.cdc. gov/travel/food-drink-risks.htm)*. NSF International is an independent, not-for-profit company that tests and certifies some water filters and purifiers. Since this is a voluntary certification process that costs the manufacturer significant money, not all manufacturers submit their product for certification testing, so lack of certification does *not* mean that the product is not effective. You can search to see if a particular product is NSF certified on their Web site *(www.nsf.org)*.

🌿 **TRICKS OF THE TRAIL**

Filter and purifier contamination If the filter takes a serious fall, it could crack internally. If the filter inside cracks, unfiltered water can flow through the crack. Some water filters come as sealed cartridges, making it impossible to inspect the actual filter cartridge for cracks. Treat your filter with care, and if it takes a significant impact, replace it.

The intake hose from a water filter/purifier has been submerged in unfiltered water. Treat this hose as "contaminated" and keep it in a separate plastic bag.

Any filter or purifier serves a collection point for nasty microorganisms, so when cleaning or changing your filter/purifier, be careful — especially if you are with individuals with impaired immune systems. Handle your filter or purifier cartridge with gloves, dispose of the used cartridge and gloves carefully, and wash your hands scrupulously afterward. This is one advantage of sealed filters.

COLLECTING AND STORING WATER IN COLD WEATHER

Water Purification in Cold Weather

Water purification methods are more limited in the wintertime owing to the temperature sensitivity of some of the methods. Clean snow is generally assumed to be free of harmful microorganisms, so you don't need to purify or treat it for things like *Giardia*. If you are taking water from a lake or stream, you should purify it in some way.

- **Boiling** This will always work in winter. The downside is that you need to bring enough fuel (more weight) to boil the water. If you have access to running water (lake or stream), you will still use less fuel to boil this for purification than you would to melt snow for water.
- **Filtration** Using a filtration pump system can be difficult in subfreezing temperatures. Water can freeze in the filter, preventing it from working. Also, as the water freezes it expands and may crack the filter, rendering it inoperable or, even worse, transmitting harmful microorganisms into your system. For these reasons, filters should be used with caution in the winter. You need to be able to keep the filter from freezing.

- **Chemical treatments** (iodination or chlorination) These methods are *not* recommended in winter because they are ineffective at low temperatures. Use these methods *only* if the water has been preheated to about 60°F (16°C).

Getting water in the wintertime can either be really easy or really hard. If local water sources like lakes and streams are not frozen, you have ample supplies. If there is snow on the ground, you've got a ready source of water—simply melt the snow with your stove. If lakes and streams are frozen, you may be chopping holes in the ice to find something to drink. There are a few important considerations for dealing with winter water.

- **Do not eat snow!** It takes an incredible amount of energy to transfer water from one state to another (solid to liquid). You are burning up too many calories to do this, which can lead to hypothermia. By volume it takes about 10 quarts/liters of snow to make 1 quart/liter of water, so you would have to eat/melt 10 quarts of snow to get 1 quart/liter of water, all the while using up a lot of body heat.
- **Getting water** Filling pots and water bottles from a stream or lake can become a major expedition in itself. Make sure that the area you plan to get water from is secure. Avoid steep banks that might lead to a plunge and make sure any ice is sufficiently stable to hold your weight. Also, make sure you don't get your gloves soaked with icy water. A loop of string tied tightly around your water bottle neck or held on with duct tape will allow you to lower a bottle in by hand or with a ski pole, ice axe, or branch. Don't trust pot grips on a large pot; with mittens you can lose your grip and your pot. Fill the pot up part way and then use a water bottle to top it off. If you've cut through the ice, mark the area so you can find it next time and perhaps have to do less chopping.
- **Melting snow** Snow can be melted on a fire or stove to make water. Start with some water in the bottom of your pot and add snow to the water slowly to create a slush mixture, and keep adding more snow as it melts. You'll need about 10 quarts of snow to make 1 quart of water (10 liters to 1 liter), so you'll need to have an adequate snow supply close to your stove. Clean snow does not need to be purified. Avoid using snow that has any sort of color. We all know what "yellow snow" is. Snow can also be turned different colors, like pink ("watermelon snow") by different species of algae that live in snow; some forms of algae can be toxic.
- **Winter solar water collector** You can easily create a solar water collector that will melt snow. In a spot that will remain sunny for several hours, dig out a pit in the snow about 2 feet across and 1 foot deep (0.6 meters

by 0.4 meters). If possible, line this depression with a foam pad or other insulation (not essential but it speeds the process). Spread a dark plastic bag (trashbag) over the depression, forming a shallow dish pan. Pack clean snow all around the raised margins of the pit. The black plastic absorbs the sun's energy, melting the snow, and water collects in the depression.

PREVENTING YOUR WATER FROM FREEZING

You should have a water bottle with a wide mouth; otherwise, the opening will easily freeze. During the day, carry at least one bottle next to your body. Your body heat will keep it from freezing and the bottle is handy to rehydrate yourself throughout the day. Insulated water bottle holders are available for this. Other water bottles can be kept upside down in an insulated container (sock, etc.). Being upside down will keep the mouth of the bottle from freezing.

A cold water bottle may have ice crystals in the threads when you close it. As the bottle heats up from body temperature, the ice may melt, causing the cap to loosen; also, the lid may expand with heat, causing leakage. Keep the lid tightly closed or water will leak all over the place.

At night keep your water bottles in your sleeping bag to prevent them from freezing. If you use a water bladder/tube system there is a good chance that water, particularly in the tube, will freeze. Keep the bladder itself insulated in your pack. Some manufacturers also make neoprene insulating covers for the tubes. I've found that the bite valve still freezes up, but a couple of bites usually breaks up the ice crystals and I can start drinking.

To store water overnight, fill a pot with water, place a lid on top, and bury the pot under about a foot (0.3 meters) of snow. Snow is a great insulator (lots of dead air space) and will keep the water from completely freezing, even in subzero temperatures.

CHAPTER 5

Leave No Trace Hiking and Camping

We all have different goals for traveling in the wilderness, but one thing that I think we all share is a desire to see it remain wild. Like any precious object, wilderness is fragile. Leave No Trace camping is an attitude that should pervade every aspect of your trip, from your first look at the guidebook to assembling food and equipment, from where you hike to how you set up your campsite and clean up before you leave. By learning about the ecosystem you are traveling in you can practice the best techniques for preserving it in the wild state that we all go to enjoy. Only through such practices can we protect these wonderful places for ourselves and future wilderness travelers.

Leave No Trace Center for Outdoor Ethics logo

The Leave No Trace Program is a national awareness campaign developed by the National Outdoor Leadership School, the U.S. Forest Service, U.S. Fish and Wildlife Service, the Bureau of Land Management, and other agencies. It is designed to provide backcountry travelers with the most up-to-date information about how to travel in different wilderness ecosystems without disturbing the natural world. The Leave No Trace Program is managed by the nonprofit Leave No Trace Center for Outdoor Ethics *(www.leavenotrace.org)*. Look for the Leave No Trace logo on outdoor equipment and reading material. For more information, see their Web site. I want to thank Leave No Trace Center for Outdoor Ethics for granting permission to use their Leave No Trace principles in this chapter.

GENERAL PRINCIPLES

There are seven general principles for Leave No Trace that apply to trips in any ecosystem. The specific techniques that you use to implement these principles vary from one ecosystem to the next, so it is critical to understand the details of how to apply the principles to where you are actually traveling. These are the principles that apply to all wilderness travel:

- Plan ahead and prepare.
- Travel and camp on durable surfaces.
- Dispose of waste properly.
- Minimize campfire impacts.

- Leave what you find.
- Respect wildlife.
- Be considerate of other visitors.

It's not possible in this book to cover *all* the techniques for *all* the different ecosystems you may be traveling to. Most three-season backpackers in the United States and Canada will be traveling in temperate forest, so I'll cover those guidelines in detail. Many of these techniques are used for other ecosystems as well.

Some settings like coastal areas, high-altitude locations, and desert and winter conditions require different techniques for some practices such as disposing of human waste. The best sources for detailed practices in different ecosystems are the Skills and Ethics booklets published by Leave No Trace, *Soft Paths* by Bruce Hampton and David Cole, and *Leave a Trace* by Annette McGivney. I strongly encourage you to read information specific to the ecosystem in which you are traveling.

PLAN AHEAD AND PREPARE

When you are planning your trip, think about a number of factors that can have an impact on the environment.

- **Camping Regulations** Know the specific camping regulations for the area. Some areas may not permit fires, may require you to camp only in certain locations, or may require you to pack out human waste.
- **Group Size** The size of your group can have a significant impact on the area. Large groups may have less impact if they travel and camp in smaller groups.
- **Schedule your Trip to Avoid High-Use Times** Our wilderness areas get more crowded every year. You can avoid the crowds and help keep crowding down by going on off-peak times. Talk to area land managers about places to go and places to avoid.
- **Ecosystem and Season** Learn all you can about the ecosystem to determine how best to deal with waste products (human waste and water waste). For example, the best way to dispose of human waste in the desert is very different from the best way in alpine and glacier areas.
- **Bring Proper Equipment** Make sure you carry the proper gear for safe and efficient Leave No Trace travel and to keep yourself and your group safe. (See "The Essentials," page 21.) Bringing a stove means not having

to use up local firewood. Wearing gaiters means you aren't concerned about walking through the center of the muddy trail. (See Chapter 2, "Equipment.")

- **Plan Your Meals in Advance**   This will both reduce trash before the trip and avoid having leftovers during the trip. (See Chapter 3, "Cooking and Nutrition.")

- **Take Responsibility**   Managing your safety is another way to reduce your impact on the land and other travelers. Getting lost can mean a major search-and-rescue effort to find you as well as place searchers at risk. Practice good safety management techniques. (See Chapter 8, "Safety and Emergency Procedures.") Register your group at trailheads and leave your route plan with someone at home (see Appendix, page 412). Have the skills to match your route.

TRAVEL ON DURABLE SURFACES

TRAVEL ON EXISTING TRAILS

When in the backcountry, hike on existing trails whenever possible. Existing trails have been designed to absorb a high impact. Walk single file rather than abreast so as not to widen trails. (Walking side by side creates multiple lanes that make a trail look like an interstate highway.) On wet or muddy stretches, slop right on through rather than skirt them, to avoid creating additional side trails and unnecessary erosion (good boots and gaiters will help). Never short-cut switchbacks. Switchbacks are specifically built to minimize erosion and ease ascent or descent on steep sections. Cutting off the corners creates downhill drainage patterns that can quickly erode a trail. If a trail is impassable, walk on as many hard surfaces as possible (rocks or sand) and notify area rangers of the difficulty.

When taking a rest break, move off the trail to a durable stopping place, such as a rock outcrop, sandy area, other nonvegetated place, or a location with durable vegetation, such as dry grassland.

TRAVELLING OFF-TRAIL

If you have to travel off-trail, then by definition you are impacting the land. Know the ecosystem to understand how best to do this with as little impact as possible. The two major factors that increase how off-trail travel impacts the land are the durability of the surface and the frequency of use (how many feet are tramping on it).

Surface Durability

The concept of durability is an important one for all backcountry travelers to understand. Natural surfaces respond differently to backcountry travel. Picking the most durable path (even though it may not be the shortest path) preserves the land.

- **Rock, sand, and gravel** These surfaces are highly durable and can tolerate repeated trampling and scuffing. (However, lichens that grow on rocks are vulnerable to repeated scuffing.)
- **Ice and snow** The effect of travel across these surfaces is temporary, making them good choices for travel, assuming good safety precautions are followed and the snow layer is of sufficient depth to prevent damaging vegetation underneath the snow.
- **Vegetation** The resistance of vegetation to trampling varies. Careful decisions must be made when traveling across vegetated areas where there is no trail. Select areas of durable vegetation, or sparse vegetation that is easily avoided. Dry grasses tend to be resistant to trampling. Wet meadows and other fragile vegetation quickly show the effects of many hikers. Trampling down a path encourages people after you to take the same route and can create a new trail. As a general rule, travelers who must venture off-trail should spread out to avoid creating paths that encourage others to follow. Avoid vegetation whenever possible, especially on steep slopes where the effects of off-trail travel are magnified.

In extremely fragile areas like alpine tundra or deserts with cryptobiotic soil (see the Bibliography, page 427), it is so difficult not to have an impact that it may be best to walk single file so that only one path is created. Avoid traveling in wet or boggy areas, on steep or unstable slopes, or where wildlife disturbance is likely. This may mean traveling "out of your way" in order to protect the environment.

If you choose a route without trails, do not blaze trees, build cairns, or leave messages in the dirt (except in an emergency situation). This can be extremely confusing and even dangerous for other backcountry travelers, who may become lost following your signs. Also, it can make their wilderness experience less enjoyable.

CAMP ON DURABLE SURFACES

Selecting a campsite is probably the most difficult and critical aspect of Leave No Trace backcountry use. It's the place each day where you are going to spend the most time and therefore have the greatest impact. Choosing a campsite requires evaluating the potential site and making a judgment about whether you can use the site without damaging it further or should look for another site.

GENERAL CAMPSITE GUIDELINES

- Lug-soled hiking boots can do considerable damage to soil and vegetation. Remove hiking boots and change to soft-soled shoes such as running shoes or sandals as soon as you get to camp to reduce damage to fragile vegetation and soil.
- A backcountry campsite should be reasonably organized. If you have laundry to dry or equipment to air out, make sure these items are not in sight of other campers or hikers.
- Avoid spending more than a few days at any one campsite unless it is an established campsite.
- Leave the area as you found it or better. Do *not* trench around tents, cut live branches, or pull up plants to make a pleasant campsite. If you do clear the sleeping area of sticks, pinecones, and the like, be sure to scatter these items back over the area before you leave.

CAMPING IN HIGH-USE AREAS

High-impact areas are frequently used campsites where most of the ground vegetation has been lost to trampling. Often these sites are equipped with fire rings and other signs of human activity. In some cases, a legal or required campsite may violate some of the general guidelines for a Leave No Trace camp; it may be right next to the trail or near water. This is especially true on corridor trails like the Appalachian Trail. Research shows that it can take years for an impacted site to even begin to recover. So land managers may decide to let one site stay permanently impacted rather than have twenty moderately impacted sites in the area trying to recover.

Whenever possible, choose an already impacted site rather than creating a new site. If a site has already been highly impacted, and if you are careful, it will show little or no additional impact from your being there. Continuing to use a high-impact campsite is the lesser of two evils—maintaining one high-impact site instead of creating a new site with new damage. Leave the high-impact site in good shape so that others will choose to camp there. If it was trashed when you got there, make it look great when you leave. I've hauled plenty of garbage out from campsites I didn't even stay in.

Having a proper route plan allows enough time and energy at the end of the day to select and set up an appropriate campsite. Getting in after dark and camping at "the first place you find" can really damage an area. (See Chapter 1, "Trip Planning.")

Low or moderate-impact sites showing obvious signs of use may *eventually* recover if closed to human use. If you come to a campsite that is "just starting," don't camp there. Each time you camp on a site that is trying to recover, you interrupt or even reverse the recovery. It's best to look for a high-impact site. If you can't find one, it may be better to camp on a totally undisturbed site and carefully repair and camouflage the area to prevent other people from camping, allowing the site to recover.

CAMPING IN PRISTINE, UNDISTURBED AREAS

A pristine campsite is one that shows no signs of previous camping. People often go looking for the place "no one has been before," not realizing how much damage they can do to the environment. *Only camp in such places if you are committed to and highly skilled in Leave No Trace techniques.*

- When selecting a pristine campsite, your goal is to find the most durable site that will carry the least signs of your use. Select a site that has no vegetation (such as rock outcroppings, gravel bars, beaches, or snow) or durable vegetation cover (grassy areas, leaf-covered forest duff—with minimal plant seedlings). Avoid fragile areas.
- In pristine areas, move your campsite every night (even if only a short distance) before the impact becomes noticeable. Never spend more than a few days at a pristine backcountry campsite.
- Spread out tents and avoid walking the same route to water, cooking areas, bear bag locations, etc., to prevent the establishment of trails.
- Bring large collapsible water containers so you don't have to go back and forth as often to get water.
- When you leave, take time to naturalize the setting. Cover up scuffed areas with duff or other natural materials and brush out footprints to camouflage human activity. Disguising it well will keep someone else from camping there. This will give the area a better chance to recover.

SETTING UP CAMP

If half the fun is getting there, the other half is being there. Here are some important considerations for setting up a campsite in the wilderness:

- Before setting off to hike, be informed of local regulations pertaining to camping and hiking—for example, no camping above 3,500 feet (1,066 meters).
- Try to plan your day so you arrive at a potential site with sufficient daylight to set up a good Leave No Trace camp. Arriving tired and in the dark makes this much more difficult. Know your route well enough to start looking for potential sites early.
- Find the most resilient site to set up a camp.
- Whenever possible, choose a campsite *at least* 200 feet (61 meters)—about 70 steps—from water sources, trails, and scenic spots. The choicest camping spots are often prime areas for animal forage or for other hikers to stop and enjoy the view. Take the extra time to find a more camouflaged area. Be aware of animal trails that may be prime highways for local wildlife. This can be especially hazardous in bear country.
- Try to avoid areas with rock faces, potential water runoffs, animal trails, and sensitive vegetation.

Your first priority in setting up a campsite is to establish activity areas. Some areas will get more traffic than others, so it is important to try to set up high-traffic areas in more resilient locations. For example, the cooking area is apt to get a lot of traffic, while the food-hanging area will get very little. Consider what "highways" will be established between high-traffic areas and try to minimize impact. Taking different paths each time from one activity area to another reduces "highway" impact. The following are typical activity areas:

- **Water source area**   Large collapsible water jugs will reduce the number of trips (and trampling) you do traveling back and forth to your water source. You should locate all the major areas of your camp at least 200 feet (61 meters) from your water source.
- **Sleeping area**   Look overhead to be sure that are no dead trees or branches above ("widowmakers"). The sleeping area should be upwind of the other areas, especially in bear country.
- **Cooking/Eating area**   Since this area gets most of the traffic, select the most durable location for the kitchen. In some cases you may want to set up an eating area that is separate from the cooking area. This can help keep large numbers of people from milling around hot stoves and boiling water, which can help reduce accident potential. (See Chapter 8, "Safety and Emergency Procedures.")
- **Food-hanging area**   Preferably downwind of the sleeping area. It may be adjacent to the cooking area, since food odors will already be prevalent, or in another location.

- **Waste disposal area** This is for disposal of cooking and other waste water and should be downwind of the sleeping area, at least 200 feet (61 meters) from any water source. It can be close to the food-hanging area, since food odors may be present.
- **Washing area** This is an area for personal washing and should be an appropriate distance from the other areas.
- **Bathroom area** If you are going to use a latrine for a group or set up a toilet to pack out feces, choose a designated site downwind of the sleeping area and at least 200 feet (61 meters) away from trails or water sources. If people will be using individual catholes or a latrine, establish a general direction out of camp, preferably downwind. Individual sites should also be away from trails and at least 200 feet (61 meters) away from water sources.

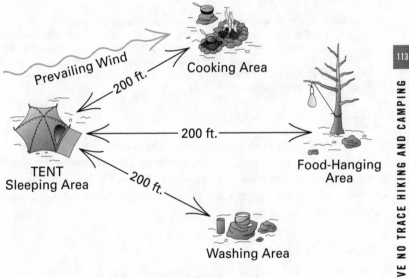

Prevailing Wind

200 ft.

Cooking Area

200 ft.

TENT
Sleeping Area

200 ft.

Food-Hanging
Area

Washing Area

Campsite Setup

If possible, set up the sleeping area, kitchen area, and food-hanging area in a triangular pattern, with about 200 feet (61 meters) on each side.

DISPOSE OF WASTE PROPERLY

DEALING WITH HUMAN WASTE

Disposing of human waste in the wilderness must be done with good judgment and common sense. Newcomers to the wilderness are often embarrassed and unsure of how to cope without a bathroom. It's a subject that most of us don't spend a lot of time talking about. However, failure to learn the proper techniques not only can damage the environment but can also lead to gastrointestinal illnesses from improper hygiene. (See "Gastrointestinal Infections," page 370; "Keeping Clean on the Trail," page 88). One of the sources for the spread of *Giardia* in backcountry water is the improper disposal of human feces.

Know your ecosystem and any camping regulations for the area. The techniques described here are the general recommendations for subalpine temperate forests in three-season conditions (spring, summer, and fall). In other ecosystems, such as glaciers, deserts, or seacoasts, the procedures may be very different.

🍁 TRICKS OF THE TRAIL

Toilet kit On group trips it's a good idea to carry a group toilet kit—a trowel for digging a cathole, toilet paper (if you are using it), and waterless hand cleaner like Purell handwashing gel all packed together and "ready to go," as it were. I also include a whistle with the trowel kit because heading off to the bathroom is one of the most common times for someone to get disoriented and lost.

URINE

Urine is "relatively" free of microorganisms (unless the individual has a kidney or urinary tract infection). As a result, urine can be considered "clean," but not sterile. The major issues with urine are the smell it leaves and the concentration of salts left behind when the water evaporates, which can attract animals.

Location

Urinate *at least 200 feet* (61 meters)—about 70 steps for an adult—away from the trail and any water sources. Urinate on rocks or in areas with thick humus layers and drainage (decaying leave piles, dirt piles). Try to avoid fragile vegetation because the acidity of urine can affect plant growth. Avoid urinating directly on plants to prevent animals from defoliating or digging up the plants for the salt. Diluting your urine with water afterward can minimize animal attraction.

Techniques

Urinating outdoors is simpler for men than for women. In her book *How to Shit in the Woods*, Kathleen Meyer devotes a whole chapter to the subject.

One technique for women is to sit on the edge of a rock or log with your feet propped up on another rock or log in front. This prevents the dreaded problem of peeing in your boots. Another technique is to use a plastic funnel to direct the urine stream. Funnels such as the Sani-Fem are made specifically for women. These can also be used with a pee bottle in a tent (handy in bad storms or cold weather).

FECES

Human feces can create a *significant* impact on the environment. Feces can contaminate water sources, spread disease, and affect other wilderness travelers, both visually and by smell. Your goal should be to prevent contamination of the environment by limiting contact between your feces and insects, animals, people, and water sources. The other goal is to maximize the ability for the feces to decompose naturally.

Fecal decomposition is affected by a number of factors—sunlight (heat), moisture, oxygen, soil pH, and soil bacteria—so different ecosystems require different methods of disposal. In most situations, the best method is to bury feces in organic soil layers or to pack it out. Burying actually slows down the decomposition, but it alleviates the problem of visual impact and reduces the chances for contaminating water sources. You'd be surprised how long feces last. Feces deposited on the surface (not buried) can carry live bacteria for 18 weeks. Research has also shown that buried feces can still contain live bacteria a year after burial. Feces left in glacial environments with little bacteria can remain there, unchanged, for years. This is one reason it is important to deposit feces well away from trails and campsites. (For more information on human waste disposal in other ecosystems, see the Bibliography.)

Remember that bacteria are likely to be on your hands after a bowel movement even when you've used toilet paper. Wash your hands after going to the bathroom to protect yourself and other members of your group from gastrointestinal infections. (See Chapter 4, "Hygiene and Water Purification.")

Locations

Find a site far enough from the trail, away from water sources, perhaps with a good view, and with abundant natural toilet paper materials. In some cases, it can involve some pretty complicated acrobatics to keep your balance and do your business.

- **Outhouses** When available, *always* use existing outhouses. Although they concentrate the smell, they minimize impact.

- **Catholes** Small pit toilets dug for individual use; these are often the best solution. The cathole means smaller, less concentrated waste disposal, usually ensuring more rapid decomposition.
- **Latrines** Larger pit toilets dug for group use; these are best if you're camping with a large group, or if you are remaining in the same camp over a number of days. You need to consider this choice carefully since this higher concentration of feces will decompose *very* slowly.

How to Dig a Cathole or Latrine

Catholes should be *at least 200 feet* (61 meters)—about 70 steps for an adult—away from streams, rivers, lakes, and marshy areas. Bacteria in feces do travel through the soil, so you want to be far enough away from a water source to allow human waste to decay without polluting the water. You should be a significant distance from trails and campsites.

Avoid digging a cathole in an obvious drainage area where water flow and erosion may unearth your deposit. In places prone to flooding (like desert canyons) or in coastal areas with tides, look for high-water marks and try to dig your cathole above that point; otherwise, a flash flood or high tide could quickly unearth your feces.

- Whenever possible, latrines or catholes should be dug in organic soil layers. Soil bacteria constitute major decomposing agents, so mix topsoil with feces before burial. In more sterile soils (sand or predominantly inorganic soil layers), subsurface moisture is often the critical factor, so feces should have a more shallow burial.
- Select an inconspicuous site away from trails and people. The more secluded, the less likely that someone else will come upon your cathole.
- Pick a site that maximizes sunlight exposure of your cathole. The heat from the sun aids the decomposition process.
- Gather any natural toilet paper and a stirring stick before digging.
- Dig a hole 6 to 8 inches deep (15 to 20 centimeters) and 4 to 6 inches in diameter (10 to 15 centimeters). If there is grassy or matted soil, cut that "topsoil patch" and set it aside. Then dig the rest of the way down piling the soil to one side. Squat over the hole (it may be best to urinate in the hole first), then have your bowel movement in the hole. Pour some of the dirt back in and "stir up" the mixture of dirt and poop to help spread the soil microbes through the poop—this will speed the decay process. Bury the feces and replace your "topsoil patch" if you have one. Cover the site with natural materials to disguise it. If you are using natural materials for toilet paper, just bury them in the hole. If you use real toilet paper, consider packing it out.

The idea behind a latrine is to concentrate the impact when you have a larger group or are using the same campsite for an extended period of time. Latrines use basically the same procedure as a cathole, except you need to dig a deeper hole. Dig a pit at least a foot deep (30 centimeters) and at least 18 inches wide (45 centimeters). Leave the pile of dirt next to the hole. After going to the bathroom, each person should cover and stir the feces with a layer of dirt. Close up the latrine before it gets too full and scatter the extra dirt. Replace your "topsoil patch" and cover the site with natural materials to disguise it.

Special Environments

Deserts   In arid environments, look for sites with maximum sun exposure for your cathole. The sun's heat will penetrate several inches through the soil, so dig your hole only 4 to 6 inches deep (10 to 15 centimeters) and the heat will eventually kill the pathogens in the feces. South-facing slopes and ridges will have greater sun exposure than other areas. In narrow canyons where there aren't a lot of "places to go," it is best to pack out feces. This is a requirement in some areas. If you use toilet paper, pack it out. Burning toilet paper in an arid environment can result in wild fires.

River Corridors   Narrow river canyons present unique Leave No Trace challenges. There may be such a narrow strip of organic soil between the river's edge and the canyon wall that depositing feces in organic soil would quickly overwhelm the area, especially at frequently used campsites. In this case, pack out your feces. Urinate away from the river's edge and people. On certain western rivers like the Colorado in the Grand Canyon, land managers require that people urinate in the river. Check with area land managers to find out the proper Leave No Trace techniques.

Coasts   If you are along the ocean, the best thing to do is urinate below the high-tide line. The urine will dissipate quickly in the huge water source. Avoid tidal pools where the urine would be concentrated until the tide comes up. It is illegal to dump feces into U.S. coastal waters, so pack out your feces or dig a cathole well above the high-tide line in organic soil to aid decomposition. Small coastal islands like the Maine Island Trail, just like narrow canyons, simply can't support the impact of buried feces. In this case, pack it out.

Winter   In the winter, urinate in the snow away from people. Cover up the yellow stain with snow before you leave. Feces can be very difficult to deal with in the winter. The best thing to do is use an outhouse if one is available.

This might be something you look for while you are planning your trip. If the ground is frozen and you can't dig a cathole, pack it out. Leaving feces on the surface causes contamination of water sources in the spring thaw as well as being extremely unsightly for other visitors.

Packing out Feces

In some locations (such as sea kayaking on coastal islands) you may need to (or be required to) pack out feces. Make sure you are familiar with the specific regulations before you go on your trip. (See Chapter 1, "Trip Planning.") If you are backpacking, this means preparing a "poop station" each time you go to the bathroom. Here are a couple of standard procedures:

Group Use A group approach is to go to the bathroom into a container that can be tightly sealed, like a surplus ammo box. Line the box with two plastic bags. After each person has a bowel movement, toss in some kitty litter or chlorine bleach to help absorb odors. (It's best if you don't urinate into the container.) Close the lid after each use. When the bag gets full, use latex gloves to tie up both bags. Place them in another clean bag, seal it, and pack it out.

Individual Collection The individual "pooper-scooper" approach is when each person collects his or her own. Turning a bag inside out and using it as a "glove" will allow you to pick up feces as long as it has a solid consistency. You can help this process by going to the bathroom into a cathole, adding dirt or sand to help solidify the mass, and then picking it up with your bag.

The Wag Bag This is a commercial "pack it out" product produced by Phillips Environmental Products *(www.thepett.com)*. It's the best product I've seen for effectively packing out feces and urine and is recommended by the American Alpine Club. The Wag Bag is a self-contained unit that includes a heavy-duty plastic bag to pee and poop in. The bag contains Pooh-Powder, a specially engineered mix of a nontoxic polymer-based absorbent (similar to what is in baby diapers), along with an organic decay catalyst as an odor neutralizer. Pooh-Powder is activated by water (or urine). The powder then becomes a gel and encapsulates the solid waste, eliminates odor, and starts the decay process.

The process is simple. Select a good location for a poop. You may want to dig a small hole to place the Wag Bag in. Pee in the bag. (If you don't need to pee, pour in about 6 ounces/177 milliliters of water to activate the Pooh-Powder.) Poop into the bag, use toilet paper (or not), and then seal up the bag.

The kit comes with a heavy-duty Ziploc-type bag to store the Wag Bag in. The Pooh-Powder will gel up to 60 fluid ounces of (1.7 liters) feces (that's a lot). A "typical" poop is 12 fluid ounces (354 milliliters), so you can reuse the bag four or five times before you have maxed it out. Don't overfill the bag.

Plastic bags, even heavy ones, have a habit of getting torn, so I pack the whole thing into a waterproof dry bag (coated nylon or vinyl) like sea kayakers use to carry gear. These have a roll-top closure and can easily be clipped to the outside of your pack (if you're nervous) or stuffed inside your pack. If you carry it in your pack, keep enough air in the dry bag when you seal it to keep it from being compressed inside your pack and thereby keep from compressing the contents inside the Wag Bag. If something bad ever did happen, it's all still inside a sealed waterproof dry bag. The waterproof bag will also give you additional protection from odor, which may start to seep out of the Wag Bag after three or four days. For you ultralighters out there, this system does add a little extra weight. But when I am packing out my poop I like the peace of mind that comes from putting it all in a dry bag. On trips where weight is not an issue, like a paddling trip, you can use a hard-shell case like an Army surplus ammo can. Pack out the entire bag and dispose of it properly after your trip. Wag Bags are made of a special plastic that is designed to decompose eventually and is EPA approved to be disposed of in sanitary landfills in all fifty states (see below for a more detailed explanation). Even though the bags decompose eventually, they should not be dumped into anything that says no plastic—pit toilets, composting toilets, outhouses, or porta-johns.

Proper Disposal of Packed-Out Feces

If you pack it out, after your trip, you need to properly dispose of feces. It's best to dispose of feces in an outhouse, a portable toilet, or a sanitary waste disposal unit like an RV collection site (found at many campgrounds) or in an approved sanitary landfill. *Never* put plastic bags in toilets, outhouses, or sanitary waste receptacles. They don't degrade and often jam pipes or suction devices. If you prefer to use a plastic bag to store your poop, dump the poop, then clean and disinfect the bag afterward with chlorine bleach before disposing of it.

TOILET PAPER

There is nothing wrong with using toilet paper in the outdoors. It's what you do with it afterward that has the impact. If you use toilet paper, use biodegradable or recycled paper, avoid paper with dyes and perfumes, and never leave toilet paper out on the ground. Here are some disposal techniques:

- **Pack it out** Use the common "pooper-scooper" approach. Take a plastic bag, invert it over your hand, and pick up the toilet paper. Fold the bag back around the toilet paper and seal it. I take a small blue plastic bag (so you don't see what's inside) for each day of the trip for toilet paper. You can also tape over a clear plastic bag with duct tape to hide the contents. Then all the bags go in one larger Ziploc bag that can be tightly sealed. Keep it in your pack away from food. Sprinkle some chlorine bleach in the Ziploc bag to help kill bacteria and odor. When you get back to "civilization," dispose of it properly as described above.
- **Burying** If you bury your toilet paper, it will decompose more quickly if it is wet. Take along your water bottle and wet the paper down or urinate on it before you bury it.
- **Tampons and pads** These should always be packed out and disposed of. (See "Women's Hygiene Issues," page 93.)

🍁 TRICKS OF THE TRAIL

Don't burn toilet paper! A number of years ago I was on a canoeing trip with friends on the Green River in Utah. As we approached the take-out at Spanish Bottom, the confluence of the Green and Colorado Rivers, we began to smell smoke. Soon clouds of thick gray smoke were pouring up the canyon. We knew a significant wildfire was burning downstream and were concerned about the fire flashing up-canyon toward us, so we paddled back upstream and camped. The next day we paddled down to find both sides of the canyon completely blackened by fire. A teenager from a camp had been burning his toilet paper when some hot ashes blew over into the dry grass and set it on fire. The fire spread quickly with the breeze, and sparks jumped across the river, burning the other side of the canyon as well. The charred remains of cottonwood trees that had provided shade for over 100 years, and dead deer and other animals trapped by the fire, were solemn reminders of the danger of burning toilet paper.

Natural Materials

Some people prefer natural materials to toilet paper because they can be used without damaging the environment. Natural materials should be disposed of with the feces (which in most cases means burying). If you are going to pack the feces out anyway, you might as well use toilet paper and pack it out as well. If you are going to use plants or other natural substances instead of toilet paper, here are some suggestions:

- Inanimate objects—Use smooth sticks, rounded rocks, fir cones, or snow.
- Use dead plants, large leaves, mosses, seaweed.

- Know your plants and avoid using toxic plants like poison ivy, poison oak, stinging nettles, or other plants with toxins or barbs.
- Avoid plants with sharp edges, like reeds and bamboo, which can cause lacerations.
- Avoid using live plants. If you must, gather plants from several locations before you start to go to the bathroom. That way you won't deplete a particular plant of too many leaves. Remove leaves only; don't uproot the entire plant. Don't pick rare species or wildflowers.

OTHER TYPES OF WASTE

MEDICAL WASTE

Any medical equipment that has been contaminated with blood or body fluids is considered medical waste and must be disposed of properly. These items should be placed in a plastic bag marked "medical waste." Sprinkle some chlorine bleach into the bag to kill any microorganisms.

Technically, this waste should *not* be disposed of with regular trash. If possible, place it in an appropriate medical-waste container when you return from your trip. Be especially aware of any sharp objects (needles, scalpels) that might be in your medical waste, since getting a needle stick can transmit infection. These should be placed in some rigid container or wrapped in cardboard and then taped to prevent injury to anyone handling the waste. (See also "Women's Hygiene Issues," page 93.)

GARBAGE

Garbage is organic food waste from cooking, including such things as fruit and vegetable peelings, leftover food, and fish viscera. Here are some guidelines for dealing with garbage:

- Minimize garbage by repacking food before your trip.
- Avoid leftover food by carefully planning your meals.
- When leftovers do occur, they should be carried out in plastic bags.
- *Don't* try to burn food unless you have a very hot fire and can completely incinerate the food. Partial burning leaves a charred food mess in the fire site that will decay and smell as well as attract animals.
- Food particles that inevitably occur in cooking should be treated like bulk leftovers and carried out. Strain the dishwater through a strainer or bandanna to separate these particles and put them in your garbage.

- Fish viscera are a natural part of the ecosystem. In high-use areas, your goal is to minimize other people's seeing or smelling them, so consider burying them in a cathole. In remote areas with few visitors, you can scatter them widely, away from camp and trails, to reduce the chance that other people will come across them. In bear country, it is important to keep fish odors safely downwind and away from people, trails, and campsites. You can scatter or bury the entrails, but do so far away from human travel areas.
- Garbage should be hung along with food, otherwise whatever critters are around will be after it.

TRASH

Trash is all the non-organic waste from the trip: paper, candy-bar wrappers, food containers etc. All of this should be packed out either for recycling or trash disposal.

WASTEWATER

There will always be some leftover water, either from cooking or personal bathing. There are two basic options: scattering or sumping. In either case, strain out any food particles for garbage. The best way to do this is to bring a small food strainer with you to collect the larger particles or use a bandanna. After straining, toss the water in a spray pattern to scatter it over a wide area. To sump the remaining wastewater, dig a small sump hole at least 200 feet (61 meters) from any water source and pour the wastewater into the hole. Replace the dirt and disguise the area by covering it with natural materials. (For resources on wastewater disposal in other ecosystems, see the Bibliography.)

AT THE END OF THE TRIP

All cans and plastic bottles that were used should be cleaned out and recycled after the trip. Cardboard containers from the original packaging should also be recycled. Depending on their condition, plastic bags or Ziploc bags can be washed out and reused. Medical waste should be disposed of properly. Garbage and trash should be thrown away. Dispose of "personal" waste like tampons and toilet paper.

MINIMIZE CAMPFIRE IMPACTS

Fires can be a wonderful part of a trip, but you really need to decide if the land can handle your having a fire. Improperly built fires definitely damage the land. A poorly built fire sterilizes the soil underneath it, and it will be years before something can grow there again—you've effectively created a little dead zone. High-use campsites are already stripped of downed, dead wood, so building a fire means foraging farther away to bring back wood. Bring a stove instead. I always plan trips with a stove, and if I find the right conditions to build a fire, I'll *think* about doing it.

Know about fire regulations in the area before you leave on your trip. In certain areas, or at certain times (like high forest-fire danger), fires may be illegal. Here are some guidelines for when it's appropriate to have a fire:

When Not to Have a Fire

- When fire danger is moderate to high. If fire danger is high, you may even have to avoid using your stove.
- When there are restrictions against fires in certain locations or above certain altitudes.
- On windy days when sparks might be dangerous, especially when the woods are dry.
- When dead wood is scarce.
- When it's solely for group bonding. Although a fire can be a very enjoyable and useful part of group bonding, even building a fire with the best Leave No Trace techniques can result in impact on the land. Often sitting around a candle can achieve the same effect.

When to Have a Fire

- When there are no land manager restrictions against fires, *and* . . .
- When fire danger is low, *and* . . .
- When you have sufficient dead wood available that its removal won't be noticeable, *and* . . .
- When the environmental conditions are not so limiting that the regeneration of wood supplies cannot keep pace with the demand (as in harsh alpine and desert environment where growing conditions are limited), *and* . . .
- When there already is an established fire ring or you have the skill to build a proper Leave No Trace fire, *or* . . .
- When your stove is not working and hot food is important for the safety of the group, *or* . . .
- When there are first-aid considerations and you need a strong heat source for the safety of an individual or for the group.

GENERAL GUIDELINES FOR FIRE BUILDING

Choose a resilient site for your fire or stove. Avoid lush meadows, fragile alpine tundra, and other areas that can be easily trampled. Try to disperse use throughout the campsite rather than concentrating activities in the cooking area. Good site selection and proper care of the cooking area and fire make effective camouflaging much easier.

Fires should be built away from tents, tarps, trees, branches, and underground root systems. They shouldn't be built in forest litter or duff. The organic layer of the soil is highly flammable and can actually smolder underground for weeks before erupting into a forest fire. (See "Forest Fires," page 246.)

Fires should *not* be ringed with rocks (unless there already is an established fire ring). To avoid permanently blackening rocks, don't build fires against rock walls. Never use river rocks for a fire ring. These rocks often contain minute amounts of water that, when heated, turn to steam and expand, causing the rocks to explode in the fire.

FIRES IN HIGHLY IMPACTED AREAS
Fire Rings

Often you may come upon one or more fire rings at a campsite. If you have decided to build a fire, use an existing ring. Pay careful attention to its location and avoid rings too close to water sources or other fragile areas. Make sure you burn your wood completely, scatter the coals and ashes, and clean all food waste and trash from the fire so that it will be attractive for the next visitors to use. If there is more than one ring at a highly impacted campsite, all but one should be dismantled.

If a fire ring is present in an area that otherwise appears to be pristine, the ring should be removed and not be used. When dismantling a fire ring, all stones should be widely dispersed and the ash should be scattered. The area should then be covered with duff and other natural materials to make it appear as natural as possible. If you can't have a safe fire without a fire ring, and there isn't one, choose not to have a fire rather than building a fire ring.

FIRES IN PRISTINE AREAS

To create a safe fire you need to keep several factors in mind. First, never build a fire directly on the top layer of organic soil (the top layer of dirt full of decomposing organic material). This layer is usually 6 to 12 inches (15 to 30 centimeters) thick and is highly flammable. A fire on this layer could smolder underground for weeks. Also, the heat from a fire can kill the microorganisms in organic soil responsible for breaking down organic matter, in effect sterilizing the soil.

Instead, fires should be created on mineral soil, which contains no organic material and is not flammable. Mineral soil is typically found below the top organic soil layer. It can also be found along riverbeds or under upturned trees or boulders. This is why it is preferable to build a mound fire above ground rather than dig a fire pit. Even if you dig down to mineral soil for your fire, you are still going *through* the organic layer. The upper levels of the pit will be sterilized, and roots and other organic material on the sides of the pit may smolder after your fire is out and buried.

METHODS OF LEAVE NO TRACE FIRE BUILDING

The Mound Fire

Mound fires can be built virtually anywhere. All that is required is a trowel or shovel, a large stuff sack, and a ground cloth or plastic trash bag (optional); see illustration.

1. Locate a good source of mineral soil. If possible, collect the mineral soil from an area that does not require excavation or is already disturbed (sandy areas, old streambeds, beneath the roots of a fallen tree).
2. Turn the stuff sack inside out and fill it with mineral soil.
3. Carry the soil to the fire site.
4. Lay the ground cloth or plastic bag as a liner on the bare ground (optional) and create a circular, flat-topped mound of mineral soil 6 to 8 inches (15 to 20 centimeters) thick. The liner is not essential but helps in the cleanup process after the fire is out. The mound insulates the ground below from the heat of the fire. The circumference of the mound should

Mound Fire

be larger than the planned size of the fire to accommodate the spreading of coals.

5. Build your fire on top of the mineral soil mound. Make sure it is thick enough to insulate the ground (and your ground cloth) from the heat. If the mound is thick enough it will not damage the plants beneath, but it won't sterilize the soil, as would a fire built directly on the ground.

6. After the fire is out, clean it up as described below. Return the mineral soil to its original location.

The Fire Pan

Another technique is to build your fire on something fireproof. Fire pans are metal pans originally developed for river running. The pan provides a site to build your fire and completely burn your wood all the way down to ashes. When finished, scatter the ashes. Fire pans are too heavy to carry on a typical backpacking trip but work well on paddling trips or if you are in an extended base camp.

Fire Stoves

One step beyond fire pans are fire stoves. These are simple wood-burning stoves that cook more efficiently than an open fire. They confine or eliminate impact to the ground beneath the fire, create a draft that concentrates heat, and provide a platform for pots to rest on. Some of these stoves evolved from research in developing countries to slow deforestation, a major issue in many areas where people still cook over open fires. There are a number of commercially produced fire stoves. They range from simple, collapsible boxes to units with battery-powered fans that perform as well as many petroleum-fueled stoves. (See "Backpacking Stoves," page 55.) Remember, using a fire stove still requires firewood. If you are in an area where firewood is scarce, use a liquid, cannister, or solid fuel stove.

BUILDING AND LIGHTING A FIRE

Building a good fire that produces sufficient heat and light while burning the least amount of fuel is a practiced art. I'll presume you've already determined that it is appropriate to have a fire and selected a good location for your Leave No Trace fire.

Firewood Selection

Gather downed, dead wood—the driest possible. In highly impacted areas you may have to travel a long way to find wood. Select your firewood from small-diameter wood lying loose on the ground in order to ensure complete, efficient burning. Use only wood that is the diameter of your wrist or smaller.

- No wood should be broken off standing trees, alive or dead. An area with discolored broken stubs and few branches within arm's reach loses much of its natural beauty.
- Saws and axes are not necessary if you use "wrist-sized" wood.
- If adequate wood is not available by acceptable means, use a stove. When in doubt, use a stove!
- Firewood is a valuable and often scarce resource, so it should not be wasted on excessively large fires. Build a small fire rather than a big fire, and just sit closer to it.

First collect *tinder*. This is light airy material that will catch a spark and light. Natural materials like dry pine needles, grasses, cattail, thistle, or man-made materials like unused toilet paper, tampons, or even cotton balls soaked in Vaseline petroleum jelly make good tinder. An airy clump about the size of a baseball should be plenty. In wet weather, securing good tinder is essential. You can also use artificial substances like stove-priming paste.

Then collect *kindling:* twigs the diameter of a pencil or smaller. Finally, collect *fuel wood:* larger pieces of wood (pencil-diameter to the diameter of your wrist). This may be big enough for the type of fire you need. If you are in a survival situation, use larger logs to keep the fire burning constantly.

Lighting the Fire

Matches, lighters, flint and steel, or a magnesium fire starter are all good ways to start your fire. For those who have practiced primitive skills, a fire can be started with a bow drill, hand drill, or mouth drill.

Tipi Fire Start with small kindling sticks in a tipi arrangement just a few inches high. Leave a small opening in the tipi, and in the open space beneath the tipi place your tinder. Light the tinder with a spark or flame. The tinder will light the kindling on fire. Continue to add larger pieces of kindling in the tipi arrangement, taking care not to smother the flame with too much fuel. You can gently blow through the tipi opening to add supplemental oxygen to the flame. Continue to add larger kindling and finally fuel wood to sustain the flame. Tipi fires concentrate the heat in one spot and burn hot and fast, so they can be good for cooking and quick warmth. For cooking you'll need to suspend your pot over the fire. In a survival situation you can feed the ends of logs into the tipi fire and slowly advance them as the ends burn.

Cross Stack Fire The cross stack fire is built by creating a rectangular base with larger kindling or fuel wood open at one or both ends. Place a layer of kindling across the base logs and then cross-stack other layers on top of that. The larger logs create air space between your kindling layers and the ground. Place your tinder beneath the cross-stacked kindling and light it. As the kindling burns, continue to cross-stack larger fuel on top. As layers burn down, you add a new layer. Cross stack fires burn with a more diffuse flame and spread the heat. They burn more slowly than a tipi fire and generate lots of coals, so they are good if you need to keep a fire going for a long time. A cross stack fire may offer a "flatter" top surface and allow you to place a pot on the wood for cooking. I don't advise building this kind of fire if you need a fire only for a short time, since it takes much longer to burn the wood down to ashes. It is a good survival fire since it burns more slowly using up less wood.

CLEAN-UP AFTER A FIRE

Burn all wood completely. Plan ahead and stop feeding your fire long before you are ready to put the fire out. Don't put a "night log" on your fire that will be only half-burned in the morning. For safety, never leave a fire unattended. When it's time for bed, the fire should be put out completely.

Let your fire burn down to white ash before dousing it thoroughly with water (untreated water is fine). Then stir all the way through the embers with a stick to make sure the fire is completely out. It should be cool enough to put your hand in the ashes when it's out. But *don't* put your hand in. White ash mixed with water makes caustic lye, which can cause chemical burns (see "Toxins," page 349). Grind up small coals into ash. Scatter the ashes over a large area away from camp. Don't bury ashes. Scatter excess firewood before leaving your campsite.

LEAVE WHAT YOU FIND
LEAVE NATURAL FEATURES UNDISTURBED

There is something incredibly exciting about finding an arrowhead or a deer skull in the wilderness. So why not leave it for the next person to be able to experience that same sense of excitement? Natural objects of beauty or interest, such as antlers, petrified wood, colored rocks, and other natural objects, should be left for others to appreciate. These objects are also an ongoing part of the ecosystem—for example, animal bones are chewed on by rodents. In many national parks, other federal lands, and hiking areas, it is *illegal* to remove natural objects.

AVOID SPREADING NON-NATIVE PLANTS AND ANIMALS

With global travel it is possible to transport species of plants and animals from their natural environment to another one in which they have no natural controls. When I was backpacking (or tramping) in New Zealand I came across the Australian possum, a marsupial herbivore about the size of a raccoon that was introduced to New Zealand in the late 1800's for the fur trade. There are no native mammal predators in New Zealand, so with no natural predators, the possum population exploded. There are now 90 million possums in New Zealand, and they have decimated native forests. The introduction of non-native species—everything from the Kadzu vine to the snakehead fish—is the second leading cause of natural habitat loss (the leading cause is worldwide land development).

- Don't bring plants from home into wild areas.
- Empty and clean your pack, tent, and other gear after every trip.
- Clean the dirt out of your boot soles, and if you headed off-road, out of your tire treads.
- Make sure that pets are immunized and their coats are free of seeds, twigs, and harmful pests such as ticks.

RESPECT CULTURAL, RELIGIOUS, AND HISTORICAL SITES

Signs of human history—ancient sites of indigenous peoples, pioneer settlements, and other relics—are another part of wilderness exploration. Save these for other visitors. Don't remove items as souvenirs. In the U.S., cultural artifacts are protected by the Archaeological Resources Protection Act. It is illegal to remove or disturb archeological sites, historic sites, or artifacts such as pot shards, arrowheads, structures, and even antique bottles found on public lands. Some of these sites have significant cultural and religious significance to native peoples. Respect their history and culture.

RESPECT WILDLIFE

The natural world has its own pace. Tuning yourself to nature's rhythms is one of the most valuable parts of being in the backcountry. Learn about wildlife through quiet observation; often you can see more by knowing about wildlife signs. (See Chapter 7, "Weather and Nature.") Remember that you are in their home and respect their needs for undisturbed territory. Disturbing animals can interfere with feeding or breeding behavior.

- **Observe wildlife from a distance** Don't come so close that they are scared or forced to flee. Avoid sudden motions and loud noise, and never chase or charge any animal. A good rule of thumb is, if you are close enough so that the animal is changing its behavior because of you, then you're too close. (See "Wildlife Observation and Animal Tracking," page 221.) Large groups can disturb wildlife, so keep your group small.
- **Avoid sensitive times and habitats** Different seasons of the year correspond to different parts of the life cycle of wildlife. At certain periods, such as mating and nesting seasons or winter hibernation, animals are extremely sensitive to outside stress. Be aware of times and/or locations and avoid disturbing wildlife.
- **Don't touch or pick up wild animals** It is stressful to the animal, and it is possible that the animal could harbor rabies or other diseases. (See "Rabies," page 352.) Sick or wounded animals can bite, peck, or scratch. Touching young animals may cause the parents to abandon them. If you find a sick animal or animal in trouble, don't approach it; notify a game warden or local ranger.
- **Keep human food/garbage away from animals** Don't feed animals; don't even leave bread crumbs and seeds for birds or squirrels. Feeding wildlife can upset the natural balance of their food chain, or make them dependent on human food (bears are a major example). One saying is "A fed bear is a dead bear." That is, if a bear gets habituated to human food, it often leads to negative human encounters, which may result in the bear's having to be killed. It would be terrible to think that your poor Leave No Trace practice led to someone being injured by a bear and the bear's having to be killed. In addition, your leftovers may carry bacteria that are harmful to animals. Secure your food and garbage so that animals can't get to it. (See "Traveling in Bear Country," page 180.)
- **Allow animals free access to water sources** Give them the buffer space they need to feel secure. Ideally, camps should be located 200 feet (61 meters) or more from existing water sources. This will minimize disturbance to wildlife and ensure that animals have access to their precious drinking water. Water is limited in arid lands, and desert travelers must strive to reduce their impact on the animals struggling for survival. Desert animals are most active at night. By avoiding water holes at night, you will be less likely to frighten animals.
- **Use careful washing and human waste disposal practices** This ensures that the environment remain pristine, is not polluted, and animals and aquatic life are not injured. Swimming in lakes or streams is okay in most instances, but in desert areas, leave scarce water holes undisturbed and unpolluted so animals may drink from them (see page 113).

BE CONSIDERATE OF OTHER VISITORS

The way in which you travel through the wilderness can have a huge impact on someone else's experience. I can think of more than one occasion when I've picked up and moved a camp because the behavior of the people nearby was simply atrocious.

- **Travel quietly** Be quiet in the backcountry, whether hiking by trail or cross-country (the exception to this rule is when traveling in bear country; see "Traveling in Bear Country," page 180). You will see more of your environment, wildlife will be less intimidated, and other hikers will appreciate the quiet. If you bring audio equipment, bring headphones, too.
- **Limit group size** Be aware of the impact you have as a group. If you are a large group, think about breaking into smaller groups to minimize your impact on the land and on other hikers.
- **Yield to livestock** Groups leading or riding livestock have the right-of-way on trails. On hills, stand on the downhill side to avoid spooking livestock. On cliff edges, stand to the inside of the trail for livestock to pass.
- **Avoid bright-colored clothing and tents** Wear muted colors to minimize your visual impact, especially if traveling with a group. (The exception is winter hiking or during hunting seasons, when visibility becomes a safety concern.)
- **Educate people if and when you can** If you see people who don't know how to properly practice Leave No Trace techniques, introduce yourself and gently offer some suggestions. You need to look to see if there is an opening to do this. Try not to seem judgmental; you may just turn people off to your message. Some people will appreciate your effort and learn from you.
- **Keep a low profile** Take your rest break off the trail on a durable surface. When possible, camp out of sight and sound of other backcountry users.
- **Pick up litter** Pick up any garbage and trash that you can along your way. Consider it your gift to the next person who hikes down the trail.
- **Choose private campsites** If you aren't in an established campsite, choose a location where trees or the landscape will shield you from others' view (their view of you and your view of them).
- **Don't impose yourself on other groups** If you are on an organized program with specific activities and an agenda like team-building activities, be mindful of when you do these to minimize impact on others. Things like pranks on another group are totally inappropriate.
- **Control your pets** Keep pets under control at all times. If your pet is not "backcountry trained," leave her at home. Be aware of leash laws and follow them.

CHAPTER 6
Wilderness Travel

Now that you're ready to hit the trail, this chapter will cover the basics of how to get around in the wilderness, from route-finding to river crossings. Let's start with the tools you need to navigate.

MAPS AND MAP READING

A map is a two-dimensional representation of the three-dimensional world using special symbols and colors to represent the earth's surface. Map reading is about learning to understand this two-dimensional "language." The most useful map for the backcountry is a topographic map, which uses markings called contour lines to simulate the three-dimensional topography of the land. For backpacking, these are much more helpful than nontopographic maps. In the United States, the U.S. Geological Survey (USGS) makes topographic maps that cover areas in great detail, and the Canada Map Office produces topographic maps of Canada. Topographic maps are indispensable if you are traveling in a remote area because they contain lots of detail. However, government topographic maps are not always accurate in displaying local marked trails. In some cases, lesser-known trails are not even shown on a topographic map. Local trail maps often have more detailed information on local trails than topographic maps. I often take both types of maps on a trip—topographic maps for the most accurate geographic information and for map and compass navigation, and a local trail map to show trails, campsites, and other features.

MAP SCALE

All maps indicate their scales in a legend, generally found in a margin. Scales are represented with two numbers in a ratio. The first number is the map distance and the second is the ground distance. The map distance is always one. A scale of 1:24,000 (be it inches, feet, or meters) means that 1 unit on the map is the equivalent of 24,000 of those same units in the real world. Since most of us don't think in hundreds of thousands of inches, the second number is typically converted into a more usable number like miles or kilometers. In this case, 1 inch on the map would equal about 2,000 feet (609 meters), and 1 centimeter on the map (0.39 inches) would equal 240 meters (787 feet).

There are large-scale maps and small-scale maps. Just remember *Large scale shows Small detail* and *Small scale shows Large detail*. The larger the second number is in the ratio, the smaller the scale of the map. A *larger scale* 1:24,000 map will show *smaller things* on the map like individual buildings and covers a *smaller area*. A *smaller scale* 1:250,000 map shows only *larger things* on the map like cities and covers a *larger* area.

When you are looking for a map, decide what scale is best for your planning in terms of the amount of detail versus the amount of area covered. The typical USGS maps used for hiking are 1:24,000 scale (also known as 7½-minute maps). Each of these maps shows an area 7½ minutes of latitude by 7½ minutes of longitude (roughly 6½ miles by 8½ miles or 10.4 kilometers by 13.6 kilometers). These maps are adequate for most backpacking trips, but if you were going on a month-long canoeing trip in northern Canada covering 500 miles you might want to use a smaller scale map that would cover greater distances and fewer details.

MAP COLORS AND SYMBOLS

USGS topographic maps use colors to designate different features.

- Black—man-made features such as roads, buildings, boundaries, etc.
- Blue—water, lakes, rivers, streams
- Brown—contour lines indicating elevation
- Green—areas with substantial vegetation (forest, scrub, etc.)
- Purple—features added to the map since the original survey: These are based on aerial photographs but have not been checked on land
- Red—major highways and boundaries of public land areas
- White—areas with little or no vegetation; white with blue lines is used to depict permanent snowfields and glaciers

In addition to colors, there are a variety of symbols and shadings that designate features on the map. The complete catalog of symbols is available at *erg.usgs.gov/isb/pubs/booklets/symbols*.

MAP LEGEND

Each map contains specific information about the area that map covers. The major features of the map legend are shown below:

- Map name
- Year of production and year of any revisions
- General location in the state
- Adjacent quadrangle maps
- Map scale
- Distance scale
- Contour interval
- Magnetic declination
- Latitude and longitude
- UTM coordinates

CONTOUR LINES

Contour lines depict the three-dimensional character of terrain on a two-dimensional surface. Just as isobars on weather maps depict lines of equal atmospheric pressure in the atmosphere, contour lines drawn on the map represent equal points of height above sea level.

On multicolored maps, contour lines are represented in brown. The map legend indicates the contour interval—the distance in feet (or meters) between each contour line. There will be heavier contour lines every fourth or fifth line, labeled with the height above sea level. The figure on page 137 illustrates how a variety of surface features can be identified from contour lines.

Big Sur, California, Three-Dimensional View Showing Contour Lines

- Steep slopes—contours are closely spaced
- Gentle slopes—contours are widely spaced
- Valleys—contours form a V shape pointing up the hill; these Vs are always an indication of a drainage path that could also be a stream or river
- Ridges—contours form a V-shape pointing down the hill
- Summits—contours form circles
- Depressions—contours are circular with lines radiating to the center

MEASURING DISTANCES

There are a number of ways to measure distance accurately on a map. One is to use a piece of string to trace the intended route. Lay the string along the route and then pull the string straight and measure it against the scale line in the map

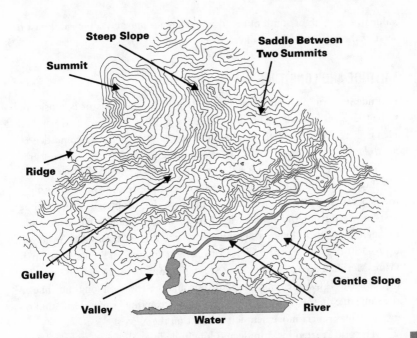

Big Sur, California, Map View Showing Contour Lines and Features

legend. Another method is to use a mathematic compass and set it at a narrow distance on the map scale, such as ½ mile, and then "walk off" your route. Depending on how accurately you measure and the scale of your map, be conservative and add 5 to 10 percent of the total distance to account for features like switchbacks, which may not appear on the map. It's better to anticipate a longer route than a shorter one. There are also map measurers with a little wheel that you roll along your route that calculates your total mileage. For winding trails the compass method is not very accurate; use a string or a map measurer.

CALCULATING LOCATION USING A COORDINATE SYSTEM

Any location on the earth can be plotted using one of several coordinate systems. The most commonly used coordinate systems are latitude and longitude and the Universal Transverse Mercator (UTM) system. In order to identify any location you have to start with some reference points. These systems use two standardized reference lines—one for north–south (the Y-axis) and another for east–west (the X-axis). You can then identify an exact location as some value to the north or south of the Y-axis reference line and some value east or west of the X-axis reference line.

LATITUDE AND LONGITUDE

Latitude lines run east and west around the earth. The Equator is considered to be 0 degrees latitude and bisects the globe into the Northern and Southern Hemispheres. Points north of the Equator are referred to as some degrees *north latitude* and points south of the equator are referred to as some degrees *south latitude*. Latitude values reflect movement up or down the Y-axis.

Longitude lines, also called meridians, run north and south, meeting at the geographic poles. Longitude lines measure the distance in degrees either east or west from the Prime Meridian (0 degrees longitude), which runs through Greenwich, England. Points east of the Prime Meridian go from zero up to 180 degrees and are referred to as *east longitude*. Points west of the Prime Meridian are referred to as *west longitude* and also go from 0 up to 180 degrees. The 180 degree east longitude line and the 180 west longitude line are the same line on the opposite side of the globe from the Prime Meridian. Longitude values reflect movement left or right on the X-axis.

The grid created by latitude and longitude lines allows us to calculate an exact point as X-axis and Y-axis coordinates. In the drawing below you can see that the point P is where the 30 degrees north latitude line and the 20 degrees west longitude line intersect.

Both latitude and longitude are measured in degrees, minutes, and seconds of arc, as follows:

1 degree = 1/360 of a circle

1 minute of arc = 1/60 of a degree

1 second of arc = 1/60 of a minute of arc

Therefore, 7½ minutes of arc (the typical area shown in a topo map) shows an area ⅛ of a degree.

Let's look at an example of latitude and longitude positioning. The latitude value is always displayed first. The location of Mt. Princeton in the Colorado Rockies is:

N 38° 44'58" W 106° 14'31"

The "N" specifies north latitude and the "W" specifies west longitude. This is read as 38 degrees 44 minutes and 58 seconds north (of the Equator) latitude and 106 degrees 14 minutes and 31 seconds west (of the Prime Meridian) longitude. Calculating location using latitude and longitude can be cumbersome because there are so many units to work with (degrees, minutes, and seconds).

UNIVERSAL TRANSVERSE MERCATOR SYSTEM

Once you understand it, the Universal Transverse Mercator (UTM) system is easier to use than the latitude-longitude system since it does not require parsing units down into degrees, minutes, and seconds. The UTM system is based on the metric system and uses meters as the unit of distance (1 meter = 3.28 feet). In the UTM grid, the world is divided into sixty zones that run north–south from pole to pole, each covering a strip 6 degrees wide in longitude at the widest point, the equator. These zones are numbered consecutively

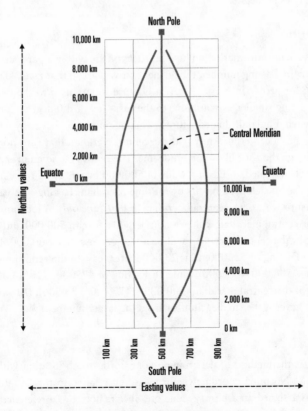

UTM Coordinate System

going east starting with Zone 1 (on the International Date Line out in the middle of the Pacific Ocean), which covers between 180° and 174° *west* longitude to Zone 60, which covers from 174° to 180° *east* longitude (so Zone 1 and 60 meet at 180° *east/west* longitude). The lower forty-eight States in the United States and Canada are covered by Zone 7 on the West Coast through Zone 22 in eastern Canada.

Each zone is oblong in shape, narrower at the top and bottom than in the middle owing to the spherical nature of the earth and what happens when you project a sphere onto a flat map. Each zone covers both the Northern and Southern Hemispheres. Each zone is divided into horizontal bands spanning 8 degrees of latitude. The letters C–M specify latitudes south of the Equator, and the letters N–X specify latitudes north of the Equator. So using just the zone number and the band letter, you can get a general region of the earth's surface. Within each zone coordinates are measured north and east of fixed reference lines in meters.

Eastings

Eastings provide information on how far east you are within a particular zone. The larger the Easting number, the farther east you are in that zone. (This gets confusing for people in North America because we are used to the longitude number getting smaller as you move to the east—toward 0 degrees longitude at Greenwich, England.) In order for the Easting number to have any meaning, each zone has a centerline known as the central meridian that runs north and south through the zone like a longitude line. The central meridian in each zone is arbitrarily assigned an Easting value of 500,000 meters east. You can think of this line as if each zone has its own Prime Meridian. Eastings are values in meters east or west of the central meridian *in that zone only*. A location that is east of the central meridian will be a number greater than 500,000 and a location west of the central meridian will be a number less than 500,000. For example, an Easting of 523000mE is 23,000 meters east of the central meridian (523,000 – 500,000 = 23,000) while an Easting of 477000mE is 23,000 meters west of the central meridian (500,000 – 477,000 = 23,000). (Always subtract whichever is the smaller number from the larger number.)

Northings

Northing is the method of determining your north–south location within the zone. UTM Northing coordinates are measured relative to the Equator. The Equator is assigned an arbitrary value of 0 meters north, as a reference for all locations north of the Equator. For locations south of the Equator, the Equator is assigned an arbitrary value of 10,000,000 meters north. This prevents locations in the Southern Hemisphere from having negative Northing values. It is possible to have duplicate Northing values within the same zone—one above the Equator and one below the Equator. To identify the correct location you typically include the letter for the latitude band after the zone number. The latitude band letter is often dropped when you know what hemisphere you are in.

UTM Map References

A complete UTM coordinate starts with the zone, followed (sometimes) by the band letter, then the full Easting value and finally the full Northing value. Always remember the order *zone* then *east* then *north*. One mnemonic to remember the correct order is Z-E-N, zone-Easting-Northing. Let's look at the summit of Mt. Princeton in UTM coordinates.

13 S 0392028E 4289705N also written as 13 S 03^{92}028mE 42^{89}705mN

Reading from left to right, the first value, *13,* represents the zone you are in. The letter (S) refers to the latitude band, so you can quickly identify a very general location on the earth with just the zone and band (hemisphere). The next set of numbers, 03^{92}028, is the Easting value showing your east–west position in the zone. The final set of numbers, 42^{89}705, is the Northing value showing your north–south position in the zone.

The central meridian of the zone is always at 500,000 meters. The 03^{92}028 means that this point is at 392,028 meters; therefore, it is west of the central meridian by 500,000 − 392,028 = 107,972 meters west. Since the location of the central meridian is known in each zone, you can calculate the line that this point is on by going 107,972 meters west of the central meridian. The 42^{89}705 means that this point is 4,289,705 meters north of the Equator. Combine these two points and you establish your coordinate location.

One of the nice parts about the UTM system is that you can use fewer numbers for a less exact location and more numbers for a more exact location. When working with UTM on a map, you typically work with the two superscript print numbers (in this case 92 and 89), which represent the key Easting and Northing values that define the grids on the map. If you use only the first two numbers of the Easting and Northing coordinate, then you define an area that is 1,000 meters by 1,000 meters (3,280 feet × 3,280 feet). As you add digits you increase the accuracy of the positioning. Think of it like a Zip code. The more digits you add, the closer in you get to the exact location. This isn't possible with the latitude-longitude coordinate system.

UTM Coordinates	Digit Resolution
92 89	4 digit—a square 1000 m by 1000m
920 897	6 digit—a square 100 m by 100m
9202 8970	8 digit—a square 10 m by 10m
92028 89705	10 digit—a square 1 m by 1m

UTM Coordinates on a Map

When you start working with UTM coordinates on a map, the notation changes a little based on the map scale. The 1:24000 map below has major UTM grid lines every 1,000 meters marked on the edges of the map. The vertical grid lines are the Easting lines and determine east–west position, and the horizontal grid lines are the Northing lines and determine north–south position. The major Northing and Easting lines are shown in regular type and the other numbers shown as superscripts (the opposite of how the UTM coordinate is written out). Label C, $^{3}92^{000}$mE, means "three hundred ninety-two thousand meters east." Since the central meridian is 500,000 meters, and this

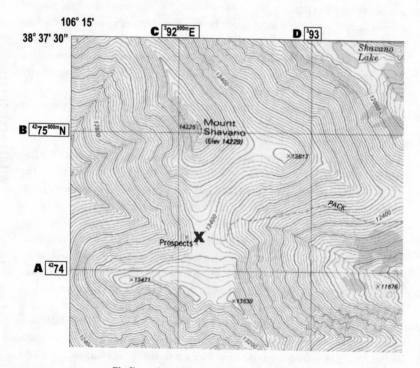

Finding a Location Using UTM Coordinates

number is lower than that, we know that this line is west of the central meridian by 108,000 meters (500,000 – 392,000 = 108,000). The D label next to it, ^{3}93, is an abbreviation for, ^{0}393^{000}mE. The two gridlines are 1,000 meters apart. Northing gridlines are measured the same way on the horizontal axis. The full Northing value of ^{42}75^{000}mN at label B means that this Northing line is 4,275,000 meters north of the Equator. The ^{42}74 shorthand at label A is 1,000 meters south.

Finding a Location with UTM

We want to locate Point X where the old prospector sites are on the south side of Mt. Shavano in Colorado. Make sure your map has UTM coordinates marked on it.

We know from the map legend that this is Zone 13. Since UTM starts with the Easting coordinate, find out which vertical Easting lines Point X is between. It's between Easting line 92 and line 93. If you just gave someone the coordinates 13 03 92E and 42 74N, it defines a 1,000-meter-square grid on a particular map, and she would know that you are talking about some point within that grid. To get a more accurate location, divide the distance between line 92 and line 93 into tenths (since UTM is based on the metric system we divide things up by 10), and estimate how many tenths east of line 92 it is. It looks about two-tenths of the 1,000 meters or 200 meters. We take that 2 and write it after the 92 for an Easting coordinate of 922.

Now do the same with the Northing coordinate. Find the line below and the line above Point X. The line below is 74 and the line above is 75. Estimate the distance north above the 74 Northing line. It looks like three-tenths of the 1,000 meters or 300 meters. Now we put the zone number and the full Easting and Northing values together for the full UTM coordinate 13 03^{92}2 42^{74}3. You can give someone else with the same map those coordinates, and they can locate that Point X on the map by finding the 92 Easting line and moving east 200 meters, then finding the 74 Northing line and moving north 300 meters.

You can make this process easier by using a UTM grid overlay. This is a piece of transparent plastic with grid markings on it, creating a series of boxes. The one shown here is from MapTools *(www.maptools.com)*. Like a map, a UTM grid overlay is based on a particular map scale, so you must use the same grid scale as your map scale (e.g., 1:24,000). Place the grid overlay on the map and line up the left grid edge with the easting gridline on your map west of Point X and the bottom grid edge along the northing gridline south of Point X. Locate which "grid box" your Point X is in. Count over along the Easting grid to find the box number Point X is in (in this case 2). In our

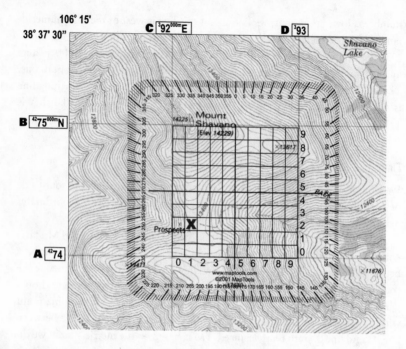

Using a Grid Overlay to Find UTM Coordinates

example, each box is 100 meters, so that box is 200 meters east of the 92 Easting line (92200). Do the same with the Northing and you get a value of 3 box (300 meters) north of the 74 (740,000) meter line. Combine the two numbers to get your Northing value of 743, so the full location is 922 743. This gives a six-digit coordinate that is accurate to within 100 meters (330 feet). To get a more accurate reading, divide the box where the X is into 10 values for Easting and Northing and add the new number to your UTM coordinate string.

USING A COMPASS

A compass consists of a magnetized metal needle that floats on a pivot point and orients to the magnetic field lines of the earth. The basic orienteering compass is composed of the following parts:

- Base plate
- Straight edge and ruler
- Direction of travel arrow

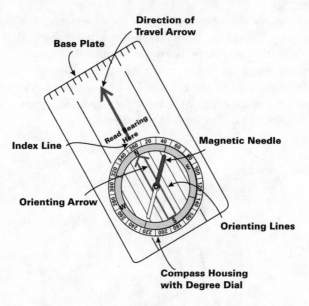

Compass

- Compass housing with 360-degree markings
- North label
- Index line
- Orienting arrow (typically red)
- Magnetic needle (north end is red)

WHAT IS NORTH?

No, this is not a silly question. There are several types of north:

True North/Map North Also known as geographic north, this is marked as ★ on a topographic map. It is the geographic North Pole, where all longitude lines meet. All maps are laid out with True North directly at the top of the map, so it is also known as Map North. Unfortunately for the wilderness traveler, True North is not at the same point on the earth as the magnetic North Pole, which is where a compass points.

Magnetic North Think of the earth as a giant magnet (it is, actually). The shape of the earth's magnetic field is roughly the same shape as the field of a bar magnet. The earth's magnetic pole doesn't correspond to the geographic

North Pole because the earth's core is molten, and the magnetic field is always shifting slightly. The red end of your compass needle is magnetized. Wherever you are, the earth's magnetic field causes the needle to rotate until it lies parallel to the lines of magnetic force in your particular location with the red end of the needle pointing to magnetic north. This is magnetic north (marked as "MN" on a topographic map). The following map shows an approximation of the lines of magnetic force for the United States.

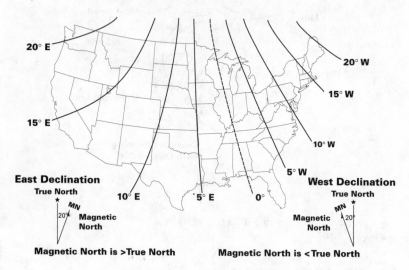

Lines of Magnetic Force in the U.S.

DECLINATION

As you can see in the illustration above, your location makes a great deal of difference in where the compass points. The angular difference between true north and magnetic north is known as the *declination* and is marked in degrees on a map. Depending on where you are, the angle between true north and magnetic north is different. In the continental United States and Canada, the angle of declination varies from about 20 degrees west in Maine to about 21 degrees east in Washington state. My trick for North America is to remember the location of the zero declination line (called the agonic line) roughly as the Mississippi River.

If you are *on* the line where the declination is 0 degrees, then you don't have to worry about declination at all, since magnetic north and map north are equivalent. (Wouldn't it be nice if all your trips were on the 0 degree of declination line?) If you are to the right of the agonic line—say, in Maine— your compass "declines" or points toward the agonic line (to the left), and hence the declination is to the west. If you are to the left of the line—say, in California—your compass "declines" or points toward the agonic line (to the right), and hence the declination is to the east.

The magnetic field lines of the earth are constantly changing, moving slowly westward (1 to 1½ degrees every five years), which is why it is important to have a recent map. Older maps will list a declination that is no longer accurate, and all your calculations using that angle will be incorrect.

🍁 TRICKS OF THE TRAIL

Caring for your compass Compasses are, of course, affected by magnetic fields. When using your compass, keep it away from metallic objects. Even a metal belt buckle can distort your magnetic reading. Also, other magnetic fields such as those found in electric motors can temporarily disorient or even permanently demagnetize the compass needle. Most compasses are made of translucent plastic. Certain chemicals and solvents like those found in products like DEET insect repellant can "eat" the paint markings off or cause the clear plastic to become cloudy.

USING A MAP AND COMPASS TOGETHER

Now that you understand the differences between True/Map North and Magnetic North, you can start to use your map and compass together.

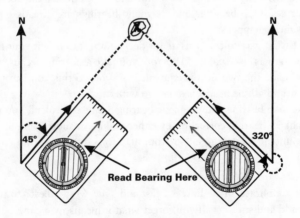

Reading a Bearing

BEARINGS

The compass is used primarily to take bearings. A bearing is a horizontal angle measured clockwise from north (either Magnetic North or True North) to some point (either a point in the real world or a point on a map). Bearings are used to locate your position or to reach a particular destination. If you are working from your map, it is called a map bearing, and the angle you are measuring is the angle measured clockwise from *True North* on your map to another point on the map. If you are taking a bearing from a real point on the landscape with a compass, you are using your compass to measure the angle clockwise from *Magnetic North* to this point on the landscape. This is called a magnetic bearing. Remember that the bearing is always measured clockwise.

MAP BEARINGS VERSUS MAGNETIC BEARINGS

Your map is an artist's rendition of the world. It displays True North, but it doesn't include magnetic fields as the real world does, so you need to make accommodations when going from your map to the real world. At the same time, the real world doesn't have a true north—it's merely a construct of the map, so you have to make accommodations when going from the north in the real world as defined by your compass to your map.

The basic principle is this: to compensate for declination, you want the map bearing and the magnetic bearing to be equivalent. There are three cases:

1. If you are lucky enough to be on the agonic line where the declination is 0 degrees, map bearings and magnetic bearings are already equivalent. This rarely happens.
2. The easiest way to compensate for declination is to orient your map with your compass (see page 151) *before* you take a bearing because then you have made the two norths equivalent. If you do this you can ignore #3 below and all the headaches that go with it.
3. If the map bearing and magnetic bearing aren't equivalent, you will need to make a bearing correction by either adding or subtracting the declination amount as you go either from map to compass or from compass to map.

I use the phrase "True East is Least and True West is Best" to remember when to add and subtract. If you forget what it means, you can "build it" as you go. I remember that true north (map north) is always the same, and it is magnetic north that shifts with declination. So any bearing I take *from the map* is based on a constant—true north. When you are going from a bearing that you have calculated on your map to a magnetic bearing and your declination is east, you *subtract* the declination from the map bearing (*least* is like *less*, which means *subtract*), so "east declination is least." If your declination is west, you *add* the declination to the map bearing (*best* is like *better*, which means *add*), so "west declination is best."

EAST DECLINATION

If your declination is east, then magnetic north is greater than true north and the map bearing is greater than the magnetic bearing. To make the two bearings equivalent, add or subtract the declination, as illustrated below:

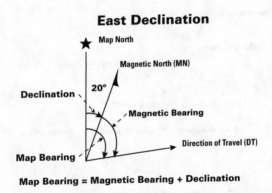

East Declination

Map Bearing = Magnetic Bearing + Declination

East Declination

- **Map Bearing to Magnetic Bearing** If you are taking a bearing from one point on your map to another point on the map with respect to *true* north, then you are working with a map bearing. To determine the magnetic bearing, *subtract* the declination from your map bearing to create the proper magnetic bearing.

  Map Bearing − Declination = Magnetic Bearing.

- **Magnetic Bearing to Map Bearing** If you use your compass to take a bearing from your current position to a point on the landscape, then you are working with a magnetic bearing. To determine your position on the map, *add* the declination from your magnetic bearing to create the proper map bearing.

Magnetic Bearing + Declination = Map Bearing.

WEST DECLINATION

If your declination is west, then magnetic north is less than true north and the map bearing is less than the magnetic bearing. As with east declination, you can make the two bearings equivalent by adding or subtracting the declination, as is illustrated below:

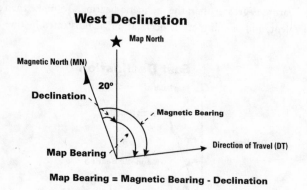

West Declination

Map Bearing = Magnetic Bearing - Declination

West Declination

- **Map Bearing to Magnetic Bearing**   If you are taking a bearing from one point on your map to another point on the map with respect to true north, then you are working with a map bearing. To determine the magnetic bearing, *add* the declination to your map bearing to create the proper magnetic bearing.

Map Bearing + Declination = Magnetic Bearing.

- **Magnetic Bearing to Map Bearing**   If you use your compass to take a bearing from your current position to a point on the landscape, then you are working with a magnetic bearing. To determine your position on the map, *subtract* the declination from your magnetic compass bearing to create the proper map bearing.

Magnetic Bearing – Declination = Map Bearing.

ADJUSTING YOUR COMPASS FOR THE LOCAL DECLINATION

Some compasses have an outer degree ring that can be unlocked with either a set screw or a latch, allowing you to reset the compass to account for declination. Normally the orienting arrow will be pointed to the N on the compass ring. You can adjust the orienting arrow so that it points to magnetic north for the declination of that particular area. Once the compass has been corrected to the local declination you won't have to add or subtract for declination because your compass is aligned to true north. This means that when the compass needle is inside the orienting arrow, the compass bearing that you read off your compass will be in relation to true north instead of magnetic north. If you have a fixed-ring compass, you can mark the declination angle on the compass baseplate with a piece of tape.

> ### 🍁 TRICKS OF THE TRAIL
>
> **Buy Your Compass for the Right Area**   In addition to the magnetic deviation east or west, compasses also show a vertical "dip" up or down. This dip varies in different parts of the world, and compasses are typically calibrated for that dip. Thus, a compass made for the Northern Hemisphere won't give accurate readings in the Southern Hemisphere. Buy your compass when you get to the country you are hiking in. Suunto makes a "global" compass that works with dip up to 20 degrees and is therefore useful in most locations around the world.

WILDERNESS NAVIGATION

Navigation in the wilderness means knowing your starting point, your destination, and traveling your route to get there.

CHECK YOUR POSITION REGULARLY

Keep your map and compass handy, and refer to them every hour or so to locate your position (more often in low visibility). Keep track of your starting time, rest breaks, lunch stops, and general hiking pace. This will also give you an idea of how far you have traveled and whether you've planned your time accurately. This is just one part of *situational awareness*. (See Chapter 8, "Safety and Emergency Procedures.")

ORIENT THE MAP

You can eliminate the need to correct for declination if you use your compass to orient the map to magnetic north each time (or if you have calibrated your compass for declination). As long as the map is oriented with respect to magnetic north, any bearings you take from map to compass or compass to map will be the same. It also helps to compare the map to the surrounding landscape if the map is oriented. You can do this by eye, using basic land features, or with your compass.

Orienting the Map Using Land Features

Lay the map on the ground or hold it horizontally. Rotate the map until recognized features on the ground roughly align with those on the map. This method is fine for general scouting of the area but not accurate enough for real navigation.

Orienting the Map Using a Compass

1. Place your compass on the map so that the side edge of the baseplate lies parallel to the east or west edge of the map, with the direction of travel arrow pointing toward the north edge of the map. The compass housing must be rotated so that the compass's orienting arrow is pointing to the top of the map (N on the compass ring is at "Read bearing here" marker).

2. Holding the compass on the map with the side edge still parallel, rotate the map *and* the compass together until the north end of the magnetic needle points to the N on the compass housing (i.e., the red north end of the magnetic needle and the orienting arrow align). This is often referred to as "boxing the needle" since the magnetic needle is inside the "box" formed by the orienting arrow. Some people also say "red in the shed" when the red end of the magnetic needle is inside the orienteering arrow on the compass, which is typically painted red. The map is now oriented with respect to magnetic north. This means that you've rotated the map so that true north on the map now points to magnetic north. Any compass bearings you take from the map can immediately be applied to the field and vice versa. This works the same way if you have a compass already adjusted for local declination.

IDENTIFY TERRAIN FEATURES

With the map oriented, look around for prominent landscape features such as mountains, valleys, lakes, and rivers. Make a mental note of the geographical features you will be traveling along and seeing during the day. If you keep the terrain in your mind, you will have a general sense of your location just by looking around.

REAL-LIFE NAVIGATION SCENARIOS

Below are some common backcountry navigation scenarios. Let's see how you can use your map and compass to follow your route.

SCENARIO 1—LOST IN THE FOG

After hiking along the trail, you bushwhack off to a nearby alpine lake to camp. When you wake up the next morning, you are fogged in. You know where you are on the map, but you don't know how to find your way out in the fog. Take a bearing on your map from your known campsite back to a known point on the trail that you can identify on the map, then follow your bearing through the fog. (You might also decide to wait out the fog if there is difficult terrain to traverse.) Should you decide to find your way out, here are the procedures:

Taking a Bearing from the Map (Map Not Oriented)

1. Lay the long edge of the compass base plate on the map, making a line from your starting point to your destination (from Point X to Point Y in the drawing). Since the base plate is parallel to the direction of travel arrow, the base plate can be used to set the direction to your destination.

2. Holding the base plate steady, rotate the compass housing until the compass orienting lines and orienting arrow are pointing to true north. You see the orienting lines and arrow are parallel to the line from A to B as well as the map gridlines. Ignore the compass needle since the bearing you are working with is based on map north.

3. Read the bearing (in degrees) from the degree dial at the index line on

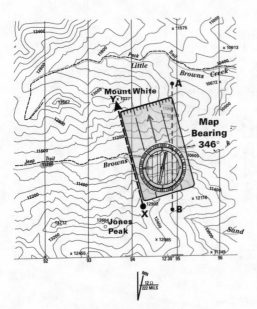

Taking a Bearing from the Map

the compass base plate (marked "Read bearing here"). In this case the map bearing is 346 degrees.

4. Now you have to correct for declination. If you are in an area with east declination, then subtract the declination angle from your map bearing to get a magnetic bearing to follow. If you are in an area with west declination, add the declination to your map bearing.

Taking a Bearing from the Map (Map Oriented to Magnetic North)

1. Orient the map with the compass (see page 151).
2. Lay the long edge of the compass base plate on the map, making a line from your starting point to your destination (from Point X to Point Y in the drawing). Since the base plate is parallel to the direction of travel arrow, the base plate can be used to set the direction to your destination.
3. Holding the base plate steady, rotate the compass housing until the orienting arrow coincides with the north end of the magnetic needle ("boxing the arrow/red in the shed").
4. Read the bearing (in degrees) from the degree dial at the index line on the compass base plate (marked "Read bearing here"). In this case the magnetic bearing is 338 degrees. The difference in degrees between this bearing and the previous bearing should be the declination for this area.

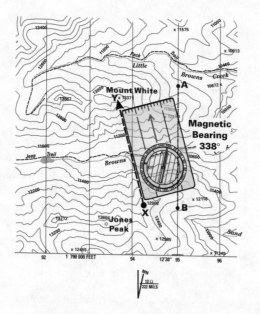

Taking a Bearing from the Compass

SCENARIO 2—HEADING TO THE SUMMIT

After hiking along the trail, you find a good campsite that is marked on the map. You see a summit ridge above the tree line that looks like a great place for photographs, but there's a valley thick with Douglas fir trees between you and the summit. Take a bearing from your current position to the summit and use that to travel through the forest. Here's your procedure:

Taking a Bearing from the Land

1. Point the direction of travel arrow of the compass toward your destination on the land.
2. Rotate the compass housing until the north-orienting arrow of the compass housing lines up with the red magnetic needle ("boxing the needle/red in the shed"). The north-orienting arrow must be pointing in the same direction as the red (north) magnetic needle.
3. Read the bearing (in degrees) from the degree dial at the index line on the compass base plate (marked "Read bearing here").

Walking a Bearing

1. After taking the bearing, hold the compass level and in front of you, so that the direction of travel arrow points to your destination.
2. Rotate your body until the magnetic needle lies directly over the orienting arrow ("boxing the needle/red in the shed"). Make sure the north end of the magnetic needle points to N on the compass housing. The direction of travel arrow on the compass now points to your destination.
3. Keeping the needle "boxed/in the shed," walk to your destination.

Walking a Line-of-Sight Bearing

Sometimes you can't see your final destination. One method for walking a bearing is to use line of sight. Walk to a visible landmark—a tree or boulder that is directly along the bearing. Then take another bearing from that landmark to the next visible landmark along the bearing and walk to that. Keep it up until you reach your destination. By going to intermediate landmarks, you minimize the chances of veering off your bearing.

SCENARIO 3—RETRACING YOUR STEPS TO CAMP

You made it to the summit and took some great photos. Now it's time to get back to your campsite. To do this you want to calculate a back bearing.

Back Bearings

Back bearings can be used either to retrace your steps or to check your position while hiking a bearing. Before you start to walk on your bearing, take a bearing 180 degrees off of the bearing you are going to walk. For example, if you are going to walk a bearing of 45 degrees, shoot a bearing directly opposite your course at 225 degrees. Locate a landmark along this opposite bearing. Walk a short distance along your bearing, then turn around and shoot a bearing back to the landmark along the opposite bearing. If you are on course, the bearing to the landmark behind you will still read 180 degrees off your bearing (in this case 225 degrees). If it doesn't, you are off course. Sailors and sea kayakers use back bearings all the time to check for lateral drift from wind or currents. Back bearings are also useful if you are heading out to a destination and then returning along the same line of travel. There are two basic formulas for calculating a back bearing:

- **When the direction of travel bearing is less than 180 degrees**

  Back Bearing (BB) = 180° + Direction of Travel Bearing (DTB)

  BB = 180° + DTB

  225° = 180° + 45°

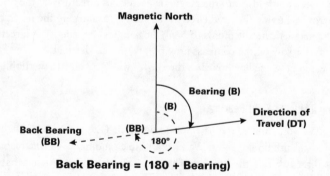

Back Bearing = (180 + Bearing)

Calculating a Back Bearing When the Bearing Is Less Than 180 Degrees

- **When the direction of travel bearing is greater than 180 degrees** If the direction of travel bearing is *more* than 180 degrees, you use a different formula (otherwise you will have a back bearing greater than 360 degrees). If we reverse the example above, let's say your bearing is 225 degrees (which is greater than 180 degrees), then your back bearing works out to 45 degrees.

Back Bearing (BB) = Direction of Travel Bearing (DTB) – 180°

BB = DTB – 180°

45° = 225° – 180°

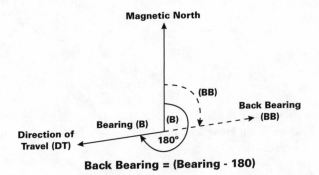

Back Bearing = (Bearing - 180)

Calculating a Back Bearing When the Bearing Is More Than 180 Degrees

Aiming Off

It's often hard to follow an exact back bearing. You veer off course somewhat. This is known as lateral drift (see page 161). Being off by just a few degrees can make a major difference after several miles (see table below). Rather than head straight for your target, it's best to calculate the direct back bearing and then deliberately set your compass bearing to aim off to the left or right side of your target. Then you'll know whether to turn right or left to get to the target.

Degrees off Course	Distance off target after 10 miles (16 kilometers)
1 degree	920 feet (280 meters)
5 degrees	4,600 feet (1,402 meters)
10 degrees	9,170 feet (2,795 meters)

Baselines

Baselines are helpful because they provide a large target to aim for. A baseline is a reference line that lies across your course. It can be a trail, cliff face, road, stream, or other feature. You can combine a baseline with aiming off to help

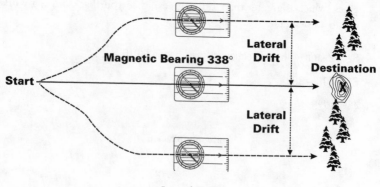

Lateral Drift

navigate. Find a baseline near your destination, then aim off of it. When you hit the baseline, you'll know which direction to turn to walk along the baseline to your destination.

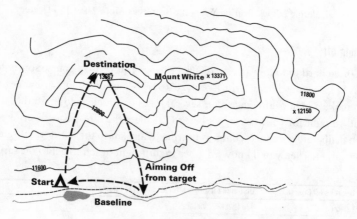

Aiming Off and Using a Baseline

SCENARIO 4—MANEUVERING AROUND OBSTACLES

You're in the midst of an incredible bushwhack and you've been diligently following a compass course, sighting from tree to tree. Up ahead there is a clearing. When you enter it, you discover a swamp. There's no way you can go straight through on your compass course. The best method for maintaining your course is to hike a rectangle around the swamp by making a series of 90 degree turns from and back to your original course. Here's your procedure:

1. Set a new bearing 90 degrees from your original heading and walk along that until you have cleared the obstacle along that axis. Remember, whenever you turn 90 degrees to the right, add 90 degrees to your course. Whenever you turn to the left, subtract 90 degrees from your course. While walking, maintain a count of paces or track the distance you travel until your next turn.
2. You have passed the length of the obstacle, so go back onto your original bearing, parallel to your original course, until you clear the obstacle along that axis.
3. Now that you've passed the width of the obstacle, it's time to hike back to your original line of travel. Set a bearing 90 degrees back to your original bearing and walk the same number of paces as you did in step 1.
4. Once you have walked off the correct distance, you are ready for your last 90 degree turn. Now turn back to your original bearing. You will be roughly along your original line of travel.

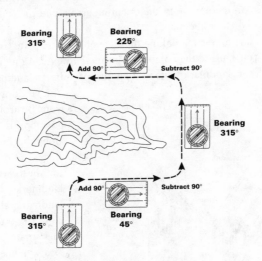

Bearing 315° **Bearing 225°**

Add 90° Subtract 90°

Bearing 315°

Add 90° Subtract 90°

Bearing 315° **Bearing 45°**

Navigating Around an Obstacle

SCENARIO 5—LOCATING YOURSELF WHEN LOST

You're hiking off-trail through the broad alpine valleys, having a deep philosophical conversation about our connection with nature—so deep that you have lost some of your own connection with nature. Suddenly, you look around and realize you don't know where you are; this alpine valley looks a lot like the last one you came through. Okay, so you're lost.

Triangulation

Triangulation is used to locate your position from compass bearings. Even if you are not sure where you are, you can find your approximate position, as long as you can identify at least two prominent landmarks (mountain, end of a lake, bridge), both on the land and on your map (see figure below). Here's your procedure:

1. Orient the map with your compass (see page 151).
2. Look around and locate prominent landmarks (preferably at least 90 degrees apart).
3. Find the landmarks on the map.
4. Take a compass bearing between you and the first landmark.
5. Place the compass on the map so that one corner of the base plate rests on the landmark.
6. Keeping the corner of the base plate on the landmark, turn the entire compass on the map until the orienting arrow and compass needle point to north on the map.
7. Draw a line on the map along the edge of the base plate from the landmark. You can use the compass base plate to extend the line on either side of the landmark, intersecting the prominent landmark symbol. You've drawn a line from B through A. Your position is somewhere along this line.

8. Repeat this procedure for the other prominent landmark. The second landmark should be as close to 90 degrees from the first as possible. Draw a line from C to the other line. Your approximate position is where the two lines intersect at Point A. This is a rough approximation of your position.

9. To make it even more ac-

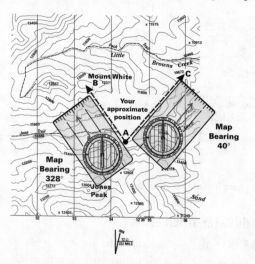

Triangulation

curate, you can repeat this process a third time to show an area bounded by three lines. If your bearings were accurate, you should be located within this triangle.

10. If you are located on a prominent feature marked on the map, such as a ridge, stream, or road, that feature can serve as a baseline, and only one calculation from a prominent landmark should be necessary. Your position will be approximately where the drawn line intersects this linear feature or baseline.

OTHER NAVIGATION TOOLS
WATCH

Wearing a watch in the backcountry is a matter of personal wilderness ethics. Many people like to let nature set the pace of the day rather than wear a watch. I may not wear my watch, but I always bring one along. There are too many times when I have needed one: to get an accurate check on how fast I am hiking; to see if my Time Control Plan is correct; and especially in first-aid and emergency situations, where timing vital signs and knowing the exact time may be essential in proper diagnosis and treatment. Watches can also be used to determine basic direction (see page 211).

ALTIMETER

An altimeter can be a useful navigation tool along with your map and compass. It is a specialized version of a barometer that measures the local atmospheric pressure of the air. This is the "weight" of the air above you. The higher you climb above sea level, the less the weight of air and the lower the pressure. Barometric pressure is measured in either inches or millibars. As you climb and descend, an altimeter monitors the changes in barometric pressure.

While you are hiking the atmospheric pressure is also constantly changing due to weather. To give you an accurate altitude reading, the altimeter must be calibrated to a known starting place. When you start your hike, find a known altitude location on your map based on contour lines, and when you are at that point you can set your altimeter to read that same elevation; it's now calibrated. As you hike, the altimeter shows the current altitude and any increase or decrease in elevation. If the overall barometric pressure in your area doesn't change due to weather, then the altimeter reading will stay accurate. However, since pressure may change, you should recalibrate your altimeter several times each day. Recalibrate, or at least look at, your altimeter reading before you go to bed. If the altimeter reads lower the next morning, then the atmospheric pressure has gone up during the night, typically indicating stable or improving weather. If the altimeter reads higher, then the atmospheric pressure has fallen, indicating potentially stormy weather. Some altimeters, once set to a known altitude, will automatically compensate for changes in barometric pressure due to weather.

You can use your altimeter as another source of information to help you locate your position or find a destination. If you are hiking up a trail and it crosses a particular altitude (contour line) at only one point, then you know where you are on that trail (based on two points of reference). Here's another situation: you know from your calibrated altimeter that you are somewhere along a contour line that lies at that elevation. You may be able to identify other clues from the landscape that you can find on the map to help you pin down exactly where you are along that contour line. Suppose you are traveling off-trail (using good Leave No Trace techniques). As you head up a ridgeline you know that there is a flat spot to camp at a certain elevation. Once you hit that elevation you can traverse along that elevation, using your altimeter to help you stay on the same contour line until you reach the flat spot.

Altimeters and altimeter watches are available for $50 to $200 dollars. Some models are prone to inaccuracies owing to temperature. Let your altimeter adjust to the ambient air temperature before taking a reading. More expensive units automatically correct for temperature changes, and some offer features like total vertical ascent and descent, altitude alarms, a separate barometer, weather trend graphs, and current temperature. You can get some of these same altitude and weather features in certain GPS receivers.

GLOBAL POSITIONING SYSTEM

The Global Positioning System (GPS) is a network of satellites in orbit above the earth. A GPS receiver is basically a radio receiver, available as a handheld unit that's easily transportable in the backcountry. The satellites transmit to the GPS receiver, which interpolates the signals into coordinate data (either latitude and longitude or UTM) that are displayed on the unit.

The GPS works just like our map and compass triangulation. Like triangulation, your GPS receiver needs to be able to "see" at least three satellites. Each satellite identifies itself, and the GPS receiver calculates how long it took to get the signal. This establishes your distance from each of the three satellites. A fourth satellite is needed to calculate your altitude. There are limitations to the accuracy of the GPS position reading. Depending on the type of receiver, GPS units are accurate from 50 feet (~15 meters) to within less than 9 feet (~3 meters). There are two enhancements that make the positioning even more accurate—differential GPS (DGPS) and Wide Area Augmentation System (WAAS). These systems include a correction signal that corrects for some of the inherent time lags in sending a radio signal from a satellite hundreds or thousands of miles away. Your GPS applies these corrections to the original satellite information. A DGPS receiver gives a position accurate from 9 to 16 feet (3 to 5 meters). A WAAS-enabled GPS receiver can read the signal and apply the correction, giving you an accuracy of less than 9 feet (3 meters). Although they can be used to determine your location very accurately and establish compass courses, don't rely on a GPS unit in place of knowledge of map and compass. Battery failure, damage to the GPS unit, or even leaving it behind at a rest stop could get you lost if you don't also have good map and compass skills. GPS units are particularly useful in locations where there no established trails or few landmarks.

There are limitations to GPS receivers. You need a clear view of the sky to get signals from multiple satellites. Bad weather, heavy tree cover, or being in a canyon all can prevent you from receiving GPS signals from multiple satellites, rendering your receiver useless. That's why you never go into the outdoors without a map and compass as well.

MAPPING SOFTWARE

Mapping software programs give you access to digital versions of topographic maps and allow you to overlay routes and waypoints (see "Global Positioning System," page 162) on the map image. The software can calculate your mileage and elevation change, giving you the information you need to more accurately determine your hiking time. You can do all of your route planning right from your computer, then download your waypoints onto your GPS receiver. There are some GPS receivers or PDAs that let you download maps so you can take your electronic map with you. Here are some of the major software titles for U.S.-based mapping:

- Delorme—Topo USA *(www.delorme.com)*
- Garmin—Mapsource United States TOPO *(www.garmin.com)*
- MapTech—Terrain Navigator *(www.maptech.com)*
- National Geographic—Topo! *(maps.nationalgeographic.com)*

MAP DATUM

Any map needs a reference to base all its locations on. Surveyors and map makers identify certain key reference points and base their measurements for all other points off of these. This is referred to as the map datum, and it is printed in the bottom left hand corner of topographic maps. It's important to understand and use the correct map datum, especially when working with maps and a GPS. When you turn on your GPS, it is set to use a default datum, and the satellites will report your position based on that datum. If your GPS reading is not based on the same reference datum as the map, then the point on the map with those coordinates is not the same point as your GPS location. So you should always set your GPS to use the datum of your map. Here are some of the major map data.

- **NAD-1927**—North American Datum 1927
- **NAD-1983**—North American Datum 1983
- **WGS-84**—World Geodetic System 1984

USING A GPS

There are a multitude of GPS receivers on the market. Different models have different control pads, display screens, and user interfaces so it isn't possible to give you detailed instructions on how to use your particular GPS. Read the instruction manual carefully. Instead I'll talk about some basic features and techniques for using a GPS.

Waypoints

A waypoint is just that—a point along your way. Say you find a great campsite or scenic spot you want to remember. You can set it as a waypoint, and your GPS will store the exact location in memory in whatever coordinate format you choose (UTM or latitude-longitude). In the future you can use the GPS to navigate back to that spot. First, you establish your current position (A) and then the GPS can indicate direction and distance from that location back to your scenic spot. Here's where you also need a map and your brain. The GPS is going to show you a direct line between your position (A) and your waypoint (B), but there could be all sorts of obstacles along that direct path, so you may still have more navigating to do.

Routes

A GPS route is a series of waypoints that you connect together to create a travel route. Once the waypoints are entered into the GPS, you can link them together, and as you hike the GPS will show you the direction from one point to the next. Obviously over a full day or multiday hike there would be an almost infinite number of individual waypoints along the route. By selecting your waypoints strategically your GPS can guide you from one waypoint to the next along your route using the "Go To" function.

When you are planning a route at home from a map, you can identify waypoints along the route that you want to go to each day, trails to take, your campsites, etc. Then you can enter these waypoints into your GPS either manually or from computer mapping software. Here's where mapping software can really help. While GPS is a great technology, the typical user interface to work with a GPS receiver is clumsy compared to a computer. Manually entering a large number of waypoints into a GPS is extremely tedious. With mapping software you identify the waypoints directly on the map on the computer screen, mark them, and then download them directly into the GPS. You can also save various routes on your computer all ready to download to your GPS.

Tracks

As you hike, most GPS units keep track of the route you hiked in what is often referred to as a "breadcrumb trail" with a track-back function. When you activate the track-back, it will help you completely retrace your route back to your starting point.

Compass and Altimeter

Some GPS units have an electronic compass that allows you to visually shoot a bearing to a location and then keeps you on course as you travel to that location. Other units include an altimeter that monitors your elevation changes and displays weather-related barometric pressure changes.

BACKCOUNTRY TRAVEL

GROUP SIZE

Hiking with a large group can be fun, but also cumbersome and slow. It seems like every five minutes someone has to stop and adjust something. Here are some considerations to help you determine ideal group size:

- **Traveling as One Large Group** *Pro:* Can be a positive group-building experience. Keeps equipment and human resources close at hand at all times. Minimizes chance of individuals getting lost. Good for groups with less experience. *Con:* Greater visual and noise impact on area and other hikers. Requires adjustment to a common pace (which could also be positive). Can compromise Leave No Trace travel, particularly if the area is pristine, and can have a greater negative impact on other hikers.

- **Splitting Into Smaller Groups** *Pro:* Reduces impact. Each subgroup still has its own equipment and human resources. Allows subgroups to form by common pace. *Con:* May need more equipment, such as first-aid kits, maps, and compasses. Each subgroup needs to have a higher skill level. Need to establish rendezvous points and definitive backup plans in case subgroups get separated or there is an emergency situation. This is one situation where walkie-talkie radios or cell phones can be helpful.

- **Traveling Alone** *Pro:* Unique wilderness experience. Reduces impact. *Con:* Limited resources immediately available if an emergency arises. May need more equipment, such as map and compass for each person. Each person must have solid backcountry skills. Group may get too spread out. Need to establish rendezvous points and times for the group to get back together. Need to have good emergency plan if someone gets lost or injured. *Note:* This is a great way to experience the wilderness, but I can't overemphasize the need for people to have solid skills and be paying attention. It is easy to let your mind wander and miss a critical trail junction. Before traveling solo, review the day's route and identify any special hazards like a river crossing that shouldn't be done solo.

CONSERVING ENERGY

Over a long day of hiking, it's important to pace yourself and conserve energy. Fatigue can significantly increase accident potential (see page 228) and drain you of energy reserves that can be crucial in an emergency. Here are a few things to keep in mind:

- Each day you should examine your route to identify difficult stretches, schedule rest stops, and estimate travel time to spots along the route. (See Chapter 1, "Trip Planning.") On a multiday trip, look at your estimates for previous days—how did your estimates compare with your actual travel time? If there is a significant difference, you may want to rethink your route.
- During the day, be aware of whether or not the group is moving according to schedule, and be prepared to alter the schedule if necessary.
- If possible, try to set your route to avoid difficult ascents or descents at the very end of the day, when everyone is tired.
- Be especially cognizant of the least experienced or least physically fit hikers, and adjust the hike accordingly.
- Make sure that you leave enough energy (and time) to set up a good Leave No Trace camp at the end of the day.

Pace

A basic test for the right hiking pace is if you can hike comfortably all day with 5-minute rest periods every hour. If you find that you need to stop or slow down more often, then you are probably hiking too fast for the trail conditions, your pack weight, or the weather. When you are hiking as a group, you need to find a pace that everyone can handle.

Finding the right pace for a group of varying abilities can be a big challenge. Body metabolism, physical condition, age, experience, size, weight, and pack weight will all have an effect on the speed at which each individual can hike. Try to set a pace at an aerobic level that everyone can maintain over a long period.

"Slinky Effect"

What often happens is that faster (or more hurried) people in a group gravitate to the front and the slower (or less hurried) people end up at the rear. This can be demoralizing to slower persons and difficult because when they catch up to the group, which has stopped to rest, the group takes off again, "dragging" the slower persons along so that they get little or no rest (aka the "slinky effect"). If the group gets too spread out, people in the rear may miss trail junctions or turns and get lost, or people in front may take a wrong turn.

Modifying the Pace

It is generally better to have slower people in the front or in the middle of the group so that the group adjusts its pace to those individuals. You want to have everyone in the group hiking at a comfortable level of exertion. Faster people should be sensitive to the pace of slower people and adjust themselves accordingly. Taking weight from a slower person and giving it to a faster person helps to even out the pace.

Rest Breaks

All groups need to take regular rest breaks in order to hike effectively throughout the day. A good schedule is about 5 minutes of rest for every hour of hiking, which will minimize lactic acid buildup in the body. Lactic acid is the by-product created when your muscles burn glucose while you exercise; it's what causes your muscles to feel sore. When you stop, lactic acid continues to be produced and remains in the system. If you stop for less than 5 minutes, this buildup is not a problem. If you stop for more than 5 minutes, you may begin to feel muscle soreness and tightening. In that case it is best to extend the stop to 20 to 30 minutes to allow the excess lactic acid to be cleared out of your system.

You should encourage everyone to rehydrate at every break. Make sure that *every* break doesn't turn into a long one, or you will need to replan your route for the day. Make regular rest breaks part of your initial trip plan.

Rhythmic Breathing

Just as you need to balance the load in your pack to carry it properly, so you need to balance the load on your cardiovascular system to hike efficiently and without strain. Keeping an even breathing rate and pattern is one of the best ways to monitor and control your energy output while hiking. You should move at a pace that allows you to breathe comfortably and be able to speak. If you are constantly gasping for breath or if you can't keep up a conversation, then you are hiking too fast for your conditioning level.

The best way to control your pace is to synchronize the rhythm of your walking with the rhythm of your breathing. As the cardiovascular load increases from steep terrain, altitude, humid weather, or a heavier pack, your breathing rate will increase. Slow your pace to regain that controlled breathing rate. When the load is reduced, you can pick up your pace again. This is the same principle that all endurance athletes use to maintain high exercise output over a long period of time. Also see "The Rest Step" below.

The Rest Step

The rest step is designed to rest the leg muscles, which are doing most of the work in hiking. As you shift your weight onto each leg, briefly lock the knee. While the knee is locked, your body weight is supported by your skeletal system rather than your leg muscles.

On very steep sections you can rest on the locked leg for several seconds or longer for greater rest. Keep in mind that the rest step should be used in conjunction with rhythmic breathing. Use the rest step to keep your breathing rate easy. If you go up steep sections too fast, your body won't get enough oxygen, and you will switch from aerobic respiration to anaerobic respiration. High-altitude mountaineers take one rest step and hold it for 30 seconds or more in order to keep their breathing rate down. It is usually better to use the rest step and continue to push slowly up a short, steep incline than to stop in the middle and then have to get started again.

HIKING TECHNIQUES
Walking Uphill

When going up a steep incline, stand up straight. This puts you in the best position to recover, should you lose your balance. Try to keep your steps small (aim for a maximum elevation gain of 6 inches/15 centimeters per step). The energy expended on two small steps is less than that for one long one. If possible, avoid going up and down over rocks or logs in stair-step fashion. If an obstacle is large, go around it if possible (but don't step off the trail to avoid obstacles). Remember to use the rest step.

Walking Downhill

Walking downhill is easier aerobically, but it can be the most strenuous part of the journey on your body. Leaning backward with a heavy pack puts the hiker off-balance and places a lot of strain especially on legs, knees, and ankles. If your foot slides forward in your boot, there is increased friction, which can lead to blisters. To help prevent foot movement in the boot, lace your boots up tightly, particularly around the ankle, before a long downhill stretch. On steep downhills, improperly fitted boots can cause "toe jams" or "boot bang" where your toes smash repeatedly into the front of the boot, which can cause blood blisters under the toenail and even toenail loss. Take small, controlled steps. Try to avoid jamming your feet into the ground as you walk—lead with your heel rather than the ball of your foot and keep your knees slightly bent to absorb the shock. (See "Hiking on Snow and Ice," page 173.)

STRETCHES FOR HIKING

Hiking is just like any other sport. It is essential to warm up and to stretch muscles *before* using them to avoid stress and possible injury. Most of us forget to stretch. We are so busy breaking camp and trying to get going that we don't take 5 minutes to warm up. If it's early in the trip, you are probably using muscles that haven't been used for a while, and stretching makes them warm and loose. Stretching at the end of the day will keep your muscles from tightening up. Keep the following in mind whenever you stretch:

- Before stretching in the morning, get your heart rate up by doing several minutes of aerobic activity—jog around camp, jump in place, swing your arms, do push-ups. It is important to have increased blood flow to the muscles *before* you start to stretch.
- Stretch slowly and smoothly; do not bounce or force stretches.
- Breathe in a controlled, slow rhythm. With each exhalation, let yourself move deeper into the stretch.
- Count during each stretch for concentration.

Everyone has his or her own repertoire of stretches. Go with your favorites and learn some from the other people on your trip. I like doing stretch circles in the morning with a group. Go around the circle and let each person share a favorite stretch. Here are a few good stretches for backpacking, from Robert Anderson's excellent book *Stretching*:

- **Squat** (lower back, shins, Achilles tendon)   Squat with your heels 8 to 12 inches apart and toes slightly pointed out. Your knees should be over your toes and arms hanging down in the middle. Hold for 30 seconds. This may be done best on a downhill slant, with something supporting the mid-back, or by holding on to a tree.
- **Quadriceps Stretch**   Stand on one foot. Grasp the ankle of the other leg with your opposite hand and pull the foot up to your butt. You should push forward with your knee so that the thigh stays vertical. Do both legs.
- **Hamstrings**   Sitting with one leg straight out, toes pointing up, and the other leg bent, slowly bend from the hip without curling back. Hold where you feel the stretch in the hamstrings. Do both legs.
- **Calf and Achilles Stretch**   Keep your toes pointing forward with the heel on the ground and the knee straight. Keeping your back straight, lean forward onto a tree and stretch your calf muscles and Achilles tendon. This also feels good with a bent knee. Do both legs.
- **Groin Stretch**   Lie on your back with your knees bent and the soles of your feet together. Let the pull of gravity do the stretching.

OFF-TRAIL HIKING

Off-trail hiking can be one of the most spectacular wilderness experiences, but it must be done thoughtfully and responsibly, maintaining the highest Leave No Trace standards.

GENERAL BACKCOUNTRY CONDITIONS

When hiking off-trail, determine the best Leave No Trace approach for the area—should you spread the group out or hike together? Also, determine if the off-trail area is an open vista where navigational landmarks will be easily seen or if it is dense forest or scrub where constant compass navigation may be necessary.

Consult the map carefully for landmarks to minimize your chances of getting lost. Since the route may zigzag to avoid thicker vegetation, you may need to take repeated compass bearings. Be aware that hiking off-trail can be slow and exhausting. If you are truly bushwhacking through dense forest or scrub, hiking may take more than twice as long as usual. Keep this in mind when estimating your travel time.

Hiking Through Thick Forest or Brush

- Choose routes that offer the least resistance by constantly looking for openings ahead.
- Move slowly and deliberately, at well-spaced intervals.
- Remember that following one another too closely can result in people being slapped in the face by whiplashed branches.
- Part foliage gently with your arms and shoulders instead of plowing through with your body and pack. This helps minimize damage to branches and foliage.
- Minimize loose gear hanging on the outside of your pack, which can get snagged on branches.
- Avoid breaking off tree limbs. Some off-trail hikes are used more than once, and you rob others of the feeling of wilderness if they know people have been there before. Also, broken branches may establish a new trail.

Hiking on Rocky Slopes and Trails

- **Minimize Rockfall Exposure** If there is a significant amount of loose rock on a slope, it is best to spread the group out. A rock kicked loose from above can be a dangerous missile heading toward hikers below. Try to avoid having one person hike directly above another. If the trail goes straight up or switchbacks up the slope, you may not be able to prevent this. With switchbacks you can gather the group at each turn before proceeding.
- **Yell "Rock"** If you kick loose a rock or object of any size, yell "Rock," loudly. Even a small rock can injure hikers below.
- **Duck** If you hear someone directly above you yelling "Rock," try to turn and face downslope so that your pack is between you and the rock. Don't look straight up into the oncoming missile.
- **Take Your Time** If you are ascending or descending a rocky or boulder-filled slope, make sure that the rock you are stepping on is solid before you shift your full body weight onto it. This applies to using trekking poles as well.
- **Vary Your Stride** There is a natural tendency to leap from rock to rock. Usually we take a short "feeler" step with the foot on our dominant side, and then take a longer step with the other leg. Vary the leg you use for takeoff and landing to prevent repetitive stress injuries.

- **Trust Your Boots** When descending steep rock bands you want maximum friction, which you achieve by having the greatest surface contact between your boot soles and the rock. Try to keep your feet flat on the rock and bend heavily at the knees. Keep your center of gravity directly over your feet, with your back reasonably straight. When ascending steep rock bands, the same principle applies. Keep your feet as flat as you can. When the slope angle gets very steep, you won't be able to bend your ankles far enough forward to keep your feet flat. Using a diagonal traverse across the rock face instead of hiking straight up may decrease the angle, or you may have to climb more on the toes of your boots. Still, make sure that your center of gravity is over your feet. If you lean too far forward or too far back, you may fall over.

Scree Slopes

Scree is loose rock debris that accumulates on slopes beneath cliffs and ridges. Think gravel to baseball-size rocks. "Scree-am" is also one of the things you may do when trying to climb up a scree slope. For every step you take up, you often slide at least a half step back down in the loose rubble. This can be really exhausting as well as hazardous since it is easy to kick lose rocks down on those below you. Going up diagonally may be easier than trying to go straight up, and having people behind you in a diagonal line means less chance for rocks to come down from someone directly above you. The best way to deal with scree slopes is the rest step and lots of patience.

Coming down scree slopes can also be difficult. The best technique is to lean back a bit and dig the heels of your boots in and keep your toe fairly level. This is the same technique as the plunge step in soft snow. (See "Hiking on Snow and Ice," page 173.) You need to be careful *not* to lock your knee as you descend or you'll put a lot of strain on the joint. Also, suddenly locking your knee can cause you to pitch-pole forwards. Like plunge-stepping in snow, keep your speed controlled. If you start going too fast, stop and regain control before you end up falling head over heels. Be careful of suddenly hitting solid ground. If your body is "expecting" some of its impact to be absorbed by the loose scree and you hit solid rock, it's going to transfer a lot a stress to your joints and can throw you off balance.

Talus Slopes

Talus slopes are similar to scree slopes, only the size of the rocks is much larger. We are talking small boulders. With talus slopes you are going to have to do lots of rock hopping. The big danger is shifting your weight onto an unstable rock that then moves underneath you. Falls can be more hazardous on talus slopes than on scree slopes. Take your time and stay balanced.

HIKING ON SNOW AND ICE

In many mountain areas there are seasonal or permanent snowfields and glaciers. If you are traveling to these areas, make sure you have the proper equipment and training to deal with hazards like avalanches, crevasses, and ice fall. A full explanation of hiking on snow and ice is beyond the scope of this book. Read a book like *Mountaineering: The Freedom of the Hills* by The Mountaineers and get training in snow and ice techniques. Here are a few basic guidelines:

- North-facing slopes get less sun and stay harder longer during the day. They also tend to have snow later in the season. South-facing slopes melt out sooner. (Reverse these trends in the Southern Hemisphere.) Based on where you are going, the terrain, the extent of snow cover, and the time of day, one slope may be better than another to hike on.
- It's often best to climb in the early hours of the day before the sun has warmed the slopes too much, or you may find yourself up to your waist in soft, wet snow. Also, as the slopes get warmer, the snow softens and the risk of rockfall and icefall increases.
- Avalanches aren't just a winter phenomenon. Warm conditions can often cause wet snow slides that can be extremely dangerous. Check with local land managers about avalanche hazard before you go. When you are on the trail, look for signs of slide activity. It's best to stay off slopes from 30 to 45 degrees when avalanche danger is high.
- The steeper the climb or harder the snow or ice, the greater your chance for a fall. An ice axe and skill in self-arrest are essential for steeper areas or where the consequences of a fall are considerable (such as above crevasses).
- On steep slopes, it may be too slippery to walk up flat-footed. If the snow is soft enough, you can kick steps into the snow. Kicking steps can be tiring, so make it as efficient as you can. Bend your lower leg at the knee and lift your heel to near 90 degrees. Let your foot drop, and the weight of gravity will do some of the work of driving the toe of your boot into the snow. Test the step with some pressure before committing all your weight to it. This also compresses the step into a better platform.

You will need to kick steps that are usable by everyone in the group, so take short steps. Periodically rotate the lead. The lead person stops, kicks steps to the side, and moves out of the way. The second person takes the lead, and the previous leader falls in at the end of the group for a well-earned rest. If the snow is hard you may have to cut steps with your ice axe or use crampons. This is an environment where heavier boots may be necessary.

- On steep snow descents, when the snow is relatively soft, you can use the plunge step. Land heel first on an extended leg (but don't lock your knee), and let your body weight drive the heel down into the soft snow. With your foot at the correct angle you create a platform just like when you kick steps going up. When you get into a rhythm, you can descend very quickly. Always keep your speed controlled. Another descent method is glissading, basically "skiing" downhill on your boots. This takes balance and practice, so always evaluate the runout below you for hazards before you try it. In both cases, you should have an ice axe and be prepared to self-arrest if you lose control.

CROSSING RIVERS

River and stream crossings can be one of the most potentially uncontrollable and dangerous situations during your trip. More backpackers are killed in stream crossings than die from snakebites. Great care must be given to planning and executing any swiftwater crossing. The two biggest factors affecting the potential danger of a crossing are the speed of the current and the depth of the river, but there are a number of other potential hazards:

- **Cold Water** can lead to hypothermia. (See "Immersion Hypothermia," page 337.)
- **Foot Entrapment** occurs when a foot is caught on the river bottom and the person is pushed over by the force of the current. Often the force of the current keeps the person from being able to stand up and the individual is held under water—a potential drowning situation.
- **Strainers** are submerged branches that will hold a person swept against them—another potential drowning situation.
- **Undercut Banks and Rocks** are also places where you can be trapped by fast water—another potential drowning situation.
- **Eddies** are areas of slower moving water found behind obstacles like boulders or on the inside of a bevel.
- **Chutes** are places where the river narrows and the water speed increases. Sometimes waves form in a chute.

Making Judgments about River Crossings

You must examine the river carefully to determine what potential hazards exist in crossing. Base your decision whether to cross on a careful examination of the river, possible crossing sites, and the strengths and abilities of the people in the group. Don't let a desire to continue on a particular route push you to make a crossing that is too hazardous. Decide whether to cross, where to cross, and how to cross. Here are questions you should ask about any river crossing:

- How deep is the water?
- How fast is it moving?
- What is the water temperature?
- Are there hazards downstream?
- Will all members of this group be able to safely negotiate this crossing? Are there non-swimmers?

Red Flags for River Crossings

If you see any of these conditions, then the crossing is potentially dangerous and you should seriously consider not crossing at that location (look for another spot or don't cross at all):

- The river is moving very quickly.
- The river is in flood (often muddy brown).
- You can't determine the water depth.
- The river level is higher than your knees and moving very swiftly.
- You can hear the sound of boulders rolling in the river.
- The river has large floating logs and obstructions that could hit hikers.
- The water is extremely cold.
- There is a significant hazard downstream, near the crossing site (i.e., strainer, waterfall).

Choosing a Site to Cross

Hike up and down along the river to find the safest place to cross. Pick a shallow stretch of water free from obstructions (boulders, partially submerged logs) and with gradual banks to facilitate easy entry and exit. Try to avoid crossing at a bend in the river because the water is usually deeper and faster on the outside of the bend, and the outside bank may be steep and difficult to climb. Outside bends are also often undercut by the current and are a prime location for strainers. The stretch of water *below* the crossing point should be long and shallow (a pool to drift into safely in case of mishap).

Crossing Locations

1. **Bad**—Riffles indicate faster water and may be difficult to cross. Above a fastwater chute, losing footing could mean getting flushed down the chute.
2. **Bad**—Above an outside bend. Deepest/fastest water on the outside.

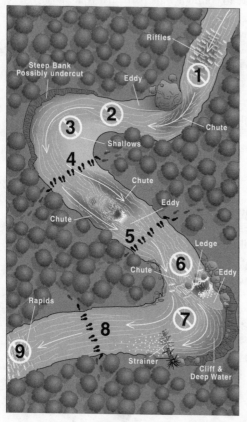

River Features

Outside bends may have steep banks and could be undercut—potential entrapment hazard.

3. **Bad**—Shallows make part of crossing easy but you still have deep water at the end of the bend and a steep bank.
4. **Good**—Below the bend, water is slowing down.
5. **Good**—Cross and take advantage of the slower water in the eddy behind the boulder.
6. **Bad**—Above a steep ledge with rapids.
7. **Bad**—Above an outside bend with a strainer—potential entrapment hazard.
8. **Good**—River is wider also probably shallower with slower water. Diagonal path across means that hikers tend to be pushed down and over to the opposite bank.
9. **Bad**—Rapids.

Important Crossing Considerations

- Know the route ahead of time and identify possible hazardous crossings. Are there alternate routes or bridges?
- How will weather impact your crossings? Is there a better time of day to cross?
- Keep your boots on (or change into sneakers or sandals, if available). They protect your feet and provide ankle support. You might take your

socks off to keep them dry, but if you have multiple crossings to do this may be too time consuming.

- Keep your pack on, but *undo the hip belt and sternum strap* so that you can jettison the pack quickly if necessary.
- Move only one foot at a time while making sure that the other foot is firmly placed, and shuffle along rather than taking big steps. Keep moving slowly. Don't cross your legs. Feel the bottom before you commit your weight to the foot (to feel and avoid potholes).
- Use a hiking stick or trekking pole as a "third leg," especially on the upstream side; walking sticks can be useful to test for dropoffs and rocks.
- Always *face upstream* while crossing solo. *If you face downstream, the force of the water could cause your legs to buckle underneath you.*
- If you feel your foot begin to get caught, fall over into the water to pull the foot out to avoid entrapment. Trying to stand may "set" the foot into the entrapment and place you at greater risk.
- If you lose your footing and are swept away, shrug out of your shoulder straps and jettison your pack. Float downstream on your back, feet first with toes on the surface. This position prevents foot entrapment. Use your legs as shock absorbers to fend off river obstacles. Actively swim to the shoreline. Don't let yourself be swept against logs, as you might be pinned against them. If you can't avoid being swept onto a river obstacle, try to clamber up onto it so that your head remains above water.
- Be extremely careful when walking on logs or boulder hopping. These places are likely to be slippery, and falls resulting in injuries are common.
- If you have a foam sleeping pad, tie it to the top of your pack. Having the pad tied on at the bottom can create too much buoyancy lifting your feet off the bottom.
- Avoid baggy pants, which offer greater resistance to the water and increase your chances of being pulled over.
- In braided rivers (rivers with multiple channels), look beyond the first crossing and make sure that you have a reasonable idea of how to continue. Sometimes one crossing leads you to one that is impassable and you have to return and try another option.
- In any deep-river crossing, position someone below the crossing point as a safety backup. Remember the principles of basic lifesaving—reach for the person, throw a line or floating object, and go in after her only as a last resort.

Crossing with a Rope

One end of a rope is securely anchored near the shoreline 5 to 6 feet (1.5 to 1.8 meters) above the river at a good crossing location. The other end is held

🍁 TRICKS OF THE TRAIL

How Deep Is Too Deep, How Fast Is Too Fast? There is no easy answer to this question, since depth and current speed interact so much. Generally any time moving water is higher than the shortest person's thighs, there can be considerable risk. You can test the speed of the current by tossing a stick in the water and trying to walk along the bank to keep pace with it. If you can't keep up, the speed is fast.

by a strong member of the group. The first person to cross holds the end of the rope above the water as she crosses; *never tie into a rope.* The person crossing and the one on the shore should both try to keep the rope up out of the water to prevent drag. Upon reaching the other side, the crossing person anchors the free end to trees or rocks 5 to 6 feet (1.5 to 1.8 meters) above the river, creating a fixed rope across the river. Group members, standing on the downstream side of the rope, and facing upstream, use the rope as a hand line and shuffle across the river. The last person (also a strong group member) unties that end of the rope and crosses as the first person. It is best to have the first and last person go across without a pack.

Crossing with a Rope

Crossing Without a Rope

There are a variety of methods for crossing a stream without a rope.

In the illustration below, the current is coming from the left, and people are moving across the river (toward the top of the page).

Triangle Method (A) With three people, you can create a "triangle of support." Each person faces inward and links arms at the shoulders, with his or her feet spread apart. The person who is downstream stays stationary while the other two rotate around that person. Then a new person becomes the downstream person, and the triangle rotation continues.

Crossing Without a Rope

Line Astern Method (B)   Form a line with three or more people extending downstream. The line should face upstream, standing one behind the other, and give one another support by hanging on to one another's waists. The upstream person moves sideways first and stops, then number two, and so forth. The first person creates a water break for the others to move into. If the current is extremely strong, the group moves simultaneously. A stick or trekking pole is very useful for the first person to help with balance, since she may have to lean upstream against the current.

Paired Crossing Method (C)   Two people face each other and link arms, with the heavier person downstream. The upstream person serves as a "water break," and the downstream person as support. The upstream person moves sideways first, supported by the downstream person, and then stops. Then the downstream person moves sideways into the "water break," or eddy created by the upstream person, and the cycle continues across the river.

Line Abreast Method   Have the whole group form a line facing the opposite bank, then move across together. There are two great methods I learned in New Zealand from the Mountain Safety Council. The first is the "clothing grab." Reach behind the back of the person on either side and grab a handful of clothing at the person's waist, then walk across the river together. You can also grab the person's pack hip belt or bottom of the shoulder strap. The advantage of these methods is that if one person loses her balance or even lets go, the person next to her can still hold her in place.

CROSSING ROADS

When we go to the backcountry, we do so to escape civilization, so we may forget that road crossings (even major interstate highways or railroad crossings) can be part of the trip route. This is especially true of long corridor trails like the Appalachian Trail and the Pacific Crest Trail. Like a river crossing, a road crossing can be hazardous, especially for a large group. Here are some things to think about:

- **Know Your Route**   Know when and where you will be required to cross a road. When will road crossings occur—midday or dusk? Also, have an idea what type of road you will be crossing. Is it a backcountry road, rarely traveled, or a busy interstate?
- **Assess the Situation**   Assess the road for the safest place to cross. You should have clear visibility down the road in both directions. If the crossing spot does not have such visibility, you may want to move to another crossing spot. If this presents a problem, locate a site that has good visibility and post a signal person there. Like a school crossing guard, the signal person lets you know when it is clear to cross. Signalers should be visible to cars, but off the road.
- **Know Your Signals**   All trip members must be clear on what signals are used to indicate safe crossing. Similar to signals used by American Whitewater for paddlers, hikers use both arms overhead to mean continue, and two arms out horizontally and waving to mean "Stop, do not cross."

Walking Along Roads

Some trail routes require you to hike along a road, perhaps for several miles, before returning to the forest. This should be evident from your trip plan, but the exact nature of the road may not be. Assess the situation for the safest place to walk. Stay well off the road on the shoulder, if there is one. If there is a safer walking area on the other side of the road, you may decide to cross and walk there. If there is no shoulder on either side of the road, it is best to walk single file on the side of the road facing oncoming traffic. Be very careful at curves, where drivers may not be able to see you.

TRAVELING IN BEAR COUNTRY

Bears are one of the great symbols of wilderness. They are majestic creatures that deserve our respect and protection. Left alone, bears generally do not pose a threat to people. Most of the problems that arise in bear-human interactions are the result of bears becoming habituated to our presence in their environment and/or becoming dependent on human food.

When traveling in bear country, there are a number of special precautions that need to be taken. The first is to be aware of the type of bear(s) you may encounter, since your behavior in a bear encounter depends on the species of bear. There are three species of bears in the United States and Canada that you might encounter: the black bear, the grizzly or brown bear, and, in northern Canada and Alaska, the polar bear.

Black Bears

Black bears are 5 to 6 feet long (152 to 183 centimeters) and weigh 200 to 500+ pounds (90 to 227+ kilograms). The color varies from black in the East to a cinnamon or black in the West. The face has a straight profile and is always brown. There is usually a small patch of white on the breast. Black bears are most active at dawn and dusk but will move about during the day. They are primarily solitary animals except when the mother is raising her cubs. She can be quite aggressive if the cubs are threatened. The black bear has poor eyesight, a fair sense of hearing, and a keen sense of smell.

Almost all black bears (except those in the Deep South) will hibernate for two to four months each winter. During this period they can be aroused quite easily and may leave the den for a few hours at a time. Bears coming out of hibernation in the spring can be unpredictable. Black bears are both omnivorous and opportunistic. They eat fruit, berries, insects, small mammals, and "people food." Black bears are quite intelligent, and quickly learn that a backcountry campsite not only means an easy meal but that a bunch of hikers banging pots aren't really a threat. This is a typical scenario that brings bears into close proximity with backcountry travelers.

Grizzly Bears

Grizzly bears are 6 to 7 feet long (180 to 213 centimeters) and weigh from 325 to 850 pounds (146 to 382 kilograms). Color ranges from yellowish to dark brown or nearly black with whitish color on the tips of hairs especially on the back, giving it a frosted appearance. The face is concave, and there is a pronounced hump at the shoulder.

Grizzlies inhabit only a small region in the continental United States and are prevalent in Alaska and portions of Canada. Their diet and feeding habits are similar to the black bear and also includes salmon. They are far more aggressive than black bears and have been known to attack and, in some rare cases, kill humans. As a result, grizzly bears can be significantly more dangerous than black bears. If you are traveling in grizzly country, talk with area land managers about special precautions and any restricted areas (for more information on bears and bear behavior, see the Bibliography).

BEAR PRECAUTIONS

- Avoid contact with bears.
- In grizzly country, it is best to travel in groups of three or more.
- Make noise when traveling in bear country to alert a bear that you are coming so it can leave.
- If a bear enters your campsite, you *might* deter it by banging pots or making loud noises. You may also try assembling the group as a large mass, swaying your arms, and making noise. Since bears have poor eyesight, they often shy away from an apparent foe that is larger than they are. If these measures fail, move well away from the bear. *Note:* If the bear is habituated to humans, almost nothing you can do will drive it away if it is hungry.
- Keep human food away from bears and other animals. This is part of good LNT practice (see Chapter 5, "Leave No Trace Hiking and Camping," and "How to Bearproof Your Camp," page 184). Keep a clean camp, and make sure cooking utensils are properly cleaned and packed away. Clean up and hang all excess or spilled food and garbage.
- Set up your cooking area downwind of your sleeping area so as not to attract a hungry bear through your camp.
- Be aware that bears and other animals tend to be more daring in areas people frequent. They become accustomed to finding food scraps left in camps by careless hikers. In particularly lean seasons, bears will seek meals wherever they can find them. Keeping a clean Leave No Trace camp helps prevent bears from becoming habituated to humans.
- In general, bears become a problem when they feel threatened (e.g., when they are cornered) or when they are traveling with their young. If you notice a cub traveling alone or with its mother, be especially cautious. Withdraw immediately.

BEAR ENCOUNTERS

If a bear charges or approaches you in an aggressive manner, it is most probably because the bear feels that you are a threat. Your actions should be designed to minimize that threat. Bear behavior is extremely complex and cannot be covered completely in this manual; if traveling in bear country, you should read a more detailed book, such as Gary Brown's *Safe Travel in Bear Country*. Here are the important points that bear experts Gary Brown and Dr. Stephen Herrero recommend:

What to Do if Approached by a Bear

Your goal is to convince the bear that you are not a threat.

- Remain calm.
- Avoid abrupt movements.
- If possible, back away slowly, still facing the bear. Stop if this appears to further agitate the bear.
- Speak to the bear in a quiet, monotone voice.
- Do *not* look directly into the bear's eyes. This is seen as a challenge and may provoke the bear.
- Do *not* run away.

What to Do if Charged by a Bear

- In most cases charges are actually a bluff and the bear will break off the charge before reaching you.
- Stand your ground. Do not run.
- If you have pepper spray, have it out and ready to use. Only use it when the bear is within 10 to 15 feet (3 to 4.5 meters). Spray directly in the bear's eyes, nose, and mouth.

What to Do if Attacked by a Bear

- If you are wearing a pack, keep it on. It may protect you.
- Lie on your stomach facing the ground. Clasp your hands behind your neck with your arms tucked close to your head to protect your head and face.
- Remain silent and motionless, even if the bear bites or claws you. If, despite being passive, the bear continues to maul you, fight back as a last resort. You should definitely fight back against a black bear. On those extremely rare occasions where the bear is attacking you to eat you, your only choice is to try and fight back.
- If the bear swats you, roll with the blow and return to your facedown position.

Bear-Attack Position

- Keep motionless and silent for at least 20 minutes or longer after the bear has left. Bears may move off and watch a victim for an hour, returning if they see movement.

🍁 TRICKS OF THE TRAIL

Pepper Spray There are a number of products on the market that spray a cayenne pepper derivative. Research indicates that such sprays are effective in deterring bears. In his book *Safe Travel in Bear Country*, Gary Brown points out that such devices have limited range (15 to 24 feet/5 to 8 meters) and must be sprayed into the sensitive mucous membranes of the bear (nose, mouth, and eyes). Therefore, it can be used only as a last resort when a bear is almost on top of you.

There are two types of pepper spray: oil-based and water-based. The oil-based sprays tend to hang in the air longer, making them more effective. In the event that you have to use it, you will have to steel yourself to wait until the very last minute and get it right in the bear's face. Shooting it off too early would be ineffective. Since bluff attacks are more common than real attacks, bears may rush at you only to veer off at the last moment. Save the pepper spray for the bear who isn't stopping.

HOW TO BEARPROOF YOUR CAMP

The goal of bearproofing your camp is to minimize odors that might attract bears and to set up safe storage areas for food and garbage away from your sleeping area and out of reach of bears and other critters. A lot of times people think that this is a big hassle and is unnecessary. You should look at this as part of Leave No Trace and protecting wildlife. There is a saying that "A fed bear is a dead bear." Bears that learn to associate easy food with humans become more and more habituated to people. Sometimes these bears become so problematic that they must be relocated or, in extreme cases, they may have to be killed.

The best way to bearproof your camp is to start with a camp setup that facilitates these goals. In *Safe Travel in Bear Country*, Gary Brown describes a basic camp setup where the sleeping area is upwind of the kitchen and food areas, and all three are at least 300 feet (100 meters) apart.

Bear bagging is a general term used for hanging your food. There are lots of other animals (raccoons, opossums, coyotes, chipmunks, and skunks) that will go after human food. In some cases, you may be camped in locations where there are no bears but still need to hang your food at night. Talk with local land managers about what the local critter population is and what precautions you should take. In areas with significant bear problems, there may be permanent food-hanging stands or containers provided by the park.

Hang up all food (except unopened canned food), pots, pans, cups, bowls, utensils, toothpaste, and garbage. On one backpacking trip in Shenandoah National Park, we diligently hung everything up. Around midnight a black bear came into camp and trotted off with someone's pack—he had left a tube of toothpaste in one of the outer pockets. Be sure your camp is clean of food scraps that may attract a bear. Suspend food and garbage in duffel bags, stuff sacks, or sealed plastic bags at least 16 feet (5 meters) above the ground and at least 8 feet (2.4 meters) from the tree trunk. The bags should hang from a point where the tree can still support them but bears and other critters will have difficulty reaching them.

Be creative and sensible with your techniques for hanging food. A 75-foot (23-meter) rope (at least ¼ inch thick or 6 millimeters), two carabiners, and stuff sacks are helpful. When using stuff sacks, don't hang the sack directly from the drawstring. Instead, wrap a rope around the neck of the sack and tie it, leaving a loop through which to clip a carabiner, which alleviates the stress on the drawcord by distributing the weight to the entire sack. Otherwise, the stuff sack is likely to rip and spill its contents onto the ground. Below are several useful methods of bear bagging. One caveat: Bears are very smart! They have figured out how to "beat" lots of these techniques.

Counterbalance Method

1. Find a tree with a live branch. The branch should be at least 15 feet (5 meters) from the ground with no object below the branch that could support a bear's weight. The point at which you will toss the rope over the branch should be at least 10 feet (3 meters) from the tree. The branch should be at least 4 inches in diameter (10 centimeters) at the tree and at least 1 inch in diameter (3 centimeters) at the rope point (see illustration). (Be aware that no system is foolproof—a bear or other animal might still be able to climb out onto the branch and raid your food supply.)

2. Separate your food and other items into two bags of roughly equal weight.

3. Throw the rope over the branch. Attach one end of the rope to one of the bags.

4. Raise the bag as high as you can up to the branch.

5. Attach the other bag to the rope as high up on the rope as you can. Leave a loop of rope at the bag for retrieval.

6. Push the second bag up to the level of the other bag with a long stick.

7. To retrieve the bags, hook the loop of rope with the stick and pull it down. Remove the bag and then lower the first bag.

Counter-Balance Method

2:1 Pulley System

This simple pulley system gives you added mechanical advantage to haul heavy loads up above critter level. Still, some bears are smart enough to know that by cutting the diagonal rope tied to the tree, they can bring down the food bag.

1. Find a tree with a live branch with the same dimensions as already described.
2. Throw the rope over the branch. Pull about two-thirds of the rope over the branch. The shorter side of the rope is End A. The longer side of the rope is End B.
3. Tie off rope End A to a tree.
4. Make a trucker's hitch (see page 192) on End B about 6 feet (2 meters) from the ground and clip Carabiner 1 into the bight of the trucker's hitch.

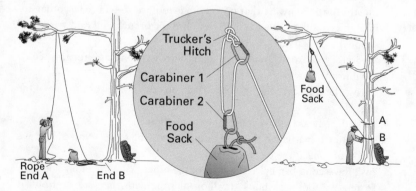

2:1 Pulley System

(If you don't use a trucker's hitch, you'll probably never get the rope loop at Carabiner 1 untied.)

5. Tie a separate piece of strong rope around the top of the food bag to clip a carabiner into.
6. Feed the running end of rope End B through Carabiner 2 and then back through Carabiner 1.
7. Attach the food bag to Carabiner 2 and pull on the free end (B) to haul the bag as high up as possible. Tie off rope End B.
8. To retrieve the bag, untie rope End B and lower the bag to the ground.

Two-Tree System

1. Find two trees with live branches with the same dimensions as already described.
2. Rig a horizontal line between the two trees at least 15 feet (5 meters) off the ground. The best way to do this is to have the rope go over a branch right where it joins the tree. The rope then runs down the side of the tree where it is tied off at Point A. Do the same on the other side, tying it off at Point B. An alternative is to tie the ends off to some other trees.
3. Throw a second rope over the horizontal rope. Attach one end of the rope to one of the bags.
4. Hoist the food bag into the air so that it is a least 12 feet (5 meters) off the ground.
5. Tie off the second rope to an adjacent tree at Point C. This can be to one of the horizontal line trees or a third tree.
6. To retrieve the bag, untie the second rope and then lower the bag. Some bears are smart enough to know that cutting the line at Point C will cause the food bag to fall.

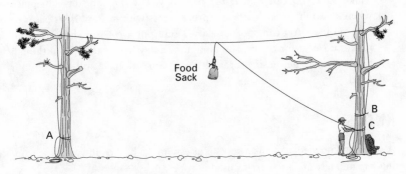

Food
Sack

A

B
C

Two-Tree System

Bear Canisters

If you are going to be traveling in a treeless area where bears are present, you will need to take additional precautions. In some cases, there may be bear boxes or bear poles to hang your food in. If not, you may want to store your food in bearproof plastic canisters on the ground. Bears have an incredible sense of smell, so they will still be able to find the canister but not open it. Don't put the canister right next to your tent! Have it away from your sleeping area.

There are a number of canisters that have proven effective, including the Bear Vault *(www.bearvault.com)*, the Bear Keg *(www.counterassault.com)*, and the Backpacker's Cache *(www.backpackerscache.com)*. Some land managers now require bear canisters in certain areas and have certain approved models. The major drawback in using a canister is weight—particularly if one person has to carry the whole container with food. Here are some suggestions for using a bear canister:

- If necessary for space, you can leave your first day's food out of the canister since you'll use it up before the end of the first day (this leaves you more room). However, keep in mind that food odors might be on your pack that will make the pack just as interesting for the bear as the canister.
- Repack the food to remove extraneous packaging. Use plastic bags when feasible and force the air out of the bags. Pack carefully. Careful packing will allow you to fit more.
- Remember to leave room in the canister for nonfood items like toothpaste and garbage that will be attractants. Your "garbage in" should be less than your "food out," so the canister should handle both as the trip progresses.
- Make sure you can find it the next day. Put the canister someplace where it won't go far if a bear starts to mess with it. Put bright paint or tape on it so you can spot it easily. Don't put a rope leash on it. That makes it easier for the bear to haul it far away from camp. Even though the bear can't get in, if it drags it away you will have still lost all your food.

KNOTS

A working knowledge of basic knots is as essential a backcountry skill as reading a map. Here are a few terms used in rope work:

- Working end—the end of the rope that is the free end, commonly called the end.
- Standing end—the fastened part of the rope; may simply be called the line or the rope.
- Bight—a simple turn of rope that does not cross itself.
- Loop—a turn of rope that does cross itself.
- Half-hitch—a loop that runs around a shaft or another piece of rope, so as to lock itself.

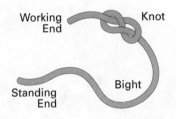

Rope and Knot Terminology

TWO HALF-HITCHES

This knot is useful for securing a rope back to itself after wrapping it around an object (e.g., a tree).

1. Take the running end around the object and then around itself and back through to create a half-hitch.
2. Repeat the loop to add a second half-hitch. You can pull a loop of rope through and leave the running end out to create a slippery half-hitch (also known as a slip knot). One tug on the running end will pull out the hitch.

Half-Hitch   **Two Half-Hitches**   **Slippery Half-Hitch**

BOWLINE

This knot is useful for tying one end of a line to something (e.g., one end of a tarp line to a tree).

1. Form a loop of rope some distance from the end of the rope.
2. Feed the running end through the loop, back around the standing part of the rope, and back through the loop.
3. To tighten, pull the running end and the standing part. Follow the old adage: "The rabbit comes out of the hole, around the tree, and back into the hole."

Bowline

TAUTLINE HITCH

This is a knot that slides and "locks" on a rope. It is excellent for a tarp line because you can adjust the tension of the rope. It can be used from one rope to itself or one rope to another.

1. Wrap the running end of the rope around the standing end with two complete wraps (additional wraps create greater friction).
2. From the lowermost wrap, bring the running end over itself, "bridging"

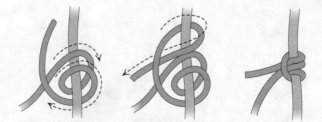

Tautline Hitch

the other wraps, back around the standing end, and then cinch the knot down.

3. When cinched, friction keeps the knot from sliding on the standing end. By loosening the "bridge," you can slide the knot up or down and reset it.

SQUARE KNOT

This knot is used for tying the ends of two ropes together, such as when you need to lengthen a tarpline. It should *not* be used if the ropes are going to be under great strain (e.g., climbing, rescue work).

1. With two ends of rope, one in each hand, lay the left side over the right side.
2. Wrap the right side over the left side.
3. Lay the right side over the left side and wrap the left side over the right side.
4. Cinch the knot down. It should be two loops of rope, "strangling" each other. If the loops aren't "strangling each other," then you have tied a granny knot, which is much harder to release after a load. The basic mnemonic is "right over left, left over right."

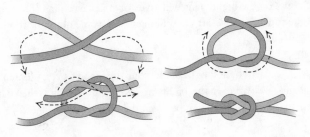

Square Knot

SHEET BEND

This knot is used to connect two different types (diameters) of rope. It should *not* be used if the ropes are going to be under great strain.

1. Create a bight in one rope. Feed the running end of the other rope through the center of the bight.
2. Bring the standing end back around behind the bight and back through the center, underneath itself.
3. Cinch the knot down by pulling on both ropes.

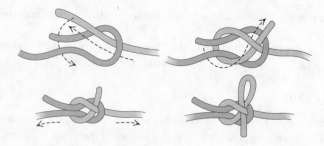

Sheet Bend

TRUCKER'S HITCH

This is useful for temporarily securing loads. It can be cinched tight and yet released easily.

1. Create a loop of rope.
2. Pull a bight of rope from the running end up through the loop.
3. Wrap the running end around an object and feed it back up through the bight you created.
4. Pull down on the bight. This will give you a 2:1 mechanical advantage to pull the rope tight. Tie off the running end to some object or to itself with two half-hitches.

Note: There will be some stretch to your rope, and as you pull tension the bight will move down. Set the bight far enough away that when you have pulled tension, there is still a gap between the bight and the object.

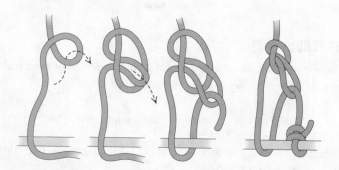

Trucker's Hitch

CHAPTER 7
Weather and Nature

WEATHER

We go to the wilderness in order to interact with the natural world. In spite of all our planning and equipment, nature ultimately sets the pace. That's why I find the backcountry such a rejuvenating experience—the longer I am there, the more I see and hear and experience. This chapter is designed to help you make better connections with the natural world—everything from understanding weather to appreciating trees and wildlife.

CLIMATE AND SEASON

Weather is a major part of the backcountry experience. Train yourself to be sensitive to weather. Watch those afternoon cumulus clouds build over the ridge on a hot, humid summer day, and think about what they might bring and where you should be if it comes. With practice, you'll be able to predict fairly well what tomorrow's and even the next day's weather will be. Before heading out on a trip you should know something about the typical weather patterns and expected temperatures.

TEMPERATURE RANGES AND TYPICAL WEATHER PATTERNS

In the temperate climate of the United States and Canada, the general temperature range from daytime low to daytime high is typically 20° to 40°F (11° to 22°C), assuming no new weather systems move in. This range increases in particular climates like deserts or at high altitudes, where the sun's heat has a greater impact on raising temperatures during the day. Coastal areas typically show milder weather due to the moderating effect of large bodies of water. Large bodies of water also can impact weather like the "lake effect snow" areas east of the Great Lakes in the United States, where in the wintertime cold air from Canada picks up moisture over the Great Lakes and dumps snow on places like Buffalo, New York. Checking regional temperature averages and weather patterns can be helpful when planning your trip. (See Chapter 1, "Trip Planning.") Charts showing average temperature highs and lows are available on the Web at sites like *www.weather.com*.

Lots of other factors play a role in temperature ranges. Cloud cover at night holds in heat minimizing the daily temperature swings while clear nights allow heat to escape and are cooler. As you go up in altitude from sea level, the temperature drops about 3.5°F (2°C) for each 1,000 feet. Let's say you live in Boulder, Colorado, at 5,344 feet (1,629 meters). It's a nice summer day in July at 80°F (26°C). At the summit of Long's Peak (14,255 feet/4,345 meters), the temperature would be 50°F (10°C). Add a potential 30°F (16°C) temperature drop at night and it can be below freezing on the summit in mid-summer.

WIND

Major weather systems are caused by the interaction of air masses. In the continental United States, weather generally travels from west to east at about 500 miles (804 kilometers) a day, moved by the prevailing westerly winds. Local winds, caused by the differential effects of heating, are described below.

MOUNTAIN WINDS

- **Valley Breezes**   These occur during the daytime. The mountains act like a heat sink and absorb solar energy during the day. As a result, the mountains heat up more quickly than the valley. Air above the mountains is heated and rises, and is replaced by cooler air flowing up from the valley.
- **Mountain Breezes**   These occur at night. The mountains act like the fins of a radiator giving off heat after the sun goes down, so they cool faster than the valley. Air along the mountains cools and flows down into the valley, creating mountain breezes. At the same time, the valley gives off heat more slowly and the air in the valley slowly rises, replaced by the cooler mountain air.

COASTAL WINDS

- **Sea Breezes**   During the day, the land warms faster than the ocean, so the air over the land heats up and rises while cooler (often moist) air from the water flows in to shore.
- **Land Breezes**   At night the land loses heat more quickly than the water. The warmer air over the water continues to rise and is replaced by cooler air blowing from the shore.

CHANGES IN WIND DIRECTION

Changes in wind direction are an important clue to incoming weather.

- **Backing wind**   When the wind direction changes *against* the path of the sun—goes from west to east moving counterclockwise—this indicates a low-pressure system and potentially bad weather. I remember this by saying, "I'd better *back up* if the wind is *backing* because bad weather may be on the way."

- **Veering wind** When the wind direction changes *to* the path of the sun—goes from east to west moving clockwise—this indicates a high-pressure system, typically associated with clear weather.

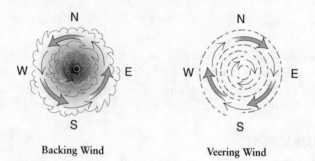

Backing Wind   Veering Wind

CLOUDS

Recognizing different cloud types is an important part of predicting incoming weather. Parcels of air contain moisture in the form of water vapor. The amount of water vapor in the air is known as the *relative humidity,* which is expressed as a percentage of the total amount of water a particular temperature of air can hold. Cooler air can hold less water than warmer air, so as a given amount of air is cooled, the relative humidity increases. When the relative humidity of any parcel of air reaches 100 percent (the saturation point), clouds will form. Clouds are classified into two major categories based on how they are formed:

- **Cumulus clouds** The typical "puffy" cloud, formed as small areas of rising air cool to the saturation point.
- **Stratus clouds** Clouds in sheets or layers, formed when a large layer of air is cooled to the saturation point.

SPECIFIC CLOUD TYPES

Clouds are also classified by their altitude. There are two basic altitude prefixes: *cirro,* or "high"; and *alto,* or "middle." The other prefix is *nimbo,* or "rain." These prefixes are combined with the basic cloud categories—cumulus or stratus—to describe the major types of clouds.

High Clouds—above 25,000 Feet (7,600 Meters)

- Cirrus—"mare's tails"; thin, whispy clouds that look like a horse's tail
- Cirrocumulus—sheets or layers of small globular clouds

- Cirrostratus—thin sheets; look like fine veils, give halos around the sun and moon

Middle Clouds—above 10,000 Feet (3,000 Meters)

- Altostratus—dense veils or sheets of gray or blue; sun or moon seen as through frosted glass
- Altocumulus—patches or layers of puffy, roll-like clouds, gray or whitish

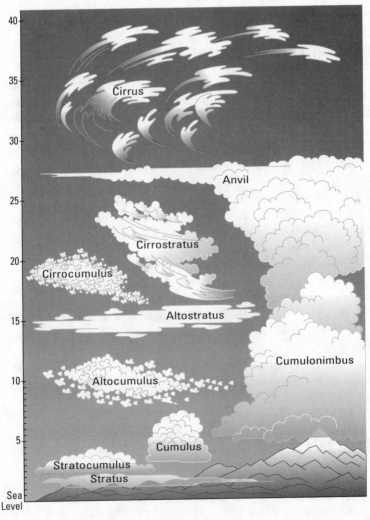

Clouds

Low Clouds—up to 6,500 Feet (1,990 Meters)

- Stratus—low uniform sheet, like fog with the base above the ground
- Nimbostratus—dark gray rain cloud
- Stratocumulus—irregular masses of clouds spread out in a rolling or puffy layer

Towering Clouds—up to 75,000 Feet (22,800 Meters)

- Cumulus—puffy, shapes change
- Cumulonimbus—thunderhead

BAROMETRIC PRESSURE

Barometric pressure is the pressure created by the weight of the atmosphere at any given point on the earth's surface. The pressure is greatest at sea level and decreases with altitude, so as you ascend to higher altitudes, the barometric pressure continues to decrease. At high altitudes, although the *percentage* of the gases is the same, the actual amount of gases in the air is less than at sea level. At 10,000 feet (3,658 meters), for example, the percentage of oxygen in the air is still the same as at sea level (21 percent), but the *number* of oxygen molecules is approximately 70 percent of what it is at sea level. This means that for every breath you take, you are getting only 70 percent of the oxygen that you'd get at sea level. This is the major cause of high-altitude illnesses. (See "Altitude Illnesses," page 380.)

Barometric pressure is an important indication of weather. Wet air is lighter than dry air, so rainy weather is associated with low-pressure systems and fair weather is associated with high pressures. A falling barometer indicates the arrival of a low-pressure system, possibly with bad weather. A rising barometer indicates the arrival of a high-pressure system, usually bringing clear weather.

If you are carrying an altimeter, you can use it to check the barometric pressure. (See "Altimeters," page 161.) Here are some natural signs of low or falling air pressure:

- Birds are not flying or are flying low. Lower barometric pressure means less dense air, which makes it harder to fly.
- Smells (especially bad ones, it seems) are more distinct because the low barometric pressure allows captive odors from plants to be more easily released. The saying is "When ditch and pond offend the nose, look for rain and storm blows."
- Smoke tends to curl downward and linger rather than dissipate.

FRONTS

When two air masses of different temperatures collide, a frontal boundary is created. Warm air rises up over cooler air, or cold air pushes underneath warm air, both causing air to be lifted up. As the air rises, it cools, and water vapor in the air condenses to form clouds. If there is enough moisture in the lifted air, there will be precipitation. The type of precipitation (rain or snow) will depend on the temperature. As fronts move through, you will usually see a change in the barometric pressure, temperature, wind direction, and cloud formation. By observing these indicators over time you can keep track of the types of systems that move through your area. The chart on page 209 shows you how to predict what types of fronts are moving through and what weather you can anticipate.

WARM FRONTS

A warm air mass coming in over a cooler air mass creates a warm front. A warm front usually covers 800 miles (1,280 kilometers) or more and slants forward riding over cooler air ahead of it. Warm fronts move very slowly, and the early signs of the warm front give advance warning of precipitation coming in 24 to 48 hours. An approaching warm front is first indicated by high wispy cirrus clouds, lowering over a period of one to two days into stratus clouds. The stratus cloud cover may continue to lower and darken, forming nimbostratus clouds, resulting in precipitation (see the following illustration). A look at the night sky can provide early warning of a coming warm front. A halo around the moon is caused by cirrus clouds; high cirrus clouds may also be indicated by twinkling stars. Since warm fronts move slowly and often cover large areas, precipitation can last for a long time—sometimes days.

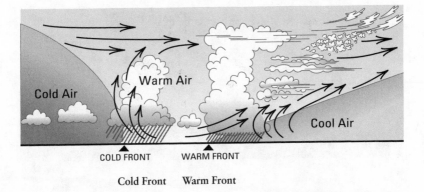

Cold Air

Warm Air

Cool Air

COLD FRONT   WARM FRONT

Cold Front   Warm Front

COLD FRONTS

A cold air mass pushing in under a warmer air mass creates a cold front. Cold fronts generally cover 100 miles (160 kilometers) or less and move much more quickly (20 to 30 mph or 32 to 48 kph) than warm fronts. Cold air is denser and heavier, causing it to sink. As a result, friction against the ground has a greater effect on the air mass. The leading edge piles up steeply, while the trailing edge slants backward. This steep leading edge pushes warmer air upward, ahead of the front. A cold front typically begins with high cumulus clouds, which will lower to form layers of stratocumulus clouds, possibly bringing precipitation. A strong cold front may push warm air up very rapidly, creating cumulonimbus clouds (thunderheads) along a narrow band at the leading edge of the front called a *squall line*. After the cold front has passed, weather is typically clear with drier, cooler air.

OCCLUDED FRONTS

An occluded front occurs when the faster-moving cold air catches up with slower-moving warmer air and lifts the warm air mass. In this case there tends to be a rapid progression of precipitation types, with nimbostratus clouds giving way to cumulonimbus clouds.

EXTREME WEATHER CONDITIONS

Extreme weather can pop up unexpectedly while you are on the trail. I've been out on trips and had hurricanes hit that were just tropical depressions off the coast of Africa when we first started out. One solution is to carry a portable weather radio so you can tune into NOAA weather alerts and get advanced warning of potential severe weather. If your group is hit by severe weather

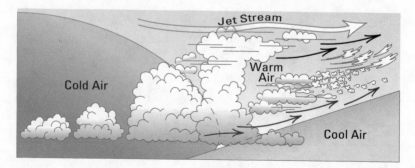

Occluded Front

conditions, your major concern is to maintain warmth and keep people dry (wet clothing can quickly lead to hypothermia). Here are the basic steps you should take:

- Concentrate immediately on everyone's being properly clothed to minimize possible hypothermia and/or frostbite. (See "Cold-Related Illnesses and Injuries" page 332.)
- Find shelter or set up camp to get out of the bad weather.
- Get people together under shelter with sleeping bags and have the group share the bags for warmth.
- If possible, get a stove working for hot drinks. Definitely have everyone eat food to restore energy and help maintain body temperature.
- Don't try to hike out in the middle of a serious storm. Better to hunker down and wait until it's over. Relocate if your current position leaves you more exposed.
- If there are strong winds, try to locate a protected area away from dead trees or trees with dead branches that may fall.
- In severe lightning storms, there is danger from both direct hits and ground currents. When lightning is close, separate the group and have people assume the lightning position (see "Lightning Dangers," page 204) until the storm has moved away.
- Wait until the storm has abated before moving camp or hiking out. Be careful of damaged tree limbs that may fall after the storm.

THUNDERSTORMS

Thunderstorms are the result of unstable moist air rising to form large cumulonimbus clouds. This can occur as part of a frontal pattern, as a cold front pushes in under a warm front, or as part of a local pattern of unstable air. Local thunderstorms begin when warm humid air rises from the ground, creating updrafts. As the air cools, it condenses to form a cumulus cloud. If the air is unstable, the updrafts continue, pulling in more warm, moist air. If enough moisture is present, the water vapor of the cloud will condense to form rain droplets. As water condenses from a gas to a liquid, it releases heat, which continues to fuel the updraft and pulls in more moist air from below. This cycle continues until significant amounts of moisture have developed. Rain and ice crystals begin to form within the cloud. When these become heavy enough, they fall, creating downdrafts within the cloud. These cool downdrafts may proceed out ahead of the storm. A sudden rush of cool air with darkening skies is often an indication of an oncoming thunderstorm.

The thunderhead continues to build in height, and the top may reach as high as 11 miles (17 kilometers). The hot air rises until it runs into the tropopause, the level in the atmosphere where the temperature is constant. The hot air can no longer rise, so the top flattens out and the cloud top forms into a classic anvil shape. Thunder and lightning may be part of the storm. As the storm matures, the precipitation descending through the cloud (rain or snow) slows and halts the updrafts, cools the cloud, and the storm eventually dissipates.

Thunderstorms are a common occurrence during the summer months in North America as the increasing heat of the summer sun and higher levels of moisture provide the fuel for frequent afternoon storms. Mountains are also a prime location for thunderstorms. As warm moist air hits the mountains, it is lifted up and over the mountains, creating updrafts that are fed by more warm moist air, beginning the cycle of thunderstorm development. In the mountains during the summer, be especially careful of afternoon thunderstorms.

THE PHYSICS OF LIGHTNING

If you remember basic physics, electrons are the tiny negatively charged particles that orbit around the atom. Most matter is electrically neutral, but you can create a charged object by transferring electrons from one object to another. This is what happens when you scuff your rubber-soled shoes across the carpet—you "scrub off" extra electrons from the carpet and develop a negative charge. Negatively charged objects are attracted to positively charged or neutral objects. If enough of a charge has built up when your hand touches a metal object, like a doorknob, a spark jumps across as the extra electrons flow from your body to the positive or neutral object. A similar process occurs with lightning.

In a mature cumulonimbus cloud, there are strong updrafts and downdrafts. Rising ice crystals and falling hail within the cloud create strong negative charges concentrated in the base of the cloud, while a layer of positive charges forms at the top. Since like charges repel each other, the negatively charged base of the cloud has an effect on the electrical charges on the ground beneath it, "pushing" the negative electrons on the ground away and leaving an area of positive charge directly beneath the cloud that follows the cloud as it moves.

Air is normally a poor conductor of electricity, but when the electrical potentials within the cloud become great enough, even air molecules will conduct electrical currents. The lightning flash is the flow of these separated positive and negative charges back together again along ionized air. Most lightning strikes occur within a cloud flowing between the areas of positive and negative charges within the cloud. You see this as cloud flashes, often referred to as *sheet lightning*.

Cloud-to-ground lightning, which accounts for only about 10–15 percent of lightning, starts as a thin stroke of negatively charged electrons from the base of the cloud that begins to zigzag down toward the ground in a forked pattern known as a *stepped leader*. The forks are created as the electrons search for the path of least resistance to the ground. This stepped leader extends tens of thousands of feet (thousand of meters) from charges in the cloud heading toward the earth. Meanwhile, the ground below the cloud is also busy. When the negatively charged stepped leader gets to within a few hundred feet (50 to 100 meters) of the ground, a positively charged upward leader or streamer leaps off the ground, typically from a tall object closer to the cloud, like a building or tree, toward the stepped leader. Actually, there may be several upward leaders, each trying to make contact, but only one will win. Any object that is tall, like a mountain peak or a tall tree, is filled with positive charge. Being near any such object means that you are likely to be affected by the splash effect of the current as it hits the ground and dissipates (the *ground current*).

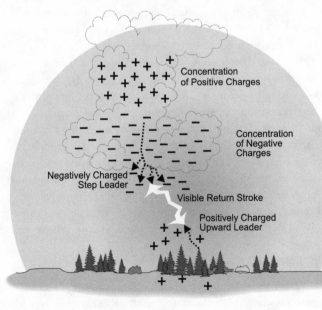

Lightning

When the stepped leader and the upward leader meet, the circuit is complete, and a rush of positive charges from the ground flows up into the cloud and negative charges flow from the cloud into the ground. This is the actual lightning flash that you see. Often there are several independent return strokes, which is why lightning seems to flicker. The stepped leader coming down from the cloud and the upward leader are fainter and happen so quickly that all we see are the return strokes. The air around the electrical charge is heated to more than 43,000°F (24,000°C), expands violently, and then contracts. This quick expansion and contraction of the air around the lightning causes air molecules to move back and forth, creating sound waves—thunder.

Storm Distance and the 30/30 Rule

Lightning often strikes out ahead of the storm, so just because the storm is not yet directly over you, don't assume that you aren't in danger. The distance of approaching lightning storms may be calculated by timing the interval between the lightning flash and the following thunder ("flash to bang"). Sound travels about one-fifth of a mile per second, so count the number of seconds between the lightning flash and the thunder, and divide by 5 to find the distance. (For kilometers, sound travels about one-third of a kilometer per second, so divide by 3.) If the thunder is within 30 seconds from the lightning, then the storm is within 6 miles (10 kilometers) of your location. This is considered the strike danger zone, and *you should start to take immediate defensive action.* It's going to take you awhile to get ready, and some storms move at 35 to 40 miles per hour (56 to 64 kilometers per hour), so the lightning can be right on top of you within minutes. Thunder can't be heard beyond about 15 miles (24 kilometers) away, so you might see a lightning flash and not hear any thunder. The storm still may be coming your way.

Lightning safety experts advise people to follow the 30/30 rule. Take immediate precautions when thunder is heard within 30 seconds of the lightning flash and wait for 30 minutes after the last thunder is heard to resume your activity. In most backcountry settings you simply can't "stop" being in the outdoors, but you should find a safe location and stay there until the storm has passed.

LIGHTNING DANGERS

Obviously, lightning storms can present significant accident potential. The primary dangers associated with cloud-to-ground lightning are direct hits, side flashes, and ground current. Before going on your trip, you need to include an assessment of general weather patterns and the potential for lightning or severe thunderstorms in your trip plan. In certain locations or at certain times of the year, thunderstorms are common.

Warning Signs of Lightning

There will always be signs of an impending storm that contains lightning. Any or all of the following may indicate the possibility of imminent lightning:

- Thunder, even without any visible lightning.
- A sudden cloudburst of enormous raindrops or huge hailstones.
- A fast-moving cold front; these often trigger thunderstorms along a squall line ahead of the front as it pushes warm moist air upward. A change in wind direction with a sudden blast of cold air is often an indication of an incoming cold front.
- Signs of highly charged air—any of the following signs is an indication of serious lightning potential: hair standing on end or crackling; crackling noises or buzzing in the air; small sparks given off around metal objects; bluish glow around objects, known as Saint Elmo's fire.

A Direct Strike

Direct lightning strikes are rare, but they do occur. Almost anything can send up an upward leader. Typically the upward leader that "wins" will come from the point with the least resistance to conducting electricity and/or the closest point to the stepped leader. High and relatively sharp points like radio antennas, mountain summits, sharp ridgelines, trees, or a standing person are most susceptible. Direct lightning strikes typically cause the heart to stop and cause serious electrical burns. (See "Basic Life Support," page 282, and "Thermal Burns," page 322.)

Side Flashes

Side flashes are extremely dangerous and account for a significant percentage of lightning injuries. As the return stroke travels to the ground, the object that sent up the upward leader may not be the best conductor of electricity. If the return stroke encounters electrical resistance it may "arc off" that object to something else looking for an easier path to ground. Depending on how well-grounded the object is, a side flash can arc 30 to 50 feet (10 to 15 meters). The arc distance for a "moderately" well-ground tree is 16 feet (5 meters). Unlike ground current, which dissipates as it spreads out, a side flash carries a full electrical current. Side flashes can arc through the air or along the ground. Standing too close to a tree that is struck by lightning can result in being hit by a side flash with the same dangerous result as a direct strike.

Ground Currents

Once the lightning hits the ground, the electrical current spreads out in all directions along the ground following numerous paths of least resistance, dissipating as it goes. This is known as ground current, and injuries from ground currents are much more frequent than direct strikes. Ground current pathways include cracks and crevices filled with water, wet rock, wet climbing ropes, root systems, and cables along the ground. In some cases the easiest path may be to "jump" across a gap of ionized air. This is known as a *spark gap*. This can occur at the openings of caves or under overhangs, where it is easier for the current to jump across the gap than to travel all the way around. If you are between the two sides of the gap, the current will flow right through you, so taking shelter at the opening of a cave may be more hazardous than being out in the open. When lightning strikes the water it dissipates in all directions; being in or on the water can put you in the path of ground current. Ground currents can be as dangerous as direct hits if you happen to be in their path and can result in thermal burns or cardiac arrest.

Protection from Lightning Strikes

To minimize your risk from lightning, your goal is to find the location that is *least likely* to send up an upward leader. Obviously, the major sources for upward leaders are things like mountain peaks, exposed ridges, and tall trees. You want to get away from these objects, but if you get too far away—out into an open field, for example—you may set yourself up as another likely source. For example, if you are near a pinnacle, stay inside a zone where your horizontal distance from the pinnacle is about one to one-half less than the pinnacle's height above you. It is best if the pinnacle is five to ten times your height to get a reasonable distance away from the potential strike location. This assumption is based on how a lightning rod works.

- Get off of summits, ridges, pinnacles, or any other place that is the highest location around. Even a few yards (meters) lower may offer some protection.
- Stay away from taller trees. If you are in a forest, try to find a group of lower trees that are less likely to be a strike site.
- If you are in the middle of an open field, the best thing to do is get into a low-lying area and assume the lightning position (see page 207).
- If you are on the water, get to shore.
- Stay out of depressions, gullies, or drainages that may have water flowing in them.

- Find a position partway down a slope. Dry or well-drained ground is best.
- Avoid caves and overhangs unless they are *clearly dry* and *spacious*. These are usually part of a larger system of cracks and fissures, which are likely conduits for ground currents, especially if they are wet. Don't seek shelter in caves, under boulders or overhangs, or in bunkers unless they are dry and unless you have at least 20 feet (6 meters) of headroom and 4 feet (2 meters) of space on every side.

Where You Want to Be

- In the lighting position.
- Crouching on top of your pack.
- Crouching on top of a boulder that is resting on top of other rocks.

What to Do in a Severe Lightning Storm

Most lightning storms move away fairly quickly. With good rain gear, you should be able to stay relatively dry until the storm has passed, even out in the open. Hypothermia could be a problem if you become wet, but that's a secondary problem compared to imminent lightning danger. Here is what you should do if you are in immediate danger from lightning:

1. **Spread Out** If the group is in an area of high lightning danger, the group should *not* wait out the storm huddled together. Split up but still be within sight of each other—20 feet (6 meters) apart or more—unless this puts some people in a site with a higher strike potential. The survival of one person whose heart or breathing has stopped as a result of a strike may depend on prompt action by companions. If you don't already know it, learn CPR (see "Basic Life Support," page 282).

2. **Assume the Lightning Position** Anytime thunder is *30 seconds* or less from the lightning, the storm is within 6 miles (10 kilometers), and you should assume a crouch position with your feet close together and your butt off the ground. Your hands should be on your knees. Don't lie down on the ground. Don't put your hands on the ground. If possible, you can crouch on top of a dry, insulating material like a foam pad or your pack. If you were in the path of a ground current, it would travel up one leg and out the other, minimizing the parts of the body affected. If a hand is on the ground, the current could just as likely flow up through the arm and out a leg traveling directly through the major organs, including your heart, potentially causing significant damage.

Lightning Myths

Contrary to popular belief, metal objects (pack frames, ice axes, climbing hardware) on the ground do not *attract* a lightning strike or ground current. The lightning has had to pass through tens of thousands of feet (thousands of meters) of air before it reaches the ground and is not going to be suddenly "pulled" in by the small amount of metal on your body or in your pack. There are usually much better objects for an upward leader. That said, don't stand right next to a huge, tall metal object like a firetower that *is* going to be a source for a an upward leader. However, metal in contact with the body can provide a path of least resistance for *ground* currents. It is best to set metal objects like pack frames and ice axes away from your body, to create a more attractive path *past* you rather than *through* you.

PREDICTING THE WEATHER

People have been making accurate short-term weather predictions long before satellites and Doppler radar. With a few regular weather observations throughout the day, you can gather enough data to make some reasonable guesses about incoming weather. Make this a part of your outdoor routine. It's best to make your observations around the same times each day: first thing in the morning, midday, and in the evening. Make your prediction for the next 24 to 48 hours, then check yourself and see how accurate you were. Base your predictions on the following list of observations:

Cloud Formations

- What types of clouds were seen?
- What direction are they moving?
- How have the clouds changed during the day?

Wind Direction and Strength

- What direction was the wind blowing?
- What strength?
- Has the direction changed? Is it veering (indicating a high-pressure system) or backing (indicating a low-pressure system)? (See "Changes in Wind Direction," page 195.)

Temperature

- Has the temperature gone noticeably up or down (beyond normal daytime fluctuations)?

Humidity

- Has the humidity changed? Increased or decreased?

Barometric Pressure

- Has the barometer changed (beyond any appropriate fluctuations for altitude changes)?

In his book *Weathering the Wilderness*, William Reifsnyder provides a simple table to help you predict upcoming weather. Apply your observations to the chart below to help you predict upcoming weather patterns.

	WARM FRONT		COLD FRONT		OCCLUDED FRONT	
Phenomenon	**Approach**	**Passage**	**Approach**	**Passage**	**Approach**	**Passage**
Pressure	Falls steadily	Levels off or falls unsteadily	Falls slowly, or rapidly if storm is intensifying	Sharp rise	Falls steadily	Rises, often not as sharply as cold front
Wind	SE; speed increases	Veers to S	S; may be squally at times	Sharp veer to SW; speed increases, gusty	E; may veer slowly to SE; speed increases	Veers to SW; speed decreases
Cloud Progression	Cirrus; cirrostratus; altostratus; nimbostratus; thickening	Stratocumulus; sometimes cumulonimbus; clearing trend	Cumulus or altocumulus; cumulonimbus in squall line	Cumulonimbus; sometimes few clouds; clearing trend	Cirrus; cirrostratus; altostratus; nimbostratus	Slow clearing; stratocumulus; altocumulus
Precipitation	Steady rain or snow starts as clouds thicken; intensifies as front approaches	Precipitation tapers off; may be showery	None or showery; intense showers or hail in prefrontal squall line	Showery; perhaps thunderstorms; rapid clearing	Steady rain or snow starts as clouds thicken, intensifies as front approaches	Precipitation tapers off slowly
Temperature	Increases slowly	Slight rise	Little change or slow rise	Sharp drop	Slow rise	Slow fall
Humidity	Increases	Increases; may level off	Steady; or slight increase	Sharp drop	Slow increase	Slow decrease
Visibility	Becomes poorer	Becomes better	Fair; may become poor in squalls	Sharp rise; becomes excellent	Becomes poorer	Becomes better

Some natural indicators of changing weather can also be found in old sayings, which have evolved through a history of observation.

"Red sky at morning, sailors take warning; red sky at night, sailor's delight." Redness in the *sky* (not redness in the clouds) is caused by light reflecting

off moisture in the air. The red color is seen *opposite* the sun. If red is seen in the sky in the morning (in the west), it means that moist air is beginning to move over you, possibly bringing precipitation. If it is seen in the evening (in the east), it means that the moisture has moved past you.

"Rainbow in the morning is a warning, at night, a delight." Rainbows are caused by sunlight reflecting off water droplets in the atmosphere, so they always occur *opposite* the sun. In North America, *most* weather systems move from west to east. A rainbow in the evening must be in the east and is reflected light from wet weather already past. A rainbow in the morning must be in the west and is reflected from wet weather moving toward you.

"When leaves show their underside, be very sure that rain betide." A period of damp air softens leaf stalks and bends them more easily in the wind as a storm approaches. This is especially true with aspen and maple leaves.

"Rain before the wind, topsail halyards you must mind. Wind before the rain, soon will make plain sail again." Rain falling ahead of a strengthening wind indicates a gale-force storm approaching. Wind ahead of a rain will die out as the rain arrives.

"No dew at night, rain by morning. No dew at morning, rain by the next day." Dew is a sign of a fair tomorrow. On a clear night, without cloud particles, moisture is released from the air and collects as dew.

NATURAL SIGNS OF DIRECTION AND TIME

DIRECTION

There are a number of clues in nature that will help you determine your direction:

- **Polaris (North Star) is always due north** The line formed by the two stars that shape the lip of the Big Dipper point to Polaris, which is the end star of the handle of the Little Dipper. It never moves, and all stars appear to revolve around Polaris (visible in the Northern Hemisphere only).
- **Sun, Moon, and Stars** All of these generally rise in the east and set in the west except the stars around Polaris, which never set (Northern Hemisphere only). The exact direction of rise and set varies with the time of year and your location.

- **Venus can be seen in the west three hours after sunset**   Except for several months out of the year, Venus is the first to appear in the evening and the last to disappear in the morning. The nonappearance months vary from year to year.

To determine direction with a watch, look at (or imagine) an analog watch and point the hour hand for the current time at the sun. South is the direction halfway between that hour hand and 12 (in the Northern Hemisphere). Remember to compensate for Daylight Savings Time. This is often easier than trying to determine the east-west passage of the sun, especially during the middle of the day.

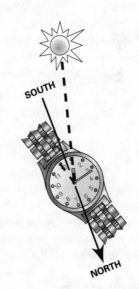

Another way to determine your direction is to make a *shadow compass*. Place a sharpened stick in the ground, point up. Mark the location of the tip of the shadow on the ground. Wait 15 to 20 minutes, and then mark the shadow tip again. Draw a line connecting these two points. This line will run east-west. Since the sun is always

Determine Direction with Your Watch

slightly south in the Northern Hemisphere and slightly north in the Southern Hemisphere, you can identify all four directions.

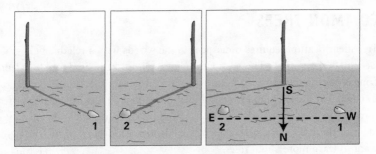

Shadow Compass

TIME

Estimate Time Using the Sun

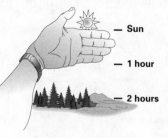

— Sun

— 1 hour

— 2 hours

Telling Time by the Sun

The sun moves about 15 degrees of arc per hour. Extend your arm with your palm facing you. With your arm extended horizontally, the width of your palm covers approximately 15 degrees. Hold your hand at the bottom of the sun and count the number of hands down to the horizon. In the morning, x hands means x hours from sunrise; in the evening y hands means y hours until sunset. This will give you an idea of the number of daylight hours remaining. If you know the time of sunrise and/or sunset, it will give you an approximate time of day. If the width of your palm (four fingers) equals an hour, then the width of each finger represents about 15 minutes. For example, suppose it is afternoon and the sun is two hands above the horizon. This means there are approximately two hours until sunset. If you know the sun sets at 6:45 P.M., it is about 4:45 P.M.

Tell Time with a Compass

Orient the compass to north. Place a thin stick upright in the center of the compass and mark the degree number where the shadow from the sun hits. Consider that north is 12:00 P.M. on this "clock." Each 15 degrees off of north is the equivalent of an hour. Add or subtract accordingly from north (12:00 P.M.). If a shadow reads 330 degrees, for example, subtract 330 from 360 for 30 degrees or 2 hours; $12 - 2 = 10:00$ A.M.

COMMON TREES

Tree identification requires time spent in the woods with a reliable field guide (see the Bibliography). This section provides a short, key-based tool for identifying some of the more common trees found across the United States and Canada. The idea behind key-based identification is to identify particular features of the tree, such as leaf structure, and follow various options until you identify the tree. Bring a thorough tree-identification book with you if you want to learn more about trees.

Trees commonly found in North America are divided into two major families: conifers and broadleaf trees. The basic differences between the two types of trees are described in the following chart. Broadleaf trees are most easily distinguished by the types of leaves and how they attach to the branch.

TREE TYPE	SEEDS	LEAF TYPE
Conifer	Have naked seeds, typically on a cone.	Most conifers are evergreen—they maintain their leaves all year. In order to reduce moisture loss through the leaves, conifers typically have long needlelike leaves with a waxy coating.
Broadleaf	Have seeds contained within an ovary.	Most broadleaf trees are deciduous—they lose their leaves once a year.

LEAF ATTACHMENT

- **Alternate** leaves are attached to alternating sites along the branch.
- **Opposite** leaves are attached to the branch directly opposite one another.

Alternate

Opposite

LEAF TYPE

Simple Leaves

A single leaf blade is joined by a woody stalk to a twig.

- **Lobed** The leaf is divided into several separate lobes.
- **Unlobed** The leaf has no lobes.

Lobed

Unlobed

Compound Leaves

A single leaf is composed of from three to several dozen leaflets that are joined to a midrib that is attached to a twig. There are two subtypes of compound leaves:

- **Palmate** leaflets are attached to the midrib at one point.
- **Pinnate** leaflets are attached at several points along the central midrib.

Palmate

Pinnate

BASIC TREE IDENTIFICATION

Does the tree have needlelike leaves? If yes, go to "Conifers," page 217. Otherwise go to "Broadleaf Trees," below.

Broadleaf Trees

Ash (Opposite; Compound; Pinnate)   Ash grows up to 80 feet (24 meters) with a very straight trunk. It has opposite compound leaves, each having three to eleven leaflets with toothed margins. Leaves are pale green and turn yellow in the fall. The fruits are single-winged seeds, which hang down in clusters. The bark is thick, furrowed, or scaly, and usually ash-colored on the branches. *Examples:* white ash, black ash, green ash.

Aspen, Quaking (Alternate; Simple; Unlobed; Toothed)   The quaking aspen grows up to 70 feet tall (21 meters). The leaves are heart-shaped and toothed. The stems are flat and are easily disturbed by a light wind, causing the familiar "quaking." The leaves are bright green and turn golden yellow in the fall. The bark is a smooth greenish-gray. Aspen are early colonizers after a fire.

Beech (Alternate; Simple; Unlobed; Toothed)   The American beech grows up

to 80 feet tall (24 meters). The beech often has a wide trunk and spreading branches. It grows well in low light, so it is often a climax species. Offspring trees can sprout from the roots of a parent tree. Leaves turn yellow and then brown in the fall and may remain on the tree all winter. The bark is smooth and light gray.

Birches (Alternate; Simple; Unlobed; Toothed)

- Paper Birch grows to 80 feet tall (24 meters). It has bright white, peeling bark with dark horizontal striations that gives it its "paper" name. The leaves are light green, heart-shaped, and toothed. They turn yellow in the fall.
- Gray Birch grows to 30 feet (9 meters). The bark is dark gray and smooth and does not peel. The leaves are alternate and arrowhead-shaped with sharp teeth. The leaves turn yellow in the fall.
- River Birch grows to 100 feet (30 meters). The leaves are diamond-shaped, and the bark peels in many layers of thin flakes.

Buckeyes (Opposite; Compound; Palmate)

- Horsechestnut grows to 80 feet tall (24 meters). Has seven to nine leaflets coming from a central rib.
- Sweet Buckeye grows to 90 feet (26 meters). Usually has five leaflets coming from a central rib.

Dogwood (Opposite; Simple; Lobed; Smooth)   Dogwood grows to 40 feet tall (12 meters). Dogwoods are known for their beautiful white or pink blossoms in springtime. The bark is a scaly gray. The leaves are opposite and oval with curving symmetrical veins. Berries are red. The leaves turn deep red in the fall.

Hickories (Alternate; Compound; Pinnate; Toothed) Hickory leaves are compound, alternate, with a terminal leaflet. Each leaf has three to seventeen (depending on the subspecies) oval, pointed, and toothed leaflets. Flowers are three-branched, slender, drooping catkins. The fruit is a nut with a husk that splits into four sections when ripe. *Examples:* shagbark hickory, pignut hickory, bitternut hickory, mockernut hickory, and pecan. The nuts of the shagbark, pecan, and mockernut are edible.

- If the bark is smooth and gray and becomes very rough and scaly on older trees, peeling off into long "shaggy" strips, it is a shagbark hickory.

Maples (Opposite; Simple; Lobed; Toothed)   There are numerous species of maple. In a few cases, the leaves are pinnately compound. Leaves turn a variety of brilliant colors in the fall. The seed is typically a pair of winged fruits in a U or V shape. These break apart and "helicopter" their way to the ground. *Examples:* sugar maple, red maple, and silver maple.

- If the notches between the lobes are U-shaped and the base of the leaf is curving, it is a sugar maple.
- If the notches between the lobes are V-shaped and the base of the leaf is not curving, it is a red maple.
- If the leaves are distinctly five-lobed and the notches between the lobes are deep, it is a silver maple.

Oak (Alternate; Simple; Unlobed; Toothed)   There are numerous species of oaks. All have alternate simple leaves and the familiar acorns. Twigs usually have clusters of buds at the tips.

- If the leaves have rounded lobes and lack teeth, it is a white oak. *Examples:* eastern white oak, valley oak.
- If the leaves have pointed lobes and bristle-pointed teeth, it is a red or black oak. *Examples:* eastern black oak, scarlet oak, northern red oak.
- If the lower branches of the tree bend downward, it is a pin oak.

Sassafras (Alternate; Simple; Lobed; Untoothed)   Sassafras grows to 50 feet  (15 meters). The leaves are the most distinguishable feature. Each tree has both unlobed leaves and two-lobed and three-lobed leaves. When crushed, the leaves give off a pleasant odor.

Sweetgum (Alternate; Simple; Lobed; Toothed)   The sweetgum grows to 100  feet (30 meters). It has star-shaped alternate leaves. The hanging fruits, a red spike-covered ball, contain the seeds. The seeds are popular with some animals, especially the red squirrel, who may have a midden (a pile) of devoured sweetgum balls under its favorite perch.

Sycamore (Alternate; Simple; Lobed; Toothed)   The sycamore grows to 100  feet (30 meters). It is easily recognized by its mottled bark. The smooth brownish bark peels off in irregular patches, leaving yellowish and whitish bark underneath. The fruit is a hairy ball that hangs from the tree. The leaves are simple, heart-shaped, with three lobes.

Tulip Tree (Alternate; Simple; Lobed; Untoothed)   The tulip tree is a tall, straight tree that typically grows to 100 feet (30 meters). The flowers of the tree look like tulips. On mature trees you will notice no branches on the lower part of the tree. The tulip tree is a fast grower and often is an earlier colonizer in cleared areas.

Conifers

Most conifers are evergreen, keeping their leaves all year round. There are a few species of conifers that are deciduous, losing their leaves in the fall. These trees include the tamarack, the western larch, and the bald cypress.

Cedars (Scale-like Needles)   The cedars found native in North America are in a different family from the true cedars found in Europe and Asia. Cedars are generally 40 to 50 feet tall (12 to 15 meters). They have tiny overlapping leaf scales typically arranged in flat sprays. Examples: western red cedar, northern white cedar.

Firs (Needles not Scale-like; Single Needles; Sharp and Four-Sided; Flat with White Bands Underneath)   Firs are 60 to 130 feet (18 to 40 meters), with needles on two sides of the branch. The needles have two silvery white bands on the underside. The cones, rather than hanging down, sit erect on the branch and have scales that are wider than they are long. *Examples:* alpine fir, balsam fir, white fir. *Note:* The Douglas fir is not a true fir but a separate species.

Hemlocks (Needles not Scale-like; Single Needles; Sharp and Four-Sided; Flat with White Bands Underneath)   Hemlocks grow from 65 to 200 feet (20 to 60 meters). The leaves have a definite fragrance. For a positive identification, just crush some of the round-tipped needles and smell. The needles are short, marked on the lower surface by two pale lines. The cones are oval, with scales as wide as they are long. *Examples:* eastern hemlock, western hemlock, Carolina hemlock.

Junipers (Scale-like Needles)   Junipers have both tiny scale-like leaves and some small, pointed needles. They grow in height from 40 to 50 feet (12 to 15 meters). The fruit, found only on female trees, is a small, firm, bluish fleshy berry. *Examples:* eastern red cedar (which is in the juniper family), common juniper, Rocky Mountain juniper, western juniper.

Pines (Needles not Scale-like; Single Needles; Needles in Bundles of 2 to 5)   Pines in North America commonly range in height up to 164 feet (50 meters). They are an evergreen with needlelike leaves in bundles of two to five. Species can be identified by the number of needles in a cluster and by the shape of the cone. The cones are usually longer than they are wide and contain the naked seeds on the hardened woody scales of flowers. There are two types of pine—soft and hard.

- If the needles are in clusters of five, the cones have a stalk, and the cones have scales without prickles, then it is a hard pine. *Example:* eastern white pine.
- If the needles are in clusters of two or three and the tree has cones with thick woody scales armed with spiny prickles, then it is a soft pine. *Examples:* jack pine, longleaf pine, pitch pine, ponderosa pine.

Spruces (Needles not Scale-like; Single Needles) Spruces are tall, tapering trees that have a wide buttress of branches at the base. Size ranges from 100 to 164 feet (30 to 50 meters). The bark is thin and scaly. Leaves are stiff, sharp evergreen needles extending out on all sides of the branch in a spiral. The cones hang down from the branch and are egg-shaped, with thin woody scales.

PLANTS

There are far too many plants to cover in this manual—vines, shrubs, wildflowers, and grasses. You should take a good field guide along to help you identify plant species (see the Bibliography). There are a few basic things about plants that you should know.

WILD EDIBLES

If you are foraging for wild edibles, you need to be able to *positively identify* the plant before eating it. Some species look very similar, and eating the wrong plant can make you very sick. Also, some wild edibles are edible only at certain stages in their development, and even then only certain parts of the plant are edible. *Know* your plant before you eat it—bring a good edible plants field guide with you.

Whenever you are collecting wild edibles, take only a few in any one spot and spread your collection out over a large area. Otherwise, you may reduce the population enough that it can't reproduce. In some locations or seasons, collecting wild edibles may be prohibited. Check with local land managers. And whenever you are collecting wild edibles, be aware of other animals that may be collecting the same thing. Berry patches, for example, can be sites for bear encounters.

PLANTS TO AVOID

There are a few plants with toxins or stings that you should definitely be able to recognize and avoid. Here are the common ones found in temperate forests:

- **Poison ivy** typically grows as a woody vine or small shrub. It has toothed leaves in groups of three and white berries. The leaves turn bright red in the fall. You may see it as a large hairy vine climbing high up the sides of trees (up to 1 to 2 inches in diameter or 5 centimeters). It typically grows in wet areas. Remember the old saying "Leaves of three, let it be." (*Note:* There is a tree that has similar-looking leaves—the box elder tree in the maple family looks similar, but it has the common winged seeds of the maple family instead of berries; poison ivy does not grow as a tree.)

- **Poison oak** is similar to poison ivy except it always grows erect (no vines).
- **Poison sumac** grows as a shrub or small tree (typically 6 to 20 feet or 2 to 6 meters). It has compound leaves composed of seven to thirteen pointed leaflets that are not toothed. The berries are white.

Poison Ivy   Poison Oak   Poison Sumac

All parts of these three plants, at all times of year, contain a toxic oil in their sap called *urushiol,* which causes skin rashes on contact. The sap can be carried on your clothing or boots, causing skin irritation long after you have passed the plant. Be especially cautious of burning wood with hairy vines. Inhaling smoke with urushiol vapors can cause the same type of reaction to the sensitive tissues of the lungs, which can result in a serious medical emergency.

- **Stinging nettles** are a 2- to 4-foot weed (0.6 to 1.2 meters) covered with coarse, stinging hairs. The hairs are on both the leaves and stem of the plant. Brushing against it breaks off tiny hairs that lodge in the skin and can be quite painful. Interestingly enough, jewelweed (aka pale touch-me-not) often grows near stinging nettles. The milky sap from crushed stems and leaves of jewelweed soothes the sting from stinging nettles. Jewelweed grows 2 to 4 feet (0.6 to 1.2 meters) high and has pale yellow-orange pendant flowers.

Stinging Nettle   Jewelweed

WILDLIFE OBSERVATION AND ANIMAL TRACKING

For me, seeing wildlife, or signs of wildlife, is one of the great joys of being in the wilderness. I remember doing a solo day hike in Zion National Park. On the way back I found a fresh set of mountain lion tracks on the trail I'd come up just a half hour earlier. I did look over my shoulder a lot on the way back down, and although I never saw him, it was still thrilling to get that close to the "ghost cat."

I started tracking animals in 1985, after taking a course from Tom Brown Jr. The art of tracking opens up your senses and makes you much more aware of your surroundings. Sometimes we are so focused in the hike itself that we miss the incredible richness of the natural world around us. Try it sometime— take your pack off and take a slow stroll through the woods. Start looking for tracks, scat (feces), and other signs of animals. You'll notice your whole pace will slow down and you'll see much more than you did before.

Animal observation and tracking is also an important part of Leave No Trace camping. You must respect animals by being nonintrusive. Getting too close to animals can have serious consequences for the animal, including abandoned young, disturbed nesting grounds, and damaged foraging areas; it may even cause the animal's death. Quick movements and loud noises are stressful to animals. Anytime an animal changes its behavior because of your presence (for example, a deer snorts at you and stamps its foot), then you are too close. In winter, many animals are already under severe stress just to stay alive. Escaping from a human could rob them of the energy they need to survive. At certain times of year, breeding and nesting areas may be off-limits for backcountry travelers. Always remember that you are only a visitor to their habitat.

Tips for Spotting Wildlife

- Look for things that stand out from the surrounding environment. In a forest, most of the outlines are oriented vertically (trees, plants), whereas animals have mostly horizontal outlines. Look for horizontal lines against the vertical as the first sign of wildlife. Also, look for parts of the animal rather than the whole animal—for example, the corner of the deer's rump.
- Blue jays or crows constantly calling in an area are a common sign of a predator, such as a fox, hawk, or owl. Look to see where the birds are concentrated.
- The best times for spotting wildlife are during the early morning and early evening hours. These are prime feeding times for herbivores and, therefore, prime hunting times for carnivores. During the day most herbivores are lying low to avoid predators, so predators snooze as well. Night is

also an active time for wildlife, although you are more likely to hear animals than see them.

Hazards of Animal Observation

- Be careful not to get too close to animals. Certain animals can be aggressive when they feel threatened. Animals that appear very docile can be ill and suddenly react. This is a common sign of rabies. (See "Rabies," page 352.)
- Whenever you are examining animal signs, be aware of the possibility of disease transmission. For example, if you are examining animal scat, *do not* use your hands. Instead, pick it apart with a stick. Bacteria in scat can cause infections, and inhaling dust from dried scat can lead to lung infections or (in the case of some rodents) to serious infections like hantavirus (see page 373).

Safety and Emergency Procedures

Emergency situations in the backcountry will tax all of your knowledge, experience, and judgment. Paul Petzoldt, the founder of the National Outdoor Leadership School (NOLS) and the Wilderness Education Association (WEA), once said, "Rules are for fools." He meant that you can't categorize situations into simple lists of problems and solutions. Each situation is unique, so as a backcountry traveler you need to assess the situation and make your own determination on the best response. This chapter identifies the issues that will help you in your assessment but should not be taken as "rules" or the only responses. Your good judgment is what keeps you safe in the backcountry.

DEALING WITH EMERGENCIES—
WHO'S IN CHARGE?

On some wilderness trips there may be organized trip leaders and participants. In this case, part of the trip leader's role is to take charge in the event of an emergency. Other trips may be a group of friends out for an adventure. In this case, there may be no assigned trip leader, and everyone shares the load and the responsibility for making decisions. While this distributed leadership model works well when deciding where to camp or how long to hike on a particular day, it is not the best approach when there is a serious problem or emergency. In the event of an emergency, the best thing is for a few people with the proper experience and training to take charge. *Before* the trip departs, the group should decide who has the skill to take over in an emergency and/or who the group is willing to delegate this responsibility to. Depending on the type of emergency, there might be different leaders. In the event of a lost person, it might be the person with the most backpacking or search-and-rescue experience. In a first-aid situation, it might be the person with the highest level of formal first-aid or medical training. For the rest of this chapter, we will consider that, in an emergency, every group has a designated emergency leader or leaders, whom I'll call trip leaders. For more on leadership and decision making see Chapter 10, "Outdoor Leadership."

Trip leaders must intimately understand certain realities about injuries and illness in the backcountry (serious or minor) if they are to deal with them effectively. Most trips are 2 to 24 hours or more from having professional medical help arrive at the accident site. The group depends on the trip leaders to take full charge of the situation—the trip leaders must care for the physiological and psychological needs of both the victim and the group. A trip leader who puts him- or herself in danger physically or emotionally for the "good of the victim" is a liability to the victim and to the group.

First and foremost, trip leaders must stay calm and inspire confidence in the group and in one another that the situation is being handled in the best way. They should talk through every step confidently and out loud; this way the leaders can fill in one another's omissions, and decisions won't be made hastily. Depending on the nature of the emergency, it may be productive to ask the group for suggestions. However, there are also times when opening up discussion interferes with necessary immediate actions.

Since each situation is unique, trip leaders must remain flexible in their responses. The key to properly responding to an emergency is to remain calm, assess the situation carefully before acting, and continue to reassess the strategy throughout. Here's a basic approach to handling emergency situations:

1. Assess the situation. Determine the nature of the emergency and what type of response is required (first aid, search for a lost person, etc.). Identify the number of people injured, missing, etc.
2. Develop a response plan (first-aid treatment, initiate search, etc.) based on the nature of the emergency and the potential risk to rescuers. Neutralize risks to the best of your ability before proceeding. Do not initiate a rescue if it is going to create more victims. Continue to reassess the situation and alter the response plan if necessary.
3. Assume leadership of the group or select someone to head the group and delegate responsibility. Group members should assist in patient care if needed, locate position on the map, set up camp, and so on.
4. Make the victim as comfortable as possible, maintain his or her body temperature, and protect the victim from the elements.
5. Make sure a trained first-aider is with the victim at all times.
6. Give the other group members something to do to get their minds off the situation and make them feel useful, such as setting up a temporary camp or preparing food and hot drinks for group members.
7. Make sure the other group members are okay. They may be suffering from shock or emotional difficulties; maintain group morale as much as possible.

HOW ACCIDENTS HAPPEN

Backcountry travel means recognizing that there are factors we cannot control, and that these factors impose potential risk. Recognizing and proactively dealing with those inherent risks is one of the challenges that make wilderness travel such a rewarding experience.

Accidents fall into two basic types: preventable accidents, which are by far the most common; and the rare unpredictable event such as a tree branch falling on someone's head. In the early 1980s, Alan Hale developed the Dynamics of Accidents Model for explaining why accidents happen in the outdoors. His work has influenced outdoor safety management ever since. Safety management is not just avoiding accident situations; it means taking a proactive stance to maintain a safe environment. It's a philosophy that should be part of everything you do in the backcountry, just like Leave No Trace camping. I've expanded Alan's model into the Risk Assessment & Safety Management System (RASM) that reflects the complex interaction between the causes of accidents and risk management.

In order to understand accidents, we have to look at the factors that lead up to them. A hazard is defined as a source of danger. There are three fundamental types of hazards in the outdoors: *environmental hazards*—including things like terrain, location, and weather; *equipment hazards*—having (or not having) the necessary equipment and food; and *human hazards*—factors like people's physical condition, medical conditions, previous experience, and emotional state. When you combine any of these types of hazards, you get an *accident potential*—the possibility that an accident may occur. That's not to say that you are going to have an accident, just that the potential to have one exists. The more hazard factors you have, the higher the accident potential. In addition, you have to look at the potential *severity* of an accident. A high accident potential for blisters isn't as worrisome as a high accident potential for a broken leg. The greater the potential severity, the more essential it is to take steps to prevent it or at least to be prepared to deal with it if it happens. You can't anticipate every possible occurrence, so you also want to focus on those things that have a higher *probability* of occurring.

ENVIRONMENTAL HAZARDS

Different environments manifest different types of hazards. The types of environmental hazards you may encounter depend on:

Activity   The hazards or potential negative consequences associated with backpacking are different from the hazards associated with whitewater kayaking or rock climbing. When you examine the particular activity, consider the physical environment in which the activity will take place. In some situations, the environment is static, relatively unchanging over time. In other activities, the environment itself may change too quickly to predict. Therefore, *static activities* are those in which the environment is relatively unchanging (e.g., hiking). *Dynamic activities* are those in which the environment itself can change very quickly in unpredictable ways (e.g., backcountry skiing and avalanches). With a dynamic activity, you may need to provide a greater margin of safety because of the unpredictability of the environment.

Season and Climate   Weather, altitude, and the possibility of weather changes have a significant impact on the accident potential. Cold, heat, rain, snow, lightning, wind, and fog can create hazardous conditions for backcountry travelers. (See "Extreme Weather Conditions," page 200.)

Remote Locations   In remote locations, you need to exercise additional precautions, since the distance from help means that you may be on your own if something goes wrong. Factor this into your plans by possibly reducing the difficulty level of your activities. This helps you take into account the increased accident potential and provides you with a greater margin of safety.

Common Environmental Hazards

- Rocky trails
- Poison ivy
- Lightning
- Bees, wasps
- Overexposure to sun
- Exposed ledges
- Cold temperatures
- Contaminated water

EQUIPMENT HAZARDS

Equipment hazards are caused by not having the correct equipment or food, by having some form of breakdown of the equipment, or by not knowing how to use the equipment properly.

Common Equipment Hazards

- Improper clothing
- Faulty stove
- Inoperative equipment
- Missing equipment

HUMAN HAZARDS

Human hazards are difficult to identify since they are often subjective matters like knowledge, judgment, and emotional state. Here are some examples of common human factor hazards that contribute to accident potential:

General Human Hazards

- Previous experience
- Physical condition

- Previous medical conditions
- No awareness of hazards
- Trying to "prove" oneself
- Fatigue
- Anxiety/fear
- Limited outdoor skills

Hazards Among Participants

- Not interested in being on the trip
- Poor communication skills
- Not willing to follow instructions
- Group lacks cooperative structure

Hazards Among Trip Leaders

- Poor teaching ability
- Inability to manage group
- Poor judgment regarding safety
- Inadequate skills to extricate self and others from hazards

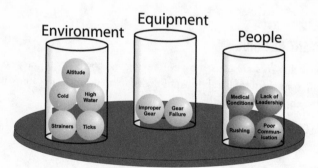

Hazard Factors

BALANCING HAZARD FACTORS WITH SAFETY FACTORS

In order to keep the accident potential down, you take proactive safety steps before and during your trip—things like leaving your route with someone before you go, talking to rangers about current conditions, checking your equipment to make sure it's in good condition. There are three general types of safety factors: equipment safety, people safety, and safety protocols.

I think of it as a balance scale. On one side of the scale are the hazard factors; on the other side of the scale are the safety factors. The more "hazard weight" on the one side, the more you have to offset it with "safety weight" on the other. (See figure on page 231.)

Equipment Safety

One of the ways that you can reduce the potential for accidents is by everyone having adequate equipment, food, and water for the conditions. Also, know how to use the equipment properly.

People Safety

By recognizing the skills and abilities that individuals bring to the group, and by developing a positive structure for group interaction, you can create positive factors that will help the group reduce their accident potential.

General Guidelines

- Know people's experience level
- Have someone trained in first aid
- Practice good communication
- Use good judgment
- Have a clear decision-making strategies for emergencies
- Make sure people's physical condition is appropriate to the trip

SAFETY PROTOCOLS/PRACTICES

As director of an outdoor program, one of my principal jobs is safety management, and one of the ways I do that is by making sure that all of our leaders have a set of operating protocols and practices. If you aren't involved with an organized outdoor program, you might ask, "Why do I need protocols? I'm just going out with friends." The answer is that everyone needs some protocols—in fact, you're already using protocols, but you probably don't think of them in those terms. For example, if you always leave your trip itinerary with a friend, you are following a protocol. Here are a few common protocols that are covered elsewhere in this book.

Sample Protocols/Practices

- Always leave your itinerary with a friend (see page 412).
- Always bring "The Essentials" (see page 21).
- Unbuckle your hip belt before crossing a deep stream (see page 177).
- Follow the 30/30 rule for lightning (see page 204).

The point of protocols is to develop patterns of behavior that will help you stay safe. It's just like an airline pilot's going down a checklist before take-off. Let me go back to Paul Petzoldt's statement "Rules are for fools." Petzoldt didn't mean not to have any rules or protocols. He meant that rules are only part of the solution. You can't have a rule or protocol already prepared for every situation you might encounter, so you still need to rely on your experience and judgment to make the right decision. Protocols are one more tool to help balance out the hazard factors.

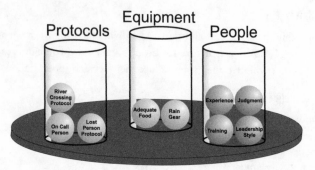

Safety Factors

Managing Accident Potential

How do you tell when the accident potential is going up, and what do you do about it? One of the techniques for keeping accident potential down is to ask yourself "What if" questions. You are at a stream crossing with fast moving water over your knees. Down below there is a downed tree (a strainer) in the river. Ask yourself, "What if someone falls in?" "How fast is the water moving?" "How far is it to the strainer?" "What is the chance that the person might get swept into the strainer?" "What would we do if the person got caught?" All of these questions are part of a worst-case scenario that will help you decide if the risk is acceptable or not. With experience you develop your instincts, that "gut feeling" that the accident potential is too high.

If we look at our Hazard and Safety Scales, we can add another piece to our design, a piston for accident potential. Increasing the "weight" of the hazard factors pushes the accident potential piston higher while increasing the "weight" of safety factors pulls the accident potential piston down. So we have

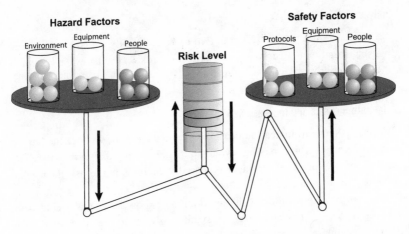

Hazard Factors Balanced by Safety Factors

a very dynamic system in which the ultimate accident potential or risk level is determined not just by the hazards but also by the safety factors you have in place. In fact, you can have a situation with very few hazards and still have a very high risk level because you have few safety factors in place. You can reduce the accident potential to a reasonable level by eliminating hazard factors and/or adding safety factors. Try both. If you still can't get the accident potential down to a level that you are comfortable with, it's time to make a new plan.

PREVENTING ACCIDENTS

Understand the Hazards

In order to prepare for the possibility of accidents, you need to anticipate and brief everyone on the trip on the potential hazards, either before or at the very beginning of the trip. By communicating information about potential hazards you make sure that everyone takes the proper safety steps to help reduce the accident potential. If there is no defined trip leader, someone should be assigned the task of researching and presenting this information to the rest of the group.

Take Responsibility

On any wilderness trip it is important that each group member accept a level of personal responsibility for maintaining a safe environment. This is true even in situations where there are defined trip leaders.

Analyze Risk on the Trail

When you are out on the trail you need to be constantly vigilant for hazards by using situational awareness and "Leader's Radar" (see below) to be aware of current conditions and hazard factors.

Eliminate Hazards and Increase Safety

When risk starts to increase, take proactive steps to either reduce the hazard factors (some of which may be beyond your control) or enhance the safety factors. Show people when accident potential is increasing and ask them what can be done to reduce it.

Example: Your group is hiking along an exposed ridge as a cold front moves through. The wind picks up significantly along the edge of the cold front, and the temperature drops from 60°F to 45°F (15°C to 7°C), then it suddenly starts to rain (environmental hazards). People are tired from the long hike (human hazard), don't have rain gear on (equipment hazard), and are starting to get wet (human hazard). You see an increasing accident potential for hypothermia from the cold and wet conditions. (See "Hypothermia," page 332.) You know that you can't do anything to reduce the new weather hazards, but you can increase the safety factors by having people add warm layers, making sure people are well-fed, keeping them active, and having everyone get on rain gear. If, after attending to all of those things, you still have a significant accident potential, then it is time to take more decisive action, such as setting up camp and getting everyone under shelter, putting people together in sleeping bags for warmth, and so on. Keep monitoring the storm for other dangers like high winds or lightning and decide if you need to move off the ridge for added safety.

SITUATIONAL AWARENESS—"LEADER'S RADAR"

Part of managing safety in the outdoors (or anywhere) is being constantly aware of the current conditions and changes in those conditions. Situational awareness is used in settings from police and firefighters to NASA space missions. In professional outdoor programs it's often referred to as "Leader's Radar." (See Chapter 10, "Outdoor Leadership.") Here are some of the things you want to be constantly "scanning" for:

- Current weather and pending weather
- Time of day (how many hours of daylight)

- How much farther to your planned destination
- Terrain and elevation (what's ahead of you and what's behind you)
- How many people in your group and where everyone is
- How far away you are from help (in your daily evacuation plan, where would you go for help)
- Your resources—equipment, food, people, etc.
- How you and everyone else in your group are doing (warmth, energy level, attitude, etc.).

ANALYZING ACCIDENTS—CLOSING THE CIRCLE

What happens if you do have an accident or near miss on the trail? After it's over, go back and examine what happened and why so that you can be better prepared to avoid such an accident in the future. Analyzing a near miss is also important because there are far more near misses than real accidents.

If a serious accident occurs, the group members may have personal emotional issues to deal with. A supportive group environment and personal counseling may be required after a severe accident. The accident analysis may need to wait until the personal healing process has begun.

In an accident analysis, you want to examine issues like:

- What were the precipitating environmental, equipment, and human hazards?
- Could any hazards have been reduced or eliminated?
- What safety factors were in place? Were they sufficient?
- Did people have the right training and experience?
- Once the accident happened, how did you respond? Could you have done anything differently?

Books like *Accidents in North American Mountaineering* and *American Whitewater River Accidents Summary* are useful guides to accident analysis (see the Bibliography).

SENDING FOR HELP

If you end up in an emergency situation, you need to evaluate your available resources and contact others if you need additional help. If a situation requires you to send for help (injury, illness, lost person), it is important to implement the following procedures:

Collect Pertinent Information

- Name, address, phone number, and age of victim.
- A written record of the patient's initial condition and current condition; description of how accident occurred—date and time; description of injuries; vital signs; and first aid performed. (See SOAP Note, page 421.)
- A copy of the Emergency Information Report (see page 419) with:
  - Location of the group on a marked map; use compass bearings if necessary
  - First-aid equipment you have on hand
  - First-aid equipment needed
  - Type of rescue or medical support you need

Call for Help

If you are carrying a phone or radio of some kind, make sure you know who to call in an emergency. Gather all the critical information *before* you call. If you have a bad connection or limited battery, make every second count. As soon as you know you have an emergency, that's the time to call for help.

Know Where to Go for Help

If you need to hike out to request help, you should be generally aware from your pre-trip planning of where to go. Locate the nearest and/or easiest place to reach: a house, ranger station, roadway, or phone. Keep in mind that reaching an isolated road in the backcountry may be the same as being in the wilderness (no houses, no phones, no cars).

Organize the Group

You need to have a plan for what the group staying behind will do—stay where they are or move to a trail junction, shelter, or roadhead—and where *exactly* they will be. If the group does move, they should leave a note at their original location stating their planned route, destination, time they departed, and estimated time of arrival. This same information should be left at any trail junctions or major intersections the group passes.

Enlist Outside Aid

If there are other hikers in the area, try to enlist their aid, whether it's hiking out for help or assisting with first aid. Remember, someone still needs to be in charge. Asking other people for help means incorporating them into *your* emergency response plan. Make this clear at the outset—otherwise, these folks may just aggravate the situation. If someone in the other group has more experience (in first aid or emergency management), you might ask that person to take over. Always make sure that the transfer of responsibility is clear. If you feel that the person is not handling the situation properly, discuss it with the individual. If you don't reach an agreement, you may have an obligation to resume control.

Hike Out for Help

Preferably, at least three people should hike out. The people who hike out should have the backcountry experience to do this safely on their own.

- Determine on a map the *best* route to obtain help—at a highway, gas station, town, store, ranger station, private home—*before* you depart! Keep in mind the weather, terrain, and potential obstacles. The best route out is *not* always the shortest distance out.
- Determine what the group remaining behind should do if help does not arrive by a certain time.
- The party going for help should have all the necessary equipment—map, compass, travel directions, food, water, clothing—to be able to travel quickly and should be prepared to bivouac. If you are far into the backcountry, hiking out could take several days.
- Travel quickly, but do *not* move at a pace that will put you at risk.
- Don't split up the party going for help. You don't need another emergency to deal with.
- On the hike out, particularly if you are hiking off trail, flag your route to make it easier for you and/or rescuers to find your way back.
- Conserve your strength in case you need to lead the rescue party back.
- The people hiking out should contact the authorities, arrange for rescue assistance, then determine what they will do—stay where they are or hike back in with the rescue personnel.

EVACUATION PROCEDURES

Evacuation is a general term for transporting someone from a trip. In most cases it's due to a medical problem, but it can also be caused by the person's deciding that the trip is no longer what she wants to do, the trip turns out to be too difficult, a psychological problem, family emergency, or the assessment by the trip leaders that the person's behavior is inappropriate or poses a threat to herself or others in the group.

If someone needs to be evacuated as the result of an injury or illness, the primary concern is for the safety and health of the patient, and the secondary one is the safety and health of the other members of the group. (Specific evacuation protocols for first-aid situations are covered in Chapter 9.) When assessing the need for an evacuation, think both of the patient's condition and how rapidly medical attention is needed. For example, it may take two hours for the patient to walk out on her own, whereas to send two people out for help (two hours), get a rescue squad to the trailhead (one hour), hike back in (two hours), and hike back out (two hours +) will mean over seven hours before the patient is evacuated. The injury may need treatment sooner than that. (Some people carry cellphones or satellite phones to try and reduce this response time, see page 64.) Carefully evaluate your resources: Do you have the necessary equipment, manpower, and experience to *safely* evacuate the person, given the person's condition and the current trail and weather conditions? If you do evacuate the person, take the time to plan the best route out, keeping in mind the patient's condition, the distance, and the terrain. Depending on the situation, you might choose the shortest route, the quickest route, or a longer route that poses less threat to the patient. Use the evacuation scenario list below and the flowchart one page 237 to determine how to deal with an evacuation situation.

POSSIBLE EVACUATION SCENARIOS

1. **Walk Out**   The person's medical condition would not be compromised by walking out. *Examples:* stomach ailment, mild allergic reaction, minor laceration.
2. **Walk Out with Assistance**   If the distance is not too great, the person may be able to hike out if carrying little or no weight and/or with assistance. This is to be attempted *only* as long as it does not aggravate the individual's condition. The person should be constantly monitored. *Examples:* stable ankle sprain, fractured forearm.
3. **Cannot Walk Out**   The injury or illness would be aggravated by walking out or movement is contraindicated. In this case, the person is either going to need to be packaged in a rescue litter and hiked out on the trail, or some form of motorized transport is required. Building a makeshift litter and transporting an injured person over difficult terrain takes a lot of skill and a lot of people. You shouldn't attempt a litter evacuation unless you have the necessary equipment, experience, and manpower; otherwise, you risk additional injury to your patient as well as placing other members of the group at risk. In that case, send for help. *Examples:* head injury, femur fracture, spinal injury.

The following flow chart will help you make the determination about how to evacuate your patient:

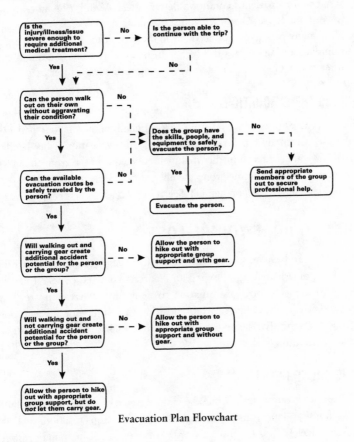

Evacuation Plan Flowchart

CHOOSING TO EVACUATE

If you have determined that it is appropriate to evacuate your patient, you need to determine whether or not you have the skills, the time, and the manpower to perform the evacuation safely. Ask yourself these questions:

- How far do you have to hike out? How long will it take (be conservative)?
- How much daylight do you have?
- What is the weather? Is it changing? For the worse?
- Can you continue to provide the necessary first-aid treatment and monitoring during the evacuation?

- Do you have the necessary equipment to properly package and transport the victim?
- What if your patient's condition deteriorates? Would it be more difficult to continue to treat her once you start hiking out?
- How many people do you have to do the evacuation? For a litter evacuation over any significant distance you should plan to have a minimum of three teams of six to eight people rotating through the litter carry.

RUNNING THE EVACUATION

Once an evacuation starts, you need to continually monitor your patient for changes to her condition. Be prepared to halt the evacuation if her condition worsens or you need to do further treatment. Someone in the group should also be monitoring the rest of the group members and the environment to be on the alert for increasing accident potential. (See "How Accidents Happen," page 225.)

WHAT TO DO IF YOU'RE LOST

Getting lost can be as simple as heading out from camp to go to the bathroom and getting disoriented or following an incorrect compass course. Keep calm and try to gather enough information to determine where you are. If you panic, the possibilities of getting more lost increase, and your accident potential rises dramatically. The best thing to do is stay where you are and properly assess the situation.

IF THE GROUP GETS LOST

If your entire group is lost, it may be embarrassing and inconvenient, but it's usually not that dangerous (unless you are in a dangerous location, such as an exposed ridgeline in a lightning storm). You have all your human resources and equipment, so if you came properly prepared, you should be able to deal with the basic survival issues (see "The Five Elements of Survival," page 250) and then work on figuring out where you are.

General Guidelines

- If you have a GPS (see "Global Positioning System," page 162), see if you can get a satellite fix on your location and then identify your position on the map. Otherwise . . .
- Identify your *last known position*. Mark the current time. Check with all group members about what they remember since that point, including landmarks, trail junctions, and signs.

- Determine how long it has been since your last known position. Subtract the time for any lunch or meal breaks to calculate your total hiking time since your last known position.
- Estimate your hiking speed and try to include time for descents and ascents. (See "Estimating Travel Times," page 12.)
- Using your last known position and the estimated elapsed hiking time, you should be able to determine how far you could have traveled since your last known point—a radius of travel. Draw a circle with a slightly larger radius (to account for inaccuracies in your estimates) on your map. This represents the possible area that you are in. You may be able to eliminate certain possibilities based on the topography. For example, there may be obvious baselines such as rivers and roads. If you have not crossed these, then at least you know where you have not been. Systematic elimination of where you *aren't* helps identify where you *are*.
- Look for any major landmarks or terrain features around you. See if you can locate those features on the map. With the map oriented, you may be able to determine a rough location with respect to local landmarks. It's essential that you be sure about your landmarks. For example, in an extremely mountainous area, it may be difficult to tell which peak is which.
- You may be able to locate your position using map and compass through triangulation (see page 160).

IF YOU OR SOMEONE IN THE GROUP GETS LOST

If you are a member of a group, and you get separated or lost from the group, it is important to follow these guidelines. The first 30 minutes of being lost is the time when people tend to make their biggest mistakes. The Mountain Rescue Association, which represents thousands of search-and-rescue mountaineers nationwide, suggests that you S.T.O.P—Sit, Think, Observe, and Plan. Don't just react. Think through your situation and make good decisions. Everyone should be briefed on these procedures at the start of the trip. (See "The Five Elements of Survival," page 250, for more details.)

- *Don't panic. Stay calm.* Your attitude is the most important factor in reducing accident potential.
- *As long as you are not in any immediate danger, stay right where you are!* As soon as the group notices that you are gone, they will begin search procedures. It is best not to wander farther. This only increases the size of the search area.
- Look and listen for the signals of rescuers and be prepared to make your own signals. Three of anything (whistles, shouts, flashes of a flashlight) are the universal distress signal. (See "Signaling for Help," page 241.)

- If for a safety reason you need to move, it is best not to move far. Go only as far as it takes to remove yourself from the immediate hazard (lightning, rockfall, avalanche, etc.). If possible, leave a note or other indication that you were there and where you went (rock cairns, arrows on the ground).
- Take stock of your resources, equipment, water, any food. These can be vitally important. Do *not* leave any equipment behind.
- It is essential that you conserve body heat and energy. Be watchful of hypothermia. Put on all of your layers of clothing before you begin to get cold. You can increase your insulation by stuffing dry leaves into the open spaces in your clothing. A survival shelter may also be useful (see page 251).
- When it gets dark, sit down and rest. If possible, build a safe fire. This will keep you warm and serve as a signal for rescuers.

IF YOU ARE HIKING ALONE AND GET LOST

Follow the steps outlined above. Of course, the cardinal rule of backpacking alone is always to let someone know where you're going and when you'll return. If you have left your trip plan with someone and the person knows who to call if you are overdue, then your best move is to stay where you are and concentrate on the survival basics (see page 250).

IDENTIFYING YOUR LOCATION

In some situations, it may be necessary to try to locate where you are or move to a safer area. You'll need to use your best judgment to decide whether to sit tight and wait for help or try and hike out on your own. Use S.T.O.P. described on page 239 before you even think of moving. One thing to keep in mind is not to move during extreme weather conditions, as you only increase your risk of hypothermia and of getting more lost. Take shelter and keep warm until the bad weather has passed. Then begin your exploration to discover where you are. Follow the general survival guidelines given on page 250. If you still have no idea where you are, and it is not appropriate to wait for help, use the following techniques described by David Seidman in *The Essential Wilderness Navigator*. You need to have a map and a compass or GPS to help.

Star Compass Search

Visualize Your Starting Point   Look around you; this is your starting point. Take "mental snapshots" (or photos if you have a digital camera). Look for obvious landmarks and jot down a few notes to help you remember. Mark your starting point somehow with a stick in the ground or a rock cairn or use a memorable boulder or tree so that you can recognize it when you return or make a quick "map" of the area. Walk around and look at your starting point from a variety of different directions so you will recognize it when you return.

Star-shaped Compass Search   Now do a quick search for landmarks to identify your location. *Taking all your gear with you,* follow a short straight-line compass course out from home base along each of the cardinal compass points (N, S, E, W) and then the intercardinal compass points (NE, NW, SE, SW). Go out on each line for 5 minutes, looking for landmarks. Write down any landmarks you find, then return to your home base following a back bearing on your compass. (See "Back Bearings," page 156.) You will end up creating a star pattern. Look at your collected landmarks and your map to see if you can now identify your location.

SIGNALING FOR HELP

Signaling for help is essential for increasing your chances of being located quickly. Here are some techniques for signaling rescuers:

- A series of three anything (whistles, flashes, etc.) is the universal signal for distress.
- Fires—during the day the smoke will be more visible. At night, the flame will be your best signal. Putting anything made of rubber will generate smoke and make a more visible fire. Burning wet wood or pine branches or leaves will also create a smoky fire, one that searchers may also be able to smell from a distance.
- Mirrors can reflect sunlight beyond the horizon up to 7 million candlepower. Hold the mirror in your hand with your arm outstretched. Sight along your arm to aim the mirror flash at particular points along the horizon. Send three flashes. Some rescue mirrors actually have a sighting hole to let you focus on a target.
- Strip signals on the ground. These can be built of rocks or tree branches or dug in the ground and are designed to be seen from the air. Make your signal big (20 feet long or 6 meters) so that it can be seen from a distance, and select a highly visible location. The universal signals are shown on the following page.

I	II	F
Require Doctor Serious Injury	**Require Medical Supplies**	**Require Food and Water**
K	X	↑
Indicate Direction to Proceed	**Unable to Proceed**	**Am Proceeding in This Direction**
▢	△	LL
Require Map and Compass	**Probably Safe to Land Here**	**All is Well**
N	Y	JL
No Negative	**Yes Affirmative**	**Do Not Understand**

Universal Emergency Signals

Lost Person Behavior

Significant research has been done on how lost people behave. According to the Mountain Rescue Association, these are some of the common behaviors:

- If a lost person finds a trail, she might start hiking, convinced she's on the way back to her last point, when in fact she might be hiking away from it.
- A lost person will rarely reverse her direction on a trail.
- Many people ignore trails and follow their own logic, traveling in a straight line. They figure they'll eventually come to a road or highway, not expecting that they may hit a cliff or an impassable river.
- Some lost people will climb/hike to the top of a hill to get a better view, only to discover that the trees obstruct any view.
- The majority of lost people will travel downhill and/or downstream under the mistaken impression that all water leads to civilization. Many times drainages lead away from civilization or to impassable areas like deep river gorges or water falls.
- Many lost people will travel at night, desperate to "find civilization" even without a flashlight.

- Most lost people will stay on a trail if they're not absolutely sure of the right direction.
- Lost people rarely move around randomly—they usually move with conviction and hope that they're heading in the right direction. This is a key feature of the psychology of lost person behavior. Under the stress and fear of being lost, people often want to *do* something rather than sitting in one place, even though moving is usually the worst thing to do.

FINDING A LOST PERSON

If you separate your group for Leave No Trace reasons or other considerations, you need to be sure that each person or subgroup has the necessary skills, equipment, and judgment to reach your intended campsite. If you aren't sure this is the case, don't split up the group. In any case, know where every member of the group is. A lost person must be considered a potential emergency situation. If you discover someone is missing, take the following steps:

Gather Information

The most important part of starting any search is to gather data. Establish where the person was last seen (known as the point last seen or PLS). What time was it? What direction was she was heading? Did she say anything about where she was going? What was she wearing? What equipment did she have with her? What was her state of mind?

Establish a Search Area

The last time the person was seen, compared with the current time, will give you an indication of how far the person *could* have traveled. Estimate the hiking speed of the person and determine how far she could have walked. Use this estimate for the radius of your circle from the PLS. This establishes your general search perimeter. The longer someone has been missing, the larger the search area. If you remember your basic math, the area inside a circle is calculated by multiplying Π (3.14) by the radius of the circle squared. Assuming that the person walked the entire time at a pace of 20 minutes per mile (1.6 kilometers), you can see in the table below how rapidly the size of the search area increases. That's why it is so important to treat a lost person as an emergency and to get rescue help quickly.

Time Missing	Distance Hiked	Area to be Searched
20 minutes	1 mile/1.6 kilometers	3.1 sq. miles/8.0 sq. kilometers
40 minutes	2 miles/3.2 kilometers	12.5 sq. miles/32.1 sq. kilometers
1 hour	3 miles/4.8 kilometers	28.2 sq. miles/72.3 sq. kilometers
2 hours	6 miles/9.6 kilometers	113 sq. miles/289.3 sq. kilometers

Make a Quick Check of Area Last Seen

If you are near the point where the person was last seen, make a quick check of the area. Shout the person's name and look around for clues.

Make a Hasty Search

If shouting does not bring a response, group members *in pairs* should perform an organized *hasty search*. Take time to plan out where searchers will go on the hasty search *before* sending them out. Look particularly in any areas that seem *probable* based on your earlier information gathering (i.e., the person was heading south out of camp, wanted to see the sunset, etc.). Identify the most likely places the person might be—nearby trails, lookout points, nearby streams or lakes, etc., and send teams to search those locations. Have search teams stop periodically and blow a whistle or shout, listen carefully for a response. The person may be injured and be unable to respond loudly, if at all. Look for visible clues such as clothing or belongings in case the person is unable to answer. There are always going to be more *clues* than victims. Search for approximately 20 to 30 minutes.

Establish an operations base camp. Build a smoky fire, make noise, blow whistles, etc., to attract the person. Communication between search teams is essential. Make sure the teams check in and provide detailed information about where they went. Documenting the search should be started right away. What time did the search begin? Where did searchers look? Keep written records and jot notes on maps. All of this can help reduce the area that needs to be searched later. As soon as possible, identify a "scent article" such as socks, underwear, or hat from the person for search dogs. Take a plastic bag and invert it over your hand. Using the bag like a glove, pick up the articles, then invert the bag over the items so your hand never comes in contact with the articles. Save this for the rescue team. Leave notes at any trailheads or other exit points telling the lost party what to do if she gets there.

Make a Secondary Search

If the hasty search does not bring results, a more systematic *secondary search* should be initiated by teams covering nearby trails, roads, water areas, and cliffs. Based on the elapsed time since the person was last seen, determine a general search perimeter, assuming an average walking speed for that person. Based on your location and resources, you will need to determine how long it will take to do a secondary search. Take time to plan out where searchers should go to cover all likely locations before sending them out. Search teams need to have all the basic survival equipment with them (water, food, clothing, rain gear) and have the experience to prevent *themselves* from getting lost. In case of darkness, all searchers should be equipped with headlights and should always be within sight of the next searcher.

Go for Help

If the secondary search does not bring results quickly (within 1 hour or so), or the possible search perimeter is too large for you to cover, you may need to send for help in order to bring in rangers or other rescue personnel for a more extensive search. (See "Signaling for Help," page 241.) This of course depends on where you are and how far away help might be. If you decide to go for help, *don't delay or "wait another hour."* Fill out the Emergency Information Report (see page 419) and follow the instructions for groups hiking out for help. As a team goes out for help or someone tries on a phone, the other members can continue the secondary search. If the person is found after the team goes for help, determine how long the help team has been gone and how long it was expected to take them to get out. *Do not* try to chase down the team if they have too much of a head start; rushing out could lead to another accident. You may need to wait for the rescue personnel to return with the team.

Perform a Line Search

A line search is the last resort in search and rescue. It is both incredibly time-consuming and requires large numbers of people. A line search should only be performed when you have narrowed down a search area with clues. If you are in a situation where you have to resort to a line search you should have already sought help from outside rescue professionals.

A line search should be performed only once you have some clues as to the person's location—a piece of clothing or gear, footprints, and so on. The "exceptions" to waiting for rescue professionals to do a line search are immediate life-threatening "lost people," like someone buried in an avalanche or trapped underwater. These "line" searches must happen in minutes.

The line search assumes that the person may not be able to respond. The line search requires the group to spread out in a line. Searchers should be close enough together (for that particular terrain and vegetation) to be able to see all the ground between themselves and the people next to them. Someone must take the role of the search commander and start the group moving forward at a controlled pace. Look for the lost person and for any clues to her whereabouts. Look behind you regularly for clues that might be behind rocks or trees. At any sign of a clue, the entire group should be told to stop while the clue is examined, and if possible identified as belonging to the missing person, and recorded in writing. Then the search line should continue. The search commander keeps track of areas searched, clues found, and moves the search line as needed.

Stopping the Search

Choosing to stop a search is a highly emotional decision. With outside help, you can rely on experts in search and rescue to take charge and bring their experience and more advanced resources to bear (such as helicopters, search dogs, and advanced search data analysis). If you are on your own, you will need to decide how long to continue the search. Bad weather, difficult terrain, or lack of sleep can place the searchers at significant risk, and you do *not* need another victim. You may need to call off your search, rest, and resume later. If the risk to others is significant, you may need to discontinue the search. If you haven't already, you should contact local rescue authorities. They may be able to restart the search, or determine that the search should be terminated.

FOREST FIRES

When traveling in the backcountry, it is important to be aware of fire hazards. Just like avalanche forecasts in the winter, many wilderness areas post seasonal fire danger levels. Check with local rangers to determine the fire danger before you go out. If the fire danger is high, you may have to reduce fire or stove use, or even reroute your trip. Fire is a complicated aspect of wilderness management. In some ecosystems, natural fires from lightning strikes are *part* of the forest ecosystem—some pinecones open and release their seeds only at temperatures of 120°F (49°C). It is only recently that land managers have come to appreciate the role that fire plays in keeping forests healthy. Fifty years of fire suppression policies have left many areas prone to devastating wildfires.

Natural fires are caused primarily by lightning strikes. However, most of the fires in the United States are caused by human activities, including campfires, smoking, debris burning, toilet paper burning, and equipment use. Assess the fire danger in an area before you go in, avoid inadvertently starting a fire, and know how to evacuate yourself to safety in the event of a fire.

THE DYNAMICS OF FOREST FIRE

Any substance that will ignite and combust is potential fuel for a fire. For a living plant, more than half of the plant's weight is water, so living plants are relatively resistant to burning. Most fires start with dry or dead fuel. Fine fuels, like dry grasses and twigs less than ¼ inch (6 millimeters) across, are easy to combust; once burning, they carry the fire to the larger fuels. As the fire spreads outward, the heat from the fire dries out the surrounding fuel and increases the likelihood that this fuel will begin to burn—this is known as *preheating*. Initially only dry, dead material burns, but once a fire is blazing, it can preheat and then burn *live* plants and trees.

In the forest, there are three basic types of fires, and most fires are some combination of these types:

- **Surface Fires** burn litter on the surface, such as grasses, small plants, shrubs, small trees, and downed limbs and branches.
- **Ground Fires** burn the duff and organic layer in the soil beneath the surface litter.
- **Crown Fires** burn the tops of trees and shrubs.

How Fire Moves

Depending on the conditions, fire can spread slowly (¼ mph or 0.4 kph) or fast (5+ mph or 8+ kph). Understanding how a fire is moving will help you determine which directions are safest and which directions are most dangerous. From the point of ignition, the fire spreads in three directions:

- **Head** (forward)   Rapidly spreads in the direction the wind is blowing
- **Flank** (at the sides)   Spreads less rapidly at right angles to the direction of the wind
- **Rear** (rearward)   Moves slowly into the wind (aka, a backing fire)

Effect of Terrain on a Fire

If the ground surface is basically flat, the flames from an already ignited area can preheat only a few trees at a time, and the fire spreads slowly. On a steep slope, flame can preheat many more trees above it, and the fire spreads much more rapidly upslope. At the top of a peak or a ridge, the flame cannot preheat trees on the down slope side away from the fire, so it rapidly uses up existing fuel and may die out.

Effect of Wind on a Fire

Any wind can significantly enhance the spread of the fire up the slope by bringing the flame closer to unburned trees and preheating them. A strong wind can do this on horizontal surfaces and steep slopes. At a peak or ridgetop, wind may actually bend the flame down the far side of the slope, preheating more fuel and allowing the fire to continue down the far side of the ridge. Winds may be part of the local weather pattern; however, a large fire often creates its own winds. As air above the fire is heated, it rises, creating convection currents (air flowing in to replace the rising air). The hotter the fire, the more air may be sucked into it, fanning the flames.

FIRE SAFETY PLAN

Fire Prevention

If the fire danger in the region is high, follow the local guidelines set by the rangers. As the fire danger increases, you may need to modify your activities, which could mean no campfires of any kind or no stove use.

Fire Evacuation

In order to escape a fire, you must first be sensitive to signs of fire. Here are general procedures for escaping a forest fire:

- Be aware of any smoke. Smoke may be evident long before the fire is actually visible. If smoke is present, ascertain the wind direction and try to locate the fire.
- If you see fire, estimate the spreading intensity, the direction of the fire, and the extent of the fire, including the effects of the wind speed, wind direction, and terrain. Keep in mind that mountain ridges often have their own up-currents and down-currents that may be moving differently from the general weather pattern of winds.
- Once you have determined the general location of a possible fire, decide if you are upwind or downwind of it. Identify as best you can the fire area on your map. Look for the nearest trailhead, road, or other connection with civilization that does *not* take you toward the fire. If you must move toward the fire, move along the *flank* or *rear* of the fire. The expansion of

the fire is much slower there, and you may have enough time to evacuate your group past the fire.

- When you have reached civilization, contact local rangers and emergency personnel. Provide them with as much detail as you can about the size and type of fire and its location. Give them your exact location and arrange for any additional transport your group may need. Also, make sure that the parking area for the vehicle is not at risk. If so, ask the rangers what they can do to help you get to and move your vehicle.

Burn Injuries

When we think of fire, we typically think of the damage caused by burns from the actual flames. However, more than just the flames are dangerous. In a forest fire, air temperatures are extremely hot. Injuries and burns can occur simply from contact with this superheated air. Inhaling this heated air can cause serious burns to lung tissue. Smoke inhalation and lung damage are also serious concerns in a fire. For first-aid treatment of smoke and fire-related injuries, see "Thermal Burns," page 314.

Fire Survival

If you are unable to escape an oncoming fire, there are only a few alternatives:

- Do your best to locate the fire and move perpendicularly away from the *flank* of the fire.
- If the surface fire is severe or approaching fast and crowning, look for the nearest large body of water and take shelter in the water. You are safer in the water, but be aware of the possibility of hypothermia from prolonged exposure to cold water.
- Go to an area with little fuel, such as a creek bed (even a dry one) or rockslide.
- Go to an area that has already burned (and hence is devoid of fuel).

FIGHTING FIRES

Don't try to put out a significant fire if you don't have the training or experience. But in some situations you might come upon a very small fire. At the initial ignition stage, you *may* be able to contain a small surface fire. Deny the fire access to additional fuel by clearing downed branches, shrubs, and duff from its path. Once you have removed the fuel source, the fire will either burn itself out or you may be able to extinguish the remaining flames by dowsing the fire with water or dirt. This may be possible, *but only if the fire is small.*

Without special training in fire fighting and the proper equipment, it is extremely difficult to put out anything but a *very* small surface fire. *Do not attempt to do so* if it means placing your group in danger. (See "How Accidents Happen," page 225.) Contact area land managers and let them know the exact location of the fire as soon as possible, even if you were able to put it out. They will most likely want to check the area.

WILDERNESS SURVIVAL

If you find yourself in an emergency situation where you are cut off from help for an extended period with limited resources, don't panic. The Mountain Rescue Association's guideline is S.T.O.P—Sit, Think, Observe, and Plan. Spend the time to take stock of the situation and your resources, and make a definitive plan. In typical situations you can survive up to three days without water and up to three weeks without food. In fact, most of the tools that you need to survive are all around you. Learning a few basic techniques and maintaining a positive attitude will cover your immediate needs for a few days to a week. Here's what to do:

- Attend to any immediate dangers—avalanche, fire, etc.
- Thoughtfully recognize the hazards of your situation and remain calm.
- Calmly assess all of your resources.
- Attend to the basic elements of survival.
- Signal for rescue.

THE FIVE ELEMENTS OF SURVIVAL

Once you acknowledge that you are in a survival situation, you should take inventory of all the food and equipment you have on hand—you may need everything. Then attend to the basic priorities of survival. In *Tom Brown's Field Guide to Wilderness Survival,* Tom Brown describes five basic survival priorities you should attend to:

1. **Attitude**   Maintaining a positive attitude is essential. You *can* survive if you stay calm, use all your available resources, and prioritize your basic needs.
2. **Shelter**   A shelter is designed to provide protection from the weather and, depending on the conditions, to protect you either from heat or cold. Hypothermia or hyperthermia are two of the greatest dangers in a survival situation. A proper shelter can prevent these situations. In a desert scenario, for example, your goal is to stay under a shelter, shaded from the effects of the sun. In cold weather situations, the shelter provides insulation from the cold.

3. **Water** Water is the most essential "nutrient" for the human body. With adequate shelter and water you can survive for weeks.
4. **Fire** In a survival situation, fire provides heat and light, and signals to rescuers.
5. **Food** Individuals in good physical condition can go for up to two to three weeks without food. Your goal in a wilderness survival situation is to be located in a matter of days, so in most cases you will be located long before food becomes a survival issue. Obtaining food is 90 percent of wilderness survival technique and is beyond the scope of this book. This includes knowledge of edible plants, tracking, hunting, stalking, trapping, and so on. (If you are interested in learning these skills, see the Bibliography.)

SHELTER

If you are in a survival situation, your first priority is to construct a shelter to protect you from the elements. Wetness, cold, and heat are your main enemies. Natural shelters, such as caves, overhangs, and rock outcrops, may protect you from rain but don't provide any insulation. They should be used only temporarily, in sudden inclement weather, until you can build a survival shelter or turn them into an insulated shelter as described below.

The Debris Hut

Tom Brown, in his book *Tom Brown's Field Guide to Wilderness Survival,* describes the debris hut as the most basic survival shelter that can be built almost anywhere. If you've ever seen a squirrel's nest up in a tree, then you understand the basics of creating a survival shelter. The nest is a ball of leaves creating dead air space. In cold conditions, this holds in body heat; in hot conditions, it keeps cooler air trapped inside. You should build your debris hut *first* so that you are prepared for any bad weather—rain, a sudden temperature drop, scorching heat—and can avoid hypothermia or hyperthermia. The following are some good places to build a debris hut:

- In a high, well-drained area, raised off the general ground level.
- In a protected area (wind makes it difficult to build a debris hut, and convection can rob you of stored hot or cool air).
- Where there is good shelter building material close at hand. This conserves energy needed for survival. Building a shelter is an energy-demanding survival activity, so you need to do it efficiently.
- No closer than 50 to 100 feet (15 to 30 meters) to water. The humid air near a water source will make you feel warmer in hot weather and colder in cool weather. The moist air also makes it difficult to dry out the

insulating materials of your debris hut, thereby reducing the maximum insulative efficiency of your shelter.

- At least 6 feet (2 meters) from your fire. A debris hut is actually a giant tinder bundle, so you need to be very careful with fire.

The debris hut consists of a central ridgepole with one end on the ground and the other lashed to a tree or propped against a stump or boulder. The ridgepole should be long enough so that you can lie completely under the length of the pole without your feet being smushed. Two angled poles come from the highest point of the ridgepole to the ground in an A-frame and form the opening. The front of the ridgepole should be high enough so that, while lying on your side, you can just barely touch the ridgepole. With this general frame in place, line branches across the ridgepole from the ground on either side for ribs. Over a good layer of branches, pile light and airy brush (pine boughs, moss, sagebrush, leaves) to act as an insulative layer. Cover the outer layer with a few light branches to keep the insulating layer from blowing away. The hut will eventually look like a dome of debris with a triangular door (see illustration). Once the hut has been built into a dome, stuff the inside with more insulative material—dried leaves, pine needles, dried grasses. You are creating a massive dead air space to provide insulation for your body. Crawl in and pack more dried materials around your body. In effect, you are creating both an insulated shelter and a sleeping bag in one.

For insulation materials, the best sources are dry vegetation such as dried grasses, ferns, and leaves. If none are available, you can use green plants. (For Leave No Trace reasons you should *only* use green plants if you are in a true survival situation.) Green plants are mostly water; just like wet clothing, a wet plant will conduct heat 25 times faster than a dry one. If the material you are using is green, you should increase the overall thickness of the hut by about one third to compensate. The actual thickness of your debris hut will depend on the temperature. In the summer, the wall should be as thick as the distance from your outstretched finger to the middle of your upper arm; in the fall (40°F or 4°C), the

Debris Hut

wall thickness should measure from your fingertip to armpit; and in the winter (17°F or –8°C), the wall should be 4 to 5 feet (1.2 to 1.5 meters) thick.

In certain regions, small critters like ticks and brown recluse spiders may end up in your hut with all the leaf litter. In a real survival situation, the idea that you might get Lyme disease from a tick is a minimal risk compared to the possibility of death from hypothermia, but if you are just practicing, you should be aware of these risks.

WATER

Water is your single most important "nutrient." You can go *only* for 24 to 72 hours without water before the effects of dehydration become apparent: impaired judgment, loss of strength and motor coordination, and increased susceptibility to hypothermia and hyperthermia. Dehydration ultimately leads to death. That's why staying hydrated is the second priority if you are in a survival situation. Whatever the water source, it is essential to *know about the purity of the water you are drinking.* (See Chapter 4, "Hygiene and Water Purification.") It may sound strange, but drinking contaminated water can be as dangerous as not drinking at all. If you get a major gastrointestinal infection from contaminated water, you can lose so much water from diarrhea or vomiting that you may die (see "Shock," page 274). In a survival situation you often will need to look for multiple sources of water. If safe water is not readily available, structure your day to conserve water. Work during the cooler morning and evening hours and rest during the hot part of the day in the shade to reduce sweating and water loss.

Rivers, Lakes, and Streams

Before going into an area, it is important to check with local land managers about water quality. The water should be clear and running quickly; standing water becomes stagnant and contaminated with microorganisms. Ask yourself what's upstream—a town, cattle ranch, campers—that could be contaminating the water source. You should assume all water is contaminated and purify it, if possible. (See "Water Purification," page 94.)

Areas devoid of vegetation may indicate contaminated or toxic water. Dead animals in the water upstream can cause contamination that will not be apparent. Observe what animals are doing—are they drinking the water? If so, it *may* be okay. But keep in mind that animals are resistant or immune to many microorganisms that we are not. It's also best to get water upstream of animal drinking areas to avoid their possible contamination of the water from things like *Giardia*. (See "Gastrointestinal Infections," page 370.)

Natural Caches

Natural caches are depressions in rocks, hollow tree stumps, and such that collect rainwater. These are less desirable than moving water, but *may* be okay if the water has recently collected. The big question is, how long has the water been sitting there? In many cases you won't know. Water that has been standing for some time often becomes stagnant and contaminated with microorganisms. Look at the water in the cache. If it is cloudy, assume it is contaminated and do not drink it *unless* you can boil or purify it. Even clear water can be contaminated, so it's best to purify all water unless it is fresh-cache rainwater. Try to avoid stirring up debris as you get water. Put a cloth in to soak up water and wring it into a container or your mouth. You can create your own rainfall caches using pots or water bottles.

Soaks

There is always water underground, even in the desert. The question is how far down and how much energy (and fluid from sweat) would be expended to reach it. In many situations, water may be close enough to the surface for you to tap it.

Look to see where there is runoff, for areas of vegetation where "watery" plants are very thick, and for moist depressions in the soil. Dig a hole at these sites and see if it fills with water. If so, you may be able to scoop the top layer. You can also stick a hollow reed or straw into the hole. The capillary action of the reed will bring the water up, leaving the debris behind.

Solar Still

You can create a solar still almost anywhere to make fresh drinking water. The solar still uses the sun's energy to extract moisture from plants or other water sources through condensation. Since the water recondenses from vapor, any microorganisms are left behind in the original water source, creating microbiologically pure water (it does not remove chemical contaminates). You need a 5 by 5-foot (1.5 by 1.5 meters) piece of clear plastic sheeting and 6 feet (2 meters) of plastic tubing. A solar still relies on moisture in the soil to work. It isn't reliable in desert situations where soil moisture in extremely low.

- Dig a pit about 3 feet deep and 4 feet across (1 by 1.2 meters) in an area with good sun exposure. Place a wide-mouthed collection container in the middle of the pit.
- Place one end of the tubing in the container and the other end on the

ground next to the pit. Place the clear plastic over the entire pit and cover the edges of the plastic with dirt to seal off the pit.

- Place a rock in the center of the plastic over the container to create a depression in the plastic. The angle of the depression should be fairly steep, about 45 degrees. The low point of the plastic sheet should be about 3 inches (8 centimeters) above the container and centered over the container so that the water will drip into it. As the sun heats up the sealed environment, the water from the ground becomes water vapor. This water vapor rises and hits the underside of the plastic sheet, where it condenses and forms droplets that roll down and drop into the container (see illustration below). The tube serves as your drinking straw.

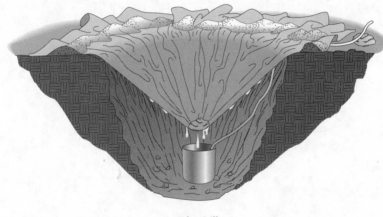

Solar Still

It will take some time to build up enough moisture in the still to start the process. The tubing allows you to suck water from the container without taking the system apart, which would just mean more time for additional water production. A solar still in a damp area will collect water for four to five days. Then simply dig a new hole and start the process again.

To increase the water production, you can "add water" to the system. Place cut green plants in the pit around the container. The sun's heat will cause their moisture to evaporate. Use edible, or at least nonpoisonous, plants—otherwise, the water that condenses may contain chemical toxins. You can also pour biologically contaminated water (like that found in an old water cache) around the edge of the pit. The water will be filtered by the dirt and distilled into biologically pure water. This technique allows you to use one still and continually "prime" it with new water.

CHAPTER 9

First Aid and Emergency Care

BACKCOUNTRY FIRST AID

Performing first aid in the backcountry may be the greatest challenge you encounter. You may be far from help and have limited first-aid supplies. Your ability to carefully examine a patient, determine a problem list, and develop a workable treatment plan may be the thing that keeps this person alive until more advanced rescue and medical care arrives. I want to thank Wilderness Medical Associates *(www.wildmed.com)* for permission to use some of their excellent teaching material in this section.

The information in this chapter is designed as reference material only, to help people who have already taken a wilderness first-aid course and CPR training. It is not a substitute for training and certification in first aid and CPR. If you have not been properly trained in these procedures, you can end up causing more harm to your patient. If you haven't taken a first-aid and CPR course, I strongly encourage you to take one before you go into the backcountry! Even a simple day trip can lead to a serious medical emergency. For a list of some organizations that offer training in wilderness first aid, see page 385. There are also a number of excellent books specifically on backcountry medicine listed in the Bibliography.

THE WILDERNESS CONTEXT

In recent years there has been new appreciation for the challenges of providing first aid in the backcountry. Minimal equipment, potentially extreme weather, and the possibility that it may be hours or days until advanced medical care arrives all create a situation comparable to "combat first aid."

In order to respond to these challenges, the Wilderness Medical Society *(www.wms.org)* and other organizations have recognized that there is a significant difference between urban first aid, where advanced medical care is often only a 911 call away and the response time is minutes, and wilderness situations where the person may be hours or days from definitive medical care. The Society defines a *wilderness context* as one that occurs more than two hours from *definitive medical care* (typically defined as a hospital emergency room or mobile paramedic emergency unit). The wilderness context also includes extended contact time with the patient (as you may be caring for this person's overall needs for hours to days) environmental hazards (keeping the person warm, dry, etc.), and coping with all of this using limited equipment. Medical professionals recognize that failure to treat certain injuries or illnesses quickly can be life-threatening or can lead to significantly greater injury. As a result, certain treatment procedures have been approved for use in the wilderness context that are *not* authorized in a typical urban situation, but *only* by those who have received wilderness first-aid instruction from an authorized source.

GOOD SAMARITAN LAWS

Whenever you talk about first aid, it is important to understand the issues of treatment and liability. If you are a licensed health-care professional (paramedic, EMT, nurse, physician, etc.), then your license establishes the parameters of what treatments you are allowed to perform and what you are not allowed to perform.

For the nonprofessional, Good Samaritan laws provide protection to render first aid to the level of their training. The Good Samaritan laws were designed to encourage people to help someone in a medical emergency without fear of being sued if something bad happens to the patient. If you have been trained and certified in CPR or wilderness first aid, and you treat someone within the guidelines of what you have been taught, the Good Samaritan laws generally protect you from a lawsuit. However, if you stray outside of that training, you expose yourself to liability. For example, if you carry medications in a first-aid kit, as a nonprofessional you are technically not permitted to give someone else a medication. This would be considered prescribing medication for someone. You can, however, inform the person of available medications that she could take, and then the person can self-administer the medication.

In a wilderness first-aid course, you may be taught techniques to use in a wilderness context that even a licensed health-care professional, like an EMT, is not authorized to do in an urban context. However, you must be extremely careful to apply your level of training to the medical context you are in. For example, if you have been properly trained in how to recognize and reduce a shoulder dislocation in a wilderness setting, you are authorized to do so only when you are in a wilderness context. Reducing a shoulder while you are in an urban setting like a playground is not appropriate since advanced medical care is less than two hours away. Rendering treatment outside of the wilderness context places you at a significant liability risk.

The bottom line is, if you are going into the backcountry, you should have solid training in wilderness first aid. Don't take a basic first-aid course designed for the urban environment. These courses will teach you only rudimentary skills like how to bandage a wound and call 911. You need the advanced skills of patient assessment, treatment techniques, and how to maintain someone for an extended period of time until advanced medical care can be reached. Using treatment procedures developed for the wilderness context is covered by the Good Samaritan law only if you have been trained in those procedures by an authorized Wilderness First Aid training program. If you have not been formally trained, then you must make the decision about how to treat your patient. Remember that the physician's motto is "Do no harm." If you are not sure what you are doing, don't blunder around or you could cause greater injury to your patient.

MAJOR BODY SYSTEMS

In order to properly evaluate a patient's medical condition, you should have a basic understanding of the three major body systems: how they function normally, what can go wrong with them, how to perform basic assessments, and what are the basic treatment protocols:

RESPIRATORY SYSTEM

Goal

Gas exchange: oxygen in and carbon dioxide out.

Problem

Respiratory failure.

Mechanisms of Injury

Airway obstruction—foreign objects (choking) or swelling (allergic reaction or asthma).

Chest wall injury.

Respiratory drive loss.

Assessment

Is air going in and out? If not, begin rescue breathing.

Rate and quality of respirations (easy or labored).

Treatment

General treatment for respiratory problems goes by the acronym PROP:

Position: Encourage the patient to rest in the position most comfortable for her. Most patients will do this on their own. If the patient is unconscious, roll her onto her side to keep the airway open.

Reassurance: Breathing difficulty is always a terrifying condition. Encourage the patient to relax, and coach her in breathing slowly and deeply.

Oxygen: If available, supplementary oxygen will increase the effectiveness of the patient's attempts to breathe.

Positive pressure ventilation: It may be necessary to assist the patient's efforts at breathing by blowing a breath into her mouth (as per rescue breathing) as she attempts to inhale.

Specific treatment of the underlying problem will vary widely. Airway obstructions should be dealt with according to your own training in basic life support (i.e., the Heimlich maneuver). If the patient is having difficulty breathing due to a chest injury, turning the patient so that she is lying on the injured side often helps relieve some respiratory difficulty.

CIRCULATORY SYSTEM

Goal
Provide an adequate supply of oxygenated blood to all body tissues (perfusion).

Problem
Shock = inadequate perfusion.

Mechanisms of Injury
Types of shock:—see Shock, page 274.

Fluid problems (loss of volume)—inadequate blood in circulation.

Pipes problems (e.g., vasodilation)—problems with blood vessels.

Pump problems (e.g., cardiac arrest)—problems with the heart muscle.

Assessment
Check for carotid pulse—if absent, begin CPR.

Check for and control major bleeding.

Secondary assessment—check distal capillary refill. See Ischemia, page 277.

Signs and symptoms of volume shock:

Increased pulse (≥100).

Increased respiration (≥24).

Pale, cool, and moist skin (as the problem progresses).

Possible loss of major quantities of body fluid.

Treatment
Volume shock is a primary life-threatening issue in the backcountry. Moderate to severe volume shock does not spontaneously improve, nor can it be definitively treated in the field. The amounts of fluid lost in these cases often cannot be replaced orally: IV fluid replacement may be necessary. Evacuation is always required.

Loss of any body fluid is ultimately reflected in reduced blood volume. Sweat, burns, vomiting, and diarrhea all lead to the same ultimate problem as bleeding. Losses from any of these sources result in exactly the same pattern of symptoms (as listed above).

Field treatment for volume shock (until the patient can be evacuated) is simple: Stop the leak. Reduce or remove the underlying cause of the volume loss—i.e., control bleeding with well-aimed direct pressure. Replace fluids if possible.

NERVOUS SYSTEM

Goal
Voluntary and involuntary control of body functions.

Problems
Inadequate perfusion to the brain.

Increasing intracranial pressure.

Spinal cord injury.

Mechanisms of Injury
Medical problems or trauma leading to swelling, inadequate perfusion.

Assessment
Level of consciousness—see AVPU scale, page 271.

Is there a mechanism for spinal injury?

Due to the tremendous potential for damage and the extreme difficulty in correctly assessing nervous system problems, any decrease in a patient's level of consciousness (anything below A on the AVPU scale) warrants evacuation (see "Vital Signs," page 270).

Other less dramatic changes in mental status (i.e., lethargy or irritability) require a bit of detective work to determine a cause and may be treatable in the field.

Wilderness Medical Associates defines seven general factors (STOPEAT) that commonly affect brain function:

Sugar—lack of blood sugar in the brain (especially an issue for a person with diabetes, see page 378).

Temperature—overheating or overcooling in the brain (see "Heatstroke," page 346, and "Hypothermia," page 332).

Oxygen—lack of oxygen in the brain.

Pressure—increasing intracranial pressure (see "Head Injury," page 306).

Electricity—electric shock, such as a lightning strike. See "Lightning Injuries," page 348.

Altitude—high altitude (which can cause lack of oxygen to the brain and brain swelling; see "Altitude Illnesses" page 380).

Toxins—various toxins (inhaled, ingested; see "Toxins," page 349).

Treatment
Ascertain the cause of the nervous system problem and treat accordingly.

ANATOMY GLOSSARY

Before we get started, here are a few general anatomy terms that will help you locate and describe an injury or illness:

- Proximal—close to the origin or point of attachment, or close to the median, or middle, line of the body
- Distal—away from the origin or point of attachment, or away from the middle line of the body
- Anterior—near the head end or toward the front plane of the body.
- Posterior—the rear plane of the body
- Medial—toward the midline of the body
- Lateral—away from the midline of the body

THE PATIENT ASSESSMENT SYSTEM

Patient assessment is the key to all medical care. You need to evaluate your patient's condition, determine what is or may be wrong, and implement an appropriate treatment plan with the equipment available. Then you need to make a judgment about whether the person can continue on the trip or whether she needs to be evacuated to definitive medical care. (See "Dealing with Emergencies—Who's In Charge?," page 224.) When in doubt, be conservative and assume the worst-case scenario.

The Patient Assessment System (PAS) is designed to provide a comprehensive approach to evaluating a patient's condition, from a minor cut to multiple traumatic injuries. Patient assessment is a complex skill that can be done well only with practice.

UNIVERSAL PRECAUTIONS FOR WORKING WITH BLOOD AND BODY FLUIDS

Before treating any patient, you need to protect yourself from exposure to blood and body fluids. There are a variety of diseases that can be transmitted from these fluids to the rescuer through contact with open cuts or mucous membranes. These include the HIV virus and hepatitis, both of which can be fatal. The basic principle of universal precautions is to always have a protective layer between you and the body fluid.

What Body Fluids Are Dangerous?

- Blood
- Blister fluid (may contain blood)
- Vaginal secretions
- Semen
- Vomit—dangerous only if the individual is vomiting up blood
- Feces, if it contains blood

What Precautions Do I Take?

The following set of universal precautions is used by hospitals and health-care organizations around the world to protect people who are exposed to body fluids. The best way to protect yourself and others is to assume that *all* body fluids are contaminated. This means *always* wearing gloves and handling contaminated items carefully. Wear disposable gloves whenever you may come in contact with body fluids. These should be handled as described below:

- Anything contaminated with body fluids (bandages, clothing, medical instruments) should be rinsed with a chlorine bleach solution (1 part bleach to 5 parts water). This will kill most microorganisms including HIV and hepatitis. Double-bag the items in two plastic bags. Do not throw out any blood-contaminated items that are sharp (e.g., syringes with needles). Owing to the risk of someone sticking herself, these items are considered medical waste. Sharp objects should be sealed in a rigid container and labeled "Medical Waste." Dispose of all medical waste properly after the trip.
- Any blood at the scene (on the ground, tarp, clothing) should be sprayed with chlorine solution.

- If you are changing a dressing, it should be considered contaminated. Dressings that have been contaminated by puslike drainage should be handled with great care to avoid spreading infection.

What About CPR?

If you need to do CPR on a patient, you should protect yourself from body fluids. Blood in the mouth, or a person vomiting blood, can be dangerous to the rescuer (and people frequently vomit during CPR). You should use a one-way valve CPR mask. The one-way valve will prevent you from inhaling or swallowing fluids from your patient and prevent your patient from being exposed to your bodily fluids.

ASSESS THE SCENE

Remember, *rescuer safety first*. Before approaching a patient, make sure that the scene is safe. You don't want more victims because people rushed foolishly into a dangerous situation. This may mean waiting for avalanche debris to settle, floodwaters to recede, etc.

- Once the situation is stabilized, approach the victim.
- Account for all victims.
- If the patient is in *imminent danger* (for example, a dangerous forest fire), you may need to move the person to another location before starting your assessment.
- Take proper precautions to maintain your safety at the scene, including wearing protective gloves (see page 265).
- Look for clues to the cause of injury.

INITIAL ASSESSMENT

The goal of the Initial (or Primary) Assessment is to identify any potentially life-threatening situations that must be dealt with immediately. The Initial Assessment is prioritized and should be performed in the following order: **A** (Airway), **B** (Breathing), **C** (Circulation), and **D** (Disability). If you find any problem in the Initial Assessment, stop the assessment and treat the patient for that problem immediately. The Initial Assessment may last only a few seconds if the patient is alert, walking around, and speaking to you. Here are the basic problems to look for when you first approach your patient:

1. ASSESS THE SCENE

Assessment

Look for causes of the accident. Survey the scene for hazards. Make sure the scene is safe for rescuers to approach. Identify the number and location of victims. Look for mechanism of injury (MOI) for spinal damage (see below). Use universal precautions for dealing with body fluids.

Approach the patient. Establish if the person is responsive and evaluate if there is a mechanism of injury (MOI) for spinal damage (see below). If the patient is unresponsive, or if you cannot rule out an MOI, then immediately control the cervical spine before continuing.

2. A = AIRWAY

Problem	Airway blocked.
Assessment	Check for a clear airway. Open the airway in accordance with your training in CPR. Look, listen, and feel for breathing.
Treatment	If not breathing, clear airway and provide Basic Life Support (page 282).

2. B = BREATHING

Problem	Patient not breathing or distressed breathing.
Assessment	Is air going in and out normally?
Treatment	If not, make sure airway is clear; provide rescue breathing.

3. C = CIRCULATION

Problem #1	No pulse.
Assessment	Check for signs of circulation.
Treatment	If there are no signs of circulation begin CPR.
Problem #2	Severe bleeding.
Assessment	Look for any signs of severe bleeding, especially under body, where blood can pool in sand or dirt.
Treatment	Control major bleeding.

4. D = DISABILITY: POSSIBLE DAMAGE TO SPINAL CORD LEADING TO PARALYSIS OR DEATH.

Problem	Possible spinal injury.

Assessment

- Mechanism of Injury: a fall or impact force that could have injured the spine.

- Unreliable patient. If the accident is unwitnessed and the person is unresponsive, lethargic, or combative—in essence, you cannot rely on her answers as truthful or accurate—you cannot rule out the possibility that there was a mechanism for spinal injury.

Treatment

Stabilization. For any patient with an unwitnessed injury or any possible mechanism for a spinal injury such as a fall, you should initially assume that an injury exists and treat as such.

- Ask the patient not to move her head and stabilize the head/neck with your hands to maintain the head and neck in a neutral, in-line position (aligned with the midline of the body).
- Keep the head and neck in a stabilized position until spinal injury can be ruled out and/or professional rescuers arrive on scene for transport.

Anything that you find within your initial assessment should be treated right away. These are all life-threatening conditions. Only after you have treated any life-threatening conditions, or ruled them all out, do you go on to evaluate and treat less serious conditions.

FOCUSED HISTORY AND PHYSICAL EXAM

Once all life-threatening conditions have been addressed, the rescuer should perform an in-depth, head-to-toe physical exam, record the patient's vital signs, and ascertain her medical history.

Patient Exam

With some practice, the rescuer can accomplish an effective and thorough exam in minutes. Except in cases of imminent danger, avoid moving an injured patient until the exam has been completed. Make the patient as comfortable as possible by assuming a professional manner, and protect the patient from inclement environmental conditions. In some cases it's preferable if the examiner is of the same gender as the patient; if that's not possible, having an observer of the same gender can help make your patient feel more comfortable. It is often convenient to have a note-taker record the findings of the patient exam, vitals, and medical history, allowing the rescuer to concentrate on the exam. For the patient exam, keep the following principles in mind:

Principles in the Patient Exam

- Identify yourself; talk to the patient; keep a calm voice; explain what you are doing. Be professional.
- Develop a relationship with your patient as the only person performing the exam and any necessary treatment.
- Avoid moving the patient unnecessarily.
- Watch the patient's face for signs of pain or discomfort.
- Keep the patient involved—ask questions about medical history and self-assessment. Give the patient a sense of control.
- A typical exam starts at the head, proceeds down the torso to the toes, and then returns to the arms. You can vary this order as conditions dictate, just make sure you cover the entire body.
- Observe for cuts, bruises, burns, or deformity. Look for discoloration and wetness. Listen and smell for anything abnormal.

- Examine the skin, muscles, and bone by feeling gently with your hands. Feel for abnormalities, wetness, and tender areas.
- Compare symmetric body parts, such as hands and feet (especially useful to detect swelling).
- Flex the joints gently to check for mobility. Be sensitive to potential injuries and stop if there is any sign of pain.

As you examine your patient, here are some of the signs and symptoms to look for, and the possible implications of those findings:

HEAD AND NECK

Examination	Signs and Symptoms	Possible Implications
Palpate scalp	Deformity; bleeding	Bump on head; skull fracture (page 309)
Check face	Bruises; bleeding	Facial fractures; skull fracture (page 309)
Ears and nose	Fluid; bruises behind ears	Bloody nose; skull fracture (page 309); increasing intracranial pressure (ICP)
Pupils	Equal in size? Responsive to light?	Increasing ICP (page 307)
Palpate face and jaw	Bruises around eyes	Increasing ICP (page 307)
Check inside mouth	Broken teeth; vomit; bleeding	Airway concerns (page 262)
Lymph nodes	Swollen	Infection
Trachea	Deviation of the trachea or neck, veins bloated and visible	Chest wall and/or lung injury; pneumothorax (pages 311–314)

UPPER TORSO

Examination	Signs and Symptoms	Possible Implications
Palpate neck and back vertebrae	Tenderness or guarding?	Spine fracture (page 302)
Palpate shoulders, shoulder blade, and collarbone	Stable? Pain?	Fracture or dislocation (pages 289–302)
Press on rib cage from top, sides, sternum	Unstable, pain, grating sound	Chest wall injury (page 311)
Breathing	Does chest wall rise symmetrically?	Flail chest (page 312)

LOWER TORSO

Examination	Signs and Symptoms	Possible Implications
Palpate four quadrants of abdomen and back under ribs	Rigidity, pain (local/general, dull ache, stabbing, burning)	Abdominal injury or illness (page 367)

Examine skin	Color; bruising; lacerations	Abdominal injury or illness
Pelvis/hips	Push from top, sides, rocking. Unstable? Pain?	Pelvic fracture; volume shock (page 275)
Genitals	Bleeding, tenderness?	Soft tissue injury; urinary tract or yeast Infection (page 376)

EXTREMITIES

Examination	Signs and Symptoms	Possible Implications
Arms, legs, hands, and feet	Unstable, decreased range of movement? Inability to bear weight, weakness? Tenderness, pain? Abnormal circulation, sensation, and movement?	Strain, sprain, fracture, dislocation (pages 287–302); soft tissue injury; nerve and/or circulatory system damage (page 305)

Performing an Abdominal Exam

The key to performing a physical exam of the abdomen is to ensure that the patient is as relaxed and comfortable as possible. Have the patient lie down in a sheltered spot, then remove or pull back any clothing covering the area. Make sure that your own hands are as warm as possible before beginning. The exam itself involves nothing more complicated than gently feeling, with fingertip pressure, all four quadrants of the abdomen (above/below and left/right of the navel).

A basic understanding of anatomy is all you need to get useful clues from this exam. Compare your findings from the patient to the way your own body feels. A normal stomach should feel soft—rigidity can indicate internal bleeding. Attempt to localize areas of tenderness exactly. Pain that can be specifically located is more suggestive of a serious condition than general and diffuse pain. Attempt to distinguish between deep pain and pain at the surface—that is, muscle pain or shallow bruises at the surface and deep pain coming from inside the peritoneal cavity. Note the location and type of pain (see page 273). If you are uncertain of your findings, assume the worst until proven otherwise and proceed accordingly.

Vital Signs

In the wilderness, you obviously don't have access to high-tech diagnostic tools, but with your five senses and a watch (one reason this is on the list of "The Essentials"; see page 21), you can gather a good deal of key diagnostic information. Vital signs are just that—they are key signs of how the body's vital systems are functioning. While each individual will have differing resting

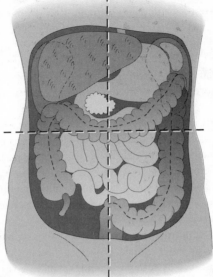

Liver	Liver
Right Kidney	Spleen
Colon	Left Kidney
Pancreas	Stomach
Gall Bladder	Colon
	Pancreas
Colon	Colon
Small Intestine	Small Intestine
Ureter	Ureter
Appendix	Major Artery
Major Artery	and Vein to
and Vein to	Left Leg
Right Leg	

Abdominal Quadrants

vital signs, it is the change in vital signs over time that may indicate injuries or illnesses, so you should measure and record vital signs on a regular basis. In cases of severe injury or illness, check vitals every 15 minutes. Vital signs include the following:

- **Heart Rate (HR)**   Record rate and strength (typical adult: 60 to 80 beats/minute).
- **Respiratory Rate (RR)**   Record rate, strength, and any unusual smell (typical adult: 12 to 20 respirations/minute, regular, unlabored).
- **Skin (SCTM)** Assess skin color (pale/normal/red), temperature (cool/normal/hot), and moisture (dry/normal/clammy/sweaty). Normal values are pink, warm, dry.
- **Level of Consciousness (LOC)**   Use the AVPU scale:
    A = Alert & Oriented—responds to questions
    - Times 4 (× 4) = oriented to person, place, time, and events (who you are, where you are, what date and time it is, what happened)
    - Times 3 (× 3) = oriented to person, place, and time
    - Times 2 (× 2) = oriented to person and place
    - Times 1 (× 1) = oriented to person

V = Verbal—responds to questions, but not completely oriented.

P = Pain—responds to painful stimuli. Rub your knuckles on the sternum or pinch the earlobes and the person will flinch.

U = Unresponsive—does not respond even to painful stimuli.

- **Temperature (T)** Record temperature. Temperature readings from the armpit (axillary) are more accurate than readings from the mouth (orally). Record which method you used. Normal reading is 98.6°F (37°C).

- **Blood pressure (BP)** Blood pressure is a measurement of the force applied to the walls of the arteries as the heart pumps blood through the body. This indicates how well the body is being perfused with blood. Blood pressure is measured with two values: the *systolic pressure* over the *diastolic pressure,* which are measured in millimeters (mm). The systolic pressure is the higher pressure, which occurs each time the heart pushes blood into the vessels. The diastolic pressure is the "base" pressure in the vessels when the heart is between beats. Without a blood pressure cuff, you cannot get an exact reading. However, checking for a pulse in the distal extremities, such as at the wrist and the ankle, gives you a general assessment of how well blood is circulating (perfusing) in all four limbs. Typically, if you get a pulse at the wrist, the systolic blood pressure should be 80 or above. Normal adult readings are 140–90mm systolic over 90–60mm diastolic.

Assessing Mental Status

There are numerous factors that can alter the person's mental status. (See "STOPEAT," page 264.) First check to make sure the person knows who she is, where she is, what day and time it is, and what happened. That gives you a basic report of the *A* in AVPU. However, the person may be able to correctly answer all these questions and still have impaired higher brain function (for example, someone under the influence of alcohol, a hypothermic person, or someone with high-altitude illness). To check higher reasoning, ask the person a question that requires her to do some calculation, like counting backwards from 100 by nines. If the person is normally able to do it and can't, you know that something is affecting her brain.

Patient History

The purpose of the patient history is to get as much information as you can that will give you clues as to the nature of the problem. Use the acronym SAMPLE to remember the categories to cover. Record everything on the SOAP Note (see page 421).

S = Symptom	Is there pain or discomfort? When was the onset of the pain? Was the onset sudden or gradual? Describe the pain: Crampy? Stabbing? Generalized? Burning? Intermittent? What aggravates it? What alleviates it? Are there nonpain-related symptoms—tiredness, weakness, dizziness, nausea?
A = Allergies	Any allergies to foods or medications, as well as urgent allergies like bee stings?
M = Medications (prescription and over-the-counter)	What is the patient currently taking and for what conditions? When did she last take it? Keep the medication with the patient in the event of an evacuation.
P = Past Relevant History	Has anything like this ever happened before? People with chronic problems often know their best treatment. Check any trip documentation, such as health history form or a medic alert tag.
L = Last Meal	When did the patient last eat and drink? What and how much? This can be very important in many cases (e.g., diabetic emergencies, heat exhaustion, hypothermia, abdominal problems).
E = Events Leading Up to Accident	What happened?

Obviously, many parts of the patient exam, vital signs, and history can be done at the same time, and each situation will determine the most important questions to ask and action to take. For example, if someone is complaining only of diarrhea and does not have a history of having fallen, it is probably not necessary to extensively check the legs for fractures.

Assessing the Patient's Pain

In his book *The Outward Bound Wilderness First-aid Manual,* Jeff Isaac defines the acronym OPQRST as a useful framework for assessing pain.

O = Onset	When did the pain begin?
P = Provoke	What provokes the pain (i.e., moving, eating)?
Q = Quality	What exactly does the pain feel like? Dull? Stabbing? Cramping?
R = Radiation	Does the pain spread to other parts of the body?
S = Severity	If 10 is the worst possible pain and 1 is very mild pain, how does this pain rate from 1 to 10?
T = Time	Does the pain change over time? Is it constant, or does it come in waves?

TREATMENT AND DOCUMENTATION
DEVELOP A TREATMENT PLAN

After you have finished your thorough examination, gathered the history, and taken vital signs, you need to put all the information together and come to some conclusions about what the problems are or might be. This is a lot like detective work. You may have a very obvious set of signs and symptoms that tell you the person has a broken wrist, or you may have a set of obscure clues about some type of unknown abdominal problem. You have to decide, based on all the information you have been able to gather, what may be wrong and what plan of action you can take in the field to treat it. By continuing to monitor and note changes, you may discover problems that were not initially apparent. As a result, it is imperative that you document all findings, including things you looked for but did not find.

The most common way to organize this information is called the SOAP Note (see below). This format is used by medical professionals around the world and is the best way for you to gather, record, and then communicate this information to outside rescuers and medical professionals. (See the sample SOAP Note form, page 421.)

S	**S**ubjective	What the patient tells you.	The patient's chief complaint, the events leading up to the accident, and medical history.
O	**O**bjective	What you found	All findings of the patient exam, vital signs, and observations of the rescuer.
A	**A**ssessment	What you think is wrong.	Problem List—a list of all problems in order of severity; for example, "probable broken ankle" or "possible appendicitis." Also includes any anticipated problems, such as "possible volume shock due to blood loss from lacerated leg."
P	**P**lan	What you intend to do.	Document all treatment given and plans for evacuation.

Definitive Care

The definitive care you provide depends upon your assessment of the patient's condition, your level of training, and the equipment you have on hand. If you are unsure about your problem list, you should assume the worst and respond accordingly. Any serious condition will require professional medical attention. In some cases, this means evacuating the patient to medical care; in other cases, it means bringing that care to the patient. (See "Evacuation Procedures," page 235.)

GENERAL FIRST-AID PRINCIPLES
SHOCK

The minimum requirement for keeping a human body functioning is the supply of oxygenated blood to all body tissues, known as perfusion. There are three primary components needed to maintain adequate perfusion: enough fluid—*blood*—to provide the pressure needed to circulate to all parts of the body; a pump—*the heart*—capable of circulating the blood; and pipes—*arteries, veins,* and *capillaries*—that can carry the blood from the heart to the rest of the body. Failure of any one of these components will compromise the body's ability to keep up perfusion. Regardless of the specific cause, any condition resulting in inadequate perfusion will result in an identical set of signs and symptoms, known as shock.

Compensatory Shock   A typical adult can lose about 1 quart (1 liter) of blood (about 15 percent of the person's total blood volume) and still be able to compensate for the loss and maintain an adequate level of perfusion. This is known as compensatory shock because the body is able to compensate. Blood loss of 15 to 30 percent is serious since the body must cut off blood flow to certain areas in order to maintain perfusion to the vital organs.

Decompensatory Shock   When blood loss is greater than 30 percent, the body is no longer able to compensate for the loss, and you will see changes to vital signs (see below). Death can occur at this point, especially if the fluid loss is rapid.

Vital Signs in Shock

The body attempts to compensate for decreased perfusion by increasing the pulse and respiration rates. The body also may decrease blood flow to the periphery (skin, arms, and legs) in order to save blood for the vital organs. (See "Shell/Core Response," page 278.) Look for the following:

- Pulse—increased (above 100/minute in adults), weak
- Respiration rate—increased, shallow
- Skin—pale, cool, and clammy
- Blood pressure—decreased in later stages
- Level of consciousness—patient in shock will generally be anxious and agitated in early stages, and become progressively less responsive as condition worsens (decreasing AVPU)
- Nausea and/or vomiting

Types of Shock

- **Volume Shock (fluid failure)**   There is not enough fluid to provide adequate perfusion. The most typical causes are significant blood loss from a wound or from dehydration (from inadequate drinking, from sweat loss due to heat, or diarrhea).

- **Vascular Shock (pipe failure)** There is not enough fluid pressure to provide adequate perfusion. Caused by massive dilation of the blood vessels. In the wilderness, common causes are an acute allergic reaction (anaphylaxis) or a spinal injury.
- **Cardiogenic Shock (pump failure)** A damaged heart that is not able to pump blood through the body adequately. This can be a chronic problem from heart disease or an immediate problem from an acute injury.

Treatment for Shock

Shock does not just happen—it must be caused by something. Identify the cause, and treat that as best you can. (See "Anaphylaxis," page 364; "Bleeding," page 278; "Fluid Balance," page 326.) Remember, all major injuries left untreated can result in shock. In many cases, it may be shock more than the precipitating injury that can lead to death. There are four basic treatments for any type of shock:

- **Stop Volume Loss** Maintain adequate perfusion by controlling bleeding.
- **Replace Fluids** Mild shock from sweating or diarrhea can be controlled and reversed with oral rehydration. Severe shock from major bleeding or persistent fluid loss will require intravenous fluid replacement and advanced medical care.
- **Oxygen** Provide supplemental oxygen if available to increase the oxygen level in the blood.
- **Position** Keep the person in a comfortable position and maintain body warmth. The best position for someone in shock (provided it doesn't complicate other injuries) is called the *Trendelenburg position*. This means having the head 6 to 10 inches (15 to 25 cm) lower than the legs. Gravity helps the blood flow back to the brain, aiding in perfusion.

    To get someone in this position you need the whole body on a slant. Don't just raise the legs; that can put pressure on the stomach and encourage nausea or vomiting. Find a slight incline and place the person head downhill or, if the person is on a backboard, you could elevate the foot section of the backboard. Do *not* put the person in this position if the patient has a possible head injury, spinal injury, or a leg injury that would be compromised by raising the legs.

SWELLING

Swelling (edema) is the body's universal response to injury and tissue damage. It serves to both increase blood flow to injured areas and isolate those areas from surrounding tissue. All swelling, regardless of cause or location, follows roughly the same pattern. Swelling occurs quickly for the first 6 hours after an injury and continues at a somewhat slower pace until approximately 24 hours after injury. Additional swelling is negligible after 24 hours. Extensive swelling can result in ischemia and tissue death. Swelling from certain injuries can be life-threatening, such as injuries to the brain, where the swelling takes place in an enclosed space (the skull).

ISCHEMIA

When blood flow (oxygen and nutrients) is cut off to body tissue, the result is ischemia. In its early stages, ischemia amounts to having an arm or leg fall asleep—the patient may feel tingling or numbness and will eventually lose sensation and movement in the limb. If ischemia continues, it ultimately results in the death of that tissue. Anything that impedes or cuts off blood flow to an area can result in ischemia, including swelling of a part of the body, damage to a blood vessel (lacerations or twists in the vessel), or a tight bandage or splint. You should always check the tissue distal to a splint or bandage for signs of ischemia.

Checking Circulation, Sensation, and Motion (CSM)

One important technique for evaluating whether a peripheral area is being adequately perfused is to check for circulation, sensation, and motion (CSM) at the distal end of the extremity. For example, with an arm fracture, you would want to check CSM at the fingers.

Distal Circulation   You can check distal circulation by checking for a pulse or by checking for capillary refill. Check capillary refill time by pressing the nail beds to blanch a spot. In healthy individuals, the blood returns and the skin at the blanch site becomes pink within 2 to 4 seconds. This nail bed test works with people of any skin color. If it takes significantly longer than this, then you know that peripheral circulation is impaired. If the person is experiencing a shell/core response (see page 278), you will see a longer capillary refill time.

Distal Sensation and Motion   You can check distal sensation by rubbing something gently along the skin and by gently poking the skin with a sharp object. You can check for motion in a number of ways, as long as moving the extremity will not compromise the injury. Compare the person's strength and ability on both sides to see if there is compromise.

- **For fingers**   Ask the person to wiggle the fingers, squeeze your hand, and spread her fingers open with resistance from your hand.

- **For toes**   Ask the person to wiggle her toes, try to lift her toes up against resistance from your hand, and try to push her toes down against resistance from your hand.

SHELL/CORE RESPONSE

One adaptation of the human body is the natural response to protect the vital organs in the torso and to protect the brain by cutting off blood flow to the extremities. In volume shock, the shell/core response minimizes blood flow to the extremities by constricting peripheral blood vessels to maintain perfusion of the vital body organs—the heart and the brain. In hypothermia (see "Hypothermia," page 332), the shell/core response conserves heat and oxygenated blood in the vital body organs, at the expense of the relatively resilient and expendable body shell (arms and legs). Patients undergoing a shell/core response will have pale and cool skin, as blood withdraws from the outer layers toward the core. Shell/core response is not, in and of itself, a medical problem, but rather indicates that the body is undergoing extreme stress from some source. As such, there is no direct treatment for the shell/core response itself. Try to determine the cause, and treat the underlying problem.

BLEEDING

Bleeding can be controlled by using the following techniques:

- **Direct pressure**   Most bleeding can be controlled by applying well-aimed direct pressure to the site of the wound. Using a gloved hand and a piece of sterile gauze (if available), apply firm pressure to the wound. It may take up to 15 minutes for bleeding to stop completely. It is absolutely essential that the site of the bleeding be located exactly when applying direct pressure. This may require cutting away clothing or wiping away blood until the wound can be seen clearly. If you can't see the wound, you don't know exactly where to apply the pressure to control the bleeding. When bleeding continues, most often it is due to pressure not being applied directly over the wound. You may have to remove your hand, reassess where the wound is, and reapply the direct pressure.
- **Elevation**   Elevate the wound above the heart, thereby decreasing the local blood pressure.

In most cases, direct pressure and elevation will stop the bleeding. If it does not, you may need to use these techniques in addition:

- **Pressure points** are where arteries lie close to the surface and over a bone so that the artery can be compressed against the underlying bone. There are two major pressure points: the brachial artery in the arm and the femoral artery in the leg. The *brachial artery* is on the inside of the upper arm. Compress it by holding the patient's arm with your thumb on the outside of the arm and your fingers on the inside compressing the artery. The *femoral artery* is in the groin area. Use the heel of your hand and press fairly hard on the crease between the pelvis and the leg. Pressure points can be used in addition to direct pressure to slow blood flow to distal areas.
- **Pressure bandages** are for rare situations when the rescuer has difficulty holding sustained direct pressure over the area, such as with a very large laceration. Place sterile dressings on the wound area and then tightly wrap a gauze dressing on top to create the local pressure. The gauze dressing must cover a wide area so as to avoid impinging blood flow to the entire limb.
- **Tourniquets** are *rarely* necessary except in situations of complete or partial amputation of a limb. You should resort to a tourniquet only when *all* other techniques have failed and continued blood loss will cause death—for example, if you have severe arterial bleeding that you can't visualize adequately to apply direct pressure and you are afraid that your patient will "bleed out." Anytime you use a tourniquet, you risk ischemia to the tissues below the tourniquet and potential loss of the limb. If it's "lose the limb to save the life," consider a tourniquet. Tourniquets should be applied only to the upper arm or upper leg. Use a wide band and tighten it just enough to stop the blood flow, then try to stop the bleeding with the methods above. If you use a tourniquet, mark the time you applied it. Leave it on for as little time as possible (only up to 45 minutes) and note the time you remove it. Relieve the pressure on the tourniquet slowly to prevent sudden blood flow from dislodging clots that have formed.

WOUND CARE

These are general principles for wound care. For specific types of wounds, see "Soft Tissue Injuries," page 317.

Cleaning a Wound

Make sure the bleeding has stopped. Clean around the wound with soap and water, or use a dilute povidone iodine solution (10% solution = 1 part povidone iodine to 10 parts water). To make the solution, add approximately 1 inch (2 cm) of povidone iodine ointment to 1 liter of water and allow it to dissolve. (Do *not* use 2 percent tincture of iodine, which is used for drinking water purification; this causes burns.) Irrigate the wound itself with a forceful flow of sterile water or povidone iodine solution, preferably using a an irrigation syringe. If you don't have a syringe, you can squeeze the solution out of a plastic bag with a small hole in the end. Irrigation helps remove any foreign material and does not damage tissues. Any foreign material, dead tissue, or even clotted blood left in the wound virtually ensures infection. If you use a povidone iodine solution, irrigate the wound again with fresh water to rinse the solution out of the wound.

We all know that alcohol stings when it gets into a wound. Antiseptics such as alcohol or tincture of iodine can damage tissues and *should not be used directly on the wound*. Antiseptics are used primarily for cleaning *around* a wound, like an alcohol swab on your skin before you are given an injection.

Wound Dressing and Bandaging

Never close a wound with tape; this increases the risk of infection. Instead, dress and bandage a wound. A bandage is usually composed of three layers, each with different functions.

- **The Inner Layer** This layer of the bandage should be made of a thin, sterile material that does not stick to the wound, such as a Tefla pad. This allows the bandage to be changed relatively painlessly without aggravating the injury. You can also use plain gauze covered with antibiotic ointment, which will prevent sticking. Put the ointment directly on the gauze, not on the wound.
- **The Dressing** The dressing should be sterile and bulky, such as simple gauze pads that have been opened and crumpled to increase their bulk, allowing them to absorb blood and fluid.
- **Outer Layer** The outer portion of a bandage holds the dressings securely in place. Materials that have some elasticity are easier to use and stay in place better than plain gauze. If protection from water is not a concern, porous tape should be used to hold the bandage in place. If the bandage has to be changed frequently, leave the old tape. Clip the tape off at the skin edges and place new tape on top of the old. This avoids the skin irritation that results from repeatedly ripping off the old tape.

To Dress and Bandage a Wound

1. Apply antibiotic ointment to the inner layer. The ointment should be applied to the dressing rather than directly to the wound. This will prevent contamination of the remaining antibiotic in the tube or bottle.
2. Apply an inner layer of nonstick gauze.

3. Apply dressing layers as needed (this may depend on the amount of bleeding and the size of the wound).
4. Apply the bandage. It should be tight enough to hold the dressings in place but not so tight as to impede circulation. Check CSM—circulation, sensation, and movement—distal to the wound to make sure the bandage is not too tight. Be aware that swelling may occur up to 24 hours after the injury occurred.
5. Change the dressing as needed and check the area for signs of infection.

WOUND INFECTION

It takes time for bacteria to infect a wound. A wound that is healing normally may appear red and swollen for 24 to 48 hours after the injury. Wound infection generally sets in two to four days after the injury. Any wound that remains red and swollen after 48 hours, or that becomes more swollen and painful, should be considered infected. In *The Outward Bound Wilderness First-aid Handbook,* the author defines the acronym SHARP to describe the common signs of a local infection:

S = Swelling	The area will be swollen.
H = Heat	The area will be hot to the touch.
A = Ache	The area will be painful.
R = Redness	The area will be red.
P = Pus	The wound may show pus drainage.

High-Risk Wounds for Infections

- Animal or human bites
- Crushing wounds
- Wounds near or on joints
- Punctures
- Impaled objects
- Open fractures

If a wound becomes infected, remove all dressings and re-clean the wound as described above. Re-bandage the wound. Localized infections can be serious and damage tissue or can become systemic. You may need to evacuate the patient to professional medical care.

Signs of the Infection Spreading

These are signs that the localized infection around the wound is spreading to the rest of the body. This type of systemic infection is *extremely serious and can lead to death.* Anyone showing signs of a systemic infection from a wound requires antibiotics and should be *evacuated immediately.* Here are the signs:

- High fever that develops after a wound
- Red streaks on the skin moving away from the wound and toward the heart

BASIC LIFE SUPPORT

Basic Life Support (BLS) is the fundamental skill of maintaining blood circulation and respiration for a patient whose breathing and/or heart has stopped. If there is a near-drowning, respiratory failure, heart attack, or lightning strike, the *only* thing that will keep that patient alive until definitive medical care arrives is your ability to do CPR. CPR must be initiated within minutes. (In cases of immersion hypothermia and cold water, you may have longer before any permanent damage occurs.) You should take a CPR course from the American Red Cross or the American Heart Association on a regular basis to keep your skills current. This brief review does not cover all aspects of CPR training and is *not* designed to replace a course. It assumes that you already know the basic skills and terminology. Always follow the universal precautions (see page 265), such as using a one-way valve mask, when giving CPR.

1. Is the victim conscious?

    a. Tap the person's shoulder and shout, "Are you OK?"
    b. If no response, call for help.
    c. Without moving the person, look, listen, and feel for breathing for about 5 seconds.

2. If the victim is not breathing, open the airway.

    a. Roll the victim onto her back while supporting the head and neck.
    b. Open the airway by tilting the head back and lifting the chin. If you suspect head or spinal injuries, use the jaw thrust method only.
    c. Look, listen, and feel for breathing for about 5 seconds.
    d. If there is no breathing, go to #3.

3. Give two rescue breaths.

    a. Pinch nostrils closed. Give two breaths (~2 seconds per breath).

b. If air does not go in, reposition the head to open the airway and give two rescue breaths again. If air still does not go in, straddle the patient and give abdominal thrusts. Open the mouth and look for a foreign object. Sweep it out with your finger. Open the airway again with a chin lift or jaw thrust and give two rescue breaths. If air still does not go in, continue 3a and 3b until air goes in.

4. **Check for circulation.**

   a. Locate the Adam's apple and slide two fingers down into the groove at the side of the victim's neck. Check the pulse for no more than 10 seconds (if the person is severely hypothermic, check for up to 1 minute).
   b. If there is a pulse but no breathing, proceed with rescue breathing.
   c. Open the airway and give one rescue breath about every 5 seconds. (Count 1 and 2 and 3 and 4 and 5, breathe)
   d. If there is no pulse or breathing, go to #5.

5. **Locate the breastbone.**

   a. Slide two fingers up the rib cage to the notch at the lower end of the breastbone. Place the heel of your hand just above this notch.
   b. Place your other hand on top.

6. **Chest compressions and rescue breathing.**

   a. Position your shoulders over your hands. Push straight down without bending your elbows. Push down 1½ to 2 inches (3.8 to 5 centimeters) for an adult. Give fifteen compressions.
   b. Open the airway and give two rescue breaths.
   c. Reposition for chest compressions and continue with your rate of fifteen compressions followed by two rescue breaths for about three more cycles, then stop and check for circulation as described above. If there is no sign of circulation, continue CPR.

MOVING YOUR PATIENT

There will be times when you need to move a patient, either to treat her or to quickly move her away from a dangerous situation. In many cases, you may be concerned about a possible spinal injury, so it is important to move the person as a unit, keeping the spine from bending or twisting.

When Moving a Patient

- Move a patient in small steps.
- One person should stabilize the patient's head and call when movement should occur. Make sure all rescuers are ready.
- If possible, have one person at each of the major weight centers of the body to control that area—shoulders, hips, and legs.
- If you have to "unkink" a person, move only one body weight center at a time (for example, move the hips over, then move the legs). Move each weight center slowly, and in increments, until the body is in a normal axial position.
- If you have to move the person some distance, if possible, get her into an axial (lengthwise) position and then move her along the body's long axis.
- If the person is suspected of having a spinal injury, you should immobilize the neck using a cervical collar and the spine with a backboard (if possible) before moving.

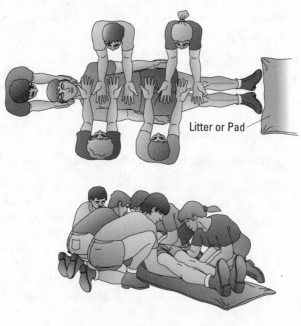

In-line Drag

The In-line Drag

The in-line drag can be used to move a person a short distance.

1. Have one person at the head controlling the head and neck and at least one person at each of the major weight centers (shoulders, hips, and legs).

2. The person at the head checks to see that everyone is ready, and on her command, the group lifts the patient to the same level and moves slowly forward. Depending on the distance to be moved, this may be a drag just above the ground, or the group may need to stand up and carry the person over a longer distance.

The Log Roll

The log roll is used to roll a patient onto her side or onto a backboard.

1. Rescuer 1, at the head, stabilizes the head and neck throughout the log roll and gives all commands about when to move.
2. Rescuer 2 kneels at the patient's chest and reaches across to the shoulder and upper arm of the patient.
3. Rescuer 3 kneels beside the patient's waist and reaches across to the lower back and pelvis.
4. Rescuer 1 gives the command, "Roll on three: one, two, three," and the rescuers slowly roll the patient toward them, keeping the body in align-

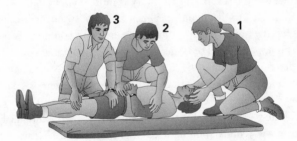

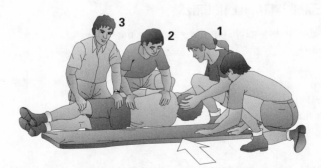

The Log Roll

ment. Rescuer 1 supports the head and maintains alignment with the spine while the other rescuers roll the body as a unit. Once the patient is on her side, Rescuer 4 can place a backboard or foam pad underneath the patient.

5. Rescuer 1 gives the command, "Lower on three: one, two, three," and the procedure is reversed. The patient is slowly lowered back while the rescuers keep the spine in alignment.

Log rolls can be done with fewer than four rescuers, if necessary. It is important to make sure that the entire spine is kept in line as the patient is rolled.

MUSCULOSKELETAL SYSTEM INJURIES

Injuries to the musculoskeletal system—strains, sprains, fractures, and dislocations—are the ones you are most likely to see as accidents in the backcountry. Fortunately, they also represent the area where a rescuer with minimum training can provide a great deal of help. The generic treatment for a musculoskeletal injury is to immobilize the area and to limit usage.

Assessment of the severity of an injury is more complicated. Without an X-ray it's often hard to distinguish between an ankle strain, sprain, or minor fracture, especially initially when it hurts like hell and you don't want to put any weight on it. So, instead of trying to determine something you can't in the field, first determine whether the injury is stable or unstable. A *stable injury* may be a strain, sprain, or stress fracture that doesn't prevent use. The person may be able to hike out on her own or with assistance. An *unstable injury* is an injury where the person is unable to use the extremity, a fracture, dislocation, or sprain that will require splinting (see "General Fracture Treatment," page 289) and may require a litter evacuation.

STABLE AND UNSTABLE INJURIES

Both stable and unstable injuries will show the following common signs and symptoms:

- Pain
- Tenderness
- Swelling
- Bruising

Pain is the best indicator of the appropriate level of use. If the ankle hurts too much to bear weight, then the patient should *not* be walking on it. You may need to wait for the initial pain to subside in order to determine the severity of the injury. The first few minutes after an ankle sprain the person may not be able to walk due to pain. Wait a bit and see if the pain subsides. If so let the person attempt to bear weight on the ankle. Here are the criteria that Wilderness Medical Associates uses (*www.wildmed.com*) to evaluate stable versus unstable injuries:

Signs and Symptoms	Stable Injury	Unstable Injury
Mechanism of injury	Yes	Yes
Ability to bear weight	Yes	No
Normal range of motion	Yes	No
Feeling of instability	No	Possibly
Deformity or angulation	No	Possibly
Crepitus—grating sound caused by broken bone ends rubbing together	No	Possibly
Point tenderness—tenderness at a specific point on the bone	No	Possibly
Patient felt or heard something snap or break	No	Possibly

BASIC STABLE INJURY TREATMENT

The goals in treating a stable injury are to reduce swelling and limit use. The basic treatment (called RICE) is to limit activity to that which does not cause pain, and administer anti-inflammatory medications (aspirin, ibuprofen).

R = Rest	Rest the area and limit use.
I = Ice	Apply ice, cold pack or another cold source immediately after the injury occurs—15 minutes on, then 15 minutes off, for up to 48 hours to reduce internal bleeding and control swelling. Avoid direct ice contact with the skin.
C = Compression	Add light pressure. An elastic "ACE" bandage is often helpful for sprains because it partially immobilizes the sprain and also provides some compression to limit swelling of the joint.
E = Elevation	Elevating the sprain increases the reabsorption rate of blood and edema fluid and helps limit the swelling.

STRAINS

Strains are minor muscle or tendon injuries usually brought on by sudden stress or prolonged use of a particular muscle group. Pulled muscles and tendonitis are both forms of strains. Pulled muscles tend to have a sudden onset, while tendonitis is characterized by a gradual onset of pain and stiffness. Having limber muscles is the best way to avoid such injuries. People should warm up and stretch every morning before starting the day and also stretch after long rest breaks or meal stops. (See "Stretches for Hiking," page 169.)

TENDONITIS

Tendonitis is caused by the swelling of tendons or surrounding tissue. The onset is usually gradual and results from repeated use, which causes inflammation over extended periods of time. A common scenario for hikers is tendonitis of the Achilles tendon (which runs up the back of the ankle), caused by stiff or tight high-top boots that constrict the tendon, causing inflammation and swelling. Check to make sure your boots don't create too much pressure on the Achilles tendon.

Treatment

Apply moist heat, massage, and anti-inflammatory medications (aspirin, ibuprofen) as appropriate. Also, regular stretching is beneficial. Splinting can help in the short term. Tendonitis symptoms in the Achilles tendon can sometimes be relieved by the insertion of a foam heel pad in the boot. Stretching the leather of the boot in the Achilles area may reduce the risk of inflammation.

> **🍁 TRICKS OF THE TRAIL**
>
> **Ankle-stabilizing straps** I once sprained my ankle badly on a back-country skiing trip in Colorado. At 12,000 feet (3,657 meters), there weren't a lot of options except to keep skiing. Since it was a stable injury, we used an ankle-stabilizing strap to support my ankle using two sleeping bag straps. First, make an ankle collar by wrapping one strap around the ankle just below the top of the hiking boot. Take the other strap and run it underneath the sole of the boot, up both sides of the boot between the boot and the ankle collar, and over the ankle collar on both sides to create a stirrup. Take the strap back down under the heel and secure it on the outside of the ankle by tightening the strap. This creates a rigid webbing strap that will help prevent sideways ankle flex but still allow flex front and back. Make sure that the straps aren't so tight that they inhibit circulation.

SPRAINS

A sprain is a severe stretch or tear of the tendons and/or ligaments around a joint. Sprains can be associated with fractures and/or dislocations. A sprain has symptoms similar to a fracture: constant pain, swelling, discoloration, and pain on use. Ankles, knees, and wrists are all commonly sprained. Your major evaluation is whether it is a stable or unstable injury. If you're unsure if it is a sprain or a fracture, treat it as if it were a fracture.

Treatment

The first aid is the same for any sprain—RICE, pain-free activity, and anti-inflammatory medications. Splinting also helps. Sprained ankles are most common and can be treated either with a figure-eight elastic bandage over the foot or by taping the ankle. In either case, the goal is to achieve lateral stability to prevent the ankle from rolling outward or inward. The patient should place her foot in a normal position as if she were standing up straight. The figure-eight elastic bandage is wrapped around the back of the heel, crosses under the sole of the foot, and crosses again on top of the foot. To tape an ankle, alternate pieces of tape that go under the heel and straight up the leg with ones that go from behind the ankle around to the top of the foot.

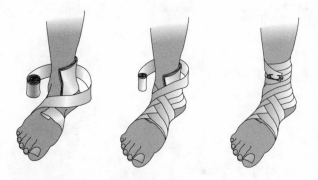

Ankle Wrap

GENERAL FRACTURE TREATMENT

SPLINTING

The purpose of a splint is to immobilize the injured area and prevent further movement and possible damage. It also helps reduce pain and swelling. There are several general principles that apply to all splinting, regardless of the location of fracture:

- If you are unsure whether it is a fracture or a sprain, assume it is a fracture.

- If the fracture is between two joints, you should immobilize the joints above and below the fracture site. If the fracture is on a joint, you should immobilize the joint above and below the fracture site.
- Immobilize the fracture in a comfortable position of normal use by creating a rigid, well-padded splint in the most comfortable position.
- Ensure that you will have access to the extremities distal to injury to be able to monitor distal CSM (see page 277).
- Make sure you have all the necessary splinting materials available *before* you begin treatment.

Splinting Basics

- Check circulation, sensation, and movement (CSM) below the fracture before you begin treatment. If you find impaired CSM, then you know that the fracture is affecting blood vessels or nerves.
- Use traction-in-position (TIP) to pull the bone back into its normal alignment. From the position the bone is in, pull gentle traction and move the broken bone back into its normal anatomical position.

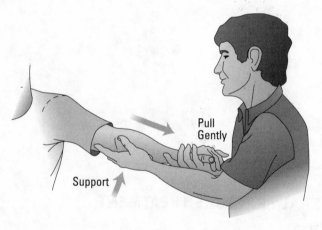

Traction in Position

- Stop traction-in-position (TIP) if you find increased resistance or significant increase in pain.
- Maintain the traction using hands-on stability.
- Apply the splint.
- Recheck circulation, sensation, and movement below the fracture site after treatment. If CSM was impaired before and is now improved, your traction-in-position and splinting has helped. If CSM was fine before and

is now impaired, your splint may be too tight or the splint may be cutting off blood flow or nerve transmission.

- Watch for shock and be prepared to treat for shock. (See "Shock," page 274.) Open fractures or fractures of the pelvis or femur can result in significant blood loss, which can lead to shock.
- Prepare to evacuate your patient.

Fracture Sites and Basic Splints

- **Skull and face**   Monitor ABCs closely. There is a possibility of head injury (see page 306) and spinal injury. Cervical collar and backboard. (See "Spinal Injuries," page 302.)
- **Neck**   Cervical collar and backboard. (See "Spinal Injuries," page 302.)
- **Jaw**   "Toothache bandage." Beware of vomiting.
- **Collarbone**   Sling and swathe.
- **Shoulder**   Sling and swathe.
- **Back**   Cervical collar and backboard. (See "Spinal Injuries," page 302.)
- **Ribs**   Sling and swathe (firmly)—monitor breathing. (See "Chest Injuries," page 311.)
- **Upper arm/elbow**   Sling and swathe or board splint.
- **Forearm, wrist, and hand**   Board splint and sling and swathe.
- **Pelvis**   Backboard with lots of padding—watch for signs of shock. (See "Shock," page 274.)
- **Femur**   Traction splint—watch for signs of shock. (See "Shock," page 274.)
- **Knee**   Splint at angle found with lots of padding.
- **Lower leg**   Splint straight with ankle at 90 degrees.
- **Ankle/foot**   Splint with the ankle at 90 degrees with big, soft splint.

Splinting Materials

The supply of splinting materials that you are already carrying with you or can find along the trail is almost endless. Here are a few suggestions of things that may be in your pack:

- Stays from internal frame packs
- Foam sleeping pads
- Tent poles
- Trekking poles
- Crazy Creek or other folding camp chairs (the entire chair, the stays that support the chair, or the foam inside the chair)
- Commercial first-aid splints like the SAM splint

SAM Splint Guidelines

The SAM Splint is a foam-covered sheet of pliable aluminum that can be molded into a variety of effective splints for different injuries. Owing to its versatility and minimal weight, it is commonly used in wilderness first-aid kits. Using a SAM splint requires some basic instruction. If the splint is flat, it has little strength. However, by creating bends in the splint, such as a fold along the long axis, it becomes quite rigid. The basic bend adds some stiffness. The reverse bend adds additional rigidity, and the T-bend creates a very rigid structure. You can also use two SAM Splints together for more rigidity. It's best to practice molding the splint to the uninjured limb first and make sure you have the correct fit so you don't have to jostle the injured limb. If you can't do this, "build" the splint on someone else of similar size in the group. For detailed information on techniques for using the SAM splint, see *www.samsplint.com*.

Basic Bend

Reverse Bend

T-Bend

Drawings courtesy of SAM Splint

Ankle

There are two different methods of using a SAM splint on an ankle; both require additional stabilization with a larger splint. Bend the SAM splint from

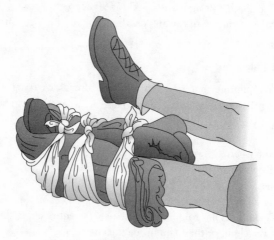

Ankle Splint

the sole of the foot up the sides of the leg in a U-shape. Pinch a tuck at the bottom of the foot to tighten the splint and stabilize the injury. Another method is to start with the middle of the splint on the sole of the foot. Wrap the splint over the top of the foot and around to the back of the ankle in a figure-eight. If two SAM splints are available, it is advisable to use both of these methods in conjunction. Additional padding can be achieved by wrapping a rolled foam pad around the lower leg. You can also create a solid ankle splint using a rolled foam pad, a camp chair, or well-padded sticks, internal frame pack stays, or tent poles.

Wrist/Forearm

The SAM splint should be folded in half lengthwise. One end of the splint should be rolled up to create a rest for the hand. Mold the SAM splint to the curvature of the arm, and pad between the split and the arm. Wrap with gauze or elastic bandage. This splint can be finished with a sling and swathe. There are numerous other methods for forearm splinting using padded boards and sticks.

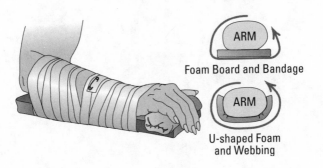

Foam Board and Bandage

U-shaped Foam
and Webbing

Forearm Splint

Elbow

The elbow should be splinted in the mid-range position. The SAM splint can be molded so that the elbow rests in the middle of the splint. The curvature of the splint can be maintained by taking tucks in the sides of the bend. Pad between the splint and the arm and wrap with gauze or an elastic bandage. Other methods include splinting to across a padded board. Apply a sling and swathe.

Elbow Splint

Sling and Swathe

The sling and swathe is used on a number of different fractures, including the collarbone, shoulder, ribs, upper arm, and to secure a lower arm splint. With the sling and swathe, it is important to immobilize the arm while maintaining comfort. Be sure to pad the neck and keep knots off the back of the neck.

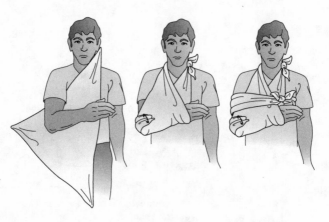

Arm Sling and Swathe

Lower Leg Splint

Splinting a leg, such as for a lower leg fracture, requires long rigid materials. Place one rigid support on each side of the leg. Due to the length of the leg you would need many SAM splints to effectively stabilize the leg. A well-padded camp chair or a rolled-up or folded foam pad and rigid objects such as branches, tent poles, trekking poles, or ice axes will effectively immobilize the leg.

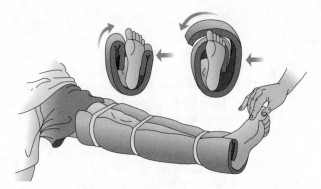

Lower Leg Splint

FRACTURES AT JOINTS

Fractures at joint sites can also include dislocations. Attempting to pull traction-in-position (TIP) can create additional damage.

Treatment

Check distal circulation, sensation, and movement (CSM). If present, these fractures should be splinted in the position they are found. Do *not* use traction-in-position (TIP) to attempt to realign the bone to its normal anatomical alignment. If distal CSM is *not* present, use TIP *only* until distal CSM returns. Then splint in this position. Stop traction-in-position (TIP) if you feel increased resistance or significant increase in pain.

ANGULATED FRACTURES

Angulated fractures are fractures of the extremities in which the bone has been broken and is now lying at an abnormal angle. These fractures present a special problem because they are almost guaranteed to interfere with normal circulation and neurological function below the fracture site. If the broken bone is not brought back to the position of normal use, the fracture may act as a tourniquet, causing ischemia and ultimately tissue death below the break.

Treatment

Check distal circulation, sensation, and movement (CSM) before treatment. These fractures should be brought back to a position of normal use by pulling traction-in-position (TIP). Grasp the bones on each side of the fracture and slowly pull in line with the bone, no matter what angle they are lying at. This procedure is best done with two people—one person holds the bone above the fracture steady while the other one slowly pulls traction. Remember, much of the pain from a broken bone arises from uncontrollable muscle contraction, so traction should reduce the pain.

After you have held traction for 10 minutes or more, the muscles should be fairly fatigued. Then slowly move the bone back into a position of normal use. Let your patient be your guide. If she says the pain is increasing, stop, hold traction, and wait until she is ready before you move again. You are in no great rush. All of the major blood vessels and nerves are surrounded by a highly sensitive layer of tissue, so you will inflict pain before you do any real damage. Your patient is relatively safe as long as you let her be your guide. Once the bone is in a position of normal use, it can be splinted like a normal fracture. Prepare to evacuate your patient.

OPEN FRACTURES

When the broken bone ends break the skin, it is called an open fracture. Open fractures may result in significant blood loss from bleeding, since the sharp bone ends may tear major blood vessels. You need to be prepared to treat for shock (see page 274). Open fractures pose significant additional complications due to the high risk of wound infection, especially if the bone is actually sticking out of the open wound.

Treatment

Treatment decisions such as whether to apply traction-in-position (TIP) should be based on the need to control bleeding. If bleeding is severe, your primary concern must be to control the bleeding to prevent volume shock. Use TIP to pull the bone ends back in, which should help control the bleeding. If you decide to draw the bones back into the body, flush them with a povidone-iodine solution or clean water first to remove all foreign material and reduce the risk of infection. (See "Wound Care," page 279.)

If bleeding is not severe, you should *not* pull to draw the bones back in. If there is no severe bleeding, the greater danger is from possible infection from drawing the bones back. Instead, use large, bulky padded dressings so as not to aggravate the fracture site. If the bone is sticking out of the wound, bleeding can often be controlled by making a "donut bandage" and applying this around the wound. (To make a donut, use at least two cravats. Wrap one around your hand several times to make a large loop. Then take the other bandage and wrap it around the first bandage.) Place the donut around the wound and secure it tightly with a wide cravat. Do not pick at, or try to push back, any exposed bone. Splint the injury as it lies. Keep in mind that you are dealing with two injuries: a fracture and a serious wound with infection potential. Prepare to evacuate your patient.

FEMUR FRACTURES AND TRACTION SPLINTS

Femur fractures must be handled slightly differently from regular fractures. The large muscles of the leg will be in spasm, causing the broken bone ends to override each other, cutting and damaging tissue. There is major risk of damage to nerves and blood vessels, including significant bleeding, and shock should always be anticipated. In order to minimize this risk, a traction splint can be used to overcome the effect of the muscle spasm and pull the bone ends back into their normal position. There is some debate about whether traction splints in wilderness field settings are actually that effective, in part due to the makeshift nature of the device. A regular splint can be used in place of a traditional splint.

Treatment

1. Roll up a foam pad lengthwise and wrap it around the leg as a splint. Secure it in place with cravats or tape.
2. To prepare for applying traction, attach traction straps over the boot or padded ankle (see illustration on page 298). Fold two cravats into long narrow bandages. Fold lengthwise, and pass one over and one behind the ankle, making sure the ends of each bandage fit snugly and flat against the ankle. The toes should remain visible or at least accessible for assessing distal circulation, sensation, and movement. You can also cut a slot in the patient's boot.
3. To construct the traction splint you need a long pole-like object (tent pole, hiking staff, ski pole, canoe paddle). It should extend from the top of the hip at least 1 foot (30 centimeters) beyond the bottom of the foot. Anchor the pole to the leg using a well-padded strap over the thigh at the hip. The distal end of the pole will need a strap that can be attached to the ankle hitch and tightened to create traction on the leg. (Practice this system on a noninjured person *before* applying it to your patient.)
4. Apply traction on the thigh by pulling the traction straps. Maintain traction by securing the traction straps to the end of the pole. Tie the traction splint to the foam pad splint already on the leg. Check distal CSM.
5. Once you have begun to pull traction on the leg, *don't* release traction. This will only result in increased injury to the surrounding vessels and tissue. Prepare to evacuate your patient. Continue to monitor distal CSM.

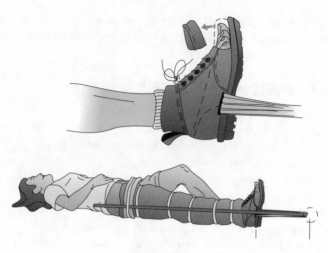

Traction Splint

DISLOCATIONS

The signs of dislocation are similar to those of a fracture: pain aggravated by motion, tenderness, swelling, discoloration, limitation of motion, and deformity of the joint. Comparison with the unaffected joint may help identify the problem. Dislocations should be treated as fractures and splinted in a comfortable position. There are three types of dislocations that can be reduced successfully in the field: shoulders, knees, and digits (fingers and toes). Keep in mind that reducing any dislocation can result in additional injury at the joint site and below. In some cases, you may not be able to distinguish between a dislocation and a fracture-dislocation where the joint is out of place *and* bone(s) are broken. Reducing a fracture-dislocation can create other medical problems. Fracture-dislocations are usually caused by a direct blow to the joint rather than an indirect force, and therefore you should *never* try to reduce a dislocation that has been caused by a direct mechanism.

Only attempt to reduce a dislocation if *all* the following conditions are true:

- The dislocation is at the shoulder, knee, or fingers.
- The dislocation was caused by an indirect mechanism (a force was applied distally to the extremity and the proximal end joint was levered out of position). Imagine grabbing the end of your finger and levering the joint out at the knuckle—this is an indirect force. Do *not* reduce the joint

if a direct force caused the injury, such as the impact from a fall (the underlying bones may also be fractured).

- There is a lack of circulation, sensation, and/or movement (CSM) of the extremity below the injured joint.
- You are more than 2 hours from more advanced medical assistance.
- You have been *properly trained* on how to reduce a dislocation *and* feel competent to attempt the procedure.

If *all* these conditions are true, field reduction is appropriate and usually successful. If reduction is delayed for more than two hours, the nerves and tissue below the injury are at risk. Failure to reduce the dislocation can result in permanent tissue damage. After reducing the dislocation, check again for circulation, sensation, and movement (CSM) of the extremity below the injured joint. If CSM has returned, then the relocation has helped save distal tissue. If not, the person is probably no worse off than before.

SHOULDER DISLOCATIONS

Shoulder dislocations can be caused either by a direct force, such as the impact of a fall onto the shoulder, or by indirect force, such as a levering force applied to the arm. Anterior shoulder dislocations happen when the head of the humerus (the upper arm bone) is forced forward (anteriorly) out of the shoulder socket. Anterior shoulder dislocations are by far the most common (98 percent of all shoulder dislocations) and are characterized by moderate to extreme pain and an obvious displacement of the arm forward from the shoulder socket. The displacement will give the shoulder a "stepped" appearance. The dislocated humeral head may be observed as a bulge anteriorly and should be palpable as well. The deltoid muscle of the upper arms looks and feels flattened. The victim usually cannot bring the arm in against the chest and cannot reach the hand of the affected side across to the other shoulder. If this is not treated quickly, the pain will worsen and the joint will begin to swell, causing additional complications later. If the dislocation is compromising nerves or circulation, tissue distal to the shoulder can be damaged. Posterior shoulder dislocations are caused by much more significant forces and often include fractures. You should *not* attempt to reduce a *posterior* shoulder dislocation.

Treatment

If a shoulder dislocation has been caused by a *direct* force, then field reduction should *not* be performed, since the possibility for a fracture-dislocation is high. In this case, the arm should be splinted, and evacuation must be initiated. Normally the most comfortable position for splinting is to secure the patient's hand to her head. To make this more comfortable for the patient, a rolled-up blanket can be secured under the armpit of the dislocation using a figure-eight bandage.

If this is an anterior dislocation and the dislocation is from an indirect force, there are several methods for reducing an anterior shoulder dislocation. Check distal CSM before performing any of these techniques, record your findings, and check again after attempting the reduction.

Boss-Holzach-Matter Self-Reduction Technique If you've dislocated your shoulder and you are by yourself or if your patient is not comfortable with you doing the reduction, the Boss-Holzach-Matter technique described by Dr. Elizabeth Joy in the *Physician and Sports Medicine Journal* is performed by the victim and is atraumatic, simple, and quick. The technique works in about 60 percent of cases. To perform the self-reduction technique, the patient sits on the ground with the knee on the same side as the shoulder dislocation bent at 90 degrees. With both of her hands clasped around the bent knee, have the patient lean backward to let gravity reduce the injury. Have the patient extend the arms completely so that the upper arm muscles aren't working. Coach your patient (or yourself) to relax as much as possible. If the reduction does not work on the first attempt, it is reasonable to try up to three times, especially if the patient is having difficulty relaxing or following instructions.

Baseball Pitch Technique Have the patient lie on her back with the injured arm along her side. While another rescuer holds on to the patient's body, pull steady, gentle traction on the arm at the elbow. Once traction has been started, *do not release it* until the dislocation has been reduced. Continue traction and slowly swing the arm so that the upper arm is in line with the shoulders. Then rotate the forearm until the arm is in the "baseball pitcher" position. At this point, the shoulder should reduce with a noticeable decrease in pain. The key to this method of reduction is to go slowly. It can sometimes take up to an hour or longer for reduction to occur. Let the patient be your guide as to how quickly to move. If there is any increase in resistance or a significant increase in pain, *stop*. Maintain the arm in that position, with traction, until the pain subsides, then continue to move the arm, this time more slowly.

Hands on Forehead Technique This technique does not require active rescuer assistance. Tell the patient to place her hands on her forehead. Then ask

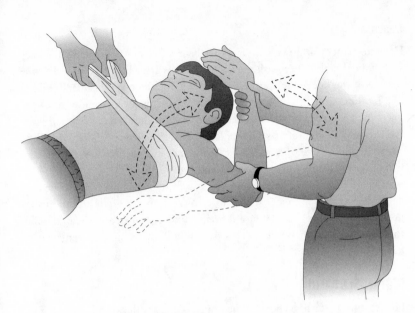

Baseball Technique for Shoulder Reduction

the patient to lie back and spread her elbows (trying to get both elbows to touch the ground). Do not physically force the patient. If the patient can get the elbows back, the shoulder most likely will suddenly pop back into place with a tremendous relief of pain.

Once the shoulder is back in the socket, be aware that the shoulder is still unstable. Immobilize it as quickly as possible using a sling and swathe. (See "Sling and Swathe," page 294.) Check distal CSM and record your findings. There can be complications associated with a dislocation, and evacuation is strongly encouraged.

KNEECAP DISLOCATION

The kneecap, or patella, is the bony plate that lies over the knee joint. It usually dislocates laterally—that is, it slips to the outside. Due to the structure of the knee, it might appear as if the patella has dislocated proximally (to the inside), but an examination of the lateral side of the leg will usually reveal that this is not the case. A dislocated patella is extremely painful and can be treated quickly and effectively in the field.

Treatment

Have the patient sit down with her knee bent. Place one hand below the knee with your thumb underneath the patient's kneecap (which has moved to the outside of the knee). Grasp the patient's ankle with your other hand, and in one motion, straighten the leg and push firmly on the outside edge of the kneecap. The kneecap will pop back into place with a sudden relief of pain. Patients may feel fine afterward, but discourage them from walking. Treat it as a severe sprain. (See "Sprains," page 288.) Since it is possible that the kneecap will dislocate again, evacuation is recommended.

Note: Dislocations to the knee joint itself (not the kneecap) can be *very* damaging to the complicated structures of the joint. Do *not* attempt to reduce a *knee* dislocation. Splint a dislocated knee joint in a position of comfort and evacuate the patient. This person will not be able to walk out on her own.

DIGIT DISLOCATION

Fingers and toes can dislocate. When this occurs, the distal end of the digit in question will be angulated with respect to the rest of the digit. Make sure that this is a dislocation and *not* a fracture or fracture-dislocation before reducing.

Treatment

Grasp the digit (finger or toe) proximally at the base with one hand and just distal of the dislocation with the other hand. Gently pull traction and pull the dislocated end of the digit back into anatomical position. The digit should then be splinted by taping it to an adjacent, uninjured digit (finger or toe).

SPINAL INJURIES

If a traumatic injury has occurred, especially something like a fall or severe impact, immediately suspect a spinal injury until you can prove otherwise. Treat any unconscious victim as if she has a spinal injury, unless you witnessed the person becoming unconscious and there was no mechanism of injury that caused the unconsciousness or occurred when the patient became unconscious. During your patient assessment you should be looking for the following:

- MOI (mechanism of injury) to the spine: any fall equal or greater than twice the height of the person; high-speed accidents; any head injury, especially if the head injury resulted in unconsciousness; any penetrating injury to the spinal region; any excessive movement to the spine, including

flexion (chin forced toward the chest), extension (head thrown backwards), compression (fall and land sitting), rotation, or lateral bending
- Numbness or tingling in the extremities
- Weakness in extremities
- Pain or tenderness anywhere along the spine
- Deformity anywhere along the spine
- Paralysis

The only way to rule out a spinal injury is if *all* of the following are true:

- You have been properly trained and certified by an authorized medical authority to evaluate spinal injuries.
- The patient is conscious and reliable.
- The patient has no sign of neurological problems. (See "The Patient Assessment System," page 264.)

The primary treatment goal for spine injuries is to stabilize the spine to prevent further damage. This can be difficult in remote settings. Individuals with specific wilderness first-aid training certified to use selective spinal stabilization may determine that stabilization isn't necessary based on their patient assessment. If you do not have this level of training, then you must operate on the assumption that a spinal injury has occurred. Professional rescue personnel will probably need to be brought in to stabilize the patient's spine on a backboard for transport.

TREATING SPINAL INJURIES

All spinal injuries are serious. Damage to any part of the spinal cord can lead to permanent paralysis or death. Injuries of the cervical spine are the most serious because nerves that control the diaphragm, which allows us to breathe, originate below the fourth vertebra of the neck (C4). If there is a cervical spinal fracture above the fourth vertebra, and the fracture damages or severs the spinal cord, the patient will no longer be able to breathe on her own ("above C4, breathe no more"). This means that the patient will require rescue breathing or CPR. A person with an unstable cervical spine injury may not have any damage to the spinal cord when you first get there. But your moving the person could damage or sever the spinal cord. That is why it is essential to check MOI when you first arrive at the scene and immediately immobilize the head and neck until you are sure that there is no spinal injury or until the entire spine has been properly immobilized with a cervical collar and a backboard.

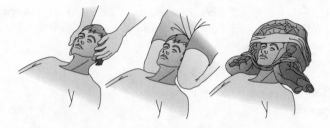

Hands-on Stable, Stabilizing the Neck

Treatment

1. The important point in treating a suspected spinal injury is to avoid moving the patient's head and neck. Ideally, the victim should not be moved unless there are serious environmental or life-threatening hazards (airway, breathing, or severe bleeding). In this case, move the person as a unit, supporting the neck at all times. (See "Log Roll" and the "In-line Drag," pages 285, 284.) The spine must be stabilized. One person should always be at the head of the patient, using traction-in-position (TIP) to maintain the head and neck in a neutral position (the position the head normally sits in relation to the spine, neither bent forward or backward). If applying a collar might cause unnecessary neck movement, or if you don't have other assistance, stabilize the head with "sandbags"—stuff sacks filled with sand or dirt—to form a moldable but rigid cradle. These are laid on either side of a supine patient's head and secured to prevent movement.

2. Apply a cervical collar to maintain the neck in a neutral position, but avoid any unnecessary movement of the patient. For improvised collars, figure out how you are going to get the cervical collar to work on *someone else* before you start applying it to your patient. Have the person be in the same position so you can practice how you will get the collar into position. A cervical collar can be improvised with a SAM splint or foam sleeping pad. Once the cervical collar has been applied, follow the instructions below for securing the rest of the spine.

3. Once the cervical collar has been applied, the rest of the spine including the pelvis needs to be immobilized. For possible spinal fractures, the entire spine is treated as one long bone, and you secure the spine from "head to tailbone." It may be difficult to fashion a proper backboard in the wilderness. External and internal pack frames or several overlapping camp chairs with sticks or pack frames may be used to create a basic backboard. Build your backboard and test it with a noninjured person. Make sure the backboard is well padded. When you are ready, you will need to use the log roll

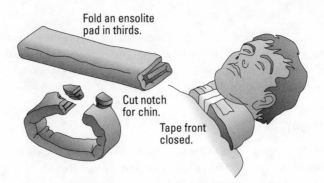

Fold an ensolite
pad in thirds.

Cut notch
for chin.

Tape front
closed.

Cervical Collar from a Foam Pad

technique (page 285) or the in-line drag technique (page 284) to get the person onto the backboard. Once on the backboard, secure the person to the backboard using duct tape, cravats, straps, belts, whatever you can find. Make sure that all straps are well padded before tightening them.

4. Remember that an improvised backboard is *not* the same as a professional rescue backboard. Don't try to use the improvised backboard to evacuate the person if it is not sturdy enough for transport; otherwise, you could seriously injure your patient. In that case wait until professional rescuers arrive.

5. In the event that the person needs to be moved (either before the application of the backboard or afterwards), you should use the log roll or the in-line drag (see pages 285, 284).

6. Treat the patient for shock and monitor until professional medical support arrives. Prepare to evacuate your patient.

CENTRAL NERVOUS SYSTEM INJURIES

Any patient who has recently suffered a blow to the head or any period of unconsciousness should be examined carefully.

FAINTING

Fainting is a temporary loss of consciousness that does *not* occur as the result of a blow to the head. This is most often the result of a sudden and temporary drop in blood pressure for any one of a number of reasons. Fainting commonly occurs in hot environments due to a combination of immobility and mild dehydration—the classic case is the soldier who faints while standing at attention. It can also be caused by low blood sugar or other factors.

Treatment

Fainting is, in and of itself, not a serious condition. Allow the patient to rest until she feels well enough to continue on. Provide fluids if dehydration is a possibility. Do a thorough assessment to make sure that a more serious problem is not the cause of the fainting.

HEAD INJURY

The term *head injury* refers to damage or trauma to *the brain itself* as opposed to the outside surface of the head (head wounds). Head wounds often bleed a lot but are not typically serious in and of themselves.

Any type of severe blow to the head is likely to cause a head injury. Look for a mechanism of injury that could have caused an impact to the brain. Head injuries can range from minor to severe. Any injury that results in swelling of the brain or internal bleeding inside the skull is considered severe and potentially life-threatening. Since there is no extra space inside the skull to accommodate this swelling or extra fluid, as the brain tissue swells it is squeezed by the skull, causing an increase in intracranial pressure (ICP, see page 307). This pressure can become so severe that the brain can't be perfused with oxygen, which can lead to death. All swelling follows the same general pattern: Swelling is fastest in the first 6 hours and continues more slowly until 24 hours after the injury, at which point it generally stops. The patient's condition will deteriorate continuously until swelling stops, so the fastest possible evacuation—preferably in the first 6 hours—is called for in cases of increasing ICP. Anyone who has suffered a severe blow to the head, particularly when associated with severe headache and vomiting, should be expected to deteriorate rapidly. Severe head injuries may also be associated with a spinal fracture. For anyone with a head injury, if you cannot rule out a spinal injury, the person should have her spine immobilized.

Assessment

In cases of head injury caused by trauma, look for tenderness and pain around the skull; for dark marks behind the ears ("battle signs"); and for dark rings that go all the way around the eyes ("raccoon eyes"). Each of these is caused by blood pooling under the skin and is a sign of a skull fracture. Also look for a clear or bloody discharge from the nose and/or ears, which may be cerebral spinal fluid leaking from a fractured skull. Do not be distracted by scalp lacerations. They bleed a lot but are minor.

General Treatment

There is no specific field treatment for a brain injury and increasing intracranial pressure (ICP) except to get the person to advanced medical care. Monitor her vitals, especially level of consciousness, closely. Whenever there is a severe blow to the head, you should assume there is a neck injury; deal with it also as a spine injury. (see "Spinal Injuries," page 302.) Vomiting is common, so monitor the patient's airway and take precautions to prevent aspiration of vomit. If the person begins to vomit, you will need to log-roll her onto her side (see "Log Roll," page 285). Head injuries alone do not cause shock; however, other injuries sustained may, especially when the injury is caused by traumatic forces. Treat for shock but do *not* elevate the legs, as it may increase intracranial pressure. Prepare to evacuate your patient. When evacuating, take into account how swelling may change over time and how that could affect your patient's condition.

INCREASING INTRACRANIAL PRESSURE (ICP)

Any person with a head injury is at risk for increasing intracranial pressure (ICP). Increasing ICP can be caused not only by trauma but also by medical problems such as a stroke, a cerebral aneurysm, or by high altitude. Increasing ICP is a serious condition and has the following signs and symptoms:

Early Signs

- Severe headache
- Dizziness
- Nausea or vomiting
- Decreasing pulse rate
- Increasing respiration rate
- Decreasing mental status (A on the AVPU scale)

Late Signs

- Changes in pupil size and reactivity to light
- Seizures
- Paralysis
- Decrease down the AVPU scale

The major thing to monitor is the level of consciousness, which will decrease as the ICP goes up. At first the patient will become disoriented, irritable, confused, and/or obnoxious. One test is to ask the person to count backwards by nines from 100; if she can't do it, you know that some part of her higher brain function is being impaired. As ICP increases the level of consciousness will decrease down through the AVPU levels (see "Patient Assessment System," page 264). You may also see deeper and faster breathing, slower pulse, flushed and warm skin, and unequal pupils. The one thing that can and must be done in the field is to carefully monitor the patient's mental status. This information is essential for proper medical treatment and should be routinely obtained and recorded about every 15 minutes.

Evaluating Possible Increasing Intracranial Pressure

These are the best ways to monitor for increasing ICP:

- Level of consciousness—monitor LOC for changes in personality, decreased mental status, and any decrease on the AVPU scale.
- Loss of ability to stand with eyes closed or walk a straight line—"sobriety test."
- Muscular weakness—compare movement at the hands and feet on both sides of the body. (See page 268.)
- Loss of sensation—compare sensation at the hands and feet on both sides of the body.

CONCUSSION

A concussion is generally a mild brain contusion (bruise) caused by an impact force to the head. Anyone who has experienced a blow to the head and who shows any of the following symptoms is considered to have a concussion:

- Loss of consciousness
- Amnesia (from before the event or after)
- Altered mental status

Concussions range from mild to severe. Anyone who has had a concussion *may* develop increasing intracranial pressure (ICP), a potentially life-threatening injury. This person must be monitored carefully for any signs of increasing ICP.

Treatment

Generally, no specific treatment is possible for a concussion. Monitor carefully for the next 24 hours for signs of increasing ICP from swelling or internal bleeding. The person does *not* need to be *constantly* kept awake but must be woken every 2 to 3 hours to be assessed. If there is any sign of decreasing AVPU, the patient should be evacuated.

SKULL FRACTURES

Skull fractures may be very difficult to diagnose and may occur with significant, little, or no brain injury. The typical signs of a fracture—pain, tenderness, swelling, and discoloration—may be masked or mimicked by contusions or lacerations in the scalp tissue overlying the skull. Fractures of the base of the skull often produce bleeding or a flow of clear fluid (cerebrospinal fluid) from the ears or nose. Make sure that any fluid is, in fact, coming from *within* the ears or nose and is not blood from a laceration of the surrounding skin. The safest course is to assume that any head injury resulting in significant unconsciousness has also fractured the skull.

Treatment

No specific treatment for skull fractures can be given in the field. Maintain an airway and contact rescue authorities for evacuation. Evaluate for the possibility of a spinal injury and treat accordingly (see "Spinal Injuries," page 302). Monitor for possible increasing ICP. Prepare to evacuate your patient.

Evacuation Guidelines for Head Injuries

Severe concussions, possible skull fractures, and any situation with increasing ICP always require evacuation of some sort; minor concussions and surface wounds to the head do not. When in doubt, evacuate the patient.

SEIZURES

Most people immediately think of epilepsy when they hear the word *seizures*, but seizures can be caused by a number of medical conditions and may occur without any prior history. If anyone on your trip has a history of seizures, make sure that she takes her medications if appropriate (most seizure patients are good about this), and remind the person that physical stress and the dietary changes of a trip can contribute to the likelihood of having a seizure. In addition to epilepsy, the acronym STOPEAT indicates the other potential causes of seizure activity.

S = Sugar	Lack of blood sugar in the brain (especially for a person with diabetes, see page 378)
T = Temperature	Overheating or overcooling in the brain (see "Heatstroke," page 346, and "Hypothermia," page 332)
O = Oxygen	Lack of oxygen in the brain (see "Shock," page 274, and "Basic LIfe Support," page 282)
P = Pressure	Increasing intracranial pressure (see "ICP," page 307)
E = Electricity	Electric shock, such as a lightning strike (see "Lightning Injuries, page 348)
A = Altitude	High altitude (see "Altitude IIInesses," page 380)
T = Toxins	Various toxins inhaled or ingested (see "Toxins," page 349)

Seizures in general have three phases: the aura, the seizure, and the post-ictal ("after seizure") phase. In the aura phase, the patient can become dazed, have a glassy look in her eyes, and seem lost. Some patients can recognize this as a warning for a seizure and will try to communicate it to you, but may not be able to speak. If you see this coming, have the patient lie down and remove everything in her way. The seizure itself may not be noticeable (person simply lies there) or it may be a grand mal (violent) seizure with uncontrolled muscle contractions all over the body. Your only concern is to prevent the patient from hurting herself by removing anything that could be in her way.

- Do *not* try to restrain a person having a seizure.
- Do *not* try to stick anything in her mouth.
- Do *not* worry if the person's jaw is clamped shut. The notion that she will choke on her tongue during a seizure is a myth. She probably isn't breathing during the seizure. Her jaw will relax and breathing will resume when the seizure has subsided. After the seizure, make sure the patient has an open airway and has resumed breathing; otherwise, begin rescue breathing. (See "Basic Life Support," page 282.)
- After the seizure, the patient will enter the post-ictal phase. She is usually very confused and lethargic, but her level of post-ictal consciousness will slowly return to normal.

Warning: Some post-ictal patients are extremely violent. They are often very disoriented and may see everything as a threat, so treat them carefully. These patients will be difficult to reason with because they are not totally conscious, although they may be able to talk to you. These patients should be kept from running around, as they have no natural sense of danger and can easily hurt themselves. Use physical restraint *only* if absolutely necessary to prevent the patient from harming herself, but do so with the utmost care. Any post-seizure patient should be examined at a medical facility. Prepare to evacuate your patient.

A seizure can be a traumatic event for the patient. Seizure patients may become incontinent (urinate or defecate in their clothing). For the person who has never had a seizure before it can be a frightening experience. Be prepared to deal with possible emotional issues after the seizure and be supportive of the person.

CHEST INJURIES

Chest injuries are typically the result of trauma. The major danger of chest injuries is the potential for damage to the underlying organs—heart, lungs, liver, kidneys, spleen, and others—which can result in life-threatening internal bleeding. Any internal injuries will be difficult to diagnose. Monitoring for changes in vital signs may be your only indication.

Basic Treatment

Any chest injury may have an impact on the person's ability to breathe. Basic first aid includes maintaining an airway and assisting the patient in breathing with PROP (see page 262).

BROKEN RIBS

Broken ribs are usually caused by a blunt trauma to the chest cavity. Due to the connective tissue and muscle surrounding the ribs, they are likely to remain in position. The patient will complain of sharp pain at the site of trauma that increases upon inspiration. Make sure that the patient's breathing is not impaired. Be wary of the possibility of a sucking chest wound (pneumothorax; see page 312). Also, watch for internal bleeding, as the force of breaking the ribs may also have damaged the nearby internal organs, such as the liver, kidneys, and spleen.

Treatment

Rib fractures cause painful breathing. As long as the pain can be controlled with pain relievers like ibuprofen, the ribs need not be splinted. If the pain cannot be controlled, splinting the chest will help stabilize the broken ribs. Either swathe the chest with broad firm cravats or tape the chest with wide pieces of tape that run parallel to the ribs and go from the sternum to the vertebrae. Monitor the vitals, especially respirations. Prepare to evacuate your patient.

FLAIL CHEST

In some cases, if several ribs are broken in multiple places, an entire section of the chest wall can come loose. This is called a flail chest, characterized by *paradoxical breathing,* or having part of the chest go in when the rest is expanding, and vice versa. This will cause extreme respiratory difficulty, and hence is an immediate life-threatening emergency. Paradoxical breathing is easiest to see when the person is lying on her back.

Treatment

Secure the flail area from moving by using bulky dressings and tape. Tape halfway around the body from the front midline to the back midline. If the person's breathing gets more labored after apply the dressing, remove it. The patient may also be helped lying on the affected side. Assist respirations with positive pressure ventilation if possible. Prepare to evacuate your patient.

CLOSED PNEUMOTHORAX/HEMOTHORAX

A *pneumothorax* occurs when the tissue of the lung wall is torn. This can occur from a rib fracture when bone ends tear the lung wall or sometimes spontaneously when a weak spot on the lung ruptures. The danger of this injury is that the space between the lung and the chest wall (pleural space) fills with air from the punctured lung, which causes the lung itself to start to collapse. *This is an immediate life-threatening emergency.* Look for bruising on the chest wall to indicate an injury site, pain upon inspiration, pain upon palpation, difficulty breathing, increasing anxiety, a feeling of "suffocation," decreased breath sounds on the affected side, rapid pulse, and pale, cool, clammy skin. A *hemothorax* is a similar condition but involves internal bleeding that causes the lung to collapse. A *hemo-pneumothorax* is both air and internal bleeding. Treatment for all three conditions is the same.

Treatment

Treat the victim as you would a patient with a fractured rib. Stabilize the fracture site with a swathe or lay the victim on her affected side (this helps limit the amount of air escaping from the lung into the pleural space). Keep in mind that a pneumothorax is often caused by a large force that might also cause spinal injury. If spinal injury is suspected, treat for spinal injury (see "Spinal Injuries," page 302.) Monitor the vital signs continuously, especially breathing, to see if it is getting worse. Give oxygen if available. In most cases the problem will reach a point where it doesn't get any worse. However, there is the possibility of the patient developing a *tension pneumothorax* (see below). Since the condition could get worse, this is a potentially life-threatning situation. Prepare to evacuate your patient.

OPEN PNEUMOTHORAX—SUCKING CHEST WOUND

An open pneumothorax is just like a closed pnuemothorax except it is an open wound caused by trauma that has punctured the wall of the lung. This can be caused by a broken rib or by a deep chest wound. It is often called a "sucking" chest wound from the sound of air rushing through the chest wall. If not treated immediately, air will begin to fill the space between the lungs and the chest wall (pleural space), causing the lung on that side to collapse. The person will have difficulty breathing, increasing anxiety ("sense of suffocating"), rapid pulse, and pale, cool, clammy skin. There may be a moist sucking sound from the open wound and/or a bubbling of fluid at the wound site. *This is an immediate life-threatening emergency.*

Treatment

The goal of treatment for a sucking chest wound is to close the hole immediately. Cover it immediately with your gloved hand. Then find an occlusive dressing (a piece of plastic bag, aluminum foil)—something that won't let air or water in or out. Find the hole, cover it with a small square piece of the occlusive dressing, and tape three sides of the square closed. Leave the bottom end or a corner open. As the patient inhales, the occlusive dressing is sucked against the hole, sealing it off and preventing additional air from entering. As the patient exhales, air *may* be pushed out. If the patient's breathing becomes *more* labored after applying dressing, then seal it completely on all sides. Lay the patient on her affected side (unless spinal injury is suspected) and send for help. Prepare to evacuate your patient. There is a danger of a tension pneumothorax developing. (See "Tension Pneumothorax" below.)

TENSION PNEUMOTHORAX

This can occur with either open or closed injuries. This is the most serious chest injury. Air is continuing to leak from the damaged lung, completely collapsing it. The air continues to leak out and has nowhere to go, so it starts to compress the heart and the major blood vessels. At this stage the pressure of the collapsed lung may push the trachea off center (trachial deviation), and you may see bulging of the neck veins. *Death is imminent.* Anytime you have a pneumothorax or hemothorax, there is the possibility that this can occur, so you should arrange for an immediate and speedy evacuation since advanced life support may be needed right away.

In the event that this is an open pneumothorax and the collapse is caused by an open wound, there is one thing you can try. Open the occlusive dressing and try sticking your finger into the hole hoping to release the trapped air. It may not work, but it could just save the person's life. Infection, of course, could result afterward.

IMPALED OBJECT IN THE CHEST

If an object is impaled deep enough in the chest, the object may cause a sucking chest wound or pneumothorax (see page 313) or may damage other organs.

Treatment

Don't remove an impaled object in the chest unless you need to do so to evacuate the patient. (See "Impaled Objects," page 320.) The object may be serving as a cork, preventing major bleeding. Stabilize the impaled object and send for help. Monitor the vitals. Treat for shock and give PROP (see page 262). Prepare to evacuate your patient.

THERMAL BURNS

Thermal burns are damage to tissue caused by extreme heat. Typical causes are overexposure to the sun, boiling water, camp stoves, or fires. Burns are categorized based on the depth of the tissue damaged (superficial, partial thickness, and full thickness) and the percentage of the body burned. (See also "Eye Injuries," page 322.)

Principles in Treating Thermal Burns

- Remove the person from the course of heat immediately. Smother the flames if appropriate—drop and roll in a blanket, etc.
- Monitor the airway and breathing. Be very suspicious of burns to the face and neck, including soot in the mouth and nose and singed nasal hair. Burned airway tissues will swell and may block the airway. Burns to the lungs (inhaled hot gases) can cause swelling and fluid buildup in the lung tissue, which can lead to respiratory failure. Treat with PROP (see page 262) and prepare for immediate evacuation.
- For surface burns apply cold immediately to counteract the heat and to

reduce tissue damage using ice, cold water, or a cold pack. Continue to apply cold until the heat has been removed. For example, if the person spills boiling water on her leg, the heat transferred to the leg will continue to cause tissue damage until all the heat has been removed. Do *not* place ice directly onto the burn site. Wrap it in a cloth; otherwise, you could actually freeze the tissue, which would cause further tissue damage.

- Do not apply ointments to a burn that is still hot; ointments trap heat in the skin, causing additional damage.
- Treat for shock and monitor the patient's vitals.
- Gauge the depth of the burn (superficial, partial thickness, or full thickness) and percentage of the body area that has been burned.

SUPERFICIAL BURNS (FIRST-DEGREE)

Only the top layers of skin are affected. Tissue is red and mild-to-moderately painful (nerve sensation is intact). Sunburn is a typical first-degree burn. Treatment is local application of cold (see above).

PARTIAL-THICKNESS BURNS (SECOND-DEGREE)

Deeper layers of tissue are damaged. Tissue is red to pale and very painful (nerve sensation is intact). Large fluid-filled blisters may form. There may be scarring when the burn heals.

Treatment

Local application of cold (see above). Once the heat has been removed, your next goal is to deal with the wound. Infection is a risk after burns, so careful wound management is important. Wash the burn with mild soap and water (antibacterial soap is best). If blisters are present and have not popped, they should be left intact. If blisters have popped, remove the blister skin by gently cutting it away. Cover the wound with a nonstick gauze pad like Telfa covered with a thin layer of antibiotic ointment. (See "Wound Care," page 279.) If the burn area is small, you can use a dressing like 2nd Skin (see page 319) to cover the wound. Then cover with roller gauze.

FULL-THICKNESS BURNS (THIRD-DEGREE)

The full thickness of tissue is affected, which includes all layers of skin and may include muscle and bones. The burned area is white, black, or leathery. There is often no pain at the deep site of the burn, due to nerve damage. Typically the tissue outside the full-thickness burn goes to partial thickness and then superficial as you move out from the center. The most severely burned area may not hurt at all while the outer edges may be very painful.

Treatment

Use local application of cold as described above. But if a third-degree burn is large (over 5 to 10 percent of the body or the size of your stomach), and especially if the burn is on the trunk of the body, do not apply cold. At this point, the skin is burned away and the body cannot properly regulate temperature, so there is a risk of hypothermia. However, burns to the face and neck should always be cooled to make sure the airway does not swell shut.

Follow the wound care instructions for partial-thickness burns above. Once the wound is dressed, leave the burn alone unless you are out in the field for an extended period of time. In this case, you may want to immobilize the burned area so that further tissue damage does not occur through moving around.

Carefully monitor the person for signs of volume shock. Burns over a large area of the body result in significant fluid loss. Attempt to rehydrate the person. Do not force fluid down if the person is unable to swallow. Be extra careful of hypothermia—a severely burned person no longer has the ability to properly thermoregulate. Monitor closely for infection.

Evacuation Guidelines

Management of severe burns or burns to critical areas requires advanced medical care in a hospital setting. You need to evaluate the percentage of the body areas burned, the areas burned, and the depth of the burn (see illustration). You should evacuate any patient who has burns of the following types:

- Partial or full-thickness burns greater than 15 percent of the body surface are a life-threatening emergency and warrant immediate evacuation
- Burns to the lungs
- Any full-thickness burns
- Circumferential burns (burns that extend completely around a part of the body) because the area may swell and impair distal circulation
- Any serious burns to sensitive areas such as the face and neck, hands, feet, or genitals

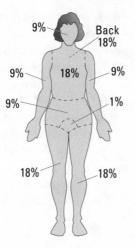

9%
Back
18%

9%   18%   9%

9%   1%

18%   18%

Burn Percentage

SOFT-TISSUE INJURIES

Soft-tissue injuries encompass any injuries to the soft tissues of the body—skin, muscles, internal organs, and so on. The primary treatment for soft-tissue injuries is to stop bleeding and properly clean and bandage the wound to minimize infection. Any more serious complications from the injuries typically need to be treated by advanced medical care.

BLISTERS

Blisters are actually highly localized second-degree burns caused by the heat of friction. They are usually found on the feet and may be the most common cause of evacuation on trips. If people pay attention to their feet and take proper precautions, most blisters can be avoided, or at least caught and treated before they become serious enough to impact your trip.

Prevention

Make sure everyone's boots fit properly and are broken in *before* the trip starts. (See "Boots," page 34.) If you know you are susceptible to blisters in a certain spot, put moleskin or tape over that area *before* you start hiking.

Treatment for Hot Spots

Before a blister forms, there will be a hot spot—a small reddened area that is essentially a first-degree burn. Get into a routine of checking for "hot spots"—

the first sign of blisters—at the start of your hike. The hot spot should be covered with a thin protective layer, such as Spenco Adhesive Kit, moleskin, or tape. Keep an eye on the area to make sure a real blister doesn't form. Tincture of Benzoin can be applied to the skin to keep the tape attached and can help toughen up the skin, which can prevent blistering. Another product that can be used to prevent blister formation is Blist-o-Ban. The Blist-o-Ban bandage looks like a blister itself. It's made up of several laminated layers of breathable plastic film bonded together, except for an area in the center. This area forms a collapsed "bubble" between the plastic sheets, allowing the plastic sheets to glide freely when lateral pressure is applied. This is just what the body is trying to do when it creates a blister. Center the dome of the Blist-o-Ban bandage over a hot spot or an already formed blister. The Blist-o-Ban bandage ends up "taking on" any friction applied to the site, minimizing further injury to the skin and dramatically reducing pain.

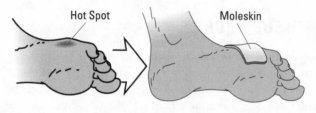

Hot Spot   Moleskin

Hot Spot Treatment

Treatment for Blisters

If the friction on a hot spot continues, eventually the top layer of skin becomes separated from the layers below. The space between the layers fills with fluid. This fluid is sterile, and so as long as the blister remains intact, you have a closed wound that does not have any risk of infection. Once the blister has popped, you have an open wound, prone to infection.

Since a popped blister is more prone to infection, you should *not* pop a blister unless the person cannot walk with the blister or walking would pop it anyway. If you must pop a blister, sterilize a needle in a flame or with alcohol and lance the blister on the edge nearest the ground, so it will drain easily. Try to have the patient do this herself. Drain the fluid and then treat it as any other open wound. Use universal precautions since blood may be present (see page 265).

To protect the blister area, build up a donut of padding around it out of moleskin or molefoam. Use as many layers as you need to keep pressure off the blister. If the blister is popped, place antibiotic ointment inside the donut

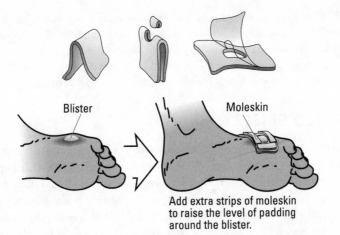

Blister | Moleskin

Add extra strips of moleskin
to raise the level of padding
around the blister.

Blister Treatment

hole and tape over the top of the donut. Blisters may need to be redressed on a daily basis. Be careful of infection. Blisters are very common and, if treated early, typically do not require evacuation unless infection sets in or the person no longer feels comfortable walking.

A popped blister is now an open wound and can become the site of an infection. There are a number of products that are effective for the treatment of open blisters. Band-Aid Advanced Healing Blister is a cushioning gel pad that works well on open blisters. Spenco 2nd Skin is another gel product on a polyethylene sheet that provides padding the open blister.

LACERATIONS

Lacerations and other wounds may be treated in the wilderness or may need advanced medical care.

Treatment

Stop the bleeding. (See "Bleeding," page 278.) Properly clean and dress the wound. Keep the dressings clean and dry. Change them every 24 hours as needed. Monitor for infection. Be prepared to evacuate your patient under the following circumstances:

- If there is a large initial blood loss.
- If there is any sign of major infection.

- If there appears to be a need for stitches—a gaping cut over ½ inch long (1.2 centimeters). Stitches should be applied within 8 to 12 hours; otherwise, the physician is likely to leave the wound open.
- If there is a laceration to the face, hands, or over a joint.
- If there is any injury to a blood vessel, ligament, or tendon.

IMPALED OBJECTS

Impaled objects can run the gamut from splinters in a finger to a tree limb protruding through the abdomen. You need to consider the forces that impaled the object and the effect the object is having on surrounding tissues. Severe bleeding, fractures, spinal injury, head injury, and major tissue damage can all occur with a deeply impaled object. The general rule is: Do *not* remove the object. The object may be acting as a cork. If you take the object out, the wound may start to bleed heavily. Furthermore, you may cause greater damage removing the object than when it first entered. You should *only* remove an impaled object if:

- Removing it is easy and safe for the patient.
- The object prevents safe transport of the patient.
- The impaled object may compromise the airway.

Treatment

The first priority is to control any bleeding that may be present. The second priority is to immobilize the object so that it will not move and cause more damage. Immobilize the object by building up pads around it or by using donuts made of bulky bandaging material, much as you would do for a blister. Be sure the object is secured in place. Prepare to evacuate your patient.

If a person has become impaled on a branch or fence post or similar object that is fairly immovable, immobilize the object in the person as best you can and then cut the object off about 6 inches (15 centimeters) from the person so you can bandage around it. Continue to immobilize the object.

MINOR IMPALED OBJECTS

These include splinters, nails, slivers of glass, fishhooks, and rock shards impaled in superficial skin tissue. In most cases, you can remove the impaled object and treat the wound. If the object is easy to remove, try to have the patient do it herself.

If the object is in deep enough to cause bleeding, check to see if the patient has had a recent tetanus shot. It should be within at least ten years or within five years if the wound is particularly dirty. If not, the patient should be evacuated to receive a tetanus booster. Ideally, the booster should be given within 24 hours. Even minor wounds can lead to serious infections. I've seen minor bug bites and lacerations result in systemic infections that could have become life-threatening. Watch for red streaks proximal from the wound and progressing toward the heart. (See "Wound Infection," page 281.)

Removing an Impaled Fishhook

Fishhooks can easily be removed in the field. Tie a piece of string about 12 inches long (30 centimeters) to the curve of the fishhook near where it enters the skin. Wrap the other end of the string around your (the rescuer's) index finger. Pull the string so that it is in line with the shank of the fish hook. Press down on the eye and shank of the fish hook with your other hand to disengage the barb. Leaving some slack in the string, give the string a sudden jerk in line with the hook. The hook should pop out. Clean and bandage the wound.

RASHES

Rashes can be caused by a variety of things, including contact dermatitis (poison ivy), friction rashes ("butt rash" or "jock itch"), or an allergic reaction. (See "Anaphylaxis," page 364, and "Animal and Insect Bites and Stings," page 352.)

POISON IVY, POISON OAK, POISON SUMAC

Contact with these plants results in a rash caused by a sap component (urushiol), which is found on all parts of the plant at all times of the year. (See "Plants to Avoid," page 219.) The sap can be carried on clothes or, on hot days, in a vapor around the plant. Scratching the rash does not spread it, but it should be discouraged because it can introduce infection or lead to scarring. The *rash* cannot be spread from person to person; however, it is possible to spread the *oil* (for example, if your boots get covered with the oil and then someone else picks up your boots). Inhaling smoke from the burning of these plants can cause the same rash on the lung surface, a serious injury that *cannot* be treated in the field. Treat lung exposure with PROP (see page 262) and prepare to evacuate your patient.

Treatment

Wash the area thoroughly and use hydrocortisone cream to combat the itch. The rash is fairly harmless, just uncomfortable, and should disappear within four to seven days. Evacuation is generally not necessary. Be aware that some people are also allergic to these plants and can have a mild or even a severe anaphylactic reaction.

FRICTION RASHES

Friction rashes are similar to hot spots. (See "Blisters," page 317.) Repeated rubbing can irritate the top layer of skin and cause a minor burn. Friction rashes are especially common around the crotch and can be partially avoided by wearing loose underwear to minimize chafing and to help the area breathe. Try to avoid wearing nylon underwear, which holds in moisture and heat.

Treatment

Have the patient apply petroleum jelly to the area of discomfort. If the itch persists, hydrocortisone cream can be used.

EYE INJURIES

Immediate attention is required for eye injuries, since even a seemingly minor abrasion can cause significant damage. It is always prudent to be conservative and evacuate any eye injury to proper medical care. When treating an eye injury, the most important thing to remember is that when one eyeball moves, so does the other. So if you need to bandage an injured eye to keep it from moving, you must bandage them both. This obviously has an impact on the person's ability to hike out.

THERMAL BURNS

A thermal eye burn should be treated as any other burn. (See "Thermal Burns," page 314.) Cool the area with water. Cover both eyes with a sterile dressing. Prepare to evacuate your patient.

SNOWBLINDNESS

"Snowblindness" is a misnomer because the injury isn't actually caused by snow; it's from the sun's rays. The major cause is overexposure (6 to 12 hours) to ultraviolet B radiation (UVB) from the sun, causing sunburn (first-degree burn) to the cornea. UVB exposure is greater at high altitudes and on snowfields and glaciers, where the UVB radiation also reflects off the snow. It can also be caused by reflected glare on water. The best protection is good sunglasses or goggles that should filter out 99 percent of UVB light. On snowfields, side shields on the glasses are also essential. In an emergency, you can create sunglasses by cutting small slits for lenses in a piece of cardboard and wearing them like glasses.

The symptoms of snowblindness are pain in the eyes, redness, swollen eyelids, pain when looking at the light, and a feeling like "sand in the eyes." Snowblindness general resolves itself in 24 to 48 hours. Remove any contact lenses and place cool compresses on the eyes. The eyes should not be exposed to additional light, so patch both eyes for 24 hours.

CHEMICAL BURNS

Any caustic chemicals in the eyes should be rinsed out using eye irrigation solution or clean water. (Don't use water treated with iodine or chlorine products.) Have the person turn her head to the side with the affected eye down, and pour the irrigation fluid from the nasal side of the eye, to keep the chemical from flowing into the other eye. Prepare to evacuate your patient.

FOREIGN OBJECTS

Foreign objects in the eye are common and can usually be removed with few complications. Pull the upper eyelid over the lashes of the lower eyelid. The lashes should be able to brush out any objects. If this does not work, try folding the upper eyelid outward over a matchstick and brushing the object out with a clean bandanna. You can also irrigate the eye as you would for a caustic burn. Irrigation is also recommended for fire ash that may get into the eye.

IMPALED OBJECTS

If someone gets a branch or other object stuck in her eye, treat it as you would any other impaled object. If possible, leave the impaled object in place, stabilize it, and bandage both eyes to limit movement. Prepare to evacuate your patient.

CONTACT LENS PROBLEMS

Periodically a contact lens will get wedged back onto the rear surface of the eyelid. Contrary to popular belief, the contact lens cannot slide to the back of the eye. It typically floats off the cornea (the clear surface of the eye) and under the eyelids. Have the person look up, down, and side to side so that you can locate it. Then gently move it back in place. *Always* clean your hands before touching a contact lens.

Contact lenses should be removed from a person who is unconscious for an extended time. With a soft lens, pinch the lens between two fingers, and it will pop out. With a hard lens, place your finger on the outer corner of the eye and pull down. The lens will pop out. Store the lenses in the appropriate solution.

NOSEBLEEDS

Nosebleeds are fairly common and come in two types: anterior bleeds (from the front of the nose, the usual variety) and posterior bleeds (from the back of the nose inside the head, more unusual). Nosebleeds may occur spontaneously, without trauma, often after a large sneeze. They are especially common in cold weather, when the air dries out the nasal membranes. Sometimes the blood flow can be very heavy at first, but you should not be alarmed, as it is generally not dangerous.

Treatment

Carefully monitor the airway, especially in patients with posterior bleeding, where there is a chance for the blood to run down the back of the throat. Have the person lean forward slightly and ask if she tastes blood. If she does, encourage her to spit it out. In the meantime, apply direct pressure by holding a piece of cloth or gauze over the nose and pinching the soft portion of the nose to apply direct pressure for 10 to 15 minutes. The bleeding will eventually subside. There should be no need for evacuation unless the person has swallowed a great deal of blood or is having difficulty breathing. Do *not* have the person lean back or lie down, as she may aspirate blood into the lungs or swallow blood, which often provokes vomiting. Most anterior nose bleeds can be treated in the field. A posterior nosebleed that doesn't stop on its own will require admission to a hospital.

If the person experiences repeated, heavy nosebleeds, there may be cause for concern. You may want to evacuate in these cases, as some more serious condition may be involved.

DENTAL PROBLEMS

Any significant dental problem will require a dentist for proper treatment. These are often painful injuries that make it difficult to eat and potentially lead to infections. In the field, there are a number of temporary treatments you can perform to hold the patient over until she can be evacuated. For extended wilderness trips, it is advisable to carry a dental emergency kit, which contains a number of special materials useful for broken teeth, lost fillings, and so on.

A patient with dental problems should eat only soft foods and cool liquids (avoid hot and cold foods) until proper dental care is available.

TOOTHACHES

Exposure of the tooth nerve, pulp, artery, or vein can cause severe pain. A toothache can also be caused by infection. (See "Infection," page 326.) Treatment is limited to pain medication and antibiotics. Avoid hot, cold, or spicy foods. Do *not* place aspirin *on* a tooth—aspirin is an acid and can cause a burn to the sensitive tissue.

BROKEN TOOTH

Tooth damage is most often associated with trauma. Thus, the possibility of associated head or neck injuries should be considered. Most important, the patient's airway should be checked, and any debris that might impede breathing, including tooth fragments or blood, should be removed.

Treatment

Position the patient on her side with the head down so that any further debris will drain out of the mouth as opposed to down the throat. If a cervical spine injury is suspected, maintain spine stability and log-roll the person onto her side (see "Log Roll," page 285) and treat for a spinal injury. (See "Spinal Injuries," page 302.) Once the patient is alert and stable, rinse her mouth with clean, cool water to flush out the remaining debris, provide some degree of pain relief, and help stop bleeding. Bleeding can be controlled with direct pressure. Fold a piece of gauze and place it on the bleeding area. Have the person hold it or bite down on the gauze for 10 to 15 minutes until the bleeding stops. A moist tea bag also works well as a packing material.

FRACTURED TOOTH

A fractured tooth that is still in place with an exposed nerve will be extremely sensitive. This can be treated temporarily by applying topical oral pain relievers to the affected area and sealing the injury with dental wax or Cavit (a temporary filling material) available in dental emergency kits until a dentist is available. Prepare to evacuate your patient.

KNOCKED-OUT TOOTH

A tooth that has been knocked out entirely may have a good chance of reattaching if it is replaced within an hour. Rinse the tooth with clean water. Avoid handling the root, which contains the delicate attachment fibers. Replace the tooth in its socket.

The replaced tooth—or any loose tooth—can be stabilized by splinting it to a neighboring tooth with dental floss or similar material. If it is not possible to replace the tooth, save the tooth and try to get the person evacuated as soon as possible. If the tooth is out and the tooth socket is bleeding, pack it as described above to place direct pressure on the tissue to stop the bleeding. You can then seal the tooth area with dental wax (found in the dental emergency kit). Prepare to evacuate your patient.

LOST FILLING

Fillings may pop out under an impact or spontaneously. If trauma is involved, follow the guidelines for a knocked-out tooth, above. If the filling has just popped out, seal the tooth area with dental wax. Prepare to evacuate your patient.

INFECTION

A cracked or broken tooth, a cavity, or a lost filling can all lead to a painful dental infection, another cause of toothache. This occurs when bacterial infection grows either at the base of a tooth or inside the tooth itself. The symptoms are local inflammation and swelling, and a marked sensitivity of the tooth or neighboring teeth.

Infections require treatment by a dentist. These are painful problems, and there is a threat of the infection spreading into the bone and sinus cavity. The only treatments available in the field during evacuation are pain relievers such as aspirin and ibuprofen. Prepare to evacuate your patient.

ENVIRONMENTAL INJURIES AND ILLNESSES
FLUID BALANCE

All the body's fluids make up one large body fluid pool. Fluid loss from any one source is reflected in the levels of all the body's other fluids. We are all losing fluid constantly, through respiration, in urine, feces, and sweat. For example, during strenuous exercise you can lose 1 to 2 quarts (liters) *per hour,* so profuse sweating will ultimately result in decreased blood volume. That means that you have to be taking 1 to 2 quarts (liters) back in each hour to stay adequately hydrated. Many hikers don't drink that much and are slowly getting fluid depleted. If a person loses enough fluid through any manner—bleeding, sweating, vomiting, or diarrhea—the end result is the same: dehydration and, potentially, volume shock (see "Shock," page 274). Adequate fluid is also critically important in hot environments to help the body thermoregulate. (See "Heat Challenge," page 342, and "Hypothermia," page 332.) Dehydration can kill.

If someone is chronically losing fluid (from continuous diarrhea or vomiting), then you can have a real emergency on your hands. Treat the cause of the fluid loss as best you can and rehydrate the patient. Be prepared to evacuate your patient.

Prevention

Dehydration is always easier to prevent than it is to treat. So it is important to ensure that all members of your group replace their regular fluid losses by drinking adequate amounts of water. (See "Basic Fluid Recommendations," page 69.) Your body absorbs fluids best when you drink frequently and in small amounts, rather than drinking large amounts at one time. It also helps with fluid absorption if you drink while eating. A pinch of salt and sugar in the water will do if no food is available. Diluted sports drinks, like Gatorade (add just enough sports drink to water to add taste), work well for this purpose.

Don't depend on feeling thirsty to tell you when to drink. Thirst is a late response of the body to fluid depletion. Once you feel thirsty, you are already low on fluids. One indicator is dry lips and mouth. The best indicator of proper fluid levels is urine output and color. You, and all the people in your group, should strive to be "copious and clear." Ample urine that is light colored to clear shows that the body has plenty of fluid. Dark urine means that the body is low on water and is trying to conserve its supply by hoarding fluid, which means that urine becomes more concentrated, thereby darker. Note that clear and copious urine can be a bad sign in Hyponatremia (see below).

HYPONATREMIA—"WATER INTOXICATION"

The body needs a certain concentration of sodium to function properly. Hyponatremia (low sodium) is caused by not having enough sodium in the bloodstream. It is usually brought about by a combination of excessive loss of body salts through sweating *combined with* a high intake of water. It is especially a concern in hot weather and desert climates. You sweat about ½ to 1 quart (500 ml to 1 liter) of water and electrolytes for every hour of activity in the heat. Sweat contains between 2 and 3.5 grams of salt per liter. Over an eight-hour day of hiking in hot weather you could lose approximately 1.8 to 2.7 grams of salt. Some hikers drink lots of water but fail to take in enough salt, slowly building up a salt imbalance. As a result you basically "dilute" your blood. Here are common signs and symptoms of hyponatremia:

- Headache
- Lightheadedness
- Weakness and fatigue
- Nausea
- Heavy sweating
- Lack of thirst
- Lower extremity cramping
- History of heavy water intake
- History of little or no food intake (especially salty foods)
- Clear and copious urination (here it's a bad sign)
- Altered mental status in severe cases (decreasing AVPU) ⁻
- Seizures in severe cases

The early signs of hyponatremia can look just like dehydration, which normally would be treated with more fluids—just the *wrong* thing for someone with hyponatremia, so review the person's history of previous fluid intake *before* giving fluid.

Treatment

Hyponatremia can be a life-threatening illness. Severe sodium imbalance can cause cerebral edema (increasing ICP), coma, and death. For mild cases, have the person rest in the shade and gradually eat salty foods. *Do not* allow the person to drink any more fluids. Changes in mental status indicate a severe case, and the person must be evacuated to advanced medical care *immediately*.

Prevention

Prevention is the key. Drinking regularly and eating salty foods on a regular basis will maintain both proper hydration and proper salt balance. Some people assume that drinking an electrolyte replacement drink is all they need. However, the amount of salt lost through sweat can be significantly higher than the amount of sodium in many electrolyte drinks. What about salt tablets? Salt tablets are *not* recommended. It's better to ingest moderate amounts of salt in food over a longer period of time than to "dump" too much salt in all at once.

Rehydration Solutions

A factor in overall fluid balance is the replacement of the body's electrolytes. In most cases, the salts found in normal food consumption are adequate for salt replacement. In the event of severe dehydration, or in high-exercise levels in hot environments, a solution of ¼ teaspoon salt and ¼ teaspoon baking soda and 4 teaspoons of sugar or honey per quart or liter of water can be used to replace lost fluid and salt. Use lukewarm fluids. Discontinue the fluids if the person becomes nauseated or vomits. Restart fluids as soon as the person can tolerate it. There are commercial rehydration packets that can be carried in your first-aid kit and added to water. Sports replacement drinks like Gatorade are too high in carbohydrates and should *not* be used for cases of severe dehydration. Diarrhea results in greater electrolyte loss than sweating, so double the quantities of each ingredient above if the fluid loss is from diarrhea.

REGULATING BODY TEMPERATURE

The body has a number of mechanisms to properly maintain its optimal core temperature of 98.6°F (37°C). Above 105°F (40°C), many body enzymes become denatured, and chemical reactions cannot take place, leading to death. Below 98.6°F (37°C), chemical reactions slow down, with various complications that can lead to death. Understanding thermoregulation is important to treating injuries related to heat or cold exposure.

How Your Body Regulates Core Temperature

- Vasodilation increases surface blood flow, which increases heat loss (when ambient temperature is less than body temperature).
- Vasoconstriction decreases blood flow to the periphery (arms and legs), decreasing heat loss.
- Sweating cools the body through evaporative cooling.
- Shivering generates heat through increase in chemical reactions required for muscle activity. Visible shivering can maximally increase surface heat production by 500 percent. However, this is limited to a few hours because of depletion of muscle glucose and the onset of fatigue. Active exercise is much more efficient at heating than shivering.

- Increasing or decreasing activity will cause corresponding increases or decreases in the body's heat production. Behavioral responses, such as putting on or taking off layers of clothing, is another way to control body temperature.

COLD CHALLENGE

Whenever you go into an environment that is colder than your body temperature, you are exposed to a cold challenge. As long as your levels of heat production and heat retention (the positive factors) are greater than the cold challenge (the negative factors), then you will be thermoregulating properly. If the cold challenge is greater than your combined heat production and heat retention, you are susceptible to a cold illness such as hypothermia or frostbite.

Cold Challenge—Negative Factors

- Temperature
- Body wetness from rain, sweat, water
- Wind (see "Windchill Index," opposite)

Heat Retention—Positive Factors

- Body size/shape—your surface-to-volume ratio affects how quickly you lose heat. Children will lose heat faster than adults.
- Insulation—type of clothing layers affects how well you retain heat.
- Body fat—amount of body fat affects how quickly you lose heat.
- Shell/core response—allows the body shell to act as a thermal barrier (see "Shell/Core Response," page 278)

Heat Production—Positive Factors

- Exercise
- Shivering

Windchill

Windchill can have a major impact on heat loss through convection. As air heated by your body is replaced with cooler air pushed by the wind, the amount of heat you can lose in a given period of time increases. This increase is comparable to the amount of heat you would lose at a colder temperature with no wind. The windchill factor takes that rate of heat loss into account and gives a comparable temperature.

Windchill Index

Wind Speed mph (kph)	Actual Temperature F° (C°) — Apparent Temperature F° (C°)

Wind Speed mph (kph)	40 (4.4)	35 (1.6)	30 (-1.1)	25 (-3.8)	20 (-6.6)	15 (-9.4)	10 (-12.2)	5 (-15)	0 (-17.7)	-5 (-20.5)	-10 (-23.3)	-15 (-26.1)	-20 (-28.2)	-25 (-31.6)	-30 (-34.4)
5 (8)	36 (2.2)	31 (-0.5)	25 (-3.8)	19 (-7.2)	13 (-10.5)	7 (-13.8)	1 (-17.2)	-5 (-20.5)	-11 (-23.8)	-16 (-26.6)	-22 (-30)	-28 (-33.3)	-34 (-36.6)	-40 (-40)	-46 (-43.3)
10 (16)	34 (1.1)	27 (-2.7)	21 (-6.1)	15 (-9.4)	9 (-12.7)	3 (-16.1)	-4 (-20)	-10 (-23.3)	-16 (-26.6)	-22 (-30)	-28 (-33.3)	-35 (-37.2)	-41 (-40.5)	-47 (-43.8)	-53 (-47.2)
15 (24)	32 (0)	25 (-3.8)	19 (-7.2)	13 (-10.5)	6 (-14.4)	0 (-17.7)	-7 (-21.6)	-13 (-25)	-19 (-28.3)	-26 (-32.2)	-32 (-35.5)	-39 (-39.4)	-45 (-42.7)	-51 (-46.1)	-58 (-50)
20 (32)	30 (-1.1)	24 (-4.4)	17 (-8.3)	11 (-11.6)	4 (-15.5)	-2 (-18.8)	-9 (-22.7)	-15 (-26.6)	-22 (-30)	-29 (-33.8)	-35 (-37.2)	-42 (-41.1)	-48 (-44.4)	-55 (-48.3)	-61 (-51.1)
25 (40)	29 (-1.6)	23 (-5)	16 (-8.8)	9 (-12.7)	3 (-16.1)	-4 (-20)	-11 (-23.8)	-17 (-27.2)	-24 (-31.1)	-31 (-35)	-37 (-38.3)	-44 (-42.2)	-51 (-46.1)	-58 (-50)	-64 (-53.3)
30 (48)	28 (-2.2)	22 (-5.5)	15 (-9.4)	8 (-13.3)	1 (-17.2)	-5 (-20.5)	-12 (-24.4)	-19 (-28.3)	-26 (-32.2)	-33 (-36.1)	-39 (-39.4)	-46 (-43.3)	-53 (-47.2)	-60 (-51.1)	-67 (-55)
35 (56)	28 (-2.2)	21 (-6.1)	14 (-10)	7 (-13.8)	0 (-17.7)	-7 (-21.6)	-14 (-25.5)	-21 (-29.4)	-27 (-32.7)	-34 (-36.6)	-41 (-40.5)	-48 (-44.4)	-55 (-48.3)	-62 (-52.2)	-69 (-56.1)
40 (64)	27 (-2.7)	20 (-6.6)	13 (-10.5)	6 (-14.4)	-1 (-18.3)	-8 (-22.2)	-15 (-26.1)	-22 (-30)	-29 (-33.8)	-36 (-37.7)	-43 (-41.6)	-50 (-45.5)	-57 (-49.4)	-64 (-53.3)	-71 (-57.2)
45 (72)	26 (-3.3)	19 (-7.2)	12 (-11.1)	5 (-15)	-2 (-18.8)	-9 (-22.7)	-16 (-26.6)	-23 (-30.5)	-30 (-34.4)	-37 (-38.3)	-44 (-42.2)	-51 (-46.1)	-58 (-50)	-65 (-53.8)	-72 (-57.7)
50 (80)	26 (-3.3)	19 (-7.2)	12 (-11.1)	4 (-15.5)	-3 (-19.4)	-10 (-23.3)	-17 (-27.2)	-24 (-31.1)	-31 (-35)	-38 (-38.8)	-45 (-42.7)	-52 (-46.6)	-60 (-51.1)	-67 (-55)	-74 (-58.8)
55 (88)	25 (-3.8)	18 (-7.7)	11 (-11.6)	4 (-15.5)	-3 (-19.4)	-11 (-23.8)	-18 (-27.7)	-25 (-31.6)	-32 (-35.5)	-39 (-39.4)	-46 (-43.3)	-54 (-47.7)	-61 (-51.6)	-68 (-55.5)	-75 (-59.4)
60 (96)	25 (-3.8)	17 (-8.3)	10 (-12.2)	3 (-16.1)	-4 (-20)	-11 (-23.8)	-19 (-28.3)	-26 (-32.2)	-33 (-36.1)	-40 (-40)	-48 (-44.4)	-55 (-48.3)	-62 (-52.2)	-76 (-60)	-84 (-64.4)

Category	Frostbite Risk
Extreme Danger	Frostbite within 5 minutes
Danger	Frostbite within 10 minutes
Extreme Caution	Frostbite within 30 minutes
Caution	Frostbite in more than 30 minutes

FIRST AID AND EMERGENCY CARE

COLD-RELATED ILLNESSES AND INJURIES

HYPOTHERMIA

Hypothermia is a decrease in body core temperature to the point where normal body functions are impaired. (See "Shell/Core Response," page 278.) The key to combating hypothermia is prevention. Although the risks are highest during cold winter conditions, hypothermia can happen at any time of the year.

The classic example of hypothermia is the summer hiker on Mount Washington in New Hampshire, dressed in cotton shorts and a T-shirt. The weather changes rapidly. A sudden thunderstorm drops the temperature from 80°F (27°C) to 60°F (16°C) with strong wind and rain. In these conditions, hypothermia can start to occur almost immediately and become severe in less than an hour.

Prevention

Be aware of the causes of hypothermia, which are usually cool to cold temperatures combined with wetness and wind. Constantly evaluate the environmental conditions and the conditions of your group. Here are some guidelines to staying warm and avoiding hypothermia:

- Wear proper clothing. Adjust your clothing frequently so that you are neither too hot nor too cold. Choose materials that keep you warm even when wet (see Chapter 2, "Equipment.")
- Stay dry. Prevent your clothing from getting wet either from sweat or from rain or snow. Wet clothing will rob you of heat 25 times faster than dry clothing. Adjust your clothing layers to prevent overheating and too much sweat from saturating your inner layers. Have proper rain gear to protect your outer layers.
- Be aware of the impact of windchill on increasing the rate of heat loss. (See "Windchill Index," page 331.)
- Eat small amounts of food at frequent intervals to maintain the body's energy reserves. Carry carbohydrates to snack on because they provide quick energy, and protein and fat to eat before bed because they burn slowly, providing energy overnight. Try not to push yourself to your physical limits in cold weather. Always leave your body with energy in reserve.
- Stay well hydrated. Dehydration quickens hypothermia and hyperthermia, so drink enough fluids. (See "Fluid Balance," page 326.)
- Avoid caffeine. It is a vasoconstrictor that increases the chances of peripheral frostbite.

- Avoid alcohol. It is a vasodilator and increases heat loss.
- Be alert to sudden weather changes, make a quick evaluation of your group's condition, and take active steps to reduce the risk of exposure.

STAGES OF HYPOTHERMIA

Stage	Core Temperature	Signs and Symptoms
Mild	97–95°F	Shivering begins—can be mild to severe
	(36–35°C)	Unable to perform complex tasks with hands
		Hands numb
Moderate	95–90°F	Shivering becomes uncontrollable and violent
	(35–32°C)	Changes in mental status, mild confusion, higher reasoning becomes impaired; eventually becomes withdrawn, may show "paradoxical undressing"—person imagines they are warm and takes off clothing
		Muscle incoordination becomes apparent, movements slow and labored, stumbling pace
Severe	90–85°F	Shivering stops
	(32–29°C)	Skin blue or puffy
		Unable to walk, confusion, muscles become rigid
		Incoherent/irrational behavior, becomes semiconscious
		Pulse rate decreases
		Respiration rate decreases
	85–80°F	Unconscious
	(29–27°C)	Heartbeat and respiration erratic
		Pulse may not be palpable
		Cardiac and respiratory failure, death

How to Assess if Someone Is Hypothermic

- Ask the person a question that requires higher reasoning in the brain (to count backward from 100 by nines). If the person is hypothermic and it has started to effect higher brain function, she won't be able to do it. (Other conditions besides hypothermia could also be the cause; see "Assessing Mental Status," page 272; "Seizures," page 309.)
- If shivering can be stopped voluntarily, it is mild hypothermia. If shivering cannot be stopped voluntarily, it is moderate to severe hypothermia.
- If you can't get a radial pulse at the wrist, it indicates a core temperature below about 90°F (32°C). Check pulse and respirations *carefully*. Even after a full minute, you may not be able to detect a pulse or respirations and yet the person may still be alive. The body may be using a massive shell/core response to maintain basic life functions.

- A severely hypothermic person may appear dead. The person may be rigid, blue, and curled up in a fetal position. Try to open her arm up from the fetal position; if it curls back up, the person is alive. Dead muscles won't contract—only live muscles.

Treatment

Mild to Moderate Hypothermia

1. **Reduce Heat Loss** Remove patient from wind and cold, if possible. Remove all wet clothing. Make sure the person is properly clothed (dry wicking layer, fleece, and outer shell). Provide shelter. If a person is still shivering, she has the ability to rewarm herself at a rate of 4°F (2°C) per hour *if* you can stop all further heat loss.
2. **Add fuel and fluids** It is essential to keep a hypothermic person adequately hydrated and fueled. Food intake should include hot liquids, sugars, gorp. One of the best fuels is hot Jell-O, which contains both protein and sugars. (See "Food Sources," page 67.) Avoid alcohol, caffeine, or nicotine.
3. **Add heat** Put the hypothermic person in dry clothing, in a sleeping bag. In cases of mild hypothermia you can put another warm, dry person in the bag with her. In cases of moderate hypothermia, use chemical heat packs or hot water bottles (see "Add heat," opposite).
4. **Activity** Increasing physical activity will help rewarm the victim. Violent shivering is the body's way of generating heat from muscle contraction, so don't suppress shivering; instead, have the person be more active. A mildly hypothermic person can do jumping jacks or run in place, which will generate more heat than shivering will. A moderately hypothermic person is best in a sleeping bag to better trap the heat she produces. The person can increase heat production by moving arms and legs or doing isometric exercises inside the sleeping bag.

If the patient's condition improves, evacuation may not be necessary; but if her condition worsens or does not improve, prepare to evacuate your patient when she is able, or send for help.

Moderate to Severe Hypothermia

In addition to the treatment methods outlined above, a severely hypothermic person would be treated with the following:

1. **Create a hypothermia wrap around the victim** No matter how cold, if you provide a shell of total insulation around the patient, the victim can

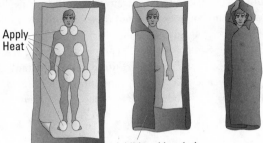

Apply
Heat

Polypropylene Blanket

Additional Insulation

Hypothermia Wrap

still internally rewarm herself more efficiently than any external rewarming you can do in the field (hospitals can obviously do a better job). Make sure the patient is dry and has a dry wicking inner layer next to the skin to minimize sweating. Use a plastic garbage bag as a diaper to prevent urine from soaking the insulation layers. The person must be protected from any moisture in the environment. Use multiple sleeping bags, blankets, clothing, foam pads, etc., to create a minimum of 4 inches (10 centimeters) of insulation all the way around the patient, especially between the patient and the ground. Use foam pads to insulate the person from the ground. Include an aluminum space blanket to help prevent radiant heat loss if you have one. Wrap the entire ensemble in something waterproof, like a tarp or tent rainfly, to protect from wind and water. Your patient will look like she is in a giant burrito with only her face exposed.

2. **Add fuel and fluids** At this stage of hypothermia, the stomach has shut down and will not digest solid food but can absorb water and dilute sugars. Give a dilute mixture of warm water with sugar every 15 minutes. Diluted hot Jell-O works best, since it is part sugar and part protein and will be absorbed directly into the bloodstream, providing the necessary calories to allow the person to rewarm herself. Do *not* give full-strength Jell-O, even in liquid form—it is too concentrated and won't be absorbed.

3. **Encourage urination** A full bladder is a place for additional heat loss, so urinating will help conserve heat. The garbage bag diaper is to allow the person to urinate inside the wrap and minimize the chilling effect.

4. **Add heat** Heat can be applied to the skin where the major arteries are near the surface—at the neck for the carotid, at the armpits for the brachial, and at the groin for the femoral artery. Research has shown that placing heat packs on the palms of the hands and the soles of the feet is

very effective. Chemical heat packs such as the Heat Wave provide 110°F (43°C) for six to ten hours. You can also use hot water bottles, warm rocks, towels, and compresses. Wrap these in cloth so as not to have the heat source directly against the skin.

5. **Rescue breathing** For a severely hypothermic person, rescue breathing (see "Basic Life Support," page 282) timed with the victim's breathing can provide supplemental oxygen and, more important, heated air going directly into the person's body core (rather then the cold environmental air).

After-Drop

After-drop is a situation in which the core temperature actually decreases during rewarming. As the shell (the arms and legs) are rewarmed, the peripheral vessels in the arms and legs dilate. This dilation sends very cold blood filled with metabolic waste products from the shell into the core, further decreasing the core temperature. It is not possible to *prevent* after-drop, but *slow* controlled rewarming, the kind the person's body is doing on its own in a hypothermia wrap, minimizes the negative effect.

After-drop is why you don't apply direct heat sources to the person's arms and legs. This would cause major vasodilation, which would push lots of cold blood quickly back into the core, which could cause death. Avoid after-drop by applying heat to the specific areas mentioned above *only!*

Evacuation Guidelines

You should not attempt to evacuate someone in a state of severe hypothermia. Moving the person can cause the heart to stop. Send for advanced medical care or wait until the condition stabilizes. If evacuation is delayed, it is recommended to put two warm rescuers inside the hypothermia wrap, one on either side of the person.

Hypothermia and CPR

When a person is in severe hypothermia, she may *appear* to be dead: cold, blue skin; fixed and dilated pupils; no discernible pulse or breathing; comatose and unresponsive to any stimuli; rigid muscles. As a rescuer, you may not be sure, so your job is to rewarm the person and do CPR if indicated. Treatment follows the saying "a hypothermic patient is never cold and dead, only warm and dead."

1. Make sure you do a complete assessment of heart rate before beginning CPR. Remember, the heart rate may be 2 to 3 per minute and the breath-

ing rate one breath every thirty seconds. During severe hypothermia, the heart is hyperexcitable, and mechanical stimulation (including CPR, moving the patient, or after-drop; see pages 334–336) may result in ventricular fibrillation, leading to death. As a result, CPR itself may be contraindicated for some hypothermia situations. Also, instituting cardiac compressions while the heart is still beating on its own may lead to life-threatening arrhythmias. Check the carotid pulse for a longer time period (up to a full minute) to ascertain if there is some slow heartbeat. Even though the heart is beating very slowly, it is filling completely and distributing blood fairly effectively. External cardiac compressions are only 20 to 30 percent effective. Thus, the body may be able to satisfy its reduced circulatory needs with only two to three beats per minute. *Be sure the pulse is absent before beginning CPR.* Once you start doing CPR, you will need to continue as you rewarm the person.

2. Ventilation (air being moved in and out of the lungs) may have stopped, but respiration (oxygen and carbon dioxide exchange in the blood) may continue. The oxygen demands for the body have been so diminished with hypothermia that the body may be able to survive for some time using only the oxygen that is already in the body. If ventilation has stopped, artificial ventilation (rescue breathing) may be started to increase available oxygen. In addition, blowing warm air into the person's lungs may assist in internal rewarming.

3. Perform CPR procedures (see "Basic Life Support," page 282):
   - Check radial pulse; between 91° and 86°F (33° and 30°C) this pulse disappears.
   - Check for carotid pulse; wait at least a full minute to check for very slow heartbeat.
   - If there is a pulse but no breathing or slow breathing, give rescue breathing (also adds heat).
   - If there is no discernible heartbeat, begin CPR and be prepared to continue—persons with hypothermia have been given CPR for up to 3.5 hours and have recovered with *no* neurological damage.
   - Begin active rewarming as described above.

IMMERSION HYPOTHERMIA

Cold water can kill. Since the body loses heat 25 times faster in water, immersion hypothermia occurs at a much faster rate than land-based hypothermia. In 50°F (10°C) water, a person can be shivering uncontrollably in 15 minutes and can be unconscious in 30 minutes (see chart below). Be extremely vigilant in cold water, such as during stream crossings.

EXPECTED SURVIVAL TIME IN COLD WATER

Water Temperature	Exhaustion or Unconsciousness in Expected Survival Time	
70–80°F (21–27°C)	3–12 hours	3 hours–indefinitely
60–70°F (16–21°C)	2–7 hours	2–40 hours
50–60°F (10–16°C)	1–2 hours	1–6 hours
40–50°F (4–10°C)	30–60 minutes	1–3 hours
32.5–40°F (0–44°C)	15–30 minutes	30–90 minutes
<=32°F (<=0°C)	Under 15 minutes	Under 15–45 minutes

Treatment

Treatment for immersion hypothermia is the same as hypothermia described above. In cold-water immersion hypothermia, the shell/core response may occur so rapidly that there is sufficient oxygen in the blood to maintain basic body functioning over an extended period of time. What this means is that someone submerged in cold water can be put into a sort of "metabolic ice-box" where oxygen needs are significantly reduced. Many people have been trained that after 6 minutes without breathing or CPR, a person will have irreparable brain damage. However, with sudden cold-water immersions there have been successful resuscitations after over 40 minutes of submersion. Immersion hypothermia victims should be treated aggressively. Rewarm the patient with a hypothermia wrap and be prepared to give CPR.

FROSTBITE AND OTHER COLD-WEATHER TISSUE INJURIES

In addition to hypothermia, cold weather can cause injuries to the periphery (skin and muscle tissue). The following are factors in peripheral cold injuries:

- Low ambient temperature
- Windchill
- Moisture
- Insulation
- Contact with metal or supercooled liquids (like liquid stove fuel)
- Exposed skin
- Vasodilation
- Vasoconstriction
- Previous cold injuries
- Constricting garments
- Local pressure

- Cramped position
- Body type
- Dehydration
- Gender (men do worse in cold than women because they generally have less subcutaneous body fat)
- Caloric intake
- Alcohol, caffeine, nicotine, and some medications
- Pre-existing medical conditions (diabetes, Raynaud's syndrome)

Frostbite

Everyone has experienced the "cold hands, cold feet" phenomenon known as a cold response. The body reduces circulation to the area to prevent heat loss. The area may be pale, cold, and numb. This may resolve itself spontaneously once heat or insulation is added.

The next, more serious stage is frostbite. Frostbite is a localized freezing of tissue caused by the shunting of blood away from cold areas of the body. As tissue begins to freeze, ice crystals are formed within the cells. As fluids inside the cells freeze, fluid from outside the cells enters. Cells may rupture from the increased water and/or from tearing by the ice crystals. *Do not rub frostbitten tissue;* it causes the ice crystals to tear the cells, creating additional tissue damage. As the ice melts, there is an influx of salts into the tissue, further damaging the cell membranes. Cell destruction results in tissue death and loss of tissue. Areas of the body and areas with a high surface-to-volume ratio—ears, nose, fingers, and toes—are the most susceptible.

Superficial frostbite, also known as frostnip, involves freezing of only the top layers of skin tissue (similar to a superficial burn). It is generally reversible. The skin will be pale and waxy. The tissue will feel numb. Most typically seen on cheeks, earlobes, fingers, and toes.

Superficial frostbite can be rewarmed in the field using skin-to-skin contact or by breathing warm air or placing a warm object on the affected part. Hands may be placed under the armpits, breathe warm air into your fingers, and cold feet can be placed on someone else's belly or under an armpit. *Never rub frostbitten areas.* Avoid placing the affected part near a strong heat source, since the lack of feeling could prevent you from experiencing the pain from burning the tissue. After rewarming, the skin may turn red and later peel like sunburned skin. Keep the area from being frozen again; it will only add to the damage until the skin has time to heal. Ibuprofen or other painkillers will ease pain. Lotions with aloe applied to the skin encourage healing.

Partial thickness frostbite involves freezing of partial layers of skin tissue (similar to a partial thickness burn). The top layer feels hard and rubbery and may dent when you push on it, but deeper tissue is still soft. The tissue may feel numb or there may be no sensation at all. Blisters may form up to 48 hours after rewarming. If the blister fluid is clear, it indicates that the tissue damage did not go very deep. If the blister fluid is red, it indicates the presence of deeper damage. If the fluid is deep red or purple, like a bruise, the damage is significant and tissue loss is likely.

Full thickness frostbite involves deep tissue freezing of all the skin layers and can include freezing of muscle and/or bone. It is very difficult to rewarm the appendage without some damage occurring. The skin will be pale and feel "wooden" all the way through. The tissue may feel numb or there may be no sensation at all. Blisters may form after rewarming as described above.

Treatment of Partial and Full Thickness Frostbite

Remove constricting clothing. Rewarming is accomplished by immersion of the affected part into a water bath of 104° to 108°F (40° to 42°C). *Additional tissue damage will result if the water is any hotter.* Monitor the temperature carefully with a thermometer. Place the appendage in the water and continue to monitor the water temperature. This temperature will drop, so additional warm water will need to be added to maintain the 104° to 108°F (40° to 42°C) temperature. *Do not* add this warm water directly to the injured area. The water will need to be circulated fairly constantly to maintain an even temperature. The affected area should be immersed for 25 to 40 minutes. Thawing is complete when the part is pliable and color and sensation have returned. Discontinue the warm-water bath when thawing is complete. Once the area is rewarmed, there can be *significant* pain. Therefore, it's best to administer pain medications *before* beginning the rewarming process.

- Do *not* use dry heat like a fire or blow dryer to rewarm. It cannot be effectively maintained at 104° to 108°F (37° to 42°C) and can cause burns, further damaging the tissues.
- Blisters may form after rewarming. They should be protected from the cold because they are very likely to refreeze. Wrap them in sterile dressings. If the blisters are ruptured, use an antibiotic ointment and a sterile dressing.

- Once rewarming is complete, the injured area should be wrapped in sterile gauze and protected from movement and further cold.
- Once a body part has been rewarmed, *it should not be used.* Also, it is essential that the part can be kept from refreezing. Refreezing *after* rewarming causes even greater tissue damage and may result in extensive loss of tissue. If you cannot *guarantee* that the tissue will stay unfrozen after rewarming, it is best *not to rewarm it.* Keeping it frozen may not cause as much additional damage as rewarming and subsequent refreezing will.

Prevention of Frostbite

Even on three-season trips, superficial frostbite is possible. Keep an eye on one another. You can't see frostnip on your own nose, cheeks, and ears, and need others to tell you when they see a problem developing. Keep well fed, and stay well hydrated. Rewarm cold parts early. In cold weather, check yourself for numbness frequently. People may be unaware or unwilling to let on that they are starting to get cold, and hypothermia increases the possibility for frostbite. Avoid caffeine (a vasoconstrictor, which increases chances of frostbite) and alcohol (a vasodilator, which increases heat loss and chance of hypothermia).

> #### 🍁 TRICKS OF THE TRAIL
>
> **"Instant" Frostbite** In temperatures below freezing you need to be extremely careful.
> - Liquids such as white gas can "supercool" in the winter (drop below their freezing point but not freeze). White gas also evaporates quickly into the air. Spilling supercooled white gas on exposed skin leads to instant frostbite from evaporative cooling. Always wear gloves when handling fuel.
> - Touching metal with bare skin can cause the moisture on your skin to freeze to the metal. (In really cold conditions, even metal eyeglass frames can be a problem.) When you pull away, you may leave a layer of skin behind. Don't touch very cold metal with bare skin.

IMMERSION FOOT OR TRENCHFOOT

Immersion foot, or trenchfoot, is caused by prolonged exposure of the feet to cool, wet conditions. The name trenchfoot comes from World War I, where it was a common injury to soldiers in the wet trenches. The body senses that it is losing heat rapidly and uses the shell/core response to reduce peripheral blood flow to that area and prevent further heat loss. Too little oxygen is going to the foot. Damage to the foot can occur in as little as 12 hours of exposure. Initially the skin is cold, and white or bluish. The patient may complain of tenderness or numbness. After the foot rewarms and blood flow returns, the skin is initially reddened with numbness, tingling pain, and itching. Blisters may form. Some tissue may die and slough off. In severe cases, immersion foot can involve the toes, heels, or entire foot and result in extensive tissue loss. Immersion foot causes permanent damage to the circulatory system, making the person more prone to cold-related injuries in that area in the future. It can occur at temperatures as high as 60°F (16°C) if the feet are constantly wet.

Treatment

Wash and dry the feet carefully. Rewarm gently with skin-to-skin contact and elevate the foot slightly above the patient's heart. Pain and itching are common complaints. Pain medications may help. The severity of the damage won't be apparent for 12 to 24 hours. Have the person see a doctor.

Prevention

Keep feet dry by wearing appropriate footwear. Check your feet regularly to see if they are wet. If your feet get wet (through sweating or immersion), stop and dry your feet and put on dry socks. Periodic air-drying, elevation, and massage will also help. Change socks at least once a day (both liner and outer socks), and do not sleep with wet socks. Be careful of tight socks or tight boots, which can further impair peripheral circulation. Canoeists and kayakers wearing water-soaked shoes or booties for extended periods need to be especially careful.

HEAT-RELATED ILLNESSES

HEAT CHALLENGE

In hot weather, especially with high humidity, you can lose a great deal of body fluid through exercise. This can lead to a variety of heat-related illnesses, including heat exhaustion and heatstroke. Balanced against this heat challenge is your body's methods of passive and active heat loss. When the heat challenge is greater than heat loss (positive factors), you are at risk for a heat-related injury. In order to reduce the risk, you need to either decrease the heat challenge or increase your heat loss. Maintaining proper fluid balance is a central part of exercising in a heat challenge.

Heat Challenge—Negative Factors

- Temperature
- Exercise
- Humidity (see "Heat Index," page 344)
- Body wetness from sweating, rain, or water

Passive Heat Loss—Positive Factors

- Body size/shape—your surface-to-volume ratio affects how quickly you lose heat
- Insulation—type of clothing affects how you lose heat
- Body fat—amount of body fat affects how quickly you lose heat
- Shell/core response—allows the body shell to act as a thermal barrier

Active Heat Loss—Positive Factors

- Radiant heat from the body
- Sweating—ability to sweat is limited by fluid levels and your level of fitness
- Wind (see "Windchill Index," page 331)

Heat illnesses are the result of elevated body temperatures due to an inability to dissipate the body's heat and/or a decreased fluid level. Always remember that mild heat illnesses have the potential of becoming life-threatening emergencies if not treated properly.

The Heat Index

Ambient temperature is not the only factor in creating the potential for heat injuries; humidity is also important. Our bodies rely on the evaporation of sweat as a major method of cooling, so high humidity in the air around you reduces your ability to evaporate sweat and cool the body, increasing the risk of heat illnesses. On a 90°F (32° Celsius) day with 90 percent humidity, not a lot of your sweat evaporates since the air is already almost completely saturated with water vapor. According to the National Weather Service, the Heat Index is an accurate measure of how hot it really feels when the relative humidity is added to the actual air temperature. The measurements are based on being in the shade in light wind conditions. If you are in direct sunlight, it can increase by 15°F (9° C). Also, if there is a strong wind continuously blowing hot air onto you, it can increase the Heat Index even more.

HEAT INDEX

RELATIVE HUMIDITY (%)

Apparent Temperature F° (C°)

Actual Temperature F° (C°)	40%	45%	50%	55%	60%	65%	70%	75%	80%	85%	90%	95%	100%
110 (47)	136 (58)												
108 (43)	130 (54)	137 (58)											
106 (41)	124 (51)	130 (54)	137 (58)										
104 (40)	119 (48)	124 (51)	131 (55)	137 (58)									
102 (39)	114 (46)	119 (48)	124 (51)	130 (54)	137 (58)								
100 (38)	109 (43)	114 (46)	118 (48)	124 (51)	129 (54)	136 (58)							
98 (37)	105 (41)	109 (43)	113 (45)	117 (47)	123 (51)	128 (53)	134 (57)						
96 (36)	101 (38)	104 (40)	108 (42)	112 (44)	116 (47)	121 (49)	126 (52)	132 (56)					
94 (34)	97 (36)	100 (38)	103 (39)	106 (41)	110 (43)	114 (46)	119 (48)	124 (51)	129 (54)	135 (57)			
92 (33)	94 (34)	96 (36)	99 (37)	101 (38)	105 (41)	108 (42)	112 (44)	116 (47)	121 (49)	126 (52)	131 (55)		
90 (32)	91 (33)	93 (34)	95 (35)	97 (36)	100 (38)	103 (39)	106 (41)	109 (43)	113 (45)	117 (47)	122 (50)	127 (53)	132 (56)
88 (31)	88 (31)	89 (32)	91 (33)	93 (34)	95 (35)	98 (37)	100 (38)	103 (39)	106 (41)	110 (43)	113 (45)	117 (47)	121 (49)
86 (30)	85 (29)	87 (31)	88 (31)	89 (32)	91 (33)	93 (34)	95 (35)	97 (36)	100 (38)	102 (39)	105 (41)	108 (42)	112 (44)
84 (29)	83 (28)	84 (29)	85 (29)	86 (30)	88 (31)	89 (32)	90 (32)	92 (33)	94 (34)	96 (36)	98 (37)	100 (38)	103 (39)
82 (28)	81 (27)	82 (28)	83 (28)	84 (29)	84 (29)	85 (29)	86 (30)	88 (31)	89 (32)	90 (32)	91 (33)	93 (34)	95 (35)
80 (27)	80 (27)	80 (27)	81 (27)	81 (27)	82 (28)	82 (28)	83 (28)	84 (29)	84 (29)	85 (29)	86 (30)	86 (30)	87 (31)

Category	Heat Index	Possible heat disorders for people in high risk groups
Extreme Danger	130° F or higher (54° C or higher)	Heatstroke highly likely with continued exposure.
Danger	105 - 129° F (41 - 54° C)	Heat cramps, and/or heat exhaustion likely. Heatstroke possible with prolonged exposure and/or physical activity.
Extreme Caution	90 - 105° F (32 - 41° C)	Heat cramps, and/or heat exhaustion possible.
Caution	80 - 90° F (27 - 32° C)	Fatigue possible with prolonged exposure and/or physical activity.

Note: This chart provides guidelines for assessing the potential severity of heat stress. Individual reactions to heat will vary. Heat illnesses can occur at lower temperature than indicated on this chart. **Exposure to full sunshine can increase values up to 15° F.**

HEAT CRAMPS

Heat cramps are muscle cramps brought on by exertion and insufficient salt.

Treatment

Replace salt and fluid (see "Fluid Balance," page 326) and stretch the muscle (see "Stretches for Hiking," page 288). Kneading and pounding the muscle is less effective than stretching and probably contributes to residual soreness.

HEAT SYNCOPE

Heat syncope (fainting) is a mild form of heat illness that results from physical exertion in a hot environment. In an effort to increase heat loss, the blood vessels in the skin dilate to such an extent that blood flow to the brain is reduced, resulting in symptoms of faintness, dizziness, headache, increased pulse rate, restlessness, nausea, vomiting, and possibly even a brief loss of consciousness. Inadequate fluid replacement that leads to dehydration contributes significantly to this problem.

Treatment

Heat syncope should be treated as fainting (see page 305). The person should lie or sit down, preferably in the shade or in a cool environment. Elevate the feet and give fluids, particularly those containing salt. (See "Rehydration Solutions," page 329.) The patient should not engage in vigorous activity at least for the rest of that day. Only after she has completely restored her body fluids and salt, and has a normal urinary output, should exercise in a hot environment be resumed, and then cautiously.

HEAT EXHAUSTION

This occurs when fluid losses from sweating and respiration are greater than internal fluid reserves (volume depletion). Heat exhaustion is really a form of volume shock. The lack of fluid causes the body to constrict blood vessels, especially in the arms and legs. To understand heat exhaustion, think of a car with a radiator leak pulling a trailer up a mountain pass. There is not enough fluid in the system to cool off the engine under its current load, so the car overheats. Adding fluid solves the problem. The signs and symptoms of heat exhaustion are:

- Sweating
- Skin pale, clammy (from peripheral vasoconstriction)
- Pulse rate increased

- Respiration rate increased
- Temperature normal or slightly elevated
- Urine output decreased
- Patient feels weak, dizzy, thirsty, "sick," anxious
- Nausea and vomiting (from decreased circulation in the stomach)

Treatment

Treatment is as described for heat syncope, but the person should be *more* conservative about resuming physical activity to give the body a chance to recover. Have the person rest (lying down) in the shade. Monitor the person's temperature to make sure that it is not rising, which could be an indication of a more serious condition, heatstroke. Replace fluid with a rehydration solution. (See "Rehydration Solutions," page 329.) Drink slowly; drinking too much, too fast very often causes nausea and vomiting. Victims of heat exhaustion must be properly rehydrated and should be very careful about resuming physical activity before the body fluid level and electrolytes have been completely restored. Evacuation is not usually necessary.

Note: Heat exhaustion can become heatstroke if not properly treated. A victim of heat exhaustion should be closely monitored to make sure that her temperature does not go above 103°F (39°C). If it does, be prepared to treat the person for heatstroke (see below).

HEATSTROKE

Heatstroke is an immediate life-threatening medical emergency. A victim can die within minutes if not properly treated. Heatstroke is caused by an increase in the body's core temperature. Core temperatures over 105°F (41°C) can quickly lead to death. The rate of onset of heatstroke depends on the individual's fluid status. To understand heatstroke, think of that same car pulling a trailer up a mountain pass on a hot day. This time the radiator has plenty of fluid, but the heat challenge of the engine combined with the external temperature is too much. The engine can't get rid of the heat fast enough and the engine overheats. There are two types of heatstroke: fluid depleted (slow onset) and fluid intact (fast onset).

Fluid Depleted   The person has heat exhaustion due to fluid loss from sweating and/or inadequate fluid replacement but continues to function in a heat-challenge situation. Ultimately, the lack of fluid minimizes the body's active heat-loss capabilities to such an extent that the internal core temperature begins to rise. *Example:* a dehydrated cyclist biking on a hot day.

Fluid Intact The person is under an *extreme* heat challenge. The heat challenge overwhelms the body's active heat-loss mechanisms even though the fluid level is sufficient. This typically has a very fast onset. *Example:* a cyclist biking hard on a 104°F day (40°C).

Signs and Symptoms of Heatstroke

The key to identifying heatstroke is *hot skin*. Some victims may have hot *dry* skin; others may have hot *wet* skin because they have just moved from heat exhaustion to heatstroke. Also look for:

- Increased temperature (may be over 105°F/41°C)—skin hot to the touch
- Increased pulse rate
- Increased respiratory rate
- Decreased urine output
- Skin that is wet or dry and flushed
- Severe changes in mental status and motor/sensory changes; the person may become comatose; possibility of seizures
- Pupils that are dilated and unresponsive to light

Treatment

Efforts to reduce body temperature must begin immediately! Move the patient (gently) to a cooler spot or shade the victim. Remove excess clothing. If you have cotton clothes or the person is wearing cotton, here is one situation where cotton clothing is a good thing. Drape cotton clothes on the person. Pour water all over the person, soaking the cotton, and start fanning the person. What you are doing is using the principle of wet clothing pulling heat off 25 times faster than dry clothing and the principle of windchill to suck heat from this person as fast as possible. Put ice/cold packs on the sites of the major arteries at the neck, armpits, and groin. Massage the arms and legs vigorously. The blood in the arms and legs will cool off faster than the blood in the trunk, and massaging helps push that cooler blood back into the core (like after-drop with hypothermia).

After the temperature has been reduced to 102°F (39°C), active cooling should be reduced to avoid hypothermia (if shivering begins, it produces more heat). The patient must be monitored closely to make sure her temperature does not increase again. She will probably need fluids regardless of the type of onset. Apply basic life support (see "Basic Life Support," page 282), if needed. After heatstroke there can be serious medical problems, so this person should seek advanced medical care as soon as possible. Prepare to evacuate your patient. Monitor the patient's temperature closely during the evacuation and be prepared to treat her again if needed.

DROWNING AND NEAR DROWNING

Drowning occurs when liquid prevents gas exchange in the lungs. There are two types of drowning. Wet drowning (85 to 90 percent of drownings) occurs when the person's lungs fill with water. Dry drownings (10 to 15 percent) take place when the person swallows water and then the larynx goes into spasm and closes off, preventing breathing. No water gets into the lungs, but no air, either. The most common cause of drowning is cold water immersion resulting in loss of muscle coordination and strength. The person becomes hypothermic (see "Hypothermia," page 332) and is no longer able to swim. He or she sinks below the surface and inhales water. The gasping reflex from sudden immersion in cold water can also trigger the person to swallow water and quickly lose consciousness.

Treatment

The primary treatment is to administer CPR immediately. (See "Basic Life Support," page 282.) In cases of dry drowning, you may not be able to force air through the spasming larynx. Massaging the muscles of the throat may relax them and allow you to ventilate the patient. If cold water is involved, treat for hypothermia. Drowning can also be connected to trauma in the water, such as a diving accident or injury from a canoeing, kayaking, or rafting incident. You may also need to treat the person for a possible spinal or head injury. If you believe there is a mechanism for a spinal injury you should keep the head and neck supported and use the jaw-thrust technique while doing CPR. *Anyone who has been through a drowning or near drowning must be evacuated for advanced medical care.*

LIGHTNING INJURIES

Electrical currents can cause the heart to stop, respiration to cease, thermal burns, muscle spasms, brain and nerve damage, and initial blindness. The extent of injury depends on the amount of current, the duration of the current, and the current's path through the body. With a direct strike or side flash, the current is usually so large that the results are fatal. Ground currents can be significantly less powerful, and the current path makes a major difference.

Other injuries from lightning include ruptured eardrums and traumatic injuries. Direct strikes can literally hurl a person many feet/meters through the air. (For more information about lightning hazards and safety, see "Lightning Dangers," page 204).

Treatment

The most dangerous situation in a lightning strike is that the heart may stop beating. Be prepared to administer CPR. There is *no* danger of electrocution from touching someone who has been hit by lightning (the current is long gone). This is different from someone who is in contact with a live power line or other electrical source that is still generating current. Lightning is one of the few CPR situations where you may be able to revive someone without advanced life support (like a defibrillator and cardiac medications), so continue to do CPR as long as possible. Also, there may be electrical burns that can result in volume shock. *Anyone who has been struck by lighting or ground current must be evacuated for advanced medical care.*

TOXINS

It is often difficult to identify specific toxins in the field, so most of the treatments are for the symptoms of toxin exposure. You must carefully evaluate the type of reaction the patient is having to a toxin and determine whether evacuation is required. When in doubt, transport. Toxins may cause long-term medical problems if not properly treated.

There are four basic types of toxins based on how the poison or toxin is introduced to the body: absorbed through the skin, ingested, injected, and inhaled. The basic principle for dealing with all toxins is to *remove* and *dilute.*

- **Absorbed through the skin** For dry toxin, brush off; for wet toxin, irrigate with water.
- **Injected** Support critical body systems; give medications where appropriate.
- **Inhaled** Clean, fresh air; PROP (see page 262).
- **Ingested** If possible, administer *activated charcoal* (25 to 50 grams) mixed with water. This is what poison control centers recommend. Activated charcoal binds with whatever is in the stomach *immediately,* preventing it from being absorbed into the blood stream. The second option is to dilute the toxin with as much water as the person can drink.

For each type of toxin exposure, the general treatment should be followed with the following specific treatments. (See also "Anaphylaxis," page 364.) There are several toxic substances that you may bring with you on your trip. You should be aware of how to properly treat toxic exposure to these substances.

ACIDS AND BASES

The major danger is burnt tissue when these products are swallowed. Be aware of the possibility of swelling of the esophagus and airway, which could compromise breathing.

Treatment

Do not induce vomiting, as it could result in additional burns. Also, if any of the material is aspirated into the lungs, it could impair breathing. Carefully monitor airway, breathing, and circulation. Give activated charcoal if available. Prepare to evacuate your patient.

PETROLEUM PRODUCTS

The immediate danger in petroleum product poisoning is that the person may vomit and aspirate vapors and fluid into the lungs, which could seriously impair breathing. Carefully monitor airway, breathing, and circulation.

Treatment

Do not induce vomiting. Give activated charcoal if available. Prepare to evacuate your patient.

MEDICINES OR PLANTS

If someone takes an overdose of medication or ingests a poisonous plant, give activated charcoal if available. If that is not available, induce vomiting. If vomiting is unsuccessful, use water to dilute the poison. *Warning: Never* induce vomiting on a patient unless she is totally conscious to avoid possible aspiration. Prepare to evacuate your patient.

IODINE CRYSTALS

Iodine crystals may be used as a form of water purification. The iodine crystals are used to make a dilute iodine solution for purifying water; the crystals themselves are far too concentrated and are toxic if ingested.

Treatment—Internal Ingestion

Drink starch in water (e.g., powdered milk). The starch will neutralize any remaining iodine in the stomach. Iodine is a strong intestinal irritant and most likely will cause immediate vomiting. If the patient vomits, carefully monitor airway, breathing, and circulation.

Treatment—External Burning

For contact with skin and/or eyes, flush with water for at least 15 minutes.

CARBON MONOXIDE

Carbon monoxide is a colorless, odorless gas that is a by-product of the combustion of stove fuel. The gas can accumulate if you are cooking or using a gas lantern in an enclosed or poorly ventilated space, like a tent or a snow cave. Symptoms include severe headache, nausea and vomiting, shortness of breath, and decreased hearing. If exposure continues, it leads to unconsciousness and death.

Treatment

Prevention is the key. Don't use a stove or gas lantern in an enclosed space. If the patient is suffering from carbon monoxide poisoning, get her away from the source and into fresh air as quickly as possible. Monitor the airway and give PROP (see page 262). If not breathing, give artificial respiration. (See "Basic Life Support," page 282.)

WHITE GAS

White gas (see page 58), which is commonly used in backpacking stoves, is considered a toxic chemical. It is important to be aware of the hazards associated with the fuel and how to respond to a serious exposure.

- **Eyes** May cause irritation, discomfort, and excess redness and swelling of the eyes. *Treatment:* Flush eyes with plenty of water for several minutes. Get medical attention if eye irritation persists.
- **Skin** Prolonged or widespread skin contact may result in the absorption of potentially harmful amounts of material. May cause irritation, local redness, and possible swelling. *Treatment:* Wash skin with plenty of soap and water until all traces of material are removed. Remove and clean contaminated clothing. Get medical attention if skin irritation persists or contact has been prolonged.
- **Inhalation** Vapors or mist may cause irritation of the nose and throat,

headache, nausea, vomiting, dizziness, drowsiness, euphoria, loss of coordination, and disorientation. In poorly ventilated areas or confined spaces, unconsciousness and asphyxiation may result. *Treatment:* Remove to fresh air. If not breathing, give artificial respiration. (See "Basic Life Support," page 282.)

- **Ingestion**   If more than several mouthfuls are swallowed, abdominal discomfort, nausea, and diarrhea may occur. Aspiration may occur during swallowing or vomiting, resulting in lung damage. *Treatment: Do not induce vomiting.* Give activated charcoal, if available. Prepare to evacuate patient.

ANIMAL AND INSECT BITES AND STINGS

Animal bites and stings can transmit toxins or infections. Bites from mammals may carry rabies and/or tetanus. Depending on where you go in the world, there are a variety of poisonous snakes that can inject toxins. In North America there are only a few species that are poisonous. Finally, many insects bite, and some can inject toxins or infectious microorganisms.

RABIES

Rabies is caused by a virus carried by mammals. The rabies virus attacks the central nervous system and is *fatal* unless the victim has been protected by immunization or receives proper treatment. The virus is found in the infected animal's saliva, so infection is usually caused by animal bites. However, rabies can be contracted if the saliva comes in contact with small cuts in the skin or mucous membranes like the inside of the mouth. The major hosts for rabies are skunks and raccoons, but rabies is also found in bats, foxes, and groundhogs, as well as in livestock and domestic animals. The incubation period, from infection with the virus to the onset of symptoms, is usually two to twelve weeks but may be longer.

Rabid animals can appear either "enraged" or "docile." In the enraged stage, the animal is aggressive and excited, snapping and biting at anything, often foaming at the mouth. In the docile stage, the animal can seem very approachable, almost tame. It may be disoriented and lack coordination. Docile animals are especially dangerous because they are easily approached but can still suddenly lunge and bite. Avoid touching any dead animals because the virus can still be transmitted to your mucous membranes or any open wounds even though the animal is dead. *Do not* try to capture a possibly rabid animal because you only risk having another person bitten. Report the incident to local authorities with a description of the animal, its behavior, and location.

Treatment

First, treat the wound and stop any major bleeding. (See "Bleeding," page 278.) The best defense against rabies is aggressive wound cleaning with a povidone iodine solution as soon as possible. Rinse the wound after cleaning and use an antibiotic ointment. (See "Wound Care," page 279.) Rabies is fatal if not identified and treated. Anyone bitten by an animal should be evacuated to advanced medical care.

SNAKES

There are a number of poisonous snakes in North America. In the event of a snake bite, try to visually identify the species of snake. That is helpful to medical personnel on deciding how to treat the person. Do *not* try to catch the snake. Snakes generally strike while trying to protect themselves, so trying to capture the snake is asking for someone else to get bitten.

PIT VIPERS

The pit viper family consists of copperheads, cottonmouths, and rattlesnakes. These snakes are found mainly in the southwestern and southeastern United States. Pit vipers are recognizable by their triangular-shaped head, pupils with vertical slits, and a heat-sensing pit behind the nostril. Pit vipers leave one or two fang marks. Envenomation occurs only in 20 to 30 percent of bites. If envenomation does occur, the amount of venom transmitted determines the severity of the poisoning.

- **Mild Envenomation** is characterized by an immediate local reaction, marked by pain and swelling. The site will turn black and blue.

Poisonous Snake   Nonpoisonous Snake

- **Moderate Envenomation** has the same symptoms. In addition, swelling becomes more extensive and progresses from the bite site toward the heart.
- **Severe Envenomation** shows major swelling, increased pulse and breathing rates, headache, blurred vision, sweating, and chills.

General Snakebite Treatment

The most effective treatment is administration of the specific antivenin for that snake, which usually requires that the patient be transported to a medical facility. Thus, the most important measure to be taken after a confirmed snakebite is evacuation. A suction extractor (such as the Sawyer Extractor, *www.sawyerproducts.com*), if used within the first few minutes after the bite, can remove up to 30 percent of the venom; continue using the Extractor for 30 minutes. This suction does not involve making any cuts in the skin. Do not use the old "cut and suck" method; you only run the risk of damaging more tissue, and you won't remove much venom. The bite is a high-risk wound for infection and should be treated accordingly. (See "Wound Care," page 279.) After use, the Extractor tip should be rinsed with a bleach solution (see universal precautions, page 265). Swelling will occur, so remove constricting items below the bite such as rings. Keep the affected area at or below the level of the heart to slow circulation of the venom. Splint the area to minimize movement. A healthy adult will become ill from pit viper venom but is not likely to die. Children, infants, the elderly, and people in poor health are at greater risk. After any envenomation you should arrange for evacuation. Minimizing movement is important, so a carry-out evacuation is preferred. If that is not possible and if the person is able to walk on her own, she should do so slowly. If the person can't be evacuated, monitor her vitals and keep them at rest. Have her drink fluids frequently. Secure professional rescue help.

CORAL SNAKES

Coral snakes are found in the southern and southwestern United States. They are marked by alternating bands of red, yellow, and black. You can recognize the coral snake from the harmless scarlet king snake by remembering this rhyme: "Red on yellow, kill a fellow; red on black, venom lack." Coral snakes are not aggressive and bite only when provoked. The coral snake passes venom by chewing on the skin, as opposed to injecting from fangs, so the snake must really grab on to you and chew. If it has broken the skin, you must assume envenomation. The venom is a neurotoxin that causes nausea, rapid pulse, and rapid respiration, which can progress to respiratory failure and death. The effects of envenomation may be delayed for up to 12 hours, which is why it is sometimes ignored as a health risk.

Treatment

Follow the general snakebite treatment above. In addition, monitor respirations carefully and treat with PROP as necessary (see page 262). Be prepared to give CPR if the patient goes into respiratory failure. Arrange for evacuation sooner rather than later.

INSECTS

There are a number of poisonous spiders and other insects in the United States and Canada. In most cases, spider bites are defensive and happen when you put your hand or foot in the wrong place. Since many of the bites are painless, the person doesn't know until hours later that she has been bitten. If the bite is witnessed, capture the spider if possible and bring it back for identification. Unlike snakes, there is very little risk of envenomation for someone catching the spider.

BLACK WIDOW SPIDER

The black widow is a small black spider about 1 inch (2.5 centimeters) long found in most of the United States and Canada. The female has an hourglass shape on her abdomen, which is often red in color. Only the female is poisonous, and she carries an extremely powerful neurotoxin. Luckily, the amount of venom injected is very small, so there are very few deaths from black widow bites. The black widow delivers a low-pain bite that sometimes goes undetected. There may be a small red bump at the bite site. Symptoms appear within an hour of being bitten and include intense pain, severe cramps in the abdomen and back, headache, nausea, fever, chills, dizziness, and sweating.

Treatment

These bites are rarely fatal. If the bite site can be located, apply cold, which slows down the spread of the venom. The person should be evaluated at a hospital. An antivenin is available. Prepare to evacuate.

BROWN RECLUSE SPIDER

The brown recluse spider is the most common culprit of serious spider bites in the United States. It tends to live under rocks and bark in relatively dry places.

The spider has a dark fiddle-shaped mark on its back. The bite is often pain-less and goes unnoticed until symptoms develop, a painful red blister typically within a few hours. In some cases, the bite site shows what is called a "red, white, and blue sign." The bite site has a white central blister, surrounded by a bluish patch, then surrounded by a reddened area. Look for infection and necrosis—the liquefaction and breakdown of tissue—at the bite site. This may lead to scarring. Chills, fever, nausea, vomiting, joint ache, and rashes or hives may also appear as later signs.

Treatment

Treat the wound. Watch for infection. If possible, save the spider for identifi-cation. If skin necrosis develops, have the person seen by a physician.

HOBO SPIDER

The hobo spider is a brown spider about ½ to ¾ inch long (12 to 18 millime-ters). Hobo spider venom is similar to that of the brown recluse. It creates a blistered area that then becomes necrotic and may take several months to heal.

Treatment

Treat the wound. Watch for infection. If possible, save the spider for identifi-cation. If skin necrosis develops, have the person seen by a physician.

SCORPIONS

In North America, scorpions are found in the southwestern states and Mex-ico. There are numerous species, all of which inject a toxin from a stinger at the end of their tails. Scorpions feed at night and love crawling into things like boots and sleeping bags. In scorpion country, shake out items like your sleeping bag before going to bed, and shake out boots and clothes in the morning. During the day, scorpions hide from the sun in shaded places—under rocks, in woodpiles, and so on. Be cautious around these places. A scorpion sting is a pricking sensation followed by burning pain, swelling, numbness, tingling, and redness. Numbness may spread to the rest to the ex-tremity. The toxin from most scorpions is nonlethal and is similar in severity to a bee sting.

The most dangerous is *Centruroides sculptuatus,* also known as the bark scorpion because it hides under the bark of trees. It is a small yellow or tan species about 1 to 3 inches (2.5 to 7.6 centimeters) long. It hides in damp, cool areas under rocks, boards, fallen logs, and dead vegetation. It injects a neurotoxin that causes overstimulation of the nervous system, resulting in hyperactivity, difficulty swallowing, and respiratory distress. Pain may become severe, and the patient becomes very jittery. Fatalities can occur in children and the elderly.

Treatment

Apply ice or cool water at the sting site and clean the wound. An antihistamine will help reduce swelling. If the pain becomes severe or the patient shows nonlocalized symptoms, there is a more severe envenomation and the patient should be evacuated. In cases of *Centruroides* envenomation, an antivenin is available.

INSECT REPELLANTS

Use of insect repellants is a personal choice for backcountry travelers. In all cases, you need to weigh the risk of exposure to insects and any possible insect-borne diseases against any risks associated with using the product.

Skin Softening Products

Some skin products like Avon's SKIN-SO-SOFT have been shown to have some insect-repellant ability. These products typically repel insects for a much shorter time and therefore must be repeatedly applied.

DEET

DEET is the most prevalently used insect repellant. It is available in a number of concentrations. According to the Environmental Protection Agency and the Centers for Disease Control, DEET products are safe when used according to the directions. DEET has been widely studied, and over the long history of its use, there have been very few confirmed incidents of toxic reactions to DEET when the product is used properly. DEET can be used either directly on the skin or on clothing. However, *DEET should not be applied to skin that is then covered by clothing.*

The concentration of DEET you should use depends on the type of insect exposure. In general, use the lowest concentration of DEET for the time duration protection needed. You can always reapply it. In most cases, concentrations of 10 to 35 percent DEET provide adequate protection. The concentration is primarily related to how long the chemical provides protection before reapplication is necessary. In national testing:

Concentration	Hours of Protection
23.8% DEET	5 hours
20% DEET	4 hours
6.65% DEET	2 hours
4.75% DEET and 2% soybean oil	1 and a half hours

Higher concentration of DEET may be preferable in situations when there is rapid loss of repellant from rain, sweat, or high temperatures. Also, consider higher concentrations when you are in one of those areas where the "bugs block out the sun," like Alaska in the summer, or when you are in areas where serious disease transmission is possible from insects, especially in the tropics with malaria, yellow fever, etc.

There have been questions raised about DEET concentration and use with children. This issue has been studied by the Environmental Protection Agency, and according to both the EPA and the American Academy of Pediatrics, when used according to the directions, DEET products with a concentration of 10 percent or less appear to be as safe for children as products with a concentration of 30 percent are for adults. DEET should not be swallowed, so avoid using DEET on children's hands or around the mouth. DEET is not recommended for use on children under 2 months of age.

The Centers for Disease Control suggests *against* using products that are combination insect repellant and sunscreen. Instead, use two separate products because sunscreen requires more frequent applications, while DEET should be used sparingly. There is no problem with putting both chemicals on at the same time.

Permethrin

Permethrin is not an insect repellant; it is an insecticide, so it actually kills insects that come in contact with it. Permethrin can be used in areas that have high incidences of insect-borne diseases like Lyme disease or West Nile virus, or for people who have frequent exposure, like outdoor professionals. Permethrin is a neurotoxin that kills insects by affecting their central nervous system. It can also affect the human central nervous system and therefore should *never* be used directly on the skin. It is designed *only* for use on clothing, boots, tents, etc. Permethrin is toxic to honey bees and other beneficial insects, fish, aquatic insects, crayfish, and shrimp, so you must be extremely careful about Permethrin exposure to water sources and other animals.

Permethrin should be used only to pretreat garments before wearing. It should not be sprayed on clothing while it is being worn. To apply Permethrin, hold the spray can 6 to 8 inches (15 to 20 centimeters) from the garment and spray for about 30 seconds, coating the surface. Concentrate the spray around places like pant cuffs and other locations where ticks or other insects may enter. Hang the garment up and allow the Permethrin treatment to dry for two hours, or four hours if conditions are very humid. Once dry it lasts up to six weeks (unless the clothes are washed).

MOSQUITOES AND DISEASE

Mosquitoes are a major disease vector in many parts of the world. Since they are blood-feeders and feed on both animals and humans it is possible to transmit bacteria and viruses easily. In North America the major disease carried by mosquitoes is the West Nile Virus. Other diseases include malaria, dengue fever, yellow fever, and Rift Valley fever. Preventative medications are available for some diseases. If you are traveling into areas where mosquito-borne diseases are endemic, check with health officials or your physician to find out what precautions you should take. *The Yellow Book: Health Information for International Travel* produced by the Centers for Disease Control is an excellent resource (*www.cdc.gov/travel/yb/index.htm*).

West Nile Virus

West Nile virus has been found in all of the lower forty-eight states in the United States, as well as in much of Canada. The virus is primarily transmitted by several species of mosquitoes. It is a seasonable disease in areas where mosquitoes die off during the winter, but in warmer southern climates the disease may be present all year. Although there are millions of mosquito bites each year, the actual incidence of the disease is quite low since it is estimated that fewer than 1 percent of mosquitoes in any given area are infected with the virus and the overall risk of being bitten by an infected mosquito is low. In a small number of cases West Nile virus has been shown to be transmittable through blood and organ transfusions, but it is not spread through casual contact with an infected person.

Most people infected with West Nile virus (80 percent) will not show any symptoms at all. Up to 20 percent of the people who become infected will display symptoms that can include fever, headache, body aches, nausea, vomiting, and sometimes swollen lymph glands or a skin rash on the chest, stomach, and back. Symptoms can last from a few days to several weeks. About one in 150 people infected with West Nile virus will develop severe illness. The severe symptoms can include high fever, headache, neck stiffness, stupor, disorientation, coma, tremors, convulsions, muscle weakness, vision loss, numbness, and paralysis. These symptoms may last several weeks, and the neurological effects may be permanent. The elderly and those with compromised immune systems are most susceptible to the disease.

Prevention

The best prevention is wearing long pants, long-sleeve shirts, and a hat, and using insect repellant. In areas with high concentrations of mosquitoes it may be helpful to use mosquito netting headnets and sleep in tents. Mosquitoes are most active between dawn and dusk. Take extra care during the early morning and early evening hours. Use insect repellants (see page 357).

Treatment

There is no specific cure for West Nile virus. People with a high fever, severe headache, and muscle weakness or confusion who may have been exposed to mosquitoes should see a physician. Mild cases of infection may not require any treatment at all. More severe cases may require hospitalization to treat the symptoms.

TICKS AND TICK-BORNE ILLNESSES

Ticks can be found almost anywhere. Ticks typically "hang out" on grass and plants, waiting for an attractive warm-blooded mammal to pass by, and they hop on. So walking through brushy areas is a common way to pick up ticks. There are a number of things you can do to protect yourself against ticks. Wear long pants and light-colored clothing; button up your shirt, tuck your long pant legs into your socks, or wear gaiters. Apply insect repellant to your skin. In areas with known tick diseases, you may want to use an insecticide like Permethrin on your clothing. The best defense is to perform regular "tick checks." Adult ticks usually like to wander around the body for an hour or two before they attach, and they like to attach in a warm hairy place. Therefore, you should regularly run your fingers through your hair and closely examine your scalp and neck. Ticks can also attach in the groin, under the arms, behind the knees, in or behind the ears, or occasionally underneath women's breasts.

TREATMENT

To remove a tick with tweezers, grasp the tick's head as close to the skin as possible, paying careful attention to the *head* of the tick, which may still be under the skin. Pull it *straight* out. Do not grab the tick in the middle part of its body. Ticks may carry harmful bacteria, and squeezing their abdomen may inject the bacteria into the wound. There are also special "tick tweezers" designed to remove the tick completely. Do *not* burn or smother the tick with fluids. These methods are not effective in removing the tick and may also force infected fluid into the bloodstream. Evacuation is not necessary, but be sure to clean the area as you would any wound. (See "Wound Care," page 279.)

If possible, save the tick for identification. Place it in a plastic bag with a small amount of vegetation. There are a number of labs to which you can mail the tick to have it tested. Live ticks can be tested to see if they are carrying disease. Dead ticks can be tested for Lyme disease. Anyone who has an engorged tick removed should watch for signs of a tick-borne illness after the trip. Blood tests for some tick-borne diseases are available.

Lyme Disease

Lyme disease is an infection caused by a spiral-shaped bacterium called a spirochete. This bacterium is carried in the gut of the deer tick *Ixodes scapularis* and its cousin, the western black-legged tick. The tick becomes infected after feeding on the blood of an infected animal. Once infected, the tick can transmit the disease to its next host. Deer ticks are extremely small, with tick nymphs about the size of the period at the end of this sentence. This means that you may have been bitten without realizing it. The tick needs to feed for an extended period of time (usually 24 to 48 hours) before infection can occur. So just because you have found an attached tick does *not* mean that you have been infected. It is also possible that the tick was not carrying the disease. Most cases of infection occur between May and July, but Lyme disease has been found steadily through October, with cases reported all year long depending on location.

If you have been *bitten* by a tick, rate your risk of infection by answering these questions:

- Do I live in a Lyme disease–endemic area (an area of high incidence)?
- Is the tick I just removed either a deer tick or a western black-legged tick?
- If so, did the tick appear engorged (swollen like a balloon) vs. tiny and flattened?

According to the American Lyme Disease Foundation, if you answer yes to all three questions, then you have a significant risk for Lyme disease. If you answered yes to only one or two questions, you have a low risk.

Detecting Lyme disease can be difficult, as the symptoms associated with the early stages—fever, headache, stiffness, lethargy, and myriad other mild complaints—are often dismissed as the flu. In some cases (about 25 percent), there is a red, ringlike rash that occurs at the site of the bite. The rash is often referred to as a "bull's-eye" rash because it has a red center surrounded by a white area and then a red outer ring. Most typically, the rash expands and then fades within a few weeks after the bite. There is a blood test for Lyme disease, but it is not 100 percent accurate. The test generally produces positive results in the later stages of the disease but often turns up false-negative results in the early stages. Therefore, diagnosis in the early phase is frequently based on symptoms and the likelihood of a deer tick bite.

Early detection means early treatment when the disease is most effectively controlled with antibiotics. Left untreated, Lyme disease can result in more serious symptoms, including arthritis, facial paralysis, cardiac abnormalities, and meningitis (a potentially fatal central nervous system disorder). Since the symptoms of the disease do not appear until weeks or even months after a trip, it is *important that all group members understand the symptoms of Lyme disease* so they can seek proper medical help if they become symptomatic after the trip. For the most up-to-date information on Lyme disease, see the American Lyme Disease Foundation *(www.aldf.com)* and the Centers for Disease Control *(www.cdc.gov)*.

Rocky Mountain Spotted Fever

Don't confuse the name of the disease with its location. Ticks carrying Rocky Mountain spotted fever are found all across the United States with the highest number of cases being found in the mid-Atlantic coastal states. This disease is carried by a bacterium and can be transmitted by the bites of dog or wood ticks. The tick can pass the disease after feeding for approximately three hours. Symptoms develop three to twelve days later. Watch for mild chills, appetite loss, and a general run-down feeling. These symptoms may worsen to severe chills, fever, headaches, muscle and bone pain, and sensitivity to light. Also, a spotty red rash (hence the name) may appear, usually starting at the wrists and ankles and spreading over the rest of the body. Normal onset of these symptoms is anywhere between three and fourteen days after infection. Untreated, the mortality rate is 20 to 30 percent. Anyone who shows these signs should be evacuated. Since the symptoms of the disease may not appear until weeks after a trip, *it is important that all group members understand the symptoms* of Rocky Mountain spotted fever disease so they can seek proper medical help if they become symptomatic after the trip.

Southern Tick-Associated Rash Illness (STARI)

STARI is a rash similar to the rash of Lyme disease, associated with the bite of the lone star tick. The female lone star tick is brown in color and has a characteristic white star in the center of its back, while males have scattered spots or streaks around the margins of the body. Lone star ticks can be found from central Texas and Oklahoma eastward across the southern states and along the Atlantic coast as far north as Maine. It also may develop into a "bull's-eye" rash that is seen in Lyme disease. Anyone developing such a rash following a tick bite should see a physician.

Ehrlichiosis

Ehrlichiosis is a recently recognized tick-borne disease caused by a bacterium. The disease is similar to Rocky Mountain spotted fever and can be life-threatening. The most common symptoms are sudden high fever, tiredness, major muscle aches, severe headache, and, in some cases, a rash. Symptoms usually appear three to sixteen days after a tick bite. Ehrlichiosis can be treated with antibiotics.

Tick Paralysis

A number of species of ticks can transmit tick paralysis. It is not an infection, but a by-product of a venom in the tick's saliva that is secreted while the tick is attached. Symptoms are unsteady movement and gait (ataxia) and ascending paralysis starting in the lower extremities and moving up. Paralysis can cause loss of respiratory drive, requiring CPR and immediate evacuation. Once the tick is removed, the source of the venom is gone and the patient generally recovers completely. Children are more likely to be affected than adults. Any patient with an ascending paralysis should be carefully checked for an attached tick. Evacuate the person for evaluation.

Tularemia

Tularemia, or rabbit fever, is a bacterial disease of which the most common carriers are rabbits, although it can also be transmitted by ticks. The disease presents with flu-like symptoms and can be treated with antibiotics.

BEE, YELLOW JACKET, AND WASP STINGS

Bees, yellow jackets, hornets, wasps, and fire ants are all in the order *hymenoptera*, and their venom can be deadly for those who are allergic. In cases of a simple sting with no allergic reaction, treatment involves removing the stinger and treating the minor pain of the sting. Bees can sting only once and leave the stinger behind; yellow jackets, hornets, wasps, and fire ants can sting repeatedly and do not leave a stinger.

Treatment

If it is a bee sting, the stinger will be left behind with a venom sack. The sack continues to contract and can pump more venom in for up to 20 minutes. Be careful not to squeeze the venom sac, which would inject more venom into the wound. Use the edge of a knife blade or a credit card to flick the stinger out. With any sting, the Extractor can be used within the first few minutes to remove up to 30 percent of the venom. This can ease pain and swelling and reduce the severity of a reaction. After use, the Extractor tip should be rinsed with a bleach solution.

Local anesthetics like Sting-eze will help relieve pain at the site. To reduce itching, you can use a paste made of baking soda and water or apply Adolph's meat tenderizer for 15 to 20 minutes. Ice packs can help reduce mild swelling, and mild analgesics like Tylenol or ibuprofen can be given for pain. Be alert for any systemic allergic reaction. (See "Anaphylaxis," below.)

ANAPHYLAXIS

Anaphylaxis is a dangerous systemic allergic reaction to a foreign substance that can be life-threatening. Like other toxins, the foreign substance can enter the bloodstream through injection, inhalation, ingestion, or absorption into the skin. One of the most common causes of anaphylaxis, with one of the quickest periods of onset, is the common bee or wasp sting (injected toxin), with an onset of symptoms typically within the first 30 minutes of exposure. Allergic reactions to foods or inhaled toxins are slower, but equally dangerous. For an ingested toxin, the reaction can take up to several hours to develop.

In response to the toxin, the body releases the chemical histamine, which causes vasodilation and fluid leakage from blood vessels, resulting in swelling. In anaphylactic shock, this response is systemic, resulting in vascular shock. (See "Shock," page 274.) The greatest danger in anaphylaxis is to the patient's airway, which can swell shut, causing respiratory arrest and death.

In evaluating anaphylaxis, it is important to differentiate between a local reaction and a true systemic reaction. For a local reaction the patient's skin may be hot, with complaints of itchiness and hives appearing only at the site of the toxin. A systemic reaction is characterized by hives or swelling distant from the site or all over the body. In a systemic reaction, the airway may be constricted, causing labored respirations and wheezing. The patient's mental status will almost always be decreasing, and nausea, vomiting, and diarrhea may occur. *A systemic anaphylactic reaction can be a life-threatening emergency. The airway can swell shut, and the person can die within minutes.*

Vitals in Anaphylaxis

- Pulse rate increased
- Respiration rate increased, labored, with possible wheezing
- Blood pressure possibly decreased
- AVPU—anxious, if severe anaphylaxis, possibly V, P, or U on the AVPU scale
- Skin hot, itchy, hives
- Temperature normal

Treatment

In true anaphylaxis, the effects of the severe vasodilation must be countered. This can be most successfully done using the injectable drug epinephrine, a synthetic form of adrenalin. Epinephrine is a short-term vasoconstrictor, so it counteracts the immediate effects of the histamine. However, the histamine is still circulating in the bloodstream, and the effects of the epinephrine wear off in 15 to 20 minutes. So the patient also needs to take an antihistamine medication like Benadryl. This inactivates the histamine in the bloodstream and prevents it from causing additional vasodilation. Give the antihistamine as soon as possible since it will take some time to be absorbed in the stomach.

In severe cases, there may be a rebound of symptoms after the first dose of epinephrine wears off, especially if the antihistamine has not yet started to work, requiring additional injections of epinephrine. The patient should continue to take antihistamines for at least 10 to 12 hours after the reaction. Any cases of anaphylaxis should be evacuated for medical follow-up. In addition to these medical treatments, be prepared for basic life support and PROP (see page 262). Remember to treat the epinephrine injector needle with universal precautions as a "sharp" that should be properly disposed of as medical waste (see pages 265 and 121).

Injectable epinephrine is found in the form of injectable pens and syringes. There are two products available in the U.S., the EpiPen and the Twin-Ject. Both are spring-loaded needles that allow for self-injection of a single dose. It's often necessary to give two or more doses, so carrying more than one injector is advisable. The Twin-ject has a second dose which can be administered. Follow all instructions on the product for the proper method of injection. It is important to note that *epinephrine is a prescription drug that requires a physician's approval for use.* There are certain medical conditions where giving epinephrine might be contraindicated.

Prevention

During your trip planning, find out if anyone in your group has serious allergies to bees, foods, or other substances. Ask if she carries epinephrine, and if so, make sure she brings it along. Know where it is kept and how to administer it. If you are in an organized outdoor program, find out if your program carries epinephrine, and get trained on how to recognize anaphylaxis and how to treat it. This is covered in most wilderness first-aid courses.

CHIGGERS

Chiggers are tiny red mite larvae. They are actually too small to be seen with the naked eye. Like ticks, they hang around on plants waiting for a warm-blooded animal or person to pass by so they can jump on. Contrary to common belief, chiggers do not burrow under the skin and they do not feed on blood. Chiggers tend to crawl around for several hours before feeding. Chigger bites are typically found around the ankles, the back of the knees, the crotch, under the belt line, and in the armpits. The chigger stays on the surface of the skin and inserts its tiny mouth parts into thin areas of skin at pores or hair follicles, and then injects a digestive enzyme that breaks down the skin cells. This is what it feeds on. The enzyme causes the surrounding skin to harden, forming a kind of "straw" called a stylosome for the chigger to continue to suck up the liquefied tissue. This stylosome is what makes the characteristic red welt of the chigger bite, and they itch like crazy. After feeding, chiggers fall off, leaving the stylosome behind. The stylosome can last for a number of weeks and continue to itch, which is why people falsely believe that the chigger is buried under the skin.

Prevention is key. Regular insect repellant on your skin or Permethrin on your clothing will keep chiggers off you (see page 357). They can easily be removed by just washing with warm soapy water. If you do find chiggers, assume that the little buggers may be all over your clothing, in your sleeping bag, etc. Everything needs to be washed, or you will just get them again. That's why one welt often becomes dozens. The best treatment to control the itching is hydrocortisone ointment or Caladryl. Avoid scratching because it only irritates the stylosome more. Scratching can also cause the wound to become infected. In North America, chiggers do not transmit disease, but other species of chiggers in other parts of the world do. If you are traveling outside of North America, it is always important to find out about local insect-borne diseases before your trip.

GENERAL MEDICAL ISSUES

ABDOMINAL INJURIES AND GASTROINTESTINAL PROBLEMS

When a patient has "abdominal pain," it is exceptionally difficult to assess in the field just what the cause is. Rather than try to pin down an exact cause for abdominal pain, the goal should be simply to determine whether the problem is potentially serious and requires evacuation, or if it can be treated in the field and expected to improve. The following list of signs and symptoms, if associated with abdominal pain, warrant genuine concern and prompt evacuation:

- Presence of blood from mouth or rectum—indicates gastrointestinal bleeding
- Vomiting or diarrhea persisting for more than 24 hours—loss of fluid volume may be too great to replace in field
- Volume shock—indicates severe fluid loss from bleeding, vomiting, diarrhea, or dehydration
- Fever—indicates infection
- Tenderness/guarding—suggests internal injury
- Pain in the "pit of the stomach" not relieved by food or antacids—a classic symptom of a heart attack

Assessment of Abdominal Pain

Your approach to these problems is dictated by the mechanism of injury to the patient. If the abdominal pain is possibly the result of a traumatic injury, your assessment will focus on a physical exam. Otherwise, you will need to rely on a thorough medical history of the illness. Common sense is your greatest asset in assessing abdominal pain. Everyone has had stomachaches. Ask the patient to compare the present illness to past ones. Ask if the patient has any relevant existing illnesses or past injuries. The acronym OPQRST (see "Patient Assessment System," page 273) provides a useful framework for assessing the pain.

APPENDICITIS

Acute appendicitis is an infection and inflammation of a small pouch attached to the intestines. The typical pattern of signs and symptoms includes pain and tenderness developing over 6 to 24 hours localizing in the right lower quadrant of the patient's abdomen. Nausea and vomiting are common, and the patient may have a low-grade fever (101°F/38°C). The patient may experience *rebound pain* when you palpate the right lower quadrant (no increase in pain when you push in; pain increases when you pull out). The main concern is that the infected appendix will eventually rupture, spreading infected contents throughout the abdomen. If left untreated, infection from a ruptured appendix can result in death.

Treatment

Appendicitis requires surgery, and a ruptured appendix requires massive antibiotic treatment. If appendicitis is suspected, prepare your patient for evacuation. In the interim, monitor your patient closely.

CONSTIPATION

Constipation is the inability to have a bowel movement. Constipation occurs when too much water is absorbed from feces in the intestines. The feces become too hard to move along normally. This can be caused by a number of things, including diet, dehydration (the body needs to retain more fluid and absorbs it from stool), and lack of opportunity to take a bowel movement. It generally becomes a problem only when the situation causes discomfort.

Treatment

The first form of treatment is prevention. Make sure that all members of your group have both time and privacy enough for their own comfort whenever nature calls, whether in camp or on the trail. Remind and encourage everyone in your group to eat high-fiber foods such as dried fruit or oatmeal on a regular basis. Most important, ensure that everyone drinks a minimum of 2 to 4 quarts (2 to 4 liters) of water per day. If someone does become constipated, the patient may consider taking a laxative.

DIARRHEA OR VOMITING

There is a wide range of possible causes for diarrhea and vomiting, including viral or bacterial infection, contaminated food, food allergy, or soap in food. The major concern in the field is how quickly the body can lose large amounts of fluid. Diarrhea or vomiting for more than 24 hours can lead to dehydration and ultimately volume shock. (See "Shock," page 274.) As with abdominal pain, it may be difficult in the field to determine the exact cause. It is more important to be able to recognize the signs of a serious condition that require advanced medical care.

Conditions with Diarrhea or Vomiting that Require Evacuation

- Fever
- Presence of blood
- Volume shock
- Diarrhea or vomiting lasting longer than 24 hours
- Pain lasting longer than 24 hours
- Any abdominal pain requiring evacuation (see "Abdominal Injuries and Gastrointestinal Problems," page 367)

Treatment

Generic treatments for less serious cases of diarrhea or vomiting are essentially the same.

1. Replace lost fluids orally with clear liquids—bouillon or other clear soups, weak Gatorade, or plain water with a pinch each of salt and sugar. (See "Rehydration Solutions," page 329.) Encourage the patient to drink slowly in small sips. If you are not able to replenish fluid losses this way, or if the patient is unable to keep the fluids down, the patient will become dangerously dehydrated. In that case, treat for shock (see page 274) and prepare to evacuate the patient.
2. Once clear liquids are tolerated, move the patient to simple carbohydrates—bread, rice, tea, and toast (BRATT). Continue giving fluids. Slowly move back to a normal diet as tolerated, and continue giving fluids.

Treatment for Vomiting

In the case of vomiting, you need to carefully monitor your patient's airway to make sure that she does not aspirate vomit. Aspirated vomit in the lungs can lead to serious lung infections. If the patient is unconscious, you should place her on her side with the head down to let vomit drain from the mouth. Sweep the mouth after each bout of vomiting to clear it, and make sure that the airway is still clear. If the airway is not clear, initiate basic life support (see page 282). After dealing with the immediate problem of vomiting, you need to try and determine what is causing the vomiting. Is it stress, a bacterial or viral infection, food poisoning? Has the person suffered a head injury, etc.? Based on the information from the patient history and physical, you can then try to address the underlying cause of the vomiting.

Treatment for Diarrhea

For extended cases of diarrhea you need to continue to hydrate the person. Use the oral rehydration formula to replace the sugar and electrolytes the person is losing. (See "Rehydration Solutions," page 329.) You may want to treat the person with an anti-diarrheal drug. In the long run, you need to discover the underlying cause of the diarrhea so that it can be treated effectively. This may require evacuating the person.

GASTROINTESTINAL INFECTIONS

There are a number of infectious gastrointestinal diseases that are of particular concern to wilderness travelers. If you are traveling outside of the United States and Canada, there are other diseases that you may need to be prepared for, either with pre-trip inoculations or by taking medication during your trip. You should check with your physician for specific information. Many of these diseases may not present themselves until weeks or even months after the trip. I always recommend that anyone traveling in remote areas of the world get a stool culture for ova and parasites upon return.

GIARDIA

Giardiasis refers to a syndrome of diarrhea, excess gas, and abdominal cramping caused by *Giardia lamblia,* a water-borne parasite that is worldwide in distribution. The symptoms usually occur one to two weeks after exposure to the parasite. *This one-to-two-week time course is extremely important.* Since most trips are less than a week, people typically don't become symptomatic until after their trip. They may not associate their symptoms with being out on a wilderness trip. Also, not all people who have ingested the cysts become symptomatic, so the few who do become sick may feel the cause is something other than water that everyone was drinking. Travelers must be educated about the possibilities of *Giardia,* so if they become symptomatic, they can seek out proper medical treatment. Failure to secure treatment can cause long-term gastrointestinal problems.

Giardia is a parasite that exists in two forms: a dormant cyst and the disease-causing form, a trophozite. The cysts are quite hardy and can survive even in extremely cold water. When the cyst is ingested, it metamorphoses into a trophozite that attaches to the intestinal wall, where it lives off its host. It is the trophozite that causes the symptoms of the disease. As feces move through the large intestine, some of the trophozites are carried out, and the trophozite changes back into the inactive cyst form. These excreted cysts often reinfect other water supplies. As backcountry travel use has increased, waste from both animals and people has spread *Giardia* to various rivers and streams, causing contamination. It is essential to remember that the spread of *Giardia* is directly related to sanitation practices. Backcountry travelers usually contract *Giardia* by drinking water from untreated or improperly treated sources. Boiling, chemical treatment of the water, and commercial water-filtration systems, used properly, eradicate the parasite. (See "Water Purification," page 94.)

Symptoms of Giardia

It usually takes seven to ten days for the *Giardia* to begin functioning in the intestine. The cysts can also remain dormant in the body and suddenly begin to cause difficulty months later.

If you have any of the following symptoms for more than 24 hours, you should consult a physician. One or more of the following symptoms may continue for several weeks, and their severity may very greatly. Mention your outdoor trip and specifically mention *Giardia*. Unfortunately, some physicians are not familiar with this parasite and may misdiagnose your problem as something else.

- Diarrhea, often "explosive" and watery
- Bloating
- Gas, often described as "sulphurous"
- Violent vomiting
- Cramps
- Weight loss
- Loss of appetite

Treatment

Giardia can be cured only with appropriate antibiotic treatment. Prior to seeing a physician, the one treatment is to maintain adequate fluid intake. (See "Fluid Balance," page 326.) The diagnosis of giardiasis can be confirmed by inspecting a stool sample for the presence of the parasite. Because this test may not always identify the organism even if it is present, a physician may elect to treat you empirically for the infection. The use of antibiotics is usually highly effective in relieving symptoms and curing the disease. Failure to treat may result in long-term gastrointestinal problems.

CRYPTOSPORIDIUM AND CYCLOSPORA

Unfortunately, there are some other critters out there in the water. Both of these are *highly resistant* to iodine or chlorine but are large enough to be filtered out by a standard water filter.

Cryptosporidium is a protozoa that causes a diarrheal illness similar to *Giardia*. Symptoms include watery diarrhea, headache, abdominal cramps, nausea, vomiting, and low-grade fever that may appear two to ten days after infection. Some infected people will be asymptomatic. It is most often spread by the feces to hands and then to the mouth. Careful handwashing is the best defense. *Cyclospora* is another cause of diarrhea. It can cause a prolonged illness (average six weeks) with profound fatigue and loss of appetite and intermittent diarrhea.

Treatment

Currently, there is no effective treatment for *Cryptosporidium*. Symptoms usually last one to two weeks, at which time the body's immune system is able to stop the infection. People with normal immune systems improve without taking antibiotics or antiparasitic medications. For people with compromised immune systems, this can be a dangerous disease. See your physician. In the backcountry, your major concern is to maintain adequate fluid levels to prevent serious dehydration. Antidiarrheal medications may help with the symptoms. In the backcountry, your major concern with *Cyclospora* is to maintain adequate fluid levels to prevent serious dehydration. *Cyclospora* can be treated with antibiotics.

OTHER INFECTIOUS DISEASES

TETANUS

Tetanus (lockjaw) is a bacterial disease that affects the nervous system. Tetanus bacteria are found in soil, especially in soil contaminated with animal feces. Tetanus may also be transmitted in animal bites. The tetanus bacteria are anaerobic—they grow in the absence of oxygen. The bacteria enter the wound (like a puncture wound from a rusty nail), and then the wound closes, creating an oxygen-free environment for the bacteria to grow in. Deep puncture wounds are most hazardous, but any anaerobic wound environment can be a breeding ground for tetanus, even minor scratches. The incubation period is typically two to eight days but may range up to several weeks. Common signs and symptoms include muscular stiffness in the jaw (lockjaw), followed by neck stiffness, difficulty in swallowing, abdominal muscle rigidity, spasms, sweating, and fever. Untreated, tetanus can lead to death.

Treatment

Wounds should be thoroughly cleaned (see page 279). If the patient has not had a tetanus booster within the previous ten years, she should receive a booster, preferably on the day of injury. A booster is also recommended if it is a severe wound and it has been more than five years since the last booster.

HANTAVIRUS PULMONARY SYNDROME

Hantavirus pulmonary syndrome (HPS) is a serious, potentially deadly respiratory disease that is carried by rodents. In recent years there have been cases of hantavirus among wilderness travelers. Currently, very few actual cases have been reported, mostly in rural areas of the western United States; however, according to the Centers for Disease Control, over half the people who have contracted the disease have died. The Centers for Disease Control reports, "Hantavirus pulmonary syndrome is a rare disease, and most tourists are not at increased risk for hantavirus infection. However, visitors to rural areas and nature resorts, campers, hikers, and others who take part in activities outdoors can become exposed to rodent urine, saliva, or droppings and become infected with hantavirus. Travel to and within all areas where hantavirus infection has been reported is safe. Nevertheless, if you camp or hike in an area inhabited by rodents, you have a small risk of being exposed to infected rodents and becoming infected with hantavirus."

The most common rodent carriers are the deer mouse and the cotton rat; others include voles and chipmunks. The deer mouse is found in most of the United States and Canada except for the southeastern United States. The cotton rat is found in the southeastern and southwestern United States.

The virus is found in rodent urine, saliva, and feces. In areas with high rodent concentrations, such as nests, mist from urine or saliva or dust from feces can carry the virus. The most common way of becoming infected is by breathing in the virus through dust or mist. The disease can also be contracted from hand-to-mouth or hand-to-nose contact after handling contaminated materials and can be spread by a rodent bite. The virus can be killed with common household disinfectants such as chlorine bleach.

According to the Centers for Disease Control, symptoms of hantavirus pulmonary syndrome appear anywhere from one to five weeks after infection, but typically within two weeks. The early symptoms are similar to the flu—fatigue, fever (101 to 104°F or 38 to 40°C), and muscle aches, especially in the large muscle groups—thighs, hips, back, and sometimes shoulders. These symptoms are universal. In the late stages of the disease HPS patients develop fluid in the lungs, which quickly progresses to an inability to breathe. Patients die from respiratory failure.

If you have been on an outdoor trip and have been exposed to conditions where rodent infestation could be a problem, and you begin to develop flu-like symptoms following your trip, contact your physician immediately and inform him or her that you have been in an environment where exposure to hantavirus was a possibility. For the latest information on hantavirus, see the Centers for Disease Control Web site (*www.cdc.gov*).

Treatment

Any sudden onset of signs and symptoms such as fever, deep muscle aches, and severe shortness of breath are cause for immediate evacuation and evaluation at a medical facility. There is no specific cure or vaccine for hantavirus infection. Patients need to be hospitalized as soon as possible.

Prevention

According to the Centers for Disease Control, you can reduce the risk of infection by following these guidelines:

- Before occupying cabins or other enclosed shelters, open them up to air out. Inspect for rodents and do not use cabins if you find signs of rodent infestation.
- If you sleep outdoors, check potential campsites for rodent droppings and burrows.
- Do not pitch tents or place sleeping bags in areas in proximity to rodent feces or burrows or near possible rodent shelters (e.g., garbage dumps or woodpiles).
- Avoid coming into contact with rodents and rodent burrows or disturbing dens (such as packrat nests).
- Avoid sleeping near woodpiles or garbage areas that may be frequented by rodents.
- Try not to sleep on the bare ground. Use tents with floors. In cabins, use a cot with a sleeping surface at least 12 inches (30 centimeters) above the floor.
- Use only bottled water or water that has been disinfected by filtration, boiling, chlorination, or iodination for drinking, cooking, washing dishes, and brushing teeth.
- Store foods in rodent-proof containers and promptly discard, bury, or burn all garbage.

- Do not play with or handle rodents that show up at a campsite, even if they appear friendly.

RESPIRATORY EMERGENCIES
ASTHMA

Asthma is a chronic lung condition characterized by difficult breathing. There is always some precursor that causes the asthmatic reaction. The precursor can be an environmental component that is inhaled, such as dust, pollen, mold, or animal dander, or it can be caused by infection, exercise, cold air inhaled into the lungs, or emotional stress. Millions of people suffer from asthma, so it is possible that people on your trip may suffer from the condition. Find out about who has asthma from the Fitness and Health Information Form (see page 408) and find out what causes the asthma. Are there specific conditions you will encounter on your trip that could exacerbate the condition?

During an asthma attack swelling causes narrowing of the patient's airway and mucus builds up. The patient can typically inhale without a problem but has great difficulty exhaling. This is often heard as a wheezing sound. In severe attacks this partial airway obstruction can become almost complete.

Treatment

Mild asthma is usually treated by the patient herself using over-the-counter inhalers. These release epinephrine in a mist, dilating the airway. Moderate asthma requires prescription inhalers or other drugs. You need to initiate treatment early during the attack to prevent the person from going into acute respiratory distress. Once the airway begins to close off significantly, it is very difficult for the patient to inhale the medication from the inhaler to reverse the effects. The patient is often very agitated from lack of oxygen and a feeling of suffocation. This may cause her to breathe faster, exacerbating the problem. Coach the person to relax and breathe with control. Help the person with her inhaler. After inhaling, the patient should hold her breath for 5 to 10 seconds to allow the medication to penetrate the tissues before exhaling.

In a severe asthma attack, the person may have difficulty speaking. She is typically sitting hunched over, gasping out one or two words at a time, or the patient may be unable to speak at all. A sure sign of imminent respiratory failure is when the person says she is tired or too exhausted to breathe. *This person can die quickly.* If the patient cannot inhale her medication and is in danger of suffocation, even CPR may not help, since the rescuer will not be able to get air into the lungs. One *last-ditch* treatment at this point is an injection of epinephrine. This is the same dosage and technique as described for anaphylaxis, so the EpiPen or TwinJect can be used. (See "Anaphylaxis," page 364.) The injected epinephrine is a vasoconstrictor that reduces the swelling in the airway. This is a prescription drug and should only be used with proper training and supervision.

After the attack, monitor the patient carefully. Keep the patient well hydrated. This will help break up the mucus in the airway. Anyone suffering a severe attack should be evaluated by a physician. Additional medications and follow-up are usually required.

GENITOURINARY TRACT AND WOMEN'S HEALTH ISSUES

Infections of the genitourinary tract are more common in women. The most important way to prevent any health complications for the women on a trip is to stress the importance of attention to hygiene, proper hydration, and urination. These are the central factors in preventing urinary tract infections. Vaginitis, another common female health issue, is more directly related to stress and activity.

URINARY TRACT DISORDERS

There are a number of conditions that can affect the sensitive tissue lining of the urinary tract and bladder. The most common is a urinary tract infection (UTI). It is common in women, since the urethra is shorter and it is relatively easy for bacteria to infect the bladder. Urinary tract infections are rare in men and should be cause for evacuation. Common causes for women include:

- **Inadequate Hygiene**   Limited washing can increase bacteria levels on the skin, which can migrate to the urinary tract.
- **Dehydration**   If you become dehydrated, the body attempts to compensate by retaining more water. This limits urination and allows bacteria more time to colonize before being flushed out of the bladder.
- **Infrequent Urination**   This can be caused by dehydration or if the individual is not comfortable urinating outdoors and holds it in for a long time.
- **Trauma to the Urethra**   Vigorous activity or bruising, such as from a bike seat or climbing harness, can cause infection.

Symptoms of a mild UTI include low pelvic pain, frequent urination in small amounts, cloudy or blood-tinged urine, and pain, tingling, or burning during urination. In some cases, the condition resolves itself in two or three days. However, if the condition persists for a longer time, or symptoms are more severe, then medical care will be required. If left untreated, the condition can become more serious, including kidney infection, which can be a life-threatening condition.

Treatment

Urinary tract infections require antibiotics, so there is little you can do in the backcountry unless you are carrying prescription antibiotics. You should, therefore, return to medical care, but it does not require an emergency evacuation. In the interim, keep the external genitalia as clean as possible. Drink plenty of fluids to help flush the system. Have the person rest as much as possible. Vitamin C (1,000 milligrams, four times a day) or drinks containing vitamin C may also help. The excess vitamin C is absorbed from the blood into the bladder, lowering the pH of the bladder and making it more difficult for bacteria to grow. If the patient with symptoms of a UTI develops a fever and pain and tenderness in the lower back, suspect a kidney infection and prepare your patient for immediate evacuation.

VAGINITIS

Infection of the vagina occurs when something upsets the normal balance between the bacteria and yeast that inhabit the vagina. If one or the other grows out of control, vaginitis results. Changes in environment, tight clothing, strenuous or vigorous activity, stress, and hot, humid conditions, high-sugar diet, or using birth control pills or antibiotics can all spur an infection. Symptoms of vaginitis include redness, soreness, general itching or burning in the genital area, and vaginal discharge that is white or "cheesy." Tingling or burning sensation on urination is also common and can be confused with a urinary tract infection.

Treatment

Vaginitis requires medical treatment to cure but is not serious enough to require immediate evacuation. However, if untreated, the infection can lead to Pelvic Inflammatory Disease (PID), a more serious condition. The symptoms can be temporarily relieved by douching daily with either 2 tablespoons of a 10 percent solution of povidone iodine or 1 tablespoon of vinegar in 1 quart/liter of water.

Prevention

Keep the vaginal area clean. Avoid nylon underpants, which hold moisture. Cotton underpants are preferable because cotton allows the air to circulate, minimizing the moist environment conducive to bacterial growth. This is one of those rare occasions where cotton clothing is beneficial. Loose-fitting pants allow for better air circulation.

DIABETES

There are two basic types of diabetic emergencies described in detail below: hypoglycemia (low blood sugar), which is the more common; and hyperglycemia (high blood sugar). If you are unsure if a diabetic is hypoglycemic or hyperglycemic, go ahead and give her sugar. It can't hurt. Keep in mind that anyone in your group (she doesn't have to be diabetic) can get a mild case of hypoglycemia if not eating properly. We all know how it feels at the end of a long day, when blood sugar levels are low and we feel tired and weak.

HYPOGLYCEMIA (LOW BLOOD SUGAR)

In hypoglycemia, the patient's glucose levels are too low. This can be caused by exercising too much (burning up glucose), by not getting enough glucose (change in diet, missed meal), or by taking too much insulin. Because of its rapid onset, if hypoglycemia is not recognized early and treated by providing simple sugars and fluids, it can progress to seizures, loss of consciousness, and eventually death. Such a situation warrants speedy evacuation if symptoms do not improve after giving sugar. Signs and symptoms include:

- Increased breathing rate
- Skin cool, clammy, very sweaty
- AVPU—decreased level of consciousness, irritability, confusion
- Restlessness, shakiness
- Faintness
- Unconsciousness

Treatment

If the patient is conscious, give her sugar—sugary drinks, sweet foods, candy, etc. If the person is unconscious, place sugar on lips and under tongue and massage it into the gums (honey or syrup works well). To prevent aspiration, place the person on her side as you administer sugar. Monitor airway and breathing to make sure she does not aspirate. Some diabetics carry an injectable hormone, Glucagon, which raises low blood glucose levels. Help the patient inject the Glucagon. In severe cases the patient may develop seizures. (See "Seizures," page 309.) After a severe incident (coma, seizures), the patient should be evacuated to medical care.

HYPERGLYCEMIA (HIGH BLOOD SUGAR)

Hyperglycemia is a condition caused by a lack of insulin. It happens either when the diabetic eats too much, takes too little insulin, or does not exercise enough. The level of glucose in the blood is adequate, but there is not enough insulin to allow the glucose to be metabolized by the cells. Since glucose can't be used to fuel the cells, the body breaks fats into fatty acids for energy. Too much acid changes the blood pH, which, if left untreated, can lead to coma, cardiac arrhythmias, and death. The process happens slowly, over 12 to 48 hours, so the person usually will catch it before it proceeds too far. However, someone on fast-absorbing insulin or on an insulin pump can quickly run out of insulin and enter hyperglycemia much faster (within in one to two hours). Signs and symptoms include:

- Patient is thirsty
- Frequent urination
- Fatigue
- Nausea, possible vomiting
- Altered level of consciousness (confusion)
- Fruity breath odor
- Rapid deep breathing

Treatment

Get the patient to take her insulin medication, and monitor her. Keep the patient well hydrated. In severe cases, you may need to evacuate your patient. If the patient has lost her insulin, she will ultimately end up hyperglycemic. The only solution is to get more insulin or get her out to medical care. The best prevention of diabetic emergencies is frequent blood testing using a glucometer. It is recommended that diabetics test their blood seven times a day, but on a trip, because of the numerous changes in variables (weather, activity level, food) that impact blood glucose, testing every two hours while awake can help with the management of diabetes in the outdoors. Most diabetic emergencies can be prevented by adjusting insulin and glucose to the new environment.

ALTITUDE ILLNESSES

Reaching the summit of a high mountain peak can be one of the most exhilarating experiences of a backpacking trip. However, there are a number of potentially serious illnesses that are caused by high altitude. Understanding the physiological effects of altitude on the body is essential to a safe trip. First of all, what altitude is high?

- High altitude—8,000 to 12,000 feet above sea level (2,400 to 3,700 meters)
- Very high altitude—12,000 to 18,000 feet (3,700 to 5,500 meters)
- Extremely high altitude—18,000+ feet (5,500+ meters)

ACCLIMATIZATION

The higher the altitude, the lower the available amount of oxygen to breathe. For example, at 18,000 feet (5,500 meters), the amount of available oxygen is 50 percent less than at sea level. Given time, the body can adapt to the decrease in oxygen molecules at a specific altitude. This process is known as acclimatization and generally takes one to three days at lower altitudes and up to a week around 10,000 feet (3,000 meters). For example, if you hike to 8,000 feet (2,438 meters) and spend several days there, your body acclimatizes to 10,000 feet. If you climb to 12,000 feet (3,700 meters), your body has to acclimatize again. Remember, *everyone* acclimatizes at a different rate, so any information here should only be used as a guideline.

A number of changes take place in the body to allow you to operate with decreased levels of oxygen:

- The depth of respiration increases. You are sucking in more air to compensate.
- Breathing rate increases immediately and continues to increase over time at any given altitude, improving the oxygen level in the blood.
- Pressure in pulmonary arteries is increased, "forcing" blood into portions of the lung that are normally not used during sea level breathing.
- The body produces more red blood cells to carry oxygen. This process takes 10 to 14 days.
- The body produces more of a particular enzyme that facilitates the release of oxygen from hemoglobin to the body tissues.

Here are a few basic guideline for proper acclimatization:

- Try not to fly or drive directly to high altitude. Start below 10,000 feet (3,000 meters) and walk up.
- If you go above 10,000 feet (3,000 meters), increase your altitude by only 1,000 feet (300 meters) per day, and for every 3,000 feet (900 meters) of elevation gained, take a rest day.
- Climb high and sleep low—this is the maxim used by mountaineers. You can climb more than 1,000 feet (300 meters) in a day as long as you come back down and sleep at a lower altitude than you climbed to.
- If you begin to show symptoms of moderate altitude illness, *don't go any higher* until symptoms decrease. If symptoms remain, descend to a lower altitude.
- Different people will acclimatize at different rates. This means that you may need to adjust your group's rate of ascent to accommodate the people who are acclimatizing more slowly.
- Stay properly hydrated. The body's fluid loss increases at high altitude. Drink at least 3 to 4 quarts (3 to 4 liters) per day more in winter conditions.
- Avoid tobacco and alcohol and other depressant drugs, including barbiturates, tranquilizers, and sleeping pills. These depressants further decrease the respiratory drive, especially during sleep, resulting in a worsening of the symptoms.

It is hard to know who may be affected by altitude illnesses. There are *no* specific factors such as age, sex, or physical condition that correlate with susceptibility to altitude sickness. Some people get it, some people don't. Most people can go up to 8,000 feet (2,400 meters) with minimal effects. If you haven't been to high altitude before, it's important to be cautious. If you have been at that altitude before with no problem, you can *probably* return to that altitude without problems as long as you are properly acclimatized.

The major causes of altitude illnesses are going too high, too fast, and not giving the body proper time to acclimatize. This can actually be more of a problem for an athletically fit person than for someone who is out of shape. The fit person may be more used to pushing her body (breathing hard) and may not recognize that being winded is not as much from aerobic exercise as from lack of atmospheric oxygen.

ACUTE MOUNTAIN SICKNESS

Acute mountain sickness (AMS) is common at high altitudes. At elevations over 10,000 feet (3,048 meters), 75 percent of people will have mild to moderate symptoms. The occurrence of AMS is dependent upon the elevation, the rate of ascent, and an individual's susceptibility. Many people will experience mild AMS during the acclimatization process. Symptoms usually start 12 to 24 hours after arrival at altitude and begin to decrease in severity about the third day. When hiking, it is essential that participants communicate any symptoms of illness immediately to others on the trip.

Mild AMS

Symptoms of AMS include headache, dizziness, fatigue, shortness of breath, loss of appetite, nausea, insomnia, and a general feeling of malaise. Symptoms tend to be worse at night and when respiratory drive is decreased. Mild AMS does not interfere with normal activity, and symptoms generally subside within two to four days as the body acclimatizes. As long as the symptoms are mild and only a nuisance, ascent can continue at a moderate rate.

If symptoms become severe, the only cure is either acclimatization or descent. Symptoms of mild AMS can be treated with pain medications for headache and Acetazolamide. Both help to reduce the severity of the symptoms, but remember that reducing the symptoms is not curing the problem. Acetazolamide induces changes in the body that mimic normal acclimatization, thereby minimizing the symptoms caused by poor oxygenation. If you have symptoms of AMS, *don't* ascend higher.

Moderate AMS

Symptoms of moderate AMS include severe headache that is *not* relieved by medication, nausea and vomiting, increasing weakness and fatigue, and shortness of breath.

Note: These signs and symptoms could be caused by other problems (see "STOPEAT," page 264). You need to do a good assessment to make sure you are providing the correct treatment for the problem at hand.

At this stage, only advanced medications or descent can reverse the problem. Descending even a few hundred feet (70 to 100 meters) may help, and definite improvement will be seen in descents of 1,000 to 2,000 feet (300 to 600 meters). Twenty-four hours at the lower altitude will result in significant improvements. The person should remain at lower altitude *until* symptoms have subsided (up to three days). At this point, if the person has become acclimatized to that altitude, she can begin ascending again.

Severe AMS

The patient will display an increase in the severity of the aforementioned symptoms, including shortness of breath *at rest,* inability to walk, decreasing mental status, and fluid buildup in the lungs. *Immediately descend to lower altitudes* (2,000 to 4,000 feet or 600 to 1,200 meters). As an alternative, put the patient in a Gamow bag (see page 384). Dexamethasone, a powerful steroid, is quite effective in keeping people ambulatory while they descend to lower altitudes. This is a prescription drug that requires proper training in its use.

HIGH-ALTITUDE PULMONARY EDEMA

High-altitude pulmonary edema (HAPE) is less frequent than AMS and is more serious. HAPE results from fluid buildup in the lungs. It typically presents after three days at a specific altitude. The fluid in the lungs prevents effective oxygen exchange. HAPE usually occurs above 10,000 feet (3,000 meters) but can be seen in susceptible people at lower altitudes. As the condition becomes more severe, the level of oxygen in the bloodstream decreases. Symptoms include shortness of breath *even at rest,* tightness in the chest, marked fatigue, a feeling of impending suffocation at night, blue or gray lips or fingernail beds, weakness, and a persistent productive cough that brings up white, watery, or frothy fluid. Confusion and irrational behavior are signs that insufficient oxygen is reaching the brain, eventually leading to impaired cerebral function and death.

One of the methods for testing for HAPE is to check recovery time after exertion. Check to see how long it takes your heart rate and breathing rate to slow down to their normal levels after exercise at your home altitude. This establishes a recovery baseline. Once you are at high altitude, see how long it takes you to reach recovery. Initially, as you are acclimatizing, it will take longer, but then it should return to near your baseline. If at high altitude you find that your recovery time continues to get longer, it could mean fluid is building up in the lungs, a sign of HAPE. HAPE can be confused with other illnesses, including pneumonia or asthma. When in doubt, *assume* that it is HAPE and get the person to a lower altitude. It is common for people who develop HAPE to also develop high-altitude cerebral edema (see page 384).

Treatment

In cases of HAPE, *immediate descent is a necessary life-saving measure* (2,000 to 4,000 feet or 600 to 1,200 meters). Don't delay descent if it is at all possible. As an alternative, put the patient in a Gamow bag (see page 384) or give supplemental oxygen. Anyone suffering from HAPE must be seen by a physician for proper follow-up treatment.

HIGH-ALTITUDE CEREBRAL EDEMA

High-altitude cerebral edema (HACE) is less frequent than AMS and is more serious. HACE is the result of swelling of brain tissue from fluid leakage. It generally occurs after a week or more at high altitude. Severe cases can lead to death if not treated quickly. Symptoms include headache, loss of coordination (ataxia), weakness, and decreasing levels of consciousness, including disorientation, loss of memory, hallucinations, psychotic behavior, and coma. Normal activity is difficult, although the person may still be able to walk on her own. One test for HACE is the "sobriety test." Draw a straight line 6 feet long (2 meters) on the ground and ask the person to walk a straight line with the heel of the front foot touching the toe of the rear foot. A person with ataxia will be unable to walk a straight line. Ataxia is the most important clinical sign for determining an increasing severity HACE. This is a clear indication that *immediate descent* is required. It is important to get the person to descend before the ataxia reaches the point where she cannot walk on her own (which would necessitate a litter evacuation).

Treatment

Immediate descent is a necessary life-saving measure (2,000 to 4,000 feet or 600 to 1,200 meters). As an alternative, put the patient in a Gamow bag (see below). Dexamethasone is also effective for treating the symptoms of HACE. Anyone suffering from HACE must be seen by a physician for proper follow-up treatment.

❧ TRICKS OF THE TRAIL

Gamow Bag (pronounced ga'-mäf) This clever invention has revolutionized field treatment of high-altitude illnesses. The bag is basically a sealed chamber with a pump. The person is placed inside the bag, and it is inflated. Pumping the bag full of air effectively increases the concentration of oxygen molecules and therefore simulates a descent to lower altitude. In as little as 10 minutes, the bag can create an "atmosphere" that corresponds to that at 3,000 to 5,000 feet (915 to 1,525 meters) lower. After one to two hours in the bag, the person's body chemistry will "reset" to the lower altitude. This lasts for up to twelve hours outside of the bag, which should be enough time to walk the person down to a lower altitude and allow for further acclimatization. The bag and pump weigh about 14 pounds (6.3 kilos) and are now carried on major high-altitude expeditions. Bags can be rented for short-term trips such as treks or expeditions.

ORGANIZATIONS PROVIDING TRAINING IN WILDERNESS FIRST AID

Three of the most widely recognized organizations providing training and certification in wilderness first aid are listed below. Courses range from hours to weeks, as well as specialized courses for groups with specific backgrounds and interests. Hosted by local organizations, all three schools teach courses throughout the country, as well as the rest of the world. A basic wilderness first-aid course is typically 8 to 16 hours. Advanced versions spanning around 32 hours leave one with an excellent background for most personal trips. The minimum standard for outdoor professionals is the Wilderness First Responder Course (WFR), which is eighty hours, or Wilderness EMT (WEMT), which takes a month.

- S.O.L.O. Wilderness Medicine
www.stonehearth.com
- Wilderness Medical Associates (WMA)
www.wildmed.com
- Wilderness Medicine Institute (WMI)
wmi.nols.edu

Outdoor Leadership

OUTDOOR LEADERSHIP

Why does a backpacking book need a section on leadership? After all, you might be heading out on a trip with friends and thinking, "We're all in charge—we don't need a "leader." The reality is that *anytime* you head off into the backcountry in a group, regardless of how small and how familiar, you need to think about how leadership issues will arise on the trip—and trust me, they always do. What happens if there is a serious medical emergency or if someone gets lost? Who has the experience to deal with such an issue? In an emergency there may not be time to figure this out, and if there hasn't been prior discussion about leadership roles, it's often the most dominant person in the group who takes over, not necessarily the most skilled person. Understanding leadership is a critical piece of running a safe and successful trip.

FORMAL VERSUS INFORMAL LEADERSHIP

In many organized outdoor activities—summer camps, scouting, college outdoor programs, outdoor education programs like Outward Bound, and the National Outdoor Leadership School—there are formal leaders. These are people who have specific skills and training and whose responsibility it is to safely lead the group. Their roles and responsibilities are typically very clearly defined, and there is usually a clear expectation of the roles of the group members. Who makes decisions and how the decisions are made are ultimately determined by the designated trip leaders. It may very well be that the trip leaders shift responsibility for decisions over to the group members, but keep in mind that the leaders have made a *decision* to do so based on operating protocols and current conditions. If those conditions change, the leadership or decision-making structure may need to revert back to the trip leaders.

If you and some friends are heading out on a week-long trip, the leadership is probably more informal, but it's there nevertheless. When you think about the trip, there is evidence of leadership everywhere—someone may initiate the trip, someone gets maps and guidebooks, someone works on group equipment, food, transportation, etc. It might be the same person doing all these things, or the responsibilities might be shared among the group. Leadership is definitely present before the trip, or it would never get off the ground. Once you are on the trail, if everyone has similar knowledge and skills, daily leadership tasks like cooking, organizing rest breaks, or setting up camp may just be split up among the group. If some people have more experience than others, they may take on de facto leadership roles. Then there are those situations when something goes wrong and someone must step in and take charge at a moment's notice, like a medical emergency or a lost person.

SITUATIONAL LEADERSHIP®

What makes a good leader? That's a huge question and one that has generated loads of research and theories. In the context of outdoor leadership, the model used most often is the Situational Leadership® Model developed by Paul Hershey, Kenneth Blanchard, and Dewey Johnson in their book *Management of Organizational Behavior.*

The Situational Leadership® Model is based on the idea that there isn't one best way to lead. Instead, there are different *styles* of leadership, and the most *appropriate style* of leadership depends on the *situation*. The Situational Leadership® Model is used by organizations from NASA to Fortune 500 companies, as well as outdoor expeditionary groups.

If you dissect leadership from this perspective, there are two fundamental roles that leaders take on. One is *directive* behaviors, working to accomplish the tasks the group has set out to do like hike from A to B, set up camp, cook meals, etc. The other is *supportive* behaviors, doing things that work to bring the group together and help them work as an effective team. You can combine differing amounts of directive and supportive behaviors into four different styles of leadership, shown in the grid opposite.

High Directive/Low Supportive Behavior (Directing)

This style is characterized by *one-way communication* in which the leader takes charge and tells people what, how, when, and where to do various tasks. It's good in situations where other people in the group have little experience or in emergency situations that require immediate action. *Example:* On the first day of one of our wilderness orientation trips, the leaders have to do a lot of instruction with the group when they get into camp—everything from how to set up a tarp and hang a bear bag to lighting the stove and cooking dinner. Leaders use a task-oriented, directive style as they teach skills and direct people to various jobs in camp. Another example is in an emergency situation where quick action is essential.

High Directive/High Supportive Behavior (Coaching)

With this style most of the direction is still provided by the leader. She also uses *two-way communication* and emotional support to get the participants to accept decisions that have to be made. *Example:* The group comes to its first hazardous river crossing. The leader needs to teach the group's basic safety procedures about river crossing yet also wants the group to understand how to make a decision about crossing. With this in mind, she asks the group for suggestions about how to proceed and coaches them through the process of evaluating the risks, determining the best solution, and then carrying out the task.

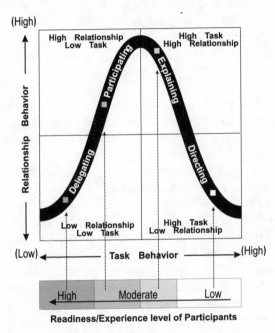

Situational Leadership® Model

Low Directive/High Supportive Behavior (Supporting)

With this style the leader and the participants now share in decision making through *two-way communication*. Participants have the basic ability and knowledge to do the task, so leaders take on a more facilitative role to encourage the effective participation of all the group members. *Example:* You are leading a backpacking trip in the Colorado Rockies. After six days on the trail, you come to open country and have a variety of options for where to hike. The leaders feel that the group has the experience to make their own decision about where to hike and camp next, so they open up the planning and decision making to the group, encouraging participation from everyone and only stepping in if there is a safety issue.

Low Directive/Low Supportive Behavior (Delegating)

This style involves letting participants "run their own show." The leaders delegate significant responsibility to the group, since the participants have become experienced and are both *willing* and *able* to take charge. *Example:* On the last day of our wilderness orientation trips, leaders typically step back and become "participants" while the group members take on all the camp setup tasks like tarps, bear bag, and cooking. The group has mastered the skills and no longer needs direction or instruction from the leaders. In fact, the group members are now the ones "initiating" things.

So how do you know which style of leadership is going to be most effective? The best style to use is based on the experience level of the group. The best way to understand Situational Leadership® is visually. In the diagram on page 389, you can see the four basic styles of leadership. Each type is in a different quadrant of the square. Along the left side of the square (Y-axis) is a measurement of the leader's supportive behaviors. Along the bottom of the square (X-axis) is a measurement of the leader's directive behaviors.

To identify the most effective style of leadership in a particular situation, determine the experience level of the group in relation to the specific task (shown in the experience rectangle), then draw a line from the participant experience level axis to the bell-shaped curve in the drawing. The intersection of the line and the bell curve indicates the most effective leadership style *for that situation*. As the group becomes more experienced in that activity, the most effective style of leadership moves left along the bell curve. This will make sense with an example.

Example   On the first day of one of our wilderness orientation canoeing trips, the group members have a low experience level with canoeing. Most have never done it before. They don't know the strokes, the terminology, or how to canoe with a partner. Also, the group is new to the area and one another. So the *most effective* leadership style will be directive. The leaders will be teaching skills, setting goals for the day, managing the group on the river, etc.

On the fourth day of the trip, the group has a high degree of experience in canoeing. They have learned how to successfully maneuver the canoes and how to work together with partners. At this point if the leaders are still using a directing style, they'd be seen as "overly bossy," and people might be frustrated with the leaders. By shifting their leadership style to supporting or delegating, the leaders will provide the group with the optimal style of leadership for that situation. Keep in mind that changing leadership styles should be gradual and should be implemented as the group is ready for the change.

If the group suddenly moves to a new activity, the experience level may suddenly drop, and the leadership style may need to change. Let's say on day five of your canoeing trip you come to your first set of rapids. The group is experienced with canoeing on flatwater but not on rapids, so the leadership style moves back to a more directive approach—teaching about whitewater, instructing people where and when to run the rapid, etc.

The important point to remember regarding Situational Leadership® is that there is no one *best* way to be a leader. Rather, from one situation to the next there is a *most effective style*. Good leaders use their "Leader's Radar" (see page 232) to analyze the situation and determine which leadership style to use.

DECISION-MAKING STRATEGIES

How decisions are made during a trip can be critical to a trip's success. Decision making, like leadership, is also situational; different situations on the trail may require different decision-making approaches.

WHO MAKES THE DECISION?

In decision making, the first thing to determine is who makes the decision. Sometimes the best person or people to make the decision are the leaders and sometimes it is other people within the group or the entire group. Determining "who" is critical because sometimes the person "in charge" is making the wrong decision. Let me give you a story to illustrate the point.

A number of years ago I organized a sixteen-day trek on the Annapurna Circuit in Nepal. There were sixteen of us, and we hired a professional guiding company to run the trip. Our Sirdar, or chief guide, had been leading treks in the Himalayas for over a decade. We were hiking in late fall and after ten days reached a camp at Thorong Phedi, 14,500 feet (4,419 meters). The next day was to be the most challenging day of the trip, hiking up to the top of the Thorong La Pass at 17,700 feet (5,394 meters) and back down to the town of Muktinath at 12,500 feet (3,810 meters). We got up at 4:00 A.M. to start hiking, only to discover that a freak early snowstorm had created whiteout conditions. You could see only about 50 feet (15 meters) in front of you. The entire mountain was covered in 6 inches (15 centimeters) of fresh snow. Half of the group wanted to go while the other half was extremely nervous. In addition, we were facing a time crunch. It had taken us ten days to hike up to this point, and we only had four days to get to our end point. If we couldn't get over the pass soon, we would miss our plane back to the states. The Sirdar assured us that it would be no trouble to cross the pass in these conditions. I was deeply concerned about hypothermia and frostbite, as well as the possibility of high-altitude illness. The clothing we had was only appropriate for around freezing, but it was below 0°F (−17°C). The Sirdar insisted that it would not be a problem. He said if anyone had trouble getting over the pass, one of the porters could carry the injured person on his back. I recognized the huge accident potential (see Chapter 8, "Safety and Emergency Procedures"), and even though I wasn't in charge, I was sure that this was an unsafe decision. I eventually convinced the Sirdar and the group that the risks were just too high, so we held off a day until the storm abated. Most of the other trekkers at Thorong Phedi that day made the same decision and waited out the storm. The few who tried to get over the pass that day did not succeed, and one trekker got frostbite of the feet so badly that he was unable to walk and had to be brought back down on a pony. This situation shows that sometimes the person with the defined role of leader may not be making the best decision.

One way of "making decisions ahead of time" is through the use of protocols (see Chapter 8, "Safety and Emergency Procedures"). In effect, a protocol has made some of the decisions for you. If you have a protocol that says "When thunder is within 30 seconds of a lightning flash you should get to a safe location and have the group get into the lightning position," then you don't need to spend time trying to decide what you are going to do when the lightning storm hits.

Before your trip goes out, it is important to come to a basic understanding of what people's skills and experience are and who and how decisions are going to be made. I might be the designated leader of the trip, but someone else in the group has more first-aid training than I do. In a medical emergency I would pass off the leadership in handling the medical issue to that person. At the same time I would take charge of managing the rest of the group and preparing for an evacuation if needed.

PLANNING OUT THE DECISION

In any decision-making situation you need to follow a basic plan:

1. Identify the situation, set goal(s), and prioritize them.
2. Brainstorm options for achieving the goal(s).
3. Evaluate the different options and examine how the options meet the goal(s).
4. Determine the decision-making strategy you are going to use to select amongst the different options from #3.

5. Decide on an option using one of the following criteria:
- Best serves highest priority goals
- Best serves all goals
- Serves goals without creating any negative outcomes
- Creates the least negative outcomes

GROUP DECISION MAKING

The first thing to determine is whether it is a decision that can and should be made by the group, or with input from the group, or if it a decision to be made solely by the leaders. During the course of a trip, there are a number of decisions that can be made by the whole group. These might include things like where to camp, which route to take, whether to rest for the afternoon or do a side hike, etc. Group decision making can be a powerful learning and growth tool for the group. To determine who should be involved in the decision, you can take the S.M.A.R.T. Decision approach by looking at:

S.M.A.R.T. Decisions

- Structure of the group—Is this a group of friends all operating on a similar level, or is this an organized trip with identified leaders?
- Motivation Level—How motivated or committed are the group members? Do they want to be involved, or would they rather others decide?
- Ability Level—What is the ability and skill level of the group members to make the decision? Do they have the knowledge and experience with river crossings to make the decision whether to cross or not?
- Risk Level—What are the potential consequences of the decision? You are at a stream crossing and you have to decide if the stream is too high and fast to cross safely. Could someone get seriously injured if the wrong decision is made?
- Time—How much time there is to make the decision? Are you on a ridge during a lighting storm? Does someone need to decide *right now* where to go, or do you have time?

DECISION-MAKING TECHNIQUES

- **Authority decides** In this case, the decision is made by the leaders by virtue of their role of being responsible for the trip or by some person determined to have the greatest knowledge about the topic. This process can be very effective when the leader(s) have significantly more knowledge than the other members of the group. It is also very efficient in terms of time. In some cases, getting feedback from the group may be essential for the leaders to have all the facts in order to make a good decision. For example, if the leaders have to decide about changing the route, they need to know the physical and mental state of all the participants. The most common scenario for this decision-making technique is a safety or emergency situation.

- **Majority vote** In this case, members of the group are polled, and the option that receives support from the greatest number in the group is chosen. This strategy works well if everyone agrees to be bound by it, and if everyone feels they have a chance to express their viewpoints and needs. However, it can lead to splintering of the group and tension. Leaders should evaluate if this method will be a positive or negative experience for the group.

- **Consensus** This is the most effective method of making a group decision in terms of members feeling included. Consensus decision making means reaching a decision that all members of the group are willing to support at some level. In order to reach this point, everyone in the group must be given ample time to express their views and time to express their disagreement with others' views. Through a process of negotiation, the group moves to an idea that everyone can support at *some* level. This process can take a great deal of time, and a "perfect consensus" is rarely reached. Make sure that you have enough time before embarking on this approach.

COMMUNICATING THE DECISION

In all of these strategies, it is important for leaders to model good listening and communication skills. Leaders may need to act as facilitators for effective communication by asking people not to interrupt others, quieting dominant members of the group, and asking quieter members to speak up.

One of the biggest causes of conflict on outdoor trips is poor communication. If leaders give the authority to make the decision to the group and then countermand the decision because the leaders disagree, you are likely to create bad feelings among the group. Avoid this problem by thinking ahead and determining what decisions are appropriate for the group to make and which ones should be made by the leaders. Leaders will also need to decide if they should be involved in the decision process with the group, or "sit it out." Sometime the presence and perceived authority of the leaders can slant the decision-making process. However, in certain situations, this can work to your advantage as a leader. Making good group decisions involves a process, which the leaders should explain and model as a norm for the group to follow.

REFLECTING ON THE EXPERIENCE

A fundamental question for each of us heading out into the outdoors is, Why are we going? What are our goals and aspirations for making the trip, and are we achieving them? As we talked about in Chapter 1, "Trip Planning," it's essential to set out the goals of the trip before going. During the trip you may want to check in about how well you are doing in the pursuit of those goals. Are you still on track? Has the trip situation and perhaps the goals changed? By reflecting on the experience we can check in on both individual and group goals and make some mid-course corrections, if needed.

As an outdoor program director, I can't stress the value of this enough. I've seen thousands of students grow from their experiences in the outdoors—developing technical skills, confidence, leadership ability, communication skills, sensitivity, and compassion for others and for the wilderness. This happens only when people reflect on what they've experienced. This is a huge topic and something that requires sensitivity and skill. I'll touch only on the basics of reflection; see the Bibliography for other resources on this subject.

WHEN TO REFLECT

Leaders need to be sensitive to when to utilize reflection techniques—both for specific individuals and for the group as a whole. Some people will be into it and others not. Here are some guidelines:

Daily

On a multiday trip it's useful to engage in at least informal check-ins with people on a regular basis. You're already doing this when you ask if someone is tired or ask when everyone would like to take a lunch break. Informal talks at the end of the day about what could be done differently, how the pace was, if people had a good or bad day, etc., can get people ready for the next day and allow you to make some adjustments, if needed.

Before a Challenge

When the group is going to be doing something readily identifiable as a challenge, it may be useful to talk and reflect beforehand about what's coming and how people are feeling about it. I remember doing a climb in the North Cascades with a friend. The knife-edged ridge that we had to traverse ahead dropped off hundreds of feet on both sides. Beyond being challenged technically, we were both really scared. By sitting down and talking about how we both felt, we settled down and were able to come up with a good strategy for dealing with the ridge and significantly reduced our accident potential (see Chapter 8, "Safety and Emergency Procedures"), which would have been very high if we'd failed to talk about how we were feeling.

After a Challenge

After a challenge people may need to sit down and reflect on the experience. This can often make or break a trip. Reflecting on the difficult parts of any journey is where the greatest potential for learning comes. Depending on logistical issues, this might happen immediately afterward or much later.

When Someone is Having Difficulty

Recognize when an individual is in a high-stress situation and needs to reflect on it. For example, someone is having real trouble keeping up with the group. You sense the person feels guilty for holding other people up. Talking with the person and having her express how she feels may be the thing that turns the trip around from a miserable experience to an extremely positive one. Sometimes this is done one-on-one, and other times it may be helpful for the whole group to be involved.

After a Critical Emergency Situation

If you have a serious emergency on the trip, like a serious near miss, injury, or even a death, it is very important at some point to process what happened. In extreme cases it is best to have a professional counselor help in the process. This is a common practice in professional organizations such as emergency service personnel, search-and-rescue teams, police, fire departments, and outdoor programs and is often referred to as *critical incident stress debriefing*. Failure to process such an experience can lead to long-term psychological problems. Call in outside professionals who are specifically trained to deal with this type of reflection.

At the End of the Trip

This is an opportunity to bring the whole experience together. It is a chance to think about how the trip went, how people worked together, etc., and can be useful for helping to set realistic goals for future trips. This is also the place where people can take what they have learned about themselves on the trail and apply it back to their daily lives. Doing some form of "final reflection" is often where the most profound learning from the trip can take place.

HOW TO REFLECT

In most cases, reflection is facilitated through group discussions prompted by questions asked by the leaders. When you are involved in a discussion, there are a number of things to keep in mind that will encourage reflection in the group:

- **Setting** Do it at a time when everyone can be focused on the task and has the energy to be actively engaged. You want people to be warm, dry, and as comfortable as possible.
- **Physical presence** It is important for the leaders to have a focused physical presence: good eye contact with participants, a focused body posture, and verbal or physical acknowledgment when someone is speaking.
- **Silence** Don't be afraid of silence after you ask a question. Silence usually means that people are thinking, both of what to say and how comfortable they feel saying it. This takes a little time. Rushing to fill the silence only interrupts the process for the participants. Wait and see what happens. If no one responds, try rephrasing the question.
- **Sequencing of questions** Ask the easy questions first, and then pose more introspective questions. If you ask really probing questions first, the conversation may go nowhere. By structuring the types of questions you ask and the order in which you ask them, you can guide the participants back through the experience and help them remember what happened and how they reacted. Finally, you can ask them to reflect on what they have learned from this trip and see how they might be able to use that knowledge in the future. Here is the basic sequence to design a series of questions for the group:

1. **What?** What happened on the trip: questions that deal with the factual experiences of the trip. These are easy to answer and help bring back memories about the experience.
2. **So What?** Questions that ask why particular events were important or had an impact. What did people feel and why? These questions require greater self-disclosure and require participants to think about their reactions to the experience.
3. **Now What?** These questions require self-assessment and ask that participants think about what comes next after this experience, how can they take what they have learned back to other parts of their lives.

Appendix

This section of the book provides forms and information for trip planning. You can download PDF versions of these files and other resources at *www.backpackersfieldmanual.com.*

THREE-SEASON BACKPACKING TRIP TEACHING PLAN

The Teaching Plan serves as an overview of all the skills needed to successfully manage your trip. If you are teaching others, use this as your "cheat sheet" to make sure you cover everything. If you are doing other wilderness activities, in different seasons or ecosystems, you may need to create your own Teaching Plan.

Equipment

- Clothing
- Layering for temperature control
- Boots
- Backpacks
  - How to pack a pack
  - Putting on a pack
  - How to wear a pack
- Group equipment

Travel Techniques

- Pacing and rhythmic breathing
- Rest step
- Contouring
- Traversing an incline
- River crossings
- Rest stops
- Map reading
- Compass use

Camp Setup

- Location—Leave No Trace
- Tarp/tent setup
- Stove use and cooking area setup
- Food and nutrition
- Cooking
- Water purification
- Hygiene

Leave No Trace

- Backcountry travel
- Garbage and food waste disposal
- Human waste disposal
- Cleaning dishes and personal bathing
- Fires

First Aid

- First-aid kit
- Foot and blister care
- Hypothermia and hyperthermia
- Adequate hydration and nutrition
- Fatigue prevention

Safety and Emergency

- Risk Assessment & Safety Management
- Environmental hazards, based on location, activity, and season
- Equipment hazards
- People hazards
- Situational awareness

WARM-WEATHER BACKPACKING EQUIPMENT LIST

This general equipment list is designed for basic multiday backpacking trips in temperate forest conditions (three-season). Typical temperature ranges would be 70's to 90's F (20° to 32° C) during the day with nighttime temperatures from 50's to 70's F (–1° to 10° C). For your own particular needs or for warmer weather or colder weather, you will need to modify this basic list.

Head

- Wool/fleece hat (optional)
- Brimmed hat (for sun protection)

Upper Body

- T-shirts as needed
- Lightweight synthetic short-sleeve shirt—polypropylene, or other hydrophobic, wicking fabric
- Lightweight synthetic long-sleeve shirt—polypropylene, or other hydrophobic, wicking fabric
- Lightweight fleece jacket/wool sweater—(e.g., Polartec 100)
- Wind jacket—nylon (can be same as rain jacket if waterproof/breathable—must fit over insulating layers)

Lower Body

- Underwear as needed
- 1 to 2 pairs of loose-fitting shorts
- Lightweight synthetic/wool long underwear bottoms—polypropylene or other hydrophobic, wicking fabric
- 1 pair long pants, loose-fitting, synthetic long pants
- Swimsuit

Feet

- 1 pair of lightweight to midweight hiking boots.
- 1 pair of running shoes, sneakers, or sandals, for around-campsite wear and/or water activities
- 2 to 3 pairs of light synthetic/polypropylene liner sock
- 2 to 3 pairs of medium-weight wool or synthetic hiking socks
- Gaiters (recommended)

Shell Layer

- Waterproof rain jacket—coated nylon or waterproof/breathable fabric
- Waterproof rain pants or rain chaps—coated nylon or waterproof/breathable fabric (optional)

Travel Gear

- External/Internal frame backpack with padded hip belt
- Pack rain cover (optional, can use a garbage bag)
- Trekking poles or hiking gear (optional)

Sleeping

- Sleeping bag—synthetic/down fill, rated to 40°F (4°C)
- 1 closed cell foam sleeping pad (⅜ in. or 9 mm) or inflatable mattress

Miscellaneous

- 2 1-quart water bottles or water bladder
- 1 unbreakable cup with handle
- 1 unbreakable bowl
- 1 spoon
- 1 bandanna, multipurpose
- 1 flashlight/headlamp with fresh batteries; rechargable batteries are fine for short trips and are more environmentally friendly
- 1 small towel
- 1 toilet kit: just the essentials, biodegradable soap, toothbrush and toothpaste, comb, sunscreen, lip balm, insect repellent
- 1 pocket knife or multi-purpose tool

- Heavy plastic garbage bags—one for sleeping bag, one for inside backpack
- 1 pair of sunglasses or clip-ons
- Glasses or contact lenses (if needed)
- Any medications you will need to take during the trip (allergy medications, etc.)

Optional

- Small notebook and pencil or ballpoint pen
- Altimeter
- Camera and film
- Books and field guides
- Folding camp chair, such as Crazy Creek
- Musical instrument
- Drawing or painting supplies

MODERATE-WEATHER BACKPACKING EQUIPMENT LIST

This is a general equipment list designed for basic multiday backpacking trips in temperate forest conditions (three-season). Typical temperature ranges are 50° to 70° F (10° to 21° C) during the day, with nighttime temperatures from 30° to 50° F (−1° to 10° C).

Head

- See "Warm-Weather Equipment List," page 400

Upper Body Layers

- Lightweight synthetic long-sleeve shirt—polypropylene or other hydrophobic wicking fabric
- Medium-weight polypropylene top or wool shirt, long sleeve
- Medium-weight fleece jacket or wool sweater (e.g., Polartec 200)
- Wind jacket, nylon (can be same as rain jacket if waterproof and breathable; must fit over insulating layers)

Hands

- Synthetic or wool glove liners

Lower Body Layers

- Underwear as needed
- Medium-weight synthetic or wool long underwear bottoms, polypropylene or other hydrophobic wicking fabric
- Lightweight wool or fleece pants (e.g., Polartec 100)

Feet

- See "Warm-Weather Equipment List," page 400

Shell Layer

- See "Warm-Weather Equipment List," page 400

Travel Gear

- See "Warm-Weather Equipment List," page 400

Sleeping

- Sleeping bag—synthetic/down fill, rated to 30° F (–1° C)
- 1 closed-cell foam sleeping pad (⅜ inch thick or 9 millimeters) or inflatable mattress

Miscellaneous

- See "Warm-Weather Equipment List," page 400

Optional

- See "Warm-Weather Equipment List," page 400

COLD-WEATHER BACKPACKING EQUIPMENT LIST

This is a general equipment list designed for basic multiday backpacking trips in temperate forest conditions (three-season). Typical temperature ranges would be approximately 30° to 50° F (0° to 10° C) during the day with nighttime temperatures approximately 0° to 30° F (–17° to 0° C).

Head

- Wool/fleece hat (must cover ears)
- Brimmed hat (for sun protection)

Upper Body

- Lightweight synthetic long-sleeve shirt—polypropylene or other hydrophobic wicking fabric
- Midweight synthetic long-sleeve shirt—polypropylene or other hydrophobic wicking fabric
- Expedition-weight synthetic long-sleeve shirt—polypropylene or other hydrophobic wicking fabric or wool
- Heavy-weight fleece jacket/wool sweater (e.g., Polartec 300)
- Wind jacket—nylon (can be same as rain jacket if waterproof-breathable—must fit over insulating layers)
- Winter parka—synthetic/down filled

Hands

- Synthetic/wool glove liners
- Synthetic/wool mittens

Lower Body

- Underwear as needed
- Midweight synthetic long underwear bottoms—polypropylene or other hydrophobic wicking fabric
- Expedition-weight synthetic long underwear bottoms—polypropylene or other hydrophobic wicking fabric
- Midweight fleece/wool pants (e.g., Polartec 200)

Feet

- 1 pair of midweight to heavy hiking boots. In colder weather you may need insulated boots such as Sorels or Army surplus "Mickey Mouse" boots or plastic shell mountaineering boots with insulated liners.
- 2 to 3 pairs of light synthetic/polypropylene liner socks.
- 2 to 3 pairs of medium-weight wool or synthetic hiking socks
- Gaiters (recommended)

Shell Layer

- See "Warm-Weather Equipment List," page 400

Travel Gear

- See "Warm-Weather Equipment List," page 400

Sleeping Gear

- See "Warm-Weather Equipment List," page 400

Miscellaneous

- See "Warm-Weather Equipment List," page 400

Optional

- See "Warm-Weather Equipment List," page 400

GENERAL GROUP EQUIPMENT LIST

This is a basic group equipment list for a three-season backpacking trip for 10 to 12 people. You may need to modify it based on the size of your group, the length and remoteness of the trip, and specific trip activities.

Shelter

- Tents or tarps and ground sheets with 75-foot tarp lines of ¼-inch braided nylon (22 meters of 6 millimeter)
- Small tarp to set up for cooking (optional)

Cooking

- Stove—one for 4 to 5 people. Carrying multiple stoves gives you more cooking options and are needed for larger groups
- Fuel bottles and fuel
- Funnel
- Strike-anywhere matches, waterproof matches, or lighter
- Nesting pots with lids—a 2-liter and 4-liter work well for groups up to 12
- Frying pan—8 to 12 inches depending on size of group
- Spatula
- Mixing spoon
- Pot gripper
- Biodegradable soap
- Strainer
- Plastic pot brush
- Ziploc/plastic bags for repacking food

Hygiene

- Water purification (have at least one backup method)
- Toilet paper (optional)
- Trowel
- Waterless hand cleanser
- Whistle
- 2 square feet aluminum foil (for tampons)
- Aspirin tablets (for tampons)
- Medical waste bag
- Chlorine bleach (for medical waste and dishwashing)
- Blue personal plastic bags for toilet paper/tampons
- Yellow plastic bags for recycling
- Heavyweight plastic trash bags (plenty—double as emergency rain gear and for hypothermia wrap)

Travel

- Compass
- Maps and guidebooks as needed
- Global Positioning Systems (GPS) receiver (optional)
- Waterproof map case (optional)

Safety

- First-aid kit
- Cellphone or satellite phone (optional)
- Personal Locator Beacon (PLB) (optional)
- Weather radio (optional)

Miscellaneous

- 75 feet of bear bag line of ¼-inch braided nylon (22 meters of 6 millimeter)
- 2 carabiners for bear-bagging
- 100 feet of parachute cord (11 meters)
- 1- or 1½-gallon collapsible water container (4–6 liter)

General Repair Kit

- Heavy-duty needles
- Stove repair parts and tools
- 30 feet of fishing line (9 meters)
- 5 safety pins
- 5 buttons
- 15 feet of duct tape on a golf pencil (5 meters)
- 3 clevis pins & split rings (repair external frame packs)
- 15 feet of #20 wire (5 meters)
- 25 feet of braided nylon cord (7 meters)
- 2-inch Fastex pack hip-belt buckle

FIRST-AID KIT

What to bring in your first aid kit depends on a lot of factors:

- Size of the group
- Length of the trip
- Remoteness of location
- Trip activities
- Your level of first-aid training
- Specific environmental hazards in the area

Here is a basic first-aid kit designed for a group of 10 out for 6 days. Remember, this equipment won't do you any good unless you have been properly trained in how to use it. Take a wilderness first-aid course before going out into the backcountry. Modify the list as needed.

When I am leading a trip I tend to be a "first-aid junkie." When I'm responsible for other people, I'd rather overpack on first-aid equipment than not have things that other people might need.

For group trips I like to pack two separate first-aid kits: a basic kit for items that are used regularly, and an emergency kit for items that are used infrequently. The emergency kit, which might include specialty items and drugs with expiration dates, is packed in a fanny pack, sealed, and dated.

There are a number of prepackaged first-aid kits on the market that allow you to select what you need for your trip.

- Adventure Medical Kits—*www.adventuremedicalkits.com*
- Atwater Carey—800-359-1646

BASIC KIT: PACKED IN A FIRST-AID POUCH
Hardware

1 box mixed Band-Aids	1 Cold Pack
10 2 × 2-inch gauze sponges	1 tweezers
6 exam gloves	1 50 sq. in. moleskin
20 triple antibiotic ointment packets	1 tube petroleum jelly
1 8 oz. tincture of benzoin	1 sunscreen
10 alcohol prep pads	1 insect repellant
1 trauma scissors	1 activated charcoal
1 1-inch adhesive tape	1 New Skin liquid bandage

EMERGENCY KIT: PACKED IN A FANNY PACK
Hardware

1 zinc oxide ointment	10 alcohol prep pads
2 combine dressing	2 3-inch Ace bandage
1 2-inch adhesive tape	1 Betadine (povidone-iodine)
10 4 × 4-inch gauze sponges	1 Inflate-a-Shield CPR mask
1 8-oz. chlorine bleach	1 bottle Polar Pure
2 Cold Packs	1 SAM splint
5 Maxi-pads	1 Extractor kit
1 box waterproof matches	6 blanket pins
2 2-inch roller gauze	2 ammonia inhalants
2 triangular bandages	1 oral thermometer
5 2 × 3-inch Telfa pads	1 Space Blanket
4 exam gloves	3 electrolyte rehydration solution

Medications

20 Tylenol/cetaphen (pain/fever)
20 ibuprofen/propinal (pain)
20 Pepto-Bismol (GI distress/diarrhea)
10 Ducolax (laxative)
10 Diarrhest (anti-diarrheal)
20 pseudophedrine/SudoTab (allergies)
1 tube hydrocortisone cream (skin rashes)
10 Sting-eze (bee sting topical analgesic)

20 Benadryl (antihistamine)
4 Epinephrine syringes (anaphylaxis)—This is a prescription drug item. Any individuals on the trip with severe allergies to such things as bee stings should bring her own. Contact your physician for more information

Reporting

3 Accident/Close Call forms
2 Information Report forms

2 SOAP Note forms
2 Emergency Information Reports

FITNESS AND HEALTH INFORMATION FORM

Gathering accurate information about the people going on your trip is important in planning a trip appropriate to the level of all participants. You need to be aware of everyone's physical condition and medical history. Here is a sample form that covers a range of such information. Add to this form if you need more information.

FIRST NAME _____   LAST NAME _____

HEIGHT:_____ inches   WEIGHT: _____ pounds

CURRENT PHYSICAL CONDITION: Please check **only one** box to rate your current physical fitness level. (See "Assessing Physical Condition" at *www.backpackersfieldmanual.com* for information on how to calculate a physical fitness score from this information.)

I. I don't participate regularly in programmed recreation sport or physical activity:

❑ Avoid walking or exertion (e.g., always use elevator, drive whenever possible instead of walking)

❑ Walk for pleasure, routinely use stairs, occasionally exercise sufficiently to cause heavy breathing or perspiration.

II. I participate regularly in recreation or work requiring modest physical activity, such as golf, horseback riding, calisthenics, gymnastics, table tennis, bowling, weight lifting, or yard work:

❑ 10 to 60 minutes per week

❑ Over one hour per week

III. I Participate regularly in heavy physical exercise (such as running or jogging, swimming, cycling, rowing, skipping rope, running in place) or engage in vigorous aerobic-type activities (such as tennis, basketball, or handball).

❑ Run less than 1 mile per week or spend less than 30 min per week in comparable physical activity.

❑ Run 1 to 5 miles per week or spend 30 to 60 min per week in comparable physical activity.

❑ Run 5 to 10 miles per week or spend 1 to 3 hours per week in comparable physical activity.

❑ Run over 10 miles per week or spend over 3 hours per week in comparable physical activity.

CURRENT EXERCISE ACTIVITY: Do you exercise regularly? ❑ No ❑ Yes If yes, list any physical activities or sports you engage in, times per week, duration, and level of intensity.

Activity	Times/Week	Approximate Time/Distance	Level of Intensity		
			❑ Leisurely	❑ Moderately	❑ Intensely
			❑ Leisurely	❑ Moderately	❑ Intensely
			❑ Leisurely	❑ Moderately	❑ Intensely

SWIMMING ABILITY: ❑ Nonswimmer ❑ Poor ❑ Fair ❑ Good ❑ Very Good

CURRENT HEALTH STATUS: Please indicate if you have any medical conditions or physical disabilities that could interfere with or limit your participation in the trip. If you are unsure, explain the trip to your physician and ask for his/her advice. If you answer yes to any of the questions below, please specify in detail section below, indicating the item number.

1. Hearing or Vision Problems (do *not* include wearing glasses or contacts)	❑ Yes	❑ No
2. Respiratory Problems (do *not* include minor ones)	❑ Yes	❑ No
3. Back Problems	❑ Yes	❑ No
4. Joint Problems (e.g., knees, ankles, hips)	❑ Yes	❑ No
5. Serious Illness or Hospitalizations in last year	❑ Yes	❑ No
6. Surgeries in last 6 months	❑ Yes	❑ No
7. Heart Problems or High Blood Pressure	❑ Yes	❑ No

8. Serious Reaction to High or Low Temperatures	❏ Yes ❏ No
9. Frequent Muscle Cramps	❏ Yes ❏ No
10. High or Low Blood Sugar	❏ Yes ❏ No
11. Seizure Disorders	❏ Yes ❏ No
12. Anemia, Bleeding tendencies or Traits	❏ Yes ❏ No
13. Psychological or Emotional Problems	❏ Yes ❏ No
14. Other	❏ Yes ❏ No

Item #	Detailed description (include restrictions, if any). Add a separate sheet if necessary.

ALLERGIES: Please indicate any allergies you have (medications, foods, etc.), your allergic reactions, and any medication required.

Allergies (check if applicable, write in others)	Reaction	Medication Required (if any)
Insect stings (bees, wasps, etc.) ❏ Yes		
Iodine or Shellfish Allergy ❏ Yes		

DIETARY RESTRICTIONS OR FOOD ALLERGIES: (Please indicate specific dietary restrictions: vegetarian, kosher, lactose intolerant, etc.)

MEDICATIONS: Please indicate any medications you are currently taking (other than allergy medications), for what condition, and whether you will need to take them during the trip. *If you need to take medications during the trip, be sure you have an ample supply.*

Medication	Condition	Do you need this during the trip?	
		❏ Yes	❏ No
		❏ Yes	❏ No

TRIP LOGISTICS PLAN

TYPE OF TRIP _____ DATES _____

LOCATION _____ LEADERS _____
DRIVING ROUTE _____ DRIVING TIME _____
STARTING POINT _____

DAY 1 ROUTE _____

PLANNED CAMP _____

MILEAGE _____ ELEVATION UP _____ ELEVATION DOWN _____ TRAVEL TIME _____
WATER LOCATIONS _____
EMERGENCY ACCESS _____

DAY 2 ROUTE _____

PLANNED CAMP _____
MILEAGE _____ ELEVATION UP _____ ELEVATION DOWN _____ TRAVEL TIME _____
WATER LOCATIONS _____
EMERGENCY ACCESS _____

DAY 3 ROUTE _____

PLANNED CAMP _____
MILEAGE _____ ELEVATION UP _____ ELEVATION DOWN _____ TRAVEL TIME _____
WATER LOCATIONS _____
EMERGENCY ACCESS _____

DAY 4 ROUTE _____

PLANNED CAMP _____
MILEAGE _____ ELEVATION UP _____ ELEVATION DOWN _____ TRAVEL TIME _____
WATER LOCATIONS _____
EMERGENCY ACCESS _____

SAFETY ISSUES

ACTIVITY HAZARDS

ENVIRONMENTAL HAZARDS (Keep in mind static vs. dynamic environments)

EQUIPMENT HAZARDS

PEOPLE HAZARDS

STEPS TO MINIMIZE ACCIDENT POTENTIALS FROM HAZARDS LISTED ABOVE:

SUBMITTED BY _____ DATE _____

Emergency Telephone Numbers

_____

TRIP SAFETY PLAN

Whenever you go on a trip, make sure that you let someone who is not going (your on-call person) know the details. Give that person a copy of your Trip Logistics Plan (above) and your Trip Safety Plan (below). Establish a time when you should be back, with a few hours leeway. Set a time after which the on-call person should contact the appropriate authorities. Make sure that he or she has the appropriate emergency phone numbers to call in case you are overdue. Call the person when you return. Whenever you are out on the trail, sign in and out on any trail registers. This helps rangers locate you in an emergency and also helps establish usage patterns for the area.

Personal Information

Full name

Home address

City

State

Postal code

Home phone

Cellular phone

Contact for Change in Plans

Full name

Home address

City

State

Postal code

Home phone

Cellular phone

Return Date

Earliest date and time

Latest date and time

If I do not return by the latest date and time listed, and I have not notified the contact above regarding a change in plans, notify the police and park security at the phone numbers below.

Emergency Contact Information

Police

Park security

Medical Information

Medical conditions

Allergies

Current medications

Members of Your Party

Name of trip leader

Home address

City

State

Postal code

Home phone

Full name

Home address

City

State

Postal code

Home phone

Transportation

What form of Transportation to Trailhead?

❏ Personal Vehicle ❏ Public Transportation ❏ Other _____

If you are driving yourself:

Vehicle 1 owner

Vehicle 1 make/model

Vehicle 1 license plate

Vehicle 2 owner

Vehicle 2 make/model

Vehicle 2 license plate

If someone is dropping you off and picking you up:

Name of person dropping off

Home phone

Alternative phone

Name of person picking up

Home phone

Alternative phone

MENU PLAN

MEAL-BY-MEAL METHOD

BREAKFAST

Trip Day	Food Items	Quantity—1 Person	Your Quantity
Day 1			
Day 2			
Day 3			

LUNCH

Trip Day	Food Items	Quantity—1 Person	Your Quantity
Day 1			
Day 2			
Day 3			

SNACKS

Trip Day	Food Items	Quantity—1 Person	Your Quantity
Day 1			
Day 2			
Day 3			

DINNER

Trip Day	Food Items	Quantity—1 Person	Your Quantity
Day 1			
Day 2			
Day 3			

RATION METHOD

BREAKFAST

Food Items	Quantity/Person/Day	Number of Days	Your Quantity

TRAIL FOODS/SNACKS

Food Items	Quantity/Person/Day	Number of Days	Your Quantity

LUNCH

Food Items	Quantity/Person/Day	Number of Days	Your Quantity

DINNER

Food Items	Quantity/Person/Day	Number of Days	Your Quantity

DESSERTS

Food Items	Quantity/Person/Day	Number of Days	Your Quantity

TRIP EXPENSES FORM

Keeping a good record of all your trip expenses is essential whether you are running an outdoor program or camping with friends who split up the costs at the end of a trip. Good record-keeping will also show you where the bulk of the costs for the trip were and may help you reduce costs for future trips.

ACTIVITY _____ DATE(S) _____

LOCATION _____

LEADER(S) _____

LEADERS _____ PARTICIPANTS _____ TOTAL NUMBER IN GROUP _____

FOOD EXPENSES: Food Purchases For _____ People For _____ Days

_____ $ _____

_____ $ _____

_____ $ _____

_____ $ _____

FOOD TOTAL = $ _____

EQUIPMENT PURCHASES:

_____ $ _____

_____ $ _____

_____ $ _____

EQUIPMENT TOTAL = $ _____

DRIVING MILEAGE:

VEHICLE #	STARTING MILEAGE	ENDING MILEAGE	TOTAL MILEAGE

GAS EXPENSES:

Amount		Amount	
$		$	
$		$	
		GAS TOTAL =	$

TOLLS:

$	$
$	$
TOLL TOTAL =	$

CAMPING/LODGING EXPENSES:

_____ $ _____

_____ $ _____

CAMPING TOTAL = $ _____

MISCELLANEOUS EXPENSES:

_____ $ _____

_____ $ _____

MISCELLANEOUS $ _____

TOTAL = _____

TRIP LOG

Location: _____

Activities: _____

Dates: _____

Starting Point: _____

Ending Point: _____

Mileage/Time	Route Traveled Trails Used	Water Availability	Terrain/Trail Conditions	Campsite
Day 1				
Day 2				
Day 3				

Permits Needed: _____

Special Regulations: _____

Ranger Station Phone: _____

Equipment Needed: _____

Maps Used: _____

Alternate Route/Activities: _____

_____

Problems with Trip: _____

_____

Places to See/Avoid: _____

_____

EMERGENCY INFORMATION REPORT

This form should be filled out if medical or evacuation assistance needs to be obtained. One copy goes with those hiking out to arrange for help; one copy stays with the patient.

DATE _____ TIME _____

LEADERS _____

ACTIVITY _____

ACCIDENT _____

NUMBER INJURED/ILL _____

VICTIM #1—NAME SEX _____ AGE _____ | _____

LOCATION OF GROUP _____ |

QUANDRANGLE MAP _____ SECTION: NE NW SE SW

EXACT LOCATION _____

TERRAIN:	• Trail	• Woods	• Field
	• Brush	• Ridgeline	• Road
SLOPE:	• Easy	• Moderate	• Steep
RESPONSE PLAN:	• Will Stay Put	• Send Messengers Out	• Evacuate to Road
	• Evacuate to Shelter	• Evacuate to Roadhead	

IF EVACUATING, GIVE DETAILS (EXACT EVACUATION POINT, ETA TO EVAC)

_____

NAMES OF MESSENGERS

_____

WHERE SHALL RESCUE TEAM MEET MESSENGERS?

_____

SOAP NOTE

VICTIM	DATE
RESCUER	TIME

SCENE DESCRIPTION

S Symptoms

A Allergies

M Medications

P Past History

L Last Meal

E Events

OBJECTIVE

EXAM:

VITAL SIGNS						
Time	Pulse	Resp.	B/P	Skin	Temp.	AVPU

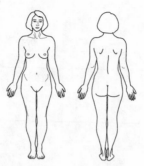

Mark Injury Locations

ASSESSMENT AND TREATMENT PLAN		
A = Assessment Plan	A´ = Anticipated Problems	P = Treatment Plan

ADDITIONAL NOTES

BIBLIOGRAPHY

If you want to learn more about the many topics covered in this book, here are some excellent resources.

Information in the age of the Internet changes rapidly. In order to keep you up to date, I have included a list of Internet resources, but remember that Web sites change. Be sure to check out the Web sites that I run: *www.backpackersfieldmanual.com,* where you'll find downloadable forms and information from the book, and *www.outdoored.com* and *www.outdoorsafety.org,* where I and other outdoor professionals post articles on outdoor education.

GENERAL INTERNET RESOURCES

Arthur Carhart National Wilderness Training Center: *carhart.wilderness.net/index.cfm*

Backpacker's Field Manual Web site: *www.backpackersfieldmanual.com*

Backpacker Magazine: www.bpbasecamp.com

GORP (Great Outdoor Recreation Pages): *www.gorp.com/*

www.outdoored.com

www.outdoorsafety.org

PARKS AND PLACES TO GO

American Discovery Trail: *www.discoverytrail.org*

Appalachian Trail: *www.appalachiantrail.org; www.nps.gov/appa*

Continental Divide Trail: *www.cdtrail.org*

Florida Trail: *www.florida-trail.org*

Ice Age Trail: *www.iceagetrail.org*

Natchez Trace Trail: *www.nps.gov/natt*

North Country Trail: *www.northcountrytrail.org*

Pacific Crest Trail: *www.pct.org*

Potomac Crest Trail: *www.nps.gov/pohe*

Usenet News Group: *groups-beta.google.com/group/ rec.outdoors.national-parks*

GOVERNMENT RESOURCES

Bureau of Land Management: *info.er.usgs.gov/doi/bureau-land-management.html*

National Avalanche Center: *www.fsavalanche.org*

National Oceanic and Atmospheric Administration (NOAA): *www.noaa.gov*

National Parks Canada: *www.parkscanada.ca*

National Park Service (NPS): *www.nps.gov*

National Snow and Ice Data Center: *nsidc.org*

U.S. Department of Agriculture Forest Service: *www.fs.fed.us*

U.S. Department of the Interior: *www.dsi.gov*

U.S. Fish & Wildlife Service: *www.fws.gov*

U.S. Geological Survey (USGS): *www.usgs.gov*

USENET NEWS GROUPS AT GOOGLE

rec.backcountry: *groups-beta.google.com/group/rec.backcountry*

rec.outdoors.camping: *groups-beta.google.com/group/rec.outdoors.camping*

rec.sport.orienteering: *groups-beta.google.com/group/rec.sport.orienteering*

rec.outdoors: *groups-beta.google.com/group/rec.outdoors*

CHAPTER 1: TRIP PLANNING

Berger, Karen. *Trailside Guide: Hiking & Backpacking*. New York: W. W. Norton & Company, 2003.

Harvey, Mark. *The NOLS Wilderness Guide*. New York: Fireside, 1999.

Jardine, Ray. *Beyond Backpacking*. Arizona City: Adventure Lore, 2001.

Logue, Victoria. *Backpacking in the 90's*. Birmingham: Menasha Ridge Press, 1993.

Schad, Jerry, and Moser, David S. *Wilderness Basics*. Seattle, WA: The Mountaineers, 1993.

Townsend, Chris. *The Backpackers Handbook*. Camden: Ragged Mountain Press, 1997.

CHAPTER 2: EQUIPMENT

Backpacker Magazine: Annual Gear Guide Issue. Emmaus: Rodale Press.

Berger, Karen. *Trailside Guide: Hiking & Backpacking*. New York: W. W. Norton & Company, 2003.

Getchell, Annie. *The Essential Outdoor Gear Manual*. Camden: Ragged Mountain Press, 2000.

Jardine, Ray. *Beyond Backpacking*. Arizona City: Adventure Lore, 2001.

Jeffrey, Kevin. *The Complete Buyers Guide to Outdoor Recreation & Equipment*. San Francisco: Foghorn Press, 1993.

MSR Whisperlite. Reprinted from MSR Whisperlite Maintenance Instructions, MSR Company, Seattle, WA.

Schad, Jerry, and Moser, David. *Wilderness Basics*. Seattle: The Mountaineers, 1992.

Tilton, Buck. *The Wilderness Medicine Newsletter*, July/August 1994.

INTERNET RESOURCES

Backpacking Light: *www.backpackinglight.com*

FabricLink: For learning about fabrics, apparel, and clothing care, *www.fabriclink.com*

Ultralight Gear: *www.thru-hiker.com*

Flying with Stove Fuel: *www.thru-hiker.com/articles.asp?subcat=2&cid=50*

CHAPTER 3: COOKING AND NUTRITION

Berger, Karen. *Hiking & Backpacking*. New York: W. W. Norton & Company, 2003.

Brunnell, Valerie, and Swain, Ralph. *The Wilderness Ranger Cookbook*. Helena: Falcon Press, 1990.

Bunnelle, Hasse. *The Backpackers Food Book*. New York: Simon & Schuster, 1981.

———. *Cooking for Camp and Trail*. San Francisco: Sierra Club Books, 1973.

Fleming, June. *The Well-Fed Backpacker*. New York: Vintage Books, 1986.

Gray, Melissa, and Tilton, Buck. *Cooking the One Burner Way*. Merrillville, IN: ICS Books, 2000.

Harvey, Mark. *The NOLS Wilderness Guide*. New York: Fireside, 1999.

Jacobson, Don. *The One Pan Gourmet*. Camden, ME: Ragged Mountain Press, 1993.

McHugh, Gretchen. *The Hungry Hiker's Book of Good Cooking*. New York: Alfred A, Knopf, 1987.

Prater, Yvonne, and Mendenhall,Ruth Dyar. *Gorp, Glop & Glue Stew*. Seattle: The Mountaineers, 1988.

Pearson, Claudia, and Clelland, Mike. *NOLS Cookery*. Harrisburg, PA: Stackpole Books, 1997.

Schad, Jerry, and Moser, David. *Wilderness Basics*. Seattle, WA: The Mountaineers, 1992.

Viehman, John. *Trailside's Trail Food*. Emmaus, PA: Rodale Press, 1993.

INTERNET RESOURCES

Food Pyramids Nutrition Source, Harvard School of Public Health: *www.hsph.harvard.edu/nutritionsource/pyramids.html*

CHAPTER 4: HYGIENE AND WATER PURIFICATION

Backer, Howard. "Field Water Disinfection," in William Forgey, *Wilderness Medicine*. Guilford: Globe Pequot 1999.

Hampton, Bruce, and David Cole. *Soft Paths*. Harrisburg: Stackpole Books, 2003.

Harvey, Mark. *The NOLS Wilderness Guide*. New York: Fireside, 1999.

Hostetter, Kristin. "The Water Filter Field Test" *Backpacker Magazine* (December 1996):56–70.

Jenkins, Mark. "What's in the Water" *Backpacker Magazine* (December 1996):56–60.

Wilkerson, James A. *Medicine for Mountaineering and Other Wilderness Activities*. Seattle, WA: The Mountaineers, 1992.

INTERNET RESOURCES

Aqua Mira Water Treatment: *www.mcnett.com*

Katadyn Water Filters & Treatment: *www.katadyn.com*

MSR & Sweetwater Water Filters: *www.msrcorp.com*

Polar Equipment, Inc: *www.polarequipment.com*

Potable Aqua: *www.pharmacalway.com*

Steripen: *www.hydro-photon.com*

Water Technology Online: *www.watertechonline.com*

Cleaning your Water Bottle – Nalge Nunc International Corporation: *www.nalgene-outdoor.com/technical/cleaning/index.html*

CHAPTER 5: LEAVE NO TRACE HIKING AND CAMPING

Hampton, Bruce, and Cole, David. *Soft Paths*. Harrisburg: Stackpole Books, 2003.

Harvey, Mark. *The NOLS Wilderness Guide*. New York: Fireside, 1999.

Hodgson, Michael. *The Basic Essentials of Minimizing Impact on the Wilderness*. Guilford: Globe Pequot, 1998.

McGiveney, Annette. *Leave No Trace*. Seattle: The Mountaineers, 2003.

Meyer, Kathleen. *How to Shit in the Woods*. Berkeley, CA: Ten Speed Press, 1994.

INTERNET RESOURCES

Cryptobiotic Soil: *www.nps.gov/care/crypto.htm*

Leave No Trace Center for Outdoor Ethics: *www.leavenotrace.org*

Phillips Environmental Products Inc: *www.thepett.com*

CHAPTER 6: WILDERNESS TRAVEL

Alter, Michael J. *Sport Stretch*. Champaign: Human Kinetics, 1997.

Anderson, Bob, and Anderson, Jean. *Stretching*. Bolinas: Shelter Publications, 2000.

Berger, Karen. *Hiking & Backpacking*. New York: W. W. Norton & Company, 2003.

Brown, Gary. *Safe Travel in Bear Country*. New York: Lyons & Burford, 1996.

Cox, Steven M., and Fulsaas, Kris. *Mountaineering: The Freedom of the Hills*. Seattle: The Mountaineers, 2003.

Fleming, June. *Staying Found: The Complete Map & Compass Handbook*. Seattle: The Mountaineers, 2001.

Geary, Don. *Using a Map & Compass*. Mechanicsburg, PA: Stackpole Books, 1995.

Harvey, Mark. *The NOLS Wilderness Guide*. New York: Fireside, 1999.

Herrero, Stephen. *Bear Attacks: Their Causes and Avoidance*. New York: Lyons Press, 2002.

Kals, W. S. *The Land Navigation Handbook*. San Francisco: Sierra Club Books, 1983.

Owen, Peter. *The Book of Outdoor Knots*. New York: Lyons Press, 1993.

Randall, Glenn. *The Outward Bound Map and Compass Handbook*. New York: Lyons Press, 1998.

Schad, Jerry, and Moser, David. *Wilderness Basics*. Seattle: The Mountaineers, 1992.

Seidman, David. *The Essential Wilderness Navigator*. Camden: Ragged Mountain Press, 2000.

Viehman, John. *Trailside's Hints & Tips for Outdoor Adventure*. Emmaus, PA: Rodale Press, 1993.

INTERNET RESOURCES

All About Map Projections: *www.eoascientific.com/cartography/aaMaps_M3_projections_Z.htm*

Bear Bag Hanging Techniques, BackpackingLight.com: *www.backpackinglight.com/cgi-bin/backpackinglight/bear_bag_hanging_technique.html?id=464nTTtg*

Eastern Slopes Grizzly Bear Project: *www.canadianrockies.net/Grizzly/index.html*

Knots, Scouting Resources UK: *www.scoutingresources.org.uk/knots_index.html*

Mapping Instructional Resources: *www.usgs.gov/education/index.html*

Maps 101—Topographic Maps, the Basics, Canadian Topographic Maps: *maps.nrcan.gc.ca/maps101/index.html*

MapTech Terrain Navigator Pro Software: *www.maptech.com*

MapTools.com: *www.maptools.com*

Sierra Interagency Black Bear Group: *www.sierrawildbear.gov*

The National Map Viewer, USGS: *nationalmap.usgs.gov/nmjump.html*

U.S. Geological Survey (USGS): *www.usgs.gov*

Using the UTM Grid System to Record Historic Sites, National Register: *www.cr.nps.gov/nr/publications/bulletins/nrb28/iNDEX.htm*

CHAPTER 7: WEATHER AND NATURE

Brown, Tom. *Tom Brown's Guide to Wild Edible and Medicinal Plants.* New York: Berkley Publishing, 1995.

Brown, Tom, Jr., with Morgan, Brandt. *Tom Brown's Field Guide to Nature Observation and Tracking.* New York: Berkley Publishing, 1988.

Burt, William, and Peterson, Roger Tory. *Peterson Field Guides: Mammals.* Boston: Houghton Mifflin, 1998.

Chartrand, Mark. *The Audubon Society Field Guide to the Night Sky.* New York: Alfred A. Knopf, 1992.

Coombes, Allen J. *Eyewitness Handbooks: Trees.* New York: Dorling Kindersley, 1992.

Halfpenny, James. *A Field Guide to Mammal Tracking in North America.* Boulder: Johnson Books, 1986.

Kricher, John, and Morrison, Gordon. *Peterson Field Guides: Eastern Forests.* Boston: Houghton Mifflin, 1998.

———. *Peterson Field Guides: Ecology of Western Forests.* Boston: Houghton Mifflin, 1993.

Ludlum, David. *The Audubon Society Field Guide to North American Weather.* New York: Alfred A. Knopf, 1991.

Murie, Olaus. *Peterson Field Guide: Animal Tracks.* Boston: Houghton Mifflin, 1998.

Peterson, Lee Allen. *A Field Guide to Edible Wild Plants.* Boston: Houghton Mifflin, 1999.

Peterson, Roger Tory. *A Field Guide to the Birds East of the Rockies.* Boston: Houghton Mifflin, 1980.

———. *A Field Guide to Western Birds.* Boston: Houghton Mifflin, 1990.

Peterson, Roger Tory, and McKenny, Margaret. *Field Guide to Wildflowers of Northeastern and North Central North America.* Boston: Houghton Mifflin, 1998.

Reifsnyder, William. *Weathering the Wilderness.* San Francisco: Sierra Club Books, 1980.

Rezendes, Paul. *Tracking and the Art of Seeing: How to Read Animal Tracks and Signs.* New York: Harper Collins, 1999.

Schad, Jerry, and David S. Moser. *Wilderness Basics.* Seattle, WA: The Mountaineers, 1993.

Steele, Frederic. *At Timberline: A Nature Guide to the Mountains of the Northeast.* Boston: Appalachian Mountain Club Books, 1982.

Stokes, Donald, and Stokes, Lillian. *A Guide to Animal Tracking and Behavior*. Boston: Little Brown, 1986.

Sutton, Ann and Myron. *National Audubon Society Nature Guide to Eastern Forests*. New York: Alfred A. Knopf, 1985.

Watts, May Thielgaard. *Master Tree Finder*. Berkeley: Nature Study Guild, 1991.

Watts, May Thielgaard. *Winter Tree Finder*. Berkeley: Nature Study Guild, 1970.

Williams, Jack. *The Weather Book*. New York: Random House, 1997.

INTERNET RESOURCES

Bear Identification, Montana Fish & Wildlife Department: *fwp.state.mt.us/bearid/default.htm*

Colorado Lightning Resource Center: *www.crh.noaa.gov/pub/ltg.shtml*

National Lightning Safety Institute: *www.lightningsafety.com*

National Weather Service: *www.nws.noaa.gov*

StarDate Online Moon Phase Calculator: *www.stardate.org/nightsky/moon*

The Weather Channel: *www.weather.com*

USA TODAY Lightning & Resources: *www.usatoday.com/weather/resources/basics/wlightning.htm*

Usenet News Group rec.birds: *groups-beta.google.com/group/rec.birds*

Usenet News Group, rec.animals.wildlife: *groups-beta.google.com/group/rec.animals.wildlife*

Usenet News Group, rec.photo.technique.nature: *groups-beta.google.com/group/rec.photo.technique.nature*

Virtual Reality Moon Phase Pictures: *tycho.usno.navy.mil/vphase.html*

CHAPTER 8: SAFETY AND EMERGENCY PROCEDURES

Brown, Tom, Jr., with Morgan, Brandt. *Tom Brown's Guide to Wilderness Survival*. New York: Berkley Books, 1989.

Fuller, Margaret. *Forest Fires*. New York: John Wiley & Sons, 1991.

Hale, Alan. "Dynamics of Accidents Model" Bellefontaine, OH: International Safety Network, 1988.

Tilton, Buck. *The Basic Essentials of Rescue from the Backcountry.* Merrillville, IN: ICS Books, 1990.

INTERNET RESOURCES

Mountain Rescue Association: *www.mra.org*

National Association for Search & Rescue (NASAR): *www.nasar.org*

OutdoorSafety.Org: *www.outdoorsafety.org*

Search & Rescue Resources on the Web: *dmoz.org/Health/Public_Health_and_Safety/Emergency_Services/Search_and_Rescue/*

Wilderness Risk Managers Committee: *wrmc.nols.edu*

CHAPTER 9: FIRST AID AND EMERGENCY CARE

Auerbach, Paul. *Medicine for the Outdoors.* New York: Lyons Press, 1997.

Bezruchka, Stephen. *Altitude Illness: Prevention & Treatment.* Seattle: The Mountaineers, 1994.

Bowman, William D., Jr., M.D. *Outdoor Emergency Care.* Boston: Jones & Bartlett, 2002.

Consumer Drug Reference 2004. Yonkers: Consumer Reports Books, 2004.

Forgey, William, M.D. *Wilderness Medical Society Practice Guidelines for Wilderness Emergency Care.* Guilford: Globe Pequot, 1998.

———. *Wilderness Medicine.* Guilford: Globe Pequot, 1999.

Gill, Paul. *The Pocket Guide to Wilderness Medicine.* New York: McGraw Hill, 1997.

Isaac, Jeff. *The Outward Bound Wilderness First-Aid Handbook.* New York: Lyons Press, 1991.

Joy, EA: Self-reduction of anterior shoulder dislocation, Phys Sportsmed 2000;28(11):65-66 2004. The McGraw Hill Companies.

Ostfeld, Richard. "The Ecology of Lyme: Disease Risk" *American Scientist,* July–August 1997: 338–346.

Schimelpfenig, Todd, and Lindsey, Linda. *NOLS Wilderness First Aid.* Harrisburg: Stackpole Books, 2000.

Tilton, Buck, and Hubbell, Frank. *Medicine for the Backcountry.* Guilford: Globe Pequot, 1999.

Tilton, Buck. *Wilderness First Responder.* Guilford: Falcon Press, 2004

Wilkerson, James A. *Medicine for Mountaineering and other Wilderness Activities.* Seattle, WA: The Mountaineers, 2001.

INTERNET RESOURCES

Altitude and Acute Mountain Sickness: *www.aescon.com/ski/medicine/mtsick.html*

American Diabetes Foundation: *www.diabetes.org*

American Lyme Disease Foundation: *www.aldf.com*

Arachnology Web Site: *www.arachnology.org*

The Asthma Corner: *www.drpaul.com/asthma/index.html*

Bjerke, Scott and Lintzenich, Anne. "Lightning Injuries," eMedicine Web site: *www.emedicine.com/med/topic2796.htm*

Centers for Disease Control: *www.cdc.gov*

Cooper, Mary Ann. "Emergent Care of Lightning and Electrical Injuries," Lightning Injury Research Web site: *tigger.uic.edu/labs/lightninginjury/index.htm*

Craig, Sandy, Hyponatremia, 2003, eMedicine Web site: *www.emedicine.com/emerg/topic275.htm*

Cryptosporidiosis Fact Sheet, Centers for Disease Control: *www.cdc.gov/ncidod/dpd/parasites/cryptosporidiosis/factsht_cryptosporidiosis.htm*

Cyclospora Fact Sheet, Centers for Disease Control: *www.cdc.gov/ncidod/dpd/parasites/cyclospora/factsht_cyclospora.htm*

Freudenrich, Craig. "How Diabetes Works," How Stuff Works Web site: *health.howstuffworks.com/diabetes1.htm*

Giardia Fact Sheet, Centers for Disease Control: *www.cdc.gov/ncidod/dpd/parasites/giardiasis/default.htm*

Guide to High Altitude Medicine, Base Camp MD: *www.basecampmd.com*

Heat Index, National Weather Service: *www.crh.noaa.gov/gjt/heat_index.htm*

Insect Repellant Use & Safety, Centers for Disease Control: *www.cdc.gov/ncidod/dvbid/westnile/qa/insect_repellent.htm*

LymeNet: *www.lymenet.org*

Medical Aspects of Lightning, NOAA Web site: *www.lightningsafety.noaa.gov/medical.htm*

Tick Photographs, Iowa State University Entomology Image Gallery: *www.ent.iastate.edu/imagegal/ticks/*

Risks from Food & Drink, Centers for Disease Control Traveler's Guide: *www.cdc.gov/travel/food-drink-risks.htm*

Sam Splint Home Page: *www.samsplint.com*

Watermelon Snow: *waynesword.palomar.edu/plaug98.htm*

Wesley, Keith MD. "Selective Spinal Immobilization": *www. wisconsinems.com/docs/Cspine.htm*

West Nile Virus Fact Sheet, Centers for Disease Control: *www.cdc.gov/ncidod/dvbid/westnile*

Wilderness Medical Society: *www.wms.org*

The Yellow Book: Health Information for International Travel, Centers for Disease Control: *www.cdc.gov/travel/yb/index.htm*

CHAPTER 10: OUTDOOR LEADERSHIP

Graham, John. *Outdoor Leadership: Technique, Common Sense & Self-Confidence.* Seattle, WA: The Mountaineers, 1997.

Hersey, Paul, Blanchard, Kenneth, Johnson, Dewey. *Management of Organization Behavior.* Saddle River, NJ: Prentice Hall, 2001.

Kosseff, Alex. *AMC Guide to Outdoor Leadership.* Boston, MA: Appalachian Mountain Club, 2003.

Simpson, Steven. *The Leader Who Is Hardly Known: Self-Less Teaching from the Chinese Tradition.* Oklahoma City, OK: Wood 'N' Barnes, 2003.

INTERNET RESOURCES

Situational Awareness, 7th Coast Guard District: *www.dirauxwest.org/TCTF/situational_awareness5.htm*

INDEX